TRANSFORMING LOSS INTO BEAUTY

TRANSFORMING LOSS INTO BEAUTY

Essays on Arabic Literature and Culture
in Honor of Magda Al-Nowaihi

Edited by
Marlé Hammond
Dana Sajdi

The American University in Cairo Press
Cairo   New York

Calligraphy: *Wa-marathin law 'annahunna dumu'un /*
lamahawna al-sutura fi-l-inshadi (Were elegies tears /
They would erase the lines of composition),
Abu al-'Ala' al-Ma'arri. Calligrapher: Ahmed Fares.

Copyright © 2008 by
The American University in Cairo Press
113 Sharia Kasr el Aini, Cairo, Egypt
420 Fifth Avenue, New York, NY 10018
www.aucpress.com

Dar el Kutub No. 3140/07
ISBN 978 977 416 102 5

1 2 3 4 5 6 7 8   12 11 10 09 08
Designed by Fatiha Bouzidi / AUC Press Design Center
Printed in Egypt

Contents

Contributors

Roger Allen is professor of Arabic language and literature at the University of Pennsylvania. He is the author of *The Arabic Novel* and *An Introduction to Arabic Literature*, and has published many translations of Arabic fiction. He is also the co-editor of *The Cambridge History of Arabic Literature: Arabic Literature in the Post-Classical Period* and the journal, *Middle Eastern Literatures*.

Dina Amin, a scholar and theater director, is assistant professor of Arabic cultural studies and theater at Villanova University. She has directed many plays in Egypt, Jordan, and the United States. Her publications include an award-winning translation of Alfred Farag's *al-Shakhs*.

Michael Beard is Chester Fritz Distinguished Professor of English at the University of North Dakota. He has produced many studies on Arabic and Persian literature, including *Hedayat's* Blind Owl *as a Western Novel* and, with Adnan Haydar, *Naked in Exile: Khalil Hawi's* Threshing Floors of Hunger. With Haydar he is just completing the translation of a collection by Adonis (Ali Ahmad Said), under the title *Mihyar of Damascus, His Songs*.

Hamid Dabashi is Hagop Kevorkian Professor of Iranian Studies and Comparative Literature at Columbia University. His celebrated works include: *Authority in Islam*; *Theology of Discontent*; *Truth and Narrative*; *Close Up: Iranian Cinema, Past, Present, Future*; *Staging a Revolution: The Art of Persuasion in the Islamic Republic of Iran*; and an edited volume, *Dreams of a Nation: On Palestinian Cinema*.

Jonathan Decter is Edmond J. Safra Professor of Sephardic Studies at Brandeis University. He is the author of *Iberian Jewish Literature: Between* *al-Andalus and Christian Europe* and the co-editor of *Studies in Arabic and Hebrew Letters in Honor of Raymond P. Scheindlin*.

Alexander Elinson is assistant professor of Arabic language and literature at Hunter College of the City of New York. He is the author of *Looking Back: The Poetics of Loss and Nostalgia in Muslim Spain, ca. 1000–1400* (forthcoming), in addition to a number of articles, book reviews, and translations.

Marlé Hammond is a British Academy Postdoctoral Fellow at Oxford University. She has published several articles on Arabic literature and is the co-editor, along with Geert Jan van Gelder, of Takhyil: *The Imaginary in Classical Arabic Poetics* (forthcoming).

András Hámori is professor of Near Eastern studies at Princeton University. He is the author of *On the Art of Medieval Arabic Literature* and *The Composition of Mutanabbi's Panegyrics to Sayf al-Dawla*. He has, in addition, published many groundbreaking articles on classical Arabic poetry and prose.

Mervat Hatem is professor of political science at Howard University. Her recent publications on gender and politics include "In the Eye of the Storm: Islamic Societies and Muslim Women in Globalization Discourses," *Comparative Studies of South Asia, Africa and the Middle East* 26, no. 1:22–35.

Wolfhart Heinrichs is James Richard Jewett Professor of Arabic at Harvard University. He has published many studies of classical Arabic literature, including *Arabische Dichtung und griechische Poetik* and *The Hand of the Northwind: Opinions on Metaphor and the Early Meaning of* Isti'ara *in Arabic Poetics*. He also specializes in Islamic law and Neo-Aramaic.

Richard Jacquemond is associate professor of modern Arabic language and literature at the University of Provence, Aix-en-Provence. He has also served as Higher Education Officer for the French Cultural Mission in Egypt. He is the author of *Conscience of the Nation: Writers, State, and Society in Modern Egypt* (AUC Press, 2008) and has translated many Arabic novels into French.

Lital Levy is currently a junior fellow at the Harvard Society of Fellows and, beginning in fall 2008, assistant professor of comparative literature at Princeton University. She has published numerous articles and book chapters on Hebrew and Arabic literatures as well as on the intellectual and cultural history of Arab Jews.

Mara Naaman is assistant professor of Arabic at Williams College. Her publications include "Invisible Ethnic: The Arab American Novels of Mona Simpson," *The Arab Novel in English*, ed. Nouri Ghana (forthcoming), and "America Undone: Sonallah Ibrahim's Intra-imperial Investigations," *Alif* 26 (2006): 71–93; 278–79.

Dana Sajdi is assistant professor of Islamic history at Boston College. She is the editor of *Ottoman Tulips, Ottoman Coffee: Leisure and Lifestyle in the Eighteenth Century*. She is currently writing a monograph on the life and work of a Damascene barber in the eighteenth century.

Christopher Stone is associate professor of Arabic and the head of the Arabic division at Hunter College of the City of New York. He is the author of *Popular Culture and Nationalism in Lebanon: The Fairouz and Rahbani Nation*. He is also a winner of the Middle East Studies Association's Malcolm H. Kerr Dissertation Award.

Acknowledgments

Many individuals have assisted us in this endeavor, and we are indebted to all of them for their moral and practical support. First, we would like to thank Samia Mehrez and Michael Beard for their help in getting this project off the ground. Samia suggested many names for our list of contributors and provided us with an Arabic transcript of Magda's Middlebury lecture; Michael offered us invaluable advice on how to approach publishers. We thank Hamid Dabashi for his moving and lyrical foreword. Lital Levy deserves special mention because it was at her instigation that this volume came about. We would also like to thank Dina Amin, who, along with other contributors to this volume, presented a "Transforming Loss" panel, which was convened in Magda's honor and chaired by George Saliba, one of her friends and colleagues at Columbia University, at the convention of the Middle Eastern Studies Association in 2005. We are indebted, furthermore, to several individuals at the American University in Cairo Press: to Neil Hewison and Chip Rossetti for their logistical support and enthusiasm, and to Klara Banaszak for her patient and rigorous editing. Last but not least, we would like to thank Fernand Cohen, Magda's husband, who has been very supportive since the project's inception and who also helped us compile a list of potential contributors. It is to Fernand, and to Magda's two children, Nadeem and Nadia, that we dedicate this volume.

Foreword

Hamid Dabashi

In the 1990s four of us at Columbia University were diagnosed with a life-threatening disease: Magda Al-Nowaihi, Edward Said, and Jeanette Wakin with cancer, and I with a congenital heart condition that required immediate open-heart surgery. This collective condition, all diagnosed within the span of a few short years, generated a sense of unspoken fragility amongst us. There was a shade of shared immanence—an implicit awareness that we all dwelt within the danger zone—that bound us together. None of us ever talked about this, but eventually the frequency of our calling on and seeing each other noticeably increased. Janet died in 1997, Magda in 2002, Edward in 2003. I have remained with their collective memory, now coalesced and sculpted into a singular vision of what once Columbia meant to me.

There is a strange serenity about an immanent death; a clarity of vision is contingent upon it, a kind of suspended enlightenment—ordinary binds and habitual banalities eventually pale and leave, the clock seems to stop ticking, you think that you have an infinity to see and sense things. It is very strange. You even feel a sense of immortality. As I recall the last few years of Magda's life, after she had been diagnosed with ovarian cancer and I had had my heart surgery, the enduring memory of my friendship with her exists as if narrated in a story, seen in a film, read in a poem, captured in a painting or a photograph. There is a sense of unreality about those last years, the memorial recollection of a walk by a sea, a stroll in a garden. I think this is what Rumi meant when he said, paraphrasing a prophetic tradition:

Go die before your death, my dear sir!
So you won't suffer the pain of dying—

A kind of death that plunges you into a light, not
A kind of death that plunges you into a grave.

Magda and I became close friends almost immediately after she came
to Columbia for her job talk in the spring of 1993. "Hold this while I kill
myself," she said half-jokingly after her talk, giving me her umbrella so
that she could light a cigarette. It was a rainy day and we were walking
out of Hamilton Hall, where she had just given one of her spectacular
performances: without so much as glancing at her paper, she gave a talk
of such exquisite subtlety, confidence, and command it was as if she
had been reading from a polished and published paper sent to her on a
teleprompter—full, grammatical, sinuous sentences, with multiple subordinate clauses, coming out of her mouth as if someone else sitting in her
mind was reading off a text and using her face as a mask.

I was part of the search committee that was responsible for hir-
ing Magda. There was a certain necessary formality in the course of our
first official encounter that we both needed to and did observe. I have a
visual memory of that formality in my mind—choreographed, courteous,
and confident. We both knew then and there that we had a moral affinity
which spoke through the professional formality. In the subtle subtext of
our mutual awareness, we agreed that, as far as the job was concerned, she
was the best there was and knew more about modern and classical Arabic
literature (and literature in general) than all our expectations combined.
Magda did not wear her erudition on her sleeve. Her intelligence over-
shadowed her vast and exquisite knowledge of literature. She was always
a few steps ahead of every conversation. Her eyes spoke faster, her gaze
probed deeper, than her articulate diction betrayed.

Mourning Magda, Edward, and Janet, I have come to understand what
Rumi meant when he said, "You, my brother, are all intelligence/The rest
is just bone and cartilage," or what Forough Farrokhzad meant when she
said, "Remember the flight! / The bird is mortal." Magda, like a few other
people whom I have loved and admired and now lost, has become integral
to my critical intelligence. I see and hear with her eyes and ears. Time and
again, particularly in moments of crisis and trauma since she died, I have
thought that if Magda were here, she would say this or that, think thus
and propose thenceforth. But such modes of thinking are all a manner of
speech, a narrative device, for me to do precisely that—to have Magda

as part of my own readings of things, as the expanded intelligence of my senses. She taught her students directly. Between the fall of 1994 when she joined us and 2 June 2002 when she died, she was singularly committed to her students. In them she wrote her books, planted the seeds of her critical intelligence, and heard the echo of her own creative mind. But the rest of us she taught indirectly, sideways, by creatively insinuating her sharp wit into our critical character. Mourning Magda has taught me that bereavement is the growing pain of our soul, the cracking sound of our bones as we reach to attain the full measures of our humanity.

There is a Persian violet (we call it *Banafsheh*) that flowers very early in the spring, lasts for a very few short days, and then withers away. Mourning a comrade, Ahmad Shamlu says in a poem that she was

A Banafsheh—
She flowered and gave the good tiding
That the winter has passed
And off she withered.

Magda Al-Nowaihi

Introduction

Marlé Hammond and Dana Sajdi

Magda Al-Nowaihi, professor of Arabic literature at Columbia University in New York City, died in June 2002 at the age of forty-four, after a long and courageous battle against ovarian cancer. Her academic breadth and versatility, combined with her charisma, acumen, and integrity, made her a formidable force in her field, and she commanded the respect of senior scholars from early in her career. This volume of essays represents the latest in a series of tributes that have recognized her career and achievements.[1] It is, of course, an academic survivors' cliché to say that she lives on, through her influence on the work of those still living. In Magda's case, however, this is especially true. Many scholars in her situation would have understandably retreated to their home offices, prioritizing their writing and research agendas. Magda chose instead to prioritize her students, and, although she did need to take some medical leave, she continued to teach and advise until the very end.

Initially, this volume was conceived as a vehicle for Magda's former students to pay homage to her, and seven of the contributors studied under her in some way: Mara Naaman, Alexander Elinson, and Marlé Hammond were among her doctoral advisees at Columbia; Dana Sajdi, Jonathan Decter, and Christopher Stone attended some of her lively graduate seminars; and Lital Levy, while a Columbia undergraduate, produced two comparative studies of Israeli and Palestinian writing under her guidance. Each one of their contributions bears Magda's imprints in rather direct ways, as would be expected since they were produced under her direction. But Magda's presence may also be felt in writings by her mentors and colleagues. This became very clear to us as editors when their positive responses to our invitations for submission rolled in, often accompanied by personal testimonials about Magda's inspirational role in their work. It is therefore with great pleasure that we include pieces by two of her teachers: Michael Beard, whom Magda credited with exposing her to the beauty of English poetry while she was an undergraduate at the American University in Cairo, and Wolfhart Heinrichs, who directed Magda's doctoral dissertation on Ibn Khafaja at Harvard. We are also proud to feature essays by her esteemed colleagues and dear friends Roger Allen, Richard Jacquemond, András Hámori, Mervat Hatem, and Dina Amin, as well as a preface by Hamid Dabashi, Magda's comrade-in-arms, whose office door just opposite Magda's in the Department of Middle East and Asian Languages and Cultures at Columbia University (MEALAC), ever adorned with colorful posters and leaflets, would remind Magda daily of one of their shared intellectual endeavors: to "subvert the dominant paradigm."

Toward the end of her tragically short career, Magda's scholarly interests began to reflect her personal experiences of loss, having had to confront in the space of a few years the deaths of her mother and her brother as well as her own diagnosis of cancer. She embarked on a project about the poetic genre of *ritha'*, or elegy, which was supposed to culminate in a book entitled *Survival Zone: Transforming Loss into Beauty in Arabic Literature*. This volume, therefore, owes its title to Magda's unfinished project, and it tackles many of the academic issues that were close to her heart, including, especially, the elegy. In other words, the present volume is an attempt to carry on with her projects, both metaphorically and, in a certain way, tangibly.

Overview

Part I, entitled "Transforming Loss," deals with the genre of elegy and its various manifestations, guises, and inversions in the Arabic tradition from pre-Islamic times to the contemporary period. A universal genre dealing with the predicament of death, elegy has a seemingly definite purpose and its own standard repertoires of images that render it a self-sufficient genre within any literary canon. As we shall see presently, however, *ritha'* in the Arabic tradition is *dialogic* on several levels: it often interacts with other poetic purposes, yielding at times to other conventions and forms and in the process undergoing structural changes that may alter elegy's basic function—evoking laughter, for example, rather than tears. It is also often celebratory, inviting comparisons with praise poetry or eulogy. Elegy addresses different audiences: the self, the community of survivors, and, most of all, the deceased. Thus the genre's dialogic and open-ended nature leads us to some of the faultlines of the Arabic literary canon, allowing a substantial number of the contributors to this volume to question certain associations and formulations as to the place of elegy within the canon and, subsequently, to the suppressions and marginalizations implicit therein. Part I of this volume deals with both universal and culturally-specific elegiac formulae. It treats elegy in a multifaceted way, underscoring the genre's particularities and characteristic tensions at the same time that it draws attention to its multitude of poetic stances and rhetorical purposes. In this section, we encounter lost loved ones, lost cities, and even lost garments.'

Part II of this volume, entitled "Crossing Boundaries," departs from the subject of elegy and deals exclusively with modern literary forms: free verse and the novel. The topics here intersect on the issues of boundaries and zone-crossing, whether generic, national, linguistic, or formal. Two chapters in this part continue to engage with issues raised earlier, such as canon formation and the criteria thereof. Many of the chapters deal with the problematic of trans-cultural translation and of how to situate 'Arabic literature' both within and without non-Arabic canons.

Part I: Transforming Loss

Part I opens, poignantly, with a previously unpublished piece on the classical elegy by Magda Al-Nowaihi herself, entitled "Elegy and the Confrontation of Death in Arabic Poetry." Originally delivered in Arabic to students at Middlebury College's summer Arabic Language Institute, it has been translated and annotated by the editors with assistance from friends and colleagues. The piece performs a double function: on the one hand it serves as an invaluable introduction to the topic of elegy in the context of classical Arabic poetics; on the other, it reminds those of us who had the pleasure of hearing her speak of her extraordinary oratorical abilities. Although its syntax and vocabulary are uncharacteristically simple, reflecting the comprehension levels of the language students she was addressing, the lecture still conveys her impressive command of the art of oratory. Her speech focuses on the Abbasid era and features a vast array of themes and images, from direct and earthly expressions of suffering and loss through to abstract and philosophical formulations on the finality of death and the nature and meaning of immortality.

In Chapter 2, "One Size Fits All," Michael Beard situates the elegy in a cross-cultural context. He takes a comparative view of the literary outcome of the experience of loss by visiting canonical elegies in the English, Ancient Greek, and Arabic traditions. He focuses on the formulaic nature and stylization implicit in elegy and pauses to consider some of its conventions and codes. He ponders one of the genre's great paradoxes — namely, that the most celebrated elegies tend to be those that depict the deceased in the least specific ways — those that, in other words, contain the least information about the deceased; hence memorialization would seem to be at odds with remembrance. He then highlights the poetry of al-Khansa', noting that her elegies emote through the intense subjectivity of the speaker's grief, rather than through a description or characterization of the deceased. Beard concludes his chapter with a discussion of the twentieth-century aversion to the standard elegiac forms.

In Chapter 3, "Notes on Abu Tammam's Elegy *Kadha fa-l-yajilla l-khatbu*" András Hámori also speaks of an aversion, this time not to elegy but to eulogy. Hámori cites the observations of the medieval critic Ibn Rashiq, who equated panegyric with elegy since both praise a human subject. A panegyric in our day and age is often met with disdain and tarnished with sycophancy, but Hámori argues that an elegy — even of a public figure — still has the power to move. He demonstrates this through an engaging analysis of a public dirge by the famous Abu Tammam (d. 842). The emotional force of a dirge that is over a millennium old bespeaks of the universality of loss.

Transforming Loss into Beauty begins its exploration of some of the specialized niches within the elegiac genre in Chapter 4, "Dead Garments, Poor Nobles, and a Handsome Youth: Notes on a Poem by al-Sanawbari." Wolfhart Heinrichs visits an unusual subject of elegy — clothing — as it is featured in a unique poem by al-Sanawbari (d. 945), whose content and structure resist characterization. The ludicrous object of the poet's lament, his own attire, described in elegiac and at times amorous codes, introduces a fair amount of humor and satire into the equation. In his analysis, Heinrichs demonstrates the poem's thematic and structural indebtedness to such diverse genres as the elegy, the love poem, and the polythematic ode.

Chapter 5, "Loss Written in Stone: Ibn Shuhayd's *Ritha'* for Cordoba and its Place in the Arabic Elegiac Tradition," then reveals that expressions of loss in the Arabic tradition are not confined to people and things, but extend to places as well. Alexander Elinson explores the Andalusian 'city-elegy' *(ritha' al-mudun)*, which developed into a full-fledged subgenre as Iberian Islamic cities fell to the Reconquista. He shows how the city-elegy is a hybrid form, combining elements of *ritha'* with elements of the polythematic *qasida*, especially with regard to the latter's opening section, the *nasib*, where the poet typically cries over the deserted encampment of a departed beloved. Elinson also compares the city-elegy to its human counterpart, finding correspondences in their cadences and in the use of repetition and naming. He ends his discussion with an analysis of Ibn Shuhayd's (d. 1035) elegy for his lost city, Cordoba.

Chapter 6 continues in the Iberian domain, but this time investigating Andalusian elegy as it is expressed in another language: Hebrew. In this chapter, "Arabic Poetics and Representations of Women in the Andalusian Hebrew Lament," Jonathan Decter discusses Hebrew laments for women and through the course of his analysis details how Arabic poetic conventions converged with Jewish cultural practices in this subgenre of classical Hebrew poetry, particularly with regard to the trope of namelessness. The theme of gender and sexuality and its intersection with poetic canons, so crucial to Decter's contribution, also carries over into the next three chapters, which begin to tackle the fact that elegies made up a large proportion of women's contributions to classical Arabic poetry.

In Chapter 7, "*Qasida, Marthiya*, and *Différance,*" Marlé Hammond explores the dialogic complexity of sexually inscribed poetic forms as they are represented by the female poet's *marthiya* (elegiac poem) and the male poet's polythematic *qasida* (heroic ode), respectively. She exploits Derrida's 'non-concept' of *différance* to compare and contrast these gendered forms without recourse to binary oppositions. Through philological analyses of canonical poems by Su'da bt. al-Shamardal, Layla al-Akhyaliya, and al-Khansa', Hammond attempts to debunk the notion that women were socially 'confined' to the elegiac genre, arguing instead that women poets chose the paradigm of the *marthiya* because it celebrates a feminine sexual impulse or posture in much the same way the heroic ode celebrates a masculine one.

But what happens to a woman whose poetic desire, so to speak, exceeds the purpose and objects of the *marthiya*? Hammond looks at Layla al-Akhyaliya precisely because her elegies have attained canonical status. Layla, however, also happens to be the first woman known to have composed a panegyric, in its classical male polythematic form, and thus to have acted as a professional poet. Although Chapter 8, "Revisiting Layla al-Akhyaliya's Trespass," inasmuch as it treats one such panegyric, represents a departure from the topic of elegy, it retains elegy as its immediate frame of reference. Here, Dana Sajdi analyzes the non-elegiac poems of Layla—precisely because they represent transgressive acts. This chapter demonstrates how Layla manipulated and appropriated the male form as she competed in the same poetic and professional field with the best male poets of her time. Sajdi then shows the ambivalence of literary critics toward Layla's unorthodox poetic career, the problematic implications of which are muted through later 'cleansing' reports that sought to expunge her excesses and preserve her memory solely as an elegist comparable to al-Khansa'.

In Chapter 9, "Writing About Life Through Loss: 'A'isha Taymur's Elegies and the Subversion of the Arabic Canon," we enter the modern era. Mervat Hatem explores the literary career of the nineteenth-century writer 'A'isha Taymur, who composed elegies to her female relatives—most famously her daughter Tawhida—to her father, and to a shaykh who may have been instrumental in her education. Although Taymur rooted herself in an ancient female poetic tradition by demonstrating a preference for the elegiac genre, she in some ways updated it for the modern world, most notably by dedicating so many of her elegies to female figures. Hatem also shows how Taymur had to contend with the critics, whose sexism, informed by contemporary trends in medicine and psychology, attributed woman's preference for lamentations to her 'unstable' nature.

Chapter 10, "Sleep in Peace: Salah 'Abd al-Sabur's Gentle Elegy to the Death of a Hero," seals the topic of elegiac poetry, but here the context is the modern nation-state and its need for human sacrifice, and the literary form is free verse. Dina Amin analyzes a public elegy by one of Egypt's most prominent twentieth-century poets, Salah 'Abd al-Sabur. The object of the elegy is a friend of the poet, an air force pilot who was killed by Israeli forces in Gaza in 1955. Amin shows how 'Abd al-Sabur paints a rich picture of the deceased which simultaneously elevates its subject to the pedestal of a willingly self-sacrificing national hero and commemorates his human, down-to-earth attributes as a teacher and friend. 'Abd al-Sabur's poem does not use classical elegiac conventions, codes, or images. Rather, it exploits a mixture of Christian and Muslim religious symbols—from the iconographic representation of Christ to references to the Qur'an—in order to imbue a secular national idiom with an interfaith construction of martyrdom.

Part II: Crossing Boundaries

Part II opens with an article by Roger Allen. In Chapter 11, "Historiography as Novel: Bensalem Himmich's *al-'Allama*," Allen considers *The Polymath* by the Moroccan novelist Bensalem Himmich in the light of its merging of history and fiction. Allen, who translated the novel into English, informs us that Himmich, a philosophy professor and author of a work on Ibn Khaldun (d. 1406), has deployed his intimate knowledge of the life and works of the North African polymath to create a personalized and intimate portrait of this historical figure alongside a fictional love story. The novel is about the last few years of Ibn Khaldun's life, after his exile from his native city. It takes the reader on Ibn Khaldun's journey in the *Mashriq* and to the scholar's famous meeting with Timur Lang. In his exposition of the novel, Allen characterizes it as a work not only of historical fiction, but of historiographical fiction, in that it appropriates historiographical literary forms. Allen explores this intersection of history, historiography, and fiction, and unveils the political ends, grounded in the present, that motivate this literary use of the historical record.

Chapter 12, "Sonallah Ibrahim's *Les années de Zeth*, or The exportability of contemporary Arabic literature," is another account of a novel from the point of view of its translator. This time it is the process of translation itself that concerns the author. Richard Jacquemond deals with the sometimes insurmountable problems the translator faces in making a text both accessible and marketable in a foreign language and culture. He does this through a critique—his own translation of Sonallah Ibrahim's masterpiece *Dhat* into French (as *Les années de Zeth*). Among the dilemmas he highlights are how to grapple with the as yet unsystematized rules of Arabic punctuation, how to translate European loanwords (that is, terminology that is itself already translated) when they are being used in the context of a satirical code, and how to handle cultural references that would not be accessible to a foreign reader—does one expunge them or explain them? Jacquemond finds no definitive answers, of course, but by highlighting the choices one is forced to make, he gives us new insight not only into the translation process but also into our reading of the original text itself.

The novel and its boundaries are taken up by the next two chapters as well. In Chapter 13, "Tawfiq al-Hakim, Yusuf al-Qa'id, and the 'Mature' Arabic Novel," Christopher Stone compares two celebrated novels, one by each of the aforementioned authors, in order to challenge the criteria by which the modern Arabic canon has classified these texts. While al-Hakim's novel is seen as representative of the Arab novel in its 'infancy,' al-Qa'id's work is said to exemplify its 'mature' stage. Unconvinced by the 'developmentalist' (and implicitly chronological and linear) positioning of the works of these two authors, Stone goes on to demonstrate that al-Hakim's work, while formally non-experimental, is in some ways a more powerful subversion of the genre upon which each is loosely based—the western detective novel.

In Chapter 14, "The Anti-Romance Antidote: Revisiting Allegories of the Nation," Mara Naaman compares and contrasts a seminal feminist novel by the Egyptian Latifa al-Zayyat with the memoirs of the American writer Mary Karr. In so doing, she challenges the nationally allegorical/apolitically libidinal boundary constructed between 'third-' and 'first-world' literatures by Frederic Jameson. True, al-Zayyat's novel is considered a national romance, but her protagonist's marginal position and feminist stance allow her to disrupt the primacy of the nation for the subjectivity of the struggle for self-actualization. Meanwhile, Karr narrates an infinitely political anti-romance that critiques and reconstructs none other than the nation. Naaman sets up a contrapuntal relationship between al-Zayyat and Karr, which sees in their respective marginal positions literary outcomes that are "hardly 'other' to each other."

Last but not least, Chapter 15, "Self-Portraits of the Other: Toward a Palestinian Poetics of Hebrew Verse," departs from the novel and returns to the Arabic influence on Hebrew poetry, this time in a modern context, to explore the linguistic and imagistic strategies employed by Palestinian poets composing in Hebrew. Lital Levy shows how these Palestinian poets use Hebrew, with its lexicon rich in Arabic cognates, to reflect and invert a linguistically alienated self that is at once both 'same' and 'other.' Similarly, on the level of spatial representation, these poets map out topographies in which one finds home in exile. In the process, Palestinian poets consciously construct an illusory self-portrait, one that includes the other within it.

Translating Loss into Beauty thus, in both its parts, reflects Magda Al-Nowaihi's depth and versatility as a scholar. Equally comfortable with classical and modern, *Mashriq* and *Maghrib*, poetry and prose, Magda engaged critically with diverse topics, subjecting them to rigorous and theoretically grounded analyses. The contributors have paid homage to her here by grappling with genres (the elegy), forms (the novel), authors (Latifa al-Zayyat, Sonallah Ibrahim, Salah 'Abd al-Sabur), and theoretical concerns (gender, sexuality, identity) near and dear to her heart. It is an apt reflection, albeit painfully incomplete. Many of her interests are of course unrepresented, and many of her friends and admirers who could have contributed are, for various reasons relating to human frailty, absent.

Before concluding, we would like to explain why we felt it was important for us to publish this volume with the American University in Cairo (AUC) Press. First, Magda had many personal ties to AUC as an institution. It is where she earned her undergraduate degree, and it is where she met her husband, Fernand Cohen. It is also where Magda's father, the late Mohamed Al-Nowaihi, taught literature for many years. In fact, it was AUC Press that published a volume in his honor over two decades ago.[2] Furthermore, by publishing this volume with AUC Press, we are reaffirming her presence in Egypt, her home country, which part of her always regretted leaving despite the tremendously successful career she made for herself at some of the most prestigious academic institutions in the United States. It is, as it were, a kind of ritual homecoming.

It would be tempting to conclude with a proper eulogy, praising Magda for her outstanding qualities, but that would make her seem somehow unreal. Instead we would like to thank her, on behalf of her students if not her colleagues, for the many instances in which she went out on a limb for us—as individuals and as members of a collective 'field'—doing her best to ensure that we found our own place and purpose in the world, and challenging us to improve standards on all fronts: these include, to name just a few examples, the time she returned early from bone-marrow transplant to prod her graduate seminar students into proposing a conference panel; the time she served on a dissertation defense committee via teleconference, despite being gravely ill; the time she took a young student from a related discipline under her wing, advising her honor's thesis when no one else was prepared to do so; and the many, many times she had the courage to give us frank assessments of our work, forcing us to confront our weaknesses and complacencies. For this we are eternally grateful.

Notes

1   These tributes include an annual prize endowed in her name at the American University in Cairo (the Magda Al-Nowaihi Graduate Student Award in Gender Studies) and two special issues of journals dedicated to her memory, namely *Edebiyat* 14, nos. 1–2 (May and November 2003), guest ed. Samah Selim, and the *Electronic Journal of Middle Eastern Studies* (Fall 2004), ed. Joseph Massad, Samia Mehrez, and Maha Yahya.
2   A.H. Green, ed., *In Quest of an Islamic Humanism: Arabic and Islamic Studies in Memory of Mohamed Al-Nowaihi* (Cairo: The American University in Cairo Press, 1984).

PART I

TRANSFORMING LOSS

1

Elegy and the Confrontation of Death in Arabic Poetry

Magda Al-Nowaihi

The following is the text of a lecture Magda delivered at the summer Arabic Language Institute of Middlebury College. Despite its simple syntax, which was entirely appropriate to her audience of language learners but which was not generally characteristic of her speaking style, the lecture conveys at least in part the warmth and charisma that Magda exuded in her public addresses. It also gives us a very rough idea of how she may have approached the elegy in her unfinished work on the subject. The speech has been translated and annotated by the editors with the help of Shahab Ahmed, Amal Jardaneh, and Geert Jan van Gelder. We would like to thank Samia Mehrez for providing us with the Arabic transcription.

Today, I am going to speak to you about a certain type of Arabic poetry—a very important type: the elegy. By elegy *(al-ritha')*, I refer to poetry written on the occasion of a person's death. That is to say that the poet, when a certain someone dies, wishes to compose a poem about his or her death. Sometimes elegy is private: when, for example, the deceased is someone who has had a close personal relationship with the poet, such as a brother, son, or husband, or someone for whom the poet felt intense affection. (Note that many women composed elegies.) And sometimes elegy is public: in this case the deceased is not necessarily someone whom the poet has known personally but who has nonetheless played a crucial role in the life of the poet and in that of his or her society, as, for example, a tribal chieftain, an army commander, a caliph, or an intellectual. Public elegy, in other words, expresses the grief of society as a whole rather than of the poet as an individual. There are also poets who composed elegies for animals—a beloved dog, cat, horse, or camel whose departure inspires an elegiac composition. Such poems are, on occasion, deeply moving. And there is yet another kind of elegy, one that is perhaps unique to Arabic poetry, and that is the elegy of the self *(ritha' al-nafs)*. The poet elegizes himself because he believes his death is imminent—perhaps he has succumbed to a fatal illness, or perhaps he finds himself imprisoned and awaiting execution. He elegizes himself, speaking about his own death. (I will give you some examples of this shortly.) To confront death is obviously tremendously difficult; for death is mysterious, unknown, and frightening. It is excruciating for everyone involved, the departed or departing and his or her friends, family, and loved ones all fear separation—*eternal* separation. But writing poetry, or literary creativity and innovation more generally, may help to confront this thing called death and the feelings and emotions that it stirs in our souls.

There is, in this regard, a lovely story about Abu Tammam (d. 842), an important Abbasid poet. For it is said that Abu Tammam, upon hearing the news of a close friend's death, asked his companions to bring him an inkstand. He then dipped his garment in the ink and proceeded to hit himself with the ink-smeared clothing, slapping himself on the cheeks, chest, and shoulders. Afterward he composed a very beautiful elegy about his deceased friend.[1] To me, this anecdote symbolizes the importance of literary and poetic composition in transporting an individual from the stage of weeping, wailing, mourning, and grieving to the stage of confrontation, creation, and invention.

Elegies have been written or composed in Arabic poetry from pre-Islamic times onward through the ages. Even now, there are important poems being composed in this genre. Here, however, I am going to focus on poetry of the Abbasid era. This is an extremely rich and fertile period, and in my view, the most beautiful Arabic poetry dates from this period. Before we begin, there are a few things we need to know about the Abbasids' view of death. Of course, as you know, by this time the Islamic religion has been firmly established in the Arabian Peninsula, Iraq, and beyond, and most people [in the region of Iraq] have embraced Islam. Islamic doctrine teaches that death is not *the end*, that there is life after death, and that, on Judgment Day, people will be resurrected to an afterlife that is eternal and free of death. Such a world view, namely that death is not an absolute end or that it is not *the end* because it is followed by another life, assists some as they confront death. Moreover, in Islamic societies, people believe that there is a kind of justice in the hereafter that is absent in the here-and-now. In this world, someone like JFK Jr.—that is a young man in his thirties or forties who is attractive, intelligent, generous, dignified, and physically strong—may die while an evil oppressive old miser lives to be ninety or even a hundred. There is no justice in this life. But Muslims believe that there is justice in the afterlife, for the evil will be punished in hell, and the good will be rewarded in paradise. This belief too will help people to some extent in their confrontation with death. Despite this, however, various views on death may be found; not everyone is in agreement. In the early days of Islam, when the Prophet first started speaking about the idea of rebirth or resurrection or life after death, not everyone was convinced by it, and this reticence is expressed in the following poetic examples.

When a poet says:

Life, then death, then resurrection
It's all nonsense, Umm 'Amr[2]

he means that the idea that we live then die then live again is a myth, not a convincing line of thought. Another poet states:

Ibn Kabsha[3] promises me that we will live
But what kind of life do corpses lead?
Is he incapable of turning death away
Reviving me only when my bones have decayed?[4]

The poet says: O Muhammad, O Messenger of God, if this God of yours is so All-Powerful and Mighty, why does he let me die and then revive me after my body and bones have decayed? Why doesn't he protect me from death in the first place? These are some of the questions that are raised—this last one dating from the period immediately following the Prophet.

But even during the Abbasid era people expressed doubts about the concept of resurrection after death. I'll give you two examples. The first is by al-Mutanabbi (d. 965), who is perhaps the greatest Arab poet:

People love to argue irreconcilably about everything but death
Yet even there they differ
Some say a man's soul emerges free, unscathed
Others say it joins man's body in the rot
He who ponders over his soul and this world
is overcome by impotence and exhaustion[5]

The poet is saying, in other words, that some people believe that body and soul die at the same time, while others believe that the body dies but the soul is saved. Anyone who seeks an explanation or solution to this will not find one. Rather, he will be exhausted and incapable of arriving at an answer. That's al-Mutanabbi. As to Abu al-'Atahiya (d. 826), an important poet of asceticism (zuhd), he finds the idea of life after death to be even scarier and more anxiety-provoking than the idea of an absolute end. He states:

If only we died and were left alone
Then death would be a relief to the living
But if, when we die, we're resurrected
We'll be held thereafter to account[6]

He means that after death we'll be asked, What did you do? and Why did you do that? and we'll be punished for our misdeeds, and that is frightening. We have all made mistakes in our lives, after all. Elsewhere Abu al-'Atahiya says:

My Lord, don't torture me
I acknowledge what I've done[7]

Don't torture me, he says, I've committed sins—I confess.
There are some important images and stylistic devices that poets use in elegies. One of the most important goals of the elegist is to achieve immortality for the deceased. How may this immortality be achieved? Via the memorable nature of beautiful poetry, because when people

remember an elegy, they also remember what the poet speaks about, namely the virtues, admirable qualities, and fine accomplishments of the deceased. And if this beautiful poetry is recited by people in the years and centuries to come, the memory of the deceased will live on, unending. In this way the deceased may achieve immortality. Abu Tammam, for example, achieved it for his friend elegized in the aforementioned poem.[8] People praised him [the deceased] and said, the one elegized in this poetry has not, and will never, die, because his memory will remain forever.

Poets have different ways of realizing immortality for the deceased. Perhaps the simplest way of doing this is to say that the deceased has now moved from the ephemeral life of this world to the everlasting one of the next. He has gone to meet God in paradise. In the following lines by Ibn al-Rumi (d. 896) that I am about to recite to you, the poet employs images and expressions of marriage in order to console a father bereaved of a daughter who was of marriageable age. The poet speaks about her death as if it is a marriage, as if she is moving into her spousal home in paradise and as if her father has secured a good dowry for her. He states:

> May God not take away a daughter
> Whom you've entrusted to a son-in-law who does not disgrace
> I hope the brideprice of paradise
> Satisfies you
> Don't despair on her account
> You've married her to a worthy husband and secured the dowry[9]

This is one way to realize immortality. Another way is to speak about how the deceased will never cease to be mentioned. The word 'mentioning' (dhikr) in Arabic is related to the word for 'memory' (dhikra). In other words, when we recall (natadhakkar) a person it means that we won't forget him. Likewise, remembering (dhikr) someone means that we speak about him a lot, for remembering and speaking about a person make him or her immortal. [Mansur] al-Namari states:

> The Nights may have stood on the verge of obliterating him
> but there is a memory of him that obliterates the Nights[10]
> The memory of this person will obliterate the Nights—in other
>   words, it will outlive time.

Among the most important means by which a person can attain this memorable status is to die an honorable death. An honorable death, in this instance, would be one that occurs in warfare, in a battle to defend one's creed, nation, or tribe. That would be considered an honorable death. There are many elegies that speak of an honorable death achieving immortality for an individual. But occasionally poets face a dilemma: what if they have to compose an elegy for an important person, a caliph, for example, and what if this important person has not died a warrior's death, and suppose he was devoid of courage and forbearance throughout his life? Take the caliph al-Amin. His life was one endless party, with wine, music, and beautiful maidens his constant companions. What, then, is a poet supposed to say? One solution rests in the somewhat amusing following lines:

> In this way the Fates surround the noble
> Amid flutes, flowers, and wine
> And between two cups they quenched his thirst
> The cup of his pleasures and the cup of Death[11]

That's a bit different than the norm.

Yet another way of realizing immortality for the deceased is to compare him to nature, to a certain time in its cycle or to one of its manifestations. Why? Because nature, as it appears to us, is constantly renewing itself. Consider the seasons: in the autumn leaves may fall off the trees, but in the spring the trees blossom once more, turning green and bearing fruit. And consider rain: it comes and goes but its traces, in the form of vegetation, flowers, trees, and so forth, stay with us all the time. For this reason, comparing the deceased with nature incorporates him or her into this ever-reinvigorating cycle of life and death. Death is not final, for, as al-Sharif al-Radi (d. 1016) says in one of his elegies:

> Move on, as Spring moves on, its trace
> lingering in every thicket and on every desert plane[12]

Spring has gone, but its vestiges remain with us, just as you O deceased one have died, but your good deeds, sweet memory, and virtues remain with us after your death.

But in elegy there is a tension between the desire to endow the deceased with immortality and the desire to recognize the stark power, cruelty, and pain of death. This is because any successful elegiac poem must express a lot of sadness and grief. It can't be merely a celebration of the personality and lasting impact of the deceased. And an elegy can't have complete faith in its power to confront and overcome death. If it did believe wholly in the idea that it could actually make the deceased immortal, then where would grief fit into it? And what about pain? Where does the pain come from? Thus the poet needs to achieve a balance, albeit a precarious one, between immortalizing the deceased and acknowledging the power of death and of time to annihilate an individual's life as well as his or her memory. Therefore, while a comparison with nature sometimes serves to assist in the immortalization of the deceased, it can also serve to convey the feeling that the deceased has vanished completely because the universal order has been upset. We cannot rely on nature's cyclical order. Our world may turn upside down, as it has in the following lines:

The stars of beneficence have plummeted, the dewy hand of
    generosity has withered
So, too, the seas of bounty dried up, after the Barmacids[13]

The Barmacids are the subjects of the elegy. And in their wake the stars have fallen, the seas become scanty, the dew dried up. Nature has been disturbed, its scales upset. Nature is, as we can see, unreliable. The entire universe is out of order.

There's another method that poets use to achieve this balance between immortalization and the acknowledgment of the power of death, and this is the very beautiful and forceful expression "as if . . . not." A poet might say, "as if he didn't do this . . . as if he didn't do that," repeating this formulation to list off everything that the deceased has accomplished. And while the poets list these deeds, they simultaneously negate them with the negative particles *lam* and *lan*.[14] In this way they repeat the characteristics, virtues, and deeds of the elegized at the same time that they negate them. Al-Mutanabbi, for example, wrote an elegy for Khawla, who was the sister of his patron Sayf al-Dawla. It is said that al-Mutanabbi and Khawla were more than just friends (that she was his lover). So he composed an elegy for her in which he repeated "as if . . . not" many times. Consider the following lines, for example (note that the poet here uses the name "Fi'la" to refer to Khawla):

> As if Fi'la's armies had not filled Diyarbakir
> [As if] she had not bestowed robes of honor
> [As if] she had not restored life to those struck with perdition
> [As if] she had not responded to a cry for help in times of calamity
>   and war[15]

Thus the poet asserts that Fi'la brimmed with life, assisted the grief-stricken, distributed robes of honor,[16] and at the same time states that it is as if she hadn't done these things. Hence an important balance is achieved between simultaneously-expressed assertions and denials.

Another element of contradiction that inserts itself in the elegist's mind involves one's perspective on time. From the vantage point of death, it seems that time comes to a decisive halt. In other words, time continues up until the moment of death, and then, with death, everything stops, including time. But the poets consider time from another angle as well, and that is the fact that it is the continuation of time which makes death inevitable. With the passing of time, each one of us will die sooner or later. How does death interact with time? How do we acknowledge that time persists and that death is an important factor in its continuity when we feel that the moment of death is an utterly painful and final cessation? Abu Tammam exhibits a certain *schadenfreude* when he states that Time, or Fate, or the Nights, or the Days, or whatever you want to call it, is itself, in the hereafter, going to die:

> The vicissitudes of Fortune may bereave me of them
> But Fortune, too, will die bereft[17]

(A 'bereft' person [*mathkul*] is one who has lost someone dear.) The poet is saying that, while today Fortune is killing my loved ones and taking them away from me, tomorrow, on the Day of Judgment, it is Fortune who will die.

Another way of treating the continuation of time against the finality of death is through repetition. Ibn al-Rumi, for example, has a certain poem where he repeats the phrase "how many a" (*ala kam*) more than twenty or thirty times in the course of ten lines. Here is the first line of the passage:

How many a great figure has time abased
Many a strong-willed one has it broken
How many has it muzzled[18]

This repetition of "how many a ... many a ... many ..." gives us the feeling of the perpetuity of time. "Many a ... many a ... many ..." runs on and on. At the same time, however, the verbs that Ibn al-Rumi chooses are all verbs of interruptions, endings, and full stops. This is what creates the balance between the perpetuity of time and the finality of death. In the following lines, al-Mutanabbi, too, expresses the idea of the oppressiveness of death, but here he sees it as an inevitable consequence of the passage of time:

People before us left their loved ones behind
Every doctor has sought, in vain, to find death's cure
They preceded us into this world and were they still here
There would be no room here for us to come and go
One moves in by stealthy repossession
The other moves out, the object of thievery[19]

In other words, at the beginning he says: We all are separated from our loved ones, because they die, and there is no cure for death—no final remedy for it; no matter how ingenious the physician, he or she won't find a cure for death. At the same time, however, the poet makes a very provocative admission: he states that if our forerunners had not died, we wouldn't be living, because our relationship with the deceased is that of the robber to the robbed, the plunderer to the plundered. We dispossess them, by force, of their place and time. If they hadn't died, we wouldn't be alive. Indeed, our life is contingent upon our loved ones' death. This is the way life works. Ancestors die so that future generations may live, and al-Mutanabbi expresses this relationship as one of theft or looting. The following dispossesses and displaces the preceding.

Al-Ma'arri (d. 1057), another prominent poet, expresses this very same idea in a celebrated elegy he composed for a jurisprudent (faqih) friend of his:

O friend! These graves of ours fill the expanses
and where are the graves from the age of 'Ad?
Lighten your tread, I do not think the face of the earth is composed
of else but these bodies.
And it is foul for us, even if a long time has passed,
to disrespect our fathers and forefathers.
Walk, if you can, gently in the air
Not trudging over the bones of worshippers.
Many a grave becomes over and again a grave
Laughing at the jamming together of rivals
And remains are buried on top of remains
Along the length of time into eternity.[20]

Al-Ma'arri wonders: What happened to the graves from the time of 'Ad? ('Ad is a prehistoric place where many are said to have died.) Where are their graves? Their graves are beneath our feet. Therefore, when we walk on the ground, we are trampling on our ancestors' heads. This debases them, of course, but what are we supposed to do if we would like life to go on? Fly in the air? Impossible. So if we accept life, we necessarily accept death, even if it means we are usurping our ancestors' time and place and trespassing on their graves. That's life, and this is the logic of our relationship with time.

The above verses treat a very important psychological theme that one finds in elegiac compositions, and this theme relates to the feeling of guilt, of sin, of culpability. It is not, of course, a rational or logical feeling, but it is very powerful nonetheless. In English we know it as 'survivor's guilt'— the feeling of guilt that we have when someone dear to us has died and we go on living. We feel a type of guilt not unlike those so well-expressed by al-Mutanabbi and al-Ma'arri. Elegists are always trying to deal with these feelings in their poems, and they have many ways of doing so. One of the principal strategies involves bringing the deceased near to them. After all, when people die, it is common for us to feel that they are very far away, in another world, in an unknown world where we can't see or hear them. But the poets wish to break down these distancing barriers between the living and the dead, and in their elegies they have different techniques for doing this. For example, they use the vocative, the second person, and the interrogative with great frequency. They address the deceased, ask questions of them, and give them orders, even though they know, of course, that the deceased do not hear them. I'll give you some examples. The first is from Ibn al-Mu'tazz (d. 908):

O dweller of the grave in the dark dusty earth
All alone, in al-Zahiriya, in the remotest part of the house,
Where are the armies you drew?
Where are the treasures you never counted?[21]

He addresses himself to the grave dweller, saying: You are in the grave, far away. The grave is dark, in the distant desert. You are by yourself, all alone. And yet, he speaks to the grave dweller as if he were standing before him. Then he asks him questions. Why? We often ask questions because we need certain information. When you students ask your teacher a question in class, you expect an answer that informs you about something. The questions here are different in that the poet does not need to know where the armies or the treasures are. He knows very well where they are. Rather, there are hidden questions behind the stated ones: Where are you? Why did you die? Why aren't you here with us? These are questions arising from denial and anger at the deceased. Once again, this feeling of anger is not logical or rational, but it is real. When we feel anger toward a deceased person who has left us, it is as if that person could have prevented his or her death.

These themes of distance, the desire for proximity, and anger toward the deceased have very beautiful expressions in elegy. I'll present you with two. The first is by Bashshar b. Burd (d. 783). These lines are, in my opinion, extremely beautiful and moving. He wrote them on the occasion of his wife's passing, when he was feeling a strong sense of loss and longing for her:

When Umm Bakr had left us,
There was sadness, followed by an intense loneliness.
My heart began to ache for something of her
to burn its fire in my chest.
I drew an image of her and sat there before it
complaining about the wailing that had overcome me
Pleading to her features in the dust

for mercy from the torture
as if she is there, listening to my anxieties
but my complaints reach only the dirt[22]

Bashshar, when his wife had died, missed his wife greatly and wanted to speak to her. So he drew her picture in the dust and began speaking and complaining to that picture. Complaining about whom? The deceased. He complains about her self to her image. And he speaks of the torturous pain of being separated from her. He knows full well that he is speaking to the dirt, but he finds that drawing her picture on the ground in some way fills a need he has to speak to her.

My second example of verses that treat the themes of distance, desire for proximity, and anger toward the deceased is from a poem by al-Sanawbari (d. 945). He expresses his anger over the death of his daughter:

I miss the sight of you, so I come
but see nothing but dirt and stone
Get yourself back home, I am oh so disappointed
at your determination to avoid it
Your home shies away from its family
and the family is afraid to go home[23]

The poem speaks about a home that has become empty and desolate. The family members hate it, and it no longer serves as their home. It's no longer their home because she's not there. The poet begs the daughter to come back home, but this, of course, is impossible.

Another technique that poets employ in elegies is to address a third party. This third party is usually a woman, an imaginary figure who either orders the poet to stop crying or beseeches him to cry more. This reflects, of course, the fact that the poet would like, on the one hand, to maintain his patience and composure in the face of death, not wishing to appear weak or defeated, and, on the other hand, to express his grief and pain. Addressing a third party who orders him to stop crying is therefore a way of coping with his internal struggle and his contradictory feelings. Abu Tammam has two lines in different poems that deal with this contradiction. In one case, he states:

My eye flows, weeping, in unrelenting grief
Leave me to it, it's not for you[24]

He says to this woman who tells him not to cry: Leave me alone—I hope you never go through the same. In another poem, he asks this female figure to do the contrary:

Repeat your wailing lament, repeat
Cry more tears, then still more again[25]

Here he asks for more crying. And, in either case, the poet depicts an internal struggle, for the woman he addresses probably exists only in his imagination.

I spoke, before, about self-elegy. This is when the poet writes about his own death. Abu al-Firas al-Hamadani (d. 968) composed an elegy for himself when he was in prison and knew he would be executed. In the poem, he does not admit to feeling fear or grief or pain for himself. He says that he doesn't fear death and that he's not particularly worried about it, but that he's concerned for his elderly mother and young daughter whom he will leave behind. That's what he's anxious about. Addressing his daughter, he says:

My little girl, don't be sad
Everyone must go
Mourn me intensely
From behind your veil
Say, when you call out to me
And I'm unable to find the words to respond,
"The Glorious Youth Abu al-Firas
never lived out his youth."[26]

Notice the contradiction: in the first line he tells her don't be upset, don't be scared, don't cry, and then he turns around in the second line and says: Mourn me, cry for me, speak to me—even if you don't hear me. And in the last line, he seems to ask her to recount his good qualities to others (tu'addid). Hence he contradicts himself. He does not own up to his own fear; rather, he transfers it to his daughter.

There is another technique that poets use to combat their feelings of guilt and blame, and that is to say that had we been able to protect the deceased we would have. Consider, for example, the case of an elegy for the caliph al-Mutawakkil. The caliph was killed in his palace one night, and it is said that his son al-Muntasir arranged his father's assassination because he wanted to take over the caliphate. The poet al-Buhturi (d. 897) was in the palace on the fatal night, and it seems that he felt guilty for not intervening to protect the caliph. Thus, in one of his elegies, he attempts to ward off his feelings of powerlessness before death by saying:

I'd defend him with my hands, but to avert the foes
the night's unarmed and its unarmored won't do
Had only my sword been in hand at the time of the killing
Then the expeditious killer would see how I'd have rushed upon him[27]

The poet tells us that he would have defended the caliph with his hands, but that it would have been to no avail. If only I had had my sword with me, he continues, I would have defeated and slaughtered the killer. Of course, this is probably a rhetorical wish; he didn't really want to have his sword in hand. Rather, he just needed to say this in an elegy to compensate for his feelings of weakness and impotence.

Now I'd like to cite examples from two poems, one by Ibn al-Rumi and one by al-Mutanabbi. In them we see how the poets deal with their feelings of culpability in completely different ways. In the case of Ibn al-Rumi, his middle son, Muhammad, had died, and he wrote a very moving elegy for him. In it he speaks with the utmost clarity about his feeling that he is to blame. (It is almost as if he had lived with us in the twentieth century and read Freud.)

My son, given over to the Earth by my own hand
What glory for the receiver, what grief for the giver[28]

He looks at the palms of his hands because it is these two hands that have buried his son. He looks at his hands, parts of his own body, and says: It is *you* who have buried this child. *You* put him in the dirt. He then makes a transition from speaking about his hands to speaking about his heart. He hates his heart. He hates it because it did not break down upon the death of the boy. He says:

I was dumbstruck that my heart did not split
even if it were harder than smooth rock[29]

Even if his heart is made of stone, he asks, how could it not be broken by the death of this innocent child? He hates his heart, just as he hates his hand. He then addresses the boy directly:

Muhammad, no delusion can console my heart
without further crippling it in grief
I see your two surviving brothers, but they
only add fuel to the fire
When they play a game you played
they inadvertently ignite a hellfire in my heart[30]

He later states:

When Death sends an infantry of men to the army
of the dead, let him conscript me[31]

Ibn al-Rumi, who had three sons, tells Muhammad that when he looks at his two surviving sons and takes pleasure in seeing them play and have fun, he hates the feeling it leaves in him. He hates the pleasure he takes in their lives and in their games. He hates that in himself. (Tragically, these two surviving sons also died during childhood, and Ibn al-Rumi buried them a few years after he buried Muhammad.) The poet also expresses a death wish: Let Death conscript me. I want to die.

Compare Ibn al-Rumi to al-Mutanabbi. Al-Mutanabbi's grandmother, who was very dear to him, died, and it is said that he was the cause of her death. Why? He had traveled far away from her and hadn't sent her any letters to give her his news. She was therefore afraid and anxious for him, and being an old, infirm woman, her health deteriorated and she died. When al-Mutanabbi got word of her death, he composed an elegy. At the beginning of the poem he speaks about his feelings of remorse and blame. He hates himself. Further on, however, due to his forceful personality, his obstinacy, and his arrogance, al-Mutanabbi transforms his internal struggle with remorse into an external one. Al-Mutanabbi is an expert at such transformations, always able to externalize any emotional conflicts or tensions. He imagines an enemy, creating one out of thin air, and then confronts and combats this enemy. (He finds this a lot easier than confronting himself.) He effects this externalization in the following lines:

> Those who find pleasure in others' misfortunes may celebrate
>   her death
> In me is born spiteful loathing for them
> It journeys outward respecting only itself
> seeking nothing but to pass judgment on its creator[32]

Who are these people who take vicarious pleasure in his grandmother's death? We don't know, and they probably don't exist but rather are created by al-Mutanabbi as external projections of his internal struggle. He later expresses that idea of accepting death, but in a completely different manner than Ibn al-Rumi. He states:

> Leave me, O World, if you wish
> Go further, O Soul, in your hatred for it
> Not a single hour has failed to be insuperable
> and I don't have a heart that gives in to oppression[33]

Here, he is saying to Death: Come and get me, I don't care. His tone is completely different than that of Ibn al-Rumi, who says he wants to die. There is negativity and resignation in Ibn al-Rumi, whereas al-Mutanabbi confronts death with violence and combativeness. It just goes to show how the poets, despite their use of techniques and expressions that are common to a certain literary genre, each have their own distinct poetic styles, showcasing their individual personalities and inclinations.

Through these poetic citations, I hope I have shown you how the elegy has the power to transform painful feelings from visceral emotional reactions into innovative and beautiful artistic creations. Al-Ma'arri states in his aforementioned poem:

Were elegies tears
they would erase the lines of composition[34]

But elegies are not tears, not a form of erasure but of composition, of literary and artistic creation. They help us to confront death. We cannot defeat death permanently, of course, but at least we may confront it and perhaps even rebel against it, in the manner of al-Mutanabbi.

Thank you.

Notes

1   Reference to this anecdote is made in Muhammad Muhyi al-Din 'Abd al-Hamid, *Ma'ahid al-tansis 'ala shawahid al-talkhis*, ed., 'Abd al-Rahim b. Ahmad al-'Abbasi, 4 pts. in 2 vols. (Cairo: Matba'at al-Sa'ada, 1947), 1.2:178–79. Note that the poem in question is analyzed by András Hámori in this volume.

2   This verse has been variously attributed to Abu Nuwas, Ibn al-Zib'ara, and Dik al-Jinn.

3   'Ibn (Abi) Kabsha' is a derogatory name for the Prophet Muhammad.

4   These verses are attributed to al-Aswad b. Ya'fur. See Muhammad b. Ahmad al-Ibshihi, *al-Mustatraf fi kull fann mustazraf*, 2 vols. (Cairo: al-Matba'a al-Saniya, 1885), 2:268.

5   Abu al-Tayyib Ahmad b. al-Husayn al-Mutanabbi, *Diwan Ibn Abi Tayyib al-Mutanabbi bi-sharh Abi al-Baqa' al-'Ukbari al-musamma bi-l-Bayan bi-sharh al-Diwan*, eds. Mustafa al-Saqqa, Ibrahim al-Ibyari, and 'Abd al-Hafiz Shalabi, 4 pts. in 2 vols. (Beirut: Dar al-Ma'rifa li-l-Tiba'a wa-l-Nashr, 1978), 1.1:95–96.

6   Isma'il b. al-Qasim Abu al-'Atahiya, *Diwan*, ed. Karam al-Bustani (Beirut: Dar Sadir, 1964), 483.

7   Ibid., 425.

8   The poem in question, that is to say the subject of the aforementioned anecdote (see note 1 above), is Abu Tammam's *ra'iya* elegizing Muhammad b. Humayd, which begins "Kadha fa-l-yajilla l-khatbu." See András Hámori's analysis of the piece in this volume.

9   Ibn al-Rumi, *Diwan*, ed. Husayn Nassar, 7 vols. (Cairo: al-Hay'a al-Misriya al-'Amma li-l-Kitab, 1973-81), 5:1819.

10 Ibn 'Abd Rabbih, *al-'Iqd al-Farid*, ed. 'Abd al-Hamid al-Tirhini, 7 vols. (Beirut: Dar al-Kutub al-'Ilmiya, 1983), 3:41.

11 The editors regret that they have not been able to identify these verses.

12 Muhammad b. al-Husayn al-Sharif al-Radi, *Diwan*, 2 vols. (Beirut: Dar Sadir, 1961), 2:385.

13 This line is attributed to Sayf b. Ibrahim. It is found in al-Tabari, *Kitab al-rusul wa-l-muluk*, ed. Muhammad Abu al-Fadl Ibrahim, 11 vols. (Cairo: Dar al-Ma'arif, 1979), 8:301.

14 *Lam* negates the past tense and *lan* the future tense.

15 Al-Mutanabbi, *Diwan*, 1.1:88.

16 This expression means that she had the authority to appoint officials.

17 Habib b. Aws al-Ta'i Abu Tammam, *Diwan*, ed. Muhyi al-Din al-Khayyat and Muhammad Jamal (Cairo: al-Markaz al-'Arabi li-l-Bahth wa-l-Nashr, 1983), 377.

18 Ibn al-Rumi, *Diwan*, 6:2303. The passage is also cited in Hamza al-Isfahani's redaction of the *Diwan* of Abu Nuwas in order to demonstrate Ibn al-Rumi's indebtedness with regard to these lines to a poem by Abu Nuwas that was itself modeled on Abu Dhu'ayb's famous elegy. See *Der Diwan des Abu Nuwas*, ed. Ewald Wagner, rev. ed., vol. 1 (Beirut and Berlin: Das Arabische Buch, 2001), 372.

19 Al-Mutanabbi, *Diwan*, 1.1:49–50.

20 Ahmad b. 'Abd Allah Abu al-'Ala' al-Ma'arri, *Sharh diwan saqt al-zand*, ed. N. Rida (Beirut: Dar Maktabat al-Haya, n.d.), 111.

21 Ibn al-Mu'tazz, Abu al-'Abbas 'Abd Allah, *Diwan*, ed. Majid Turad, 2 vols. (Beirut: Dar al-Kitab al-'Arabi, 1995), 2:293.

22 Bashshar b. Burd, *Diwan*, ed. Muhammad Tahir b. 'Ashur, 4 vols. (Tunis: al-Sharika al-Wataniya li-l-Nashr wa-l-Tawzi', 1976), 1:272.

23 Ahmad b. Muhammad al-Sanawbari, *Diwan*, ed. Ihsan 'Abbas (Beirut: Dar al-Thaqafa, 1970), 101–102.

24 Abu Tammam, *Diwan*, 359.

25 Ibid., 359.

26 Abu al-Firas al-Hamadani, *Diwan* (Beirut: Dar Ihya' al-Turath al-'Arabi), 235.

27 Al-Walid b. 'Ubayd al-Buhturi, *Diwan*, ed. Hasan Kamil al-Sayrafi, 4 vols. (Cairo Dar al-Ma'arif, n.d.), 2:1048.

28 Ibn al-Rumi, *Diwan*, 2:624.

29 Ibid., 2:625.

30 Ibid., 2:626.

31 Ibid., 2:627.

32 Al-Mutanabbi, *Diwan*, 2.4:107.

33 Ibid., 2.4:109.

34 Al-Ma'arri, *Sharh diwan saqt al-zand*, 114.

2

One Size Fits All

Michael Beard

Eight days, eight years, or eight decades, a handful
of air accumulating in the palm,
grasped from the window of a moving car,
is all we have, a stretch of time we cram
into our hungry mouths as if it were
something solid . . .

Alistair Elliot, Looking out[1]

If all we knew about the dead were what we learn from the elegiac
poetry they have inspired, our memories would be truncated and elliptical. To begin with the foundational elegies of English tradition, we
would learn from Spenser's *Pastoral Aeglogue upon the Death of Sir Phillip
Sidney Knight* only the bare minimum: "When shalt thou see among thy
shepheards al, / Any sage, so perfect?" (ll. 51–53).[2] One line lists qualities, three adjectives consistent with the historical record, but they are
hardly a full portrait: "curteous, valiant, and liberall" (l. 54). From *Lycidas*
(1638) we would learn of Milton's fellow classmate at Cambridge, Henry
King, that he died of drowning and that his fellow clergy would miss
him: "How well could I have spar'd for thee, young swain" (l. 113).[3] It is
sometimes said that Milton's Latin elegy, *Epitaphium Damonis*, written

the following year for his friend Charles Diodati, was more emotionally involved, as Diodati was a closer friend—and this may be true: the shepherd's repetition to his sheep that he is too overcome with grief to take care of them, "Ite domum impasti, domino iam non vacat, agni" [Go home unfed, for your master has no time for you, my lambs], is less controlled, more repetitious and formulaic, than anything in *Lycidas*. But we certainly don't learn much about Diodati beyond the fact that he is an elevated spirit: "nam quo dulcis abiret / sanctaque simplicitas, nam quo tua candida virtus?" [Where else should your sweet and holy simplicity have gone? Where else your unsullied virtue?] (ll. 199–200). As a portrait it's not much.

Samuel Johnson, in a famous passage from his life of Milton, says the problem with *Lycidas* is the pastoral mode: "For in this poem there is no nature, for there is nothing new. Its form is that of a pastoral, easy, vulgar, and therefore disgusting; whatever images it can supply are long ago exhausted . . . ."[4] Clearly, though, stylization can serve to focus a powerful emotional statement. An emotion we feel under the guise of a persona can be controlled, simplified, insulated, focused.[5] The pastoral elegy in its classic form allows a whole arsenal of effects: not just the distance created by the shepherd's costume, but an amplifier that turns up the volume of praise and can make it appear as though all of nature mourns the dead shepherd. The pastoral can make the sounds of wailing seem inhumanly loud and make the poet's suffering seem larger than life. This is not the same as celebrating the life of the departed subject. There may be generic forces that make it difficult for an elegy to bring the departed into real focus.[6]

Two elegies Ben Jonson wrote for a daughter who died in infancy and a son who died at the age of seven are telling in this respect. They are among the most effective lyrics from a writer who can seem phoney to the most charitable reader.

> At six months' end, she parted hence
> With safety of her innocence;
> Whose soul Heaven's Queen (whose name she bears)
> In comfort of her mother's tears,
> Hath placed amongst her virgin-train . . .[7]

As a memorial of a child dead in infancy, *On My First Daughter* doesn't really have the option of personalizing its subject beyond the reference to her name. The options that remain are rather abstract. The reference to the mother's tears suggests a dry-eyed speaker, a family spokesman bringing religious consolation. For this reason the familiar but inexplicably beautiful trope of the concluding couplet may seem by comparison more direct and more emotionally accessible because it returns us to the pagan concerns of the physical world:

This grave partakes the fleshly birth.
Which cover lightly, gentle earth.

It is a mystery why the grotesque image of the soil as a blanket doesn't come across as repellent and horrific. Perhaps we welcome it because the religious, otherworldly tone of what precedes it has made the body seem, at least in doctrinal terms, irrelevant to the poem. Perhaps it is as close as the poem comes to representing the daughter herself.

In the companion piece, *On My First Son*, Jonson shows a different category of commitment immediately:

Farewell, thou child of my right hand, and joy;
My sin was too much hope of thee, loved boy.

In part it's his choice of meter (the more elevated iambic pentameter), in part the second-person address directed to the son. Like Mary, Benjamin is named indirectly (since his name means etymologically the son of the right hand). At the same time, the poem never strays outside the enclosure of the poet's own ambition. The point of the poem is to question his own ambition, but in a poem attempting to prove itself as a poem, even paradoxically, he can hardly repudiate it.

. . . For why,
Will man lament the state he should envy?
To have so soon 'scaped world's, and flesh's rage,
And, if no other misery yet age?
Rest in soft peace, and ask, say here doth lie
Ben Jonson his best piece of poetry.

Jonson has no choice but to aim at a successfully aesthetic utterance, even at the moment when he is forced to question that enterprise. You can't help but wonder whether this is a way of saying that children are more important than one's art, or whether it demeans the son to compare the two. Is the comparison that puts his dead son and his poetic works in one category a charming pun on the multiple meanings of the word 'creation,' or is it simply troubling?

The Renaissance draws on a classical tradition of elegies and, as it uses them, the tradition remains surprisingly similar in its conceptual outlines. They seem barely Christianized. The richest vein is of course the collection of poems referred to as the *Greek Anthology*, widely circulated in the sixteenth century. These elegies may no longer be influential poems, but the selection translated by Dudley Fitts in 1938 is still in print. The elegies are among the most important poems in the anthology: an entire section (Book Seven) consists of 748 elegies, most short and epigrammatic. Among these is a whole series of poems spoken by the deceased ("I, Dionysius, lie here sixty years old. I am of Tarsus; I never married and I wish my father never had" [7.309]).[8] It is a trope that can personalize the dead, and yet only briefly. More frequently the focus is on the emotions of those left behind ("The halcyons, perchance, care for thee, Lenaeus, but they mother mourns for thee dumbly over thy cold tomb" [7.292]).[9] Among the poems of the *Greek Anthology* is one in particular admired for its delicacy and emotional precision:

> *Astèr prìn mèn élampes enì zōoîsin Heôos.*
> *Nûn dè thanōn lámpeis Hésperos en fthiménois.*
> (7.670)

W.R. Paton's prose translation hardly catches its elegance: "Of old among the living thou didst shine the Star of morn; / now shinest thou in death the Star of eve."[10] The word *astèr* (star) hangs at the beginning, before a pause, and it remains slightly separate in the reader's memory as the two lines unfold because it is the only word (except for *thanōn*, roughly 'in death') not part of the persistent pairing: *prìn* (previously) balanced by *nûn* (now), or the distributive *mèn* by its partner *dè*. The past tense verb *élampes* (you shone) is balanced by *lámpeis* (you shine), which establishes a continuity between the two realms: one line may be past tense, the other present, but the departed soul is still a star, still agent of the same verb. The star in the first line is Eôos, the goddess of morning (presumably metonymic for Eosfóros, Venus in its morning manifestation, strictly speaking a planet rather than a star), whereas Hésperos is Venus as the evening star. (There is a tradition that it was Pythagoras who first determined they were the same body.) The traditional association of heavenly bodies with persistence, with light that doesn't fade, makes this a poem of ethereal reassurance, but also a poem universal in its frame of reference. It could refer to anyone.

Shelley's translation, called by Dudley Fitts "sorry stuff when one compares it with that miraculous original,"[11] is like a lesson in the differences between the flexibility of Greek syntax and the constraints of English, where juxtaposing 'shine' and 'shone' would just be awkward:

> Thou wert the morning star among the living,
>   Ere thy fair light had fled;—
> Now, having died, thou art as Hesperus, giving
>   New splendour to the dead.[12]

The balance of "thou wert" against "thou art," "morning star" against Hesperus, remains from the original pairings, but it is Shelley's deliberate disruptions of symmetry that mark the poem. Lines two and four are additions with no specific source in the Greek text, but useful since Shelley writes for a reader who expects rhyme. "Fair light," if not pleonastic, may simply be a way to suggest a dead person of singular beauty, but one might argue that both the original and Shelley's translation have a universal quality. They could apply to pretty much anyone.

The justly celebrated pre-Islamic elegies of al-Khansa' for her brother Sakhr stem from a different tradition than the classical European one we have been tracing. They are moving and effective poems, but it is the subjectivity of the speaker and the experience of her suffering that occupy the foreground, rather than a characterization of the departed. The description in the second *bayt*, for instance, where the speaker presents herself looking at the stars in a kind of stunned reverie ("watching the stars—and I had not been charged with watching them") operates as a kind of still frame:

Ara al-nujuma wa ma kulliftu ri'yataha
wa taratan ataghashsha fadla atmari
[Watching the stars—and I had not been charged to watch them—
and anon wrapping myself in the ends of ragged robes.—trans.
Arberry][13]

The repetition of the verb *ra'a* opens up a gap between the speaker and
the outside world, with two acts of 'guarding' or 'tending,' one actual and
one imagined, which subtly open out the sense of distance governing her
pain. It is only in the third *bayt* that she describes the messenger arriving:

Wa qad sami'tu wa lam abjah bihi khabaran
muhaddithan ja'a yanmi raj'a akhbari.
Yaqulu Sakhrun muqimun thamma fi jadathin
lada al-darihi sari'un bayna ahjari [Ibid.]
[For I had heard—and it was not news to rejoice me—one making
report, who had come repeating intelligence,
Saying, "Sakhr is dwelling there in a tomb, struck to the ground
besides the grave, between certain stones."]

It is only in the sixth and seventh *bayt*s that we hear the character of the
deceased: what one remembers is the image of the spear point, appropriate
but hardly more specific than Spenser's "curteous, valiant, and liberall":

Qad kunta tahmilu qalban ghayra muhtadamin
murakkabban fi nisabin ghayra khawwari
Mithla al-sinani tudi' al-layla suratuhu
murru al-marirati hurrun wa ibn ahrari [Ibid.]
[You used to carry a heart that brooked no wrong, compounded in a
nature that was never cowardly,
Like the spear point whose (bright) shape lights up the night, (a man)
bitter in resolution, free and the son of free-men.]

The seventh *bayt* is the focal point of the poem:

Fa-sawfa abkika ma nahat mutawwaqatun
wa ma ada'at nujumu al-layli li-l-sari. [Ibid.]

It is around this statement of will, *sawfa abkika* (I shall cry for you), that the poem takes its shape. (She will mourn as long as the dove sings and the stars shine, and will never forgive the enemies who killed Sakhr.) That statement of will, a performative act of mourning whose forcefulness matches the finality of death, carries an overwhelming and anti-rhetorical intensity. The act of *buka'* which gives us one of the key words in pre-Islamic poetry is here something like an act of heroic opposition,[14] overpowering the moment when Sakhr was compared to a spear point.

A friend dies and the world without her seems different, diminished, colorless. This is enough of a human universal to be independent of cultural distinctions. Presumably this is why the tropes of consolation are limited: the dead are still alive in our thoughts; they seemed so alive before; they're alive in heaven; who will carry on their work? And yet it may surprise us that the most elegant of elegies is also the least individual; it would seem logical to emphasize how much we will miss them for the qualities that set them apart.

The phenomenon I have tried to sketch seems to present a conflict between aesthetic demands and other forces we might call ethical. There is something in the psychology of mourning that resists the question, How the survivors are doing? It is a practical and humane question; it acknowledges that the absence of the dead is final, that our attention has to shift at some point to those left behind. But it is a question which may obscure that prior, emotionally necessary, more important discussion about the dead friend's life, the specifics of what we have lost.

Whenever we write tentatively we should leave a space for dialogue, acknowledging where the reader's skepticism is likely to show up. I am aware that the phenomenon I have tried to sketch may not be representative. I can hardly claim a wide sample. Indeed, I have hardly strayed beyond the boundaries of the canonical anthology pieces. It may even be that the elegies that make their way past the sifting process into our anthologies are inevitably going to be poems in which the details of the person mourned are minimized. The act of casting sorrow in the form of a poem may work against memorializing the individual. We preserve the poems we can teach as poems, rather than those we value for their information.

I can suggest where I think the exceptions will be found, as dissatisfaction with the stylized elegiac forms seems to grow over the course of the twentieth century. Elegies like John Crowe Ransom's "Bells for John Whiteside's Daughter" (where "lightness in her footfall" is in the first stanza and specific anecdotes amplify that observation in the next two) stand as a testimony to the possibility of vivid portraiture in an elegy, though the thrust of the poem finally is on the mood of the mourners ("we are vexed at her brown study"), the shock of death.[15] More recently, Eugenio Montale's *Xenia*, the twenty-eight-part tribute to his late wife published in 1971, unrolls with intimate novelistic specificity: "Ascoltare era il solo tuo modo di vedere / Il conto del telefono s'è ridotto a ben poco" [Listening was your only way of seeing / the telephone bill has shrunk to very little.][16] But even the big public statements may find room for specificity of description, the great example being Auden's anthology piece, "In Memory of W.B. Yeats," which is both a frank assessment of his distance from Yeats ("You were silly like us") and a convincing testimony of respect.[17] As Jahan Ramazani has pointed out in *The Poetry of Mourning*, there is even a kind of competition with Yeats in Auden's memorial for him, since Auden's obvious models are elegies of Yeats: "Apparently Auden learned from Yeats that the 'personal note' of an elegy like 'In Memory of Major Robert Gregory' required that the poet not only praise the dead but also suggest their limitations."[18] The particular newness of Yeats's and Auden's approaches to the elegiac tradition fits into a wider demand for the palpable and particular that characterizes modernist poetry. The refusal to follow the grooves of a traditional discourse on death is one of many ways modernism resists or denies the accepted patterns. Dylan Thomas's famous *Refusal to Mourn the Death, by Fire, of a Child in London* confesses (surprisingly for a poet whose big statements can be ambitious and even apocalyptic) that the realm of poetry is restricted. There are some things it would be wrong to articulate:

> I shall not murder
> The mankind of her going with a grave truth
> Nor blaspheme down the stations of the breath
> With any further
> Elegy of innocence and youth.[19]

The 'grave' of "grave truth" echoes with an unusually painful wit because it is an accurate word (such words would in fact be grave in both senses—because they would be somber but also about the grave) but it could never be more than words.

The impossibility of the task poetry sets for itself is a central awareness in modernism, but what was experienced at first as an aesthetic discovery found validity in the world outside. For the European community, the experience of two world wars made it painfully clear in what great numbers people can die, numbers too great for the standard elegiac forms to grasp; it is a commonplace that in the twentieth century poetry finds itself helpless to deal with mass death. And this in turn means that room for the details of the individual's life is going to shrink even further. The absence of the individual in elegy becomes its subject. Geoffrey Hill's famous *September Song*, memorializing an unnamed ten-year-old victim of a Nazi concentration camp ("born 19.6.32—deported 24.9.42"), employs mordant understatement: "As estimated, you died."[20] In Ramazani's summary: "To elegize, Hill wryly suggests, is to enjoy one's grief, to indulge the onanistic work of mourning. 'September fattens on the vines,' but Hill refuses to integrate the child's unnatural September death into the natural death that promises cyclical renewal."[21] In other words two individuals retract from the contemporary elegy, not just the dead individual (to focus on one would obscure the others) but also the personalized voice of the poet (to speak for the dead would be an act of hubris). W.S. Merwin's very short 1970 poem *Elegy* (full text: "Who would I show it to?")[22] takes the additional step of questioning the legitimacy of the interlocutor's role in the process. If the evolution of contemporary poetry is a growing awareness of its own limitations, one result is a demand for more cunning circumlocutions rerouted around that silence. In them we may rediscover what was latent in the elegy from its earliest manifestations, a vehicle for a discussion of mortality. Rilke's *Sonnets to Orpheus* refer only indirectly to Vera Ouckama Knoop, their nominal inspiration, but the commentary on the nature of mortality and the nature of human experience, which grows over the course of the individual lyrics, is so startling and powerful that it constitutes a humanistic statement which can offer real consolation. Magda Al-Nowaihi's article on the silences in women's autobiography, those subjects not discussed by Arab women in their writings as well as the writing that simply never happened because women were not seen as fit to write it, allows us to think through the ways the silences embedded in elegies can be eloquent too. In a poem about death, silence is going to be an issue, acknowledged or not.

And yet silence is still intolerable. Reading Magda's many friends' responses to her life has encouraged me. They have been detailed and they have memorialized her in precisely the ways whose absence I have attempted to chronicle here. It is one reason to be thankful for the relative freedom of prose.

Notes

1   Alistair Elliot, *Facing Things* (Manchester: Carcanet, 1997).
2   Edmund Spenser, *The Poetical Works of Edmund Spenser*, eds. J.C. Smith and E. de Selincourt (London: Oxford University Press, 1965), 554. Text references are to lines.
3   John Milton, *Complete Poems and Major Prose*, ed. Merritt Y. Hughes (New York: Odyssey Press, 1957). Text references are to lines.
4   Samuel Johnson, *Lives of the English Poets: A Selection*, ed. John Wain (London: Everyman's Library, 1975), 88.
5   The day after Senator Paul Wellstone of Minnesota died in an airplane accident on October 25, 2002, the radio show, *Prairie Home Companion*, memorialized him. In a particularly striking decision, the most effective tribute was spoken by a fictional character. In "Guy Noir," their weekly parody of a detective story, the title character, voiced by Garrison Keillor, responds to Wellstone's death in a conversation with a bartender:

> Naw. I don't care for eulogies. Never did. People who didn't even know the guy talking about the legacy and how great he was. That's what's wrong with politics in the first place, all the yakking just for effect. All the slick guys trying to figure out what you want to hear. He was different. He was the most honest person in American politics. He won that one going away. Everything he said, from the heart. And then he goes down in a plane. ("Guy Noir," *A Prairie Home Companion*, first broadcast October 26, 2002, by Garrison Keillor, http://prairiehome.publicradio. org/programs/20021026/noir.shtml)

If anyone doubts that the pastoral tradition of the inarticulate character is still viable, this sketch is a good counterargument.
6   One generic constraint may have to do with class affiliation. Milton's two early poems dedicated to Thomas Hobson, the university 'carrier' who drove a weekly coach between Cambridge and London and died in 1631 (Milton, 64–65), are more specific and fondly personalized than elegiac poetry between colleagues.
7   Robert Cummings, ed., *Seventeenth-Century Poetry: An Annotated Anthology* (Malden, MA: Blackwell Publishers, 2000), 80.
8   *The Greek Anthology with an English Translation by W.R. Paton*, vol. 2 (London: William Heinemann, 1917), 309.

9   Dudley Fitts translates:
     You are the charge o halcyons now, it may be:
     But—oh Lenaios!—your mother
     Bends in still anguish above your empty tomb.
     (Dudley Fitts, *Poems from the Greek Anthology* [New York: New Directions, 1956],
     121)
10   Paton, vol. 2, 357, Greek original on p. 356.
11   Fitts, *Poems from the Greek Anthology*, xv.
12   Percy B. Shelley, *The Complete Poetical Works of Percy Bysshe Shelley*, ed. Thomas
     Hutchinson (London: Oxford University Press, 1965), 720.
13   A. J. Arberry, *Arabic Poetry: A Primer for Students* (Cambridge: Cambridge
     University Press, 1965), 38–39.
14   It is from Magda Al-Nowaihi's article that I learned of the Abbasid poet
     Bashshar's praise for al-Khansa', using that oddly gendered term for bravery
     "that [woman] defeated the [male] master poets (*fuhul*); she had four testicles."
     Magda M. Al-Nowaihi, "Resisting Silence in Arab Women's Autobiographies,"
     International Journal of Middle East Studies 33, no. 4 (November 2001): 477–502,
     here 479.
15   John Crowe Ransom, *Selected Poems* (A.A. Knopf: New York, 1952), 8.
16   Eugenio Montale, *Satura: 1962–1970* (Milan: Mondatori, 1971), 25.
17   W.H. Auden, *Collected Poems*, ed. Edward Mendelson (New York: Random House,
     1976), 197–98.
18   Jahan Ramazani, *The Poetry of Mourning: The Modern Elegy from Hardy to Heaney*
     (Chicago: The University of Chicago Press, 1994), 184.
19   Dylan Thomas, *The Collected Poems of Dylan Thomas* (New York: New Directions,
     1957), 112.
20   Geoffrey Hill, *Somewhere is Such a Kingdom: Poems 1952–1971* (Boston: Houghton
     Mifflin, 1975), 57.
21   Ramazani, *The Poetry of Mourning*, 7.
22   W.S. Merwin, *The Second Four Books of Poems*, reissue ed. (Port Townsend, WA:
     Copper Canyon Press, 1993). I am indebted to Ahmad Karimi-Hakkak for this
     reference.

3

Notes On Abu Tammam's Elegy
Kadha fa-l-yajilla l-khatbu

András Hámori

A thousand years on, we can't agree with the opinion recorded by Ibn Rashiq among others that there is no difference between a panegyric and an elegy, except that one addresses the living, and one the dead.[1] The attributed glories of another age turn to dust; death is unattenuated. Flattery has become repellent, but eulogy, no matter how remote in style, can be read with a willing charity. The rituals of death hold on to their power. We are touched when a father writes about the surviving brothers playing with a dead child's toys,[2] but we can be moved, this is the curious thing, by a grand, pompous, public piece as well. Such at any rate is my experience of the poem I will discuss.[3] Some of its effect is owed to the shifting patterns of rhetoric, some of it derives from the manner in which it presents the drama of time to the mind, and some from an insistent concentration on certain images.

It begins with a shock:

١ كذا فليجل الخطب وليفدح الأمر   فليس لعين لم يفض ماؤها عذر

which, in passable English, means: "If you wish to see a grave calamity, a crushing blow—here it is! There is no excuse for an eye not awash in tears."[4] With its rough, awkward grammar, the literal translation "Thus let a calamity be grave. . ." is truer to the feeling of the original. It was, it seems, an astonishing first line. Abu Tammam was chided for starting with a reference to something that has not yet been spoken of.[5] Some manuscripts retain a line that was fabricated and placed at the head of the poem to draw the sting of this attack.[6] But no commentary is needed to bring out the theatrical possibilities of that first exclamation, torn from the normal flow of speech. After it, I think the performer would have paused for a moment. For one thing, a brief silence would create a desirable tension of staged expectation, even if in the real world everyone knew who the dead person was. For another, Abu Tammam makes the next three lines into a distinct unit in sound and syntax.

وأصبح في شغل عن السفر السفر   توفيت الآمال بعد محمد   2

وذخرًا لمن أمسى وليس له ذخر   وما كان إلا مال من قل ماله   3

إذا ما استهلت أنه خلق العسر   وما كان يدري مجتدي جود كفه[7]   4

2   Hope died after Muhammad; travelers [in search of a generous man] have come to be distracted [by grief] from their travels.

3   He was wealth to those who had no wealth, a treasure to those who had come to have no treasure.

4   Whoever sought the bounty of his hand was not aware, once its showers had begun, that hardship had ever been created.

Verse 3 being a kind of explication of verse 2, *illa mala* would be spoken so as to echo and replace *al-amalu*. Verses 2 and 3 are linked by the complementary words *asbaha* and *amsa* as well. Morning and night will return in verses 12 and 13, in a grand and powerful image. *Asbaha* and *amsa* are lightly marked here, but a natural light pause after *amsa* (demanded by the secondary caesura and permitted by the syntax) gives them just enough prominence to let the later lines inspire in the listener a sense of the unfolding of some previously adumbrated event. The obvious link between verses 3 and 4 is the repetition of *wa-ma kana* at the head of each. From *ma'uha* in the first line of the poem, the syllable *ma* ties these first four lines into one great wave.

Another exclamation now leads into the story of the hero's death:

فجاج سبيل الله وانثغر الثغر ٥ ألا في سبيل الله من عطلت له

دما ضحكت عنه الأحاديث والذكر ٦ فتى كلما فاضت عيون قبيلة

فتى مات بين الطعن والضرب ميتة تقوم مقام النصر إن فاته النصر ٧

من الضرب واعتلت عليه القنا السمر ٨ وما مات حتى مات مضرب سيفه

إليه الحفاظ المر والخلق الوعر ٩ وقد كان فوت الموت سهلا فرده

هو الكفر يوم الروع أو دونه الكفر ١٠ ونفس تعاف العار حتى كأنما

وقال لها: من تحت أخمصك الحشر ١١ فأثبت في مستنقع الموت رجله

5 Oh, he died for the sake of God, this man whose death [*lahu*] has caused the mountain roads of the struggle for the sake of God to be left defenseless and the frontier regions to have their teeth broken.[8]

6 Such a man was he that the more a tribe's eyes are flooded with tears of blood, the more tales [of glory] and renown reveal him as they laugh [in delight].

7 A man who, in the midst of spear thrusts and sword strokes, died a death that will stand in the place of victory if victory has eluded him.

8 He did not die until after the edge of his sword had died of dealing blows, until the tawny spears [of the enemy] had sickened from striking upon him.

9 It would have been easy to escape death, but there had driven him back to it a grim resolve and an intractable temper

10 And a soul that loathed shame so much that on the day of battle shame seemed like unbelief or worse,

11 So that he planted his foot in the pool of death and said to it: under your hollow is the [place of] resurrection.

There is solid verbal and grammatical concatenation here.[9] The indefinite relative pronoun *man* (he who) in verse 5 is specified by *fatan*, (such a man), in verse 6, which then leads to the overlapping phrases *fatan mata* in 7, *wa-ma mata hatta* in 8, and *fawtu l-mawti* in 9. Verse 10 is not an independent sentence but a continuation of 9, and verse 11 is a resultative statement logically and syntactically dependent on verses 9 and 10. But the verbal ties are just a pleasing surface counterpart of a conceptual progression. Verses 5 and 6 inform us that the dead man died a martyr of God, and that he has also won fame among men. In the first four lines the man's generosity was extolled; now we hear about his virtues as a warrior. I think perhaps that is why in verse 6, in *fatan kullama fadat 'uyunu qabilatin daman*, the subordinate clause should remind the audience of the opening statement *(fa-laysa li-'aynin lam yafid ma'uha 'udhru)*, adding a crescendo as blood replaces water. For the first time in the poem, the syntactic caesura has shifted away from the division between halflines, to after *daman*. In performance this would certainly draw attention to *daman* and so perhaps to what is here similar to, and what is different from, line one.

After verses 5 and 6 the poem gradually provides more detail, including temporal detail. In verse 7 it makes explicit for the first time (for *a-la fi sabili l-lahi* can be employed in any number of contexts) that this man died in battle, and that he died well. In verse 8, it backtracks a bit in time, and tells us that he put up a good fight. It is noteworthy also that while in verse 7, *ta'n* and *darb* are actions whose temporal aspect is not foregrounded at all, verse 8 relates processes with marked temporal extension *(wa-ma mata hatta mata . . .)*. His sword becomes notched and their spears shatter on his armor before the hero is finished off. Verses 9 and 10 move yet farther back, looking into what might have been *(wa-qad kana fawtu l-mawti sahlan)*, but for the dead man's long-term qualities and dispositions. The last of these, *nafsun ta'afu l-'ara*, expansively described, brings us to *aw dunahu l-kufru* and so, by implication, to faith. I think in this context the expression for battle, *yawm al-raw'*, which literally means 'day of terror,' is also preparation for what follows. Having gradually moved in time farther and farther back from the man's death, now suddenly the poem introduces eternity, the one future that really counts: "So that he planted his foot in the pool of death and said to it: under your hollow is the [place of] resurrection." Then, in verses 12 and 13, there comes a violent compression of time, the climactic moment in the shifts of temporal perspective that began in verse 7:

فلم ينصرف إلا وأكفانه الأجر   غدا غدوة والحمد نسج ردائه   ١٢

١٣ تردى ثياب الموت حمرا فما أتى[10] لها الليل إلا وهي من سندس خضر

12 In the morning he went forth, his cloak woven of praise, and did not move from there except shrouded in the heavenly reward.

13 He put on the crimson robes of death, and by nightfall they were green, of [the] silk [of paradise].

It is perhaps also worth noting that while verse 12 relies on metaphor, in 13 the blood-red garment and the green silk are both quite concrete. Verse12 moves from the praise of the living to the ultimate reward wrapped in the vocabulary of death *(akfanuhu l-ajru)*, while 13 moves from the red garments of death to silks the color of life in paradise.

Abu Tammam now turns to the hero's kinsmen, a common enough pattern:

نجوم سماء خر من بينها البدر   ١٤ كأن بني نبهان يوم وفاته

وييكي عليه الجود والبأس والشعر   ١٥ يعزون عن ثاو تعزى به العلى

الى الموت حتى استشهدا هو والصبر   ١٦ وأنى لهم صبر عليه وقد مضى

ولكن كبرا أن يقال به الكبر   ١٧ فتى كان عذب الروح لا من غضاضة

وبزته نار الحرب وهو لها جمر   ١٨ فتى سلبته الخيل وهو حمى لها

بواتر فهي الآن من بعده بتر   ١٩ وقد كانت البيض المآثير في الوغى

14 On the day of his death, the Banu Nabhan were like stars in a firmament from whose midst the full moon had fallen.

15 They are offered consolation for the loss of one lying in the tomb, who is the consolation of glorious deeds, for whom generosity, valor, and poetry weep.

16 And how could they endure his loss with fortitude, now that he has gone to his death? Now that two were martyred at once: he and fortitude?

17 A man of sweet nature—not out of baseness, but from being too proud-spirited to have it said that there was pride in him.

18   A man whom the horsemen have despoiled of life although he had been their protector; whom the fire of war has plundered although he had been as live coals to that fire.

19   The glittering white blades had been sharp in battle; now, after his death, they are broken.[11]

Having a new addressee permits Abu Tammam to offer permutations on ideas and paradoxes already introduced.[12] In verse 15, "They are offered consolation for [the loss of] one lying in the tomb *(thawin)*, who is the consolation of glorious deeds" harks back to verse 6, *fatan kullama fadat 'uyunu qabilatin / daman dahikat 'anhu l-ahadithu wa-l-dhikru*. Perhaps on hearing the next line, where the dead hero's kinsmen cannot subdue their grief because fortitude was martyred along with him, the listener will recall the structure of *wa-ma mata hatta mata madribu sayfihi* from verse 8. No one will miss that in verses 17 and 18 Abu Tammam resumes the anaphora of *fatan*. From conventional components, he creates a subtle rhetorical design. A cleverly set up and cleverly off-balance structural parallel links the two verses. Both are about qualities that cancel themselves: The first says that the dead man was too proud to be thought proud—in other words, that pride begat its opposite. The second says that the valor which had made him the protector of horsemen led to them taking his life, and that the fire of war plundered him who had been the glowing embers of war. In their meanings, however, these verses are antithetical: The first describes something positive, namely the man's conscious decision not to be proud. The second relates an evil end imposed by fate. The poet, moreover, makes good use of a second difference between these verses: In the first he speaks exclusively of the man's qualities in life, in the second, of his states in life and at the moment of death. Then he speaks of swords that were sharp in battle, but are useless *(butru)* after the man's death. This allows Abu Tammam to pose two related questions about the long-range future and then, with a gnomic meditation on Time itself, to move toward the end of the poem:

٢٠   أمن بعد طيّ الحادثات محمدا   يكون لأثواب الندى أبدا نشر

٢١   إذا شجرات العرف جذت أصولها   ففي أيّ فرع يوجد الورق النضر

لعهدي به ممن يحب له الدهر　　22 لئن أبغض الدهر الخؤون لفقده

لما زالت الأيام شيمتها الغدر　　23 لئن غدرت في الروع أيامه به

لما عريت منها تميم ولا بكر　　24 لئن ألبست فيه المصيبة طيئ

يشاركنا في فقده البدو والحضر　　25 كذلك ما ننفك نفقد هالكا

20 Now that calamitous fate has gathered in Muhammad, will the robes of generosity ever be unfolded again?

21 If the roots of the tree of beneficence have been severed, on what branch might green leaves be found?

22 If guileful Time is hated because of his loss, I knew him when he was one on whose account Time was loved.

23 If his days (=warlike engagements) betrayed him in battle, it has ever been the nature of the Days (=the turns of fate) to betray.

24 If Tayyi' has been clothed in calamity because of him, neither Tamim nor Bakr have remained bare of it.

25 Thus there is no end to our losing the dead for whom settled folk and Bedouin grieve with us.[13]

Line is again joined to line in this passage. Verse 20 leads to its metaphorical variant in verse 21, cast in the form of a conditional sentence *(idha shajaratu l-'urfi judhdhat usuluha . . .)*. The verses about *dahr* and *ayyam* are conditional sentences as well, and here too Abu Tammam combines parallelism of theme *(dahr* and *ayyam)* with a subtle contrast. The line about *dahr* is in the form of a concessive sentence, as is common in *marathi*: "If guileful Time is hated because of his loss, I knew him when he was one on whose account Time was loved." In other words, although the state of affairs is now thus, it is a source of solace that it was once otherwise. When Abu Tammam goes on to speak of *ayyam*, he starts the sentence the same way *(la-in ubghida l-dahru l-kha'unu li-faqdihi* and *la-in ghadarat fi-l-raw'i ayyamuhu bihi)*, but now he brusquely abolishes the contrast between present and past: "If his days betrayed him in battle, it has ever been the nature of the Days to betray."

The series of conditional sentences continues, still with anaphora of the conditional particle, in *la-in ulbisat fihi l-musibata tayyi'un*. This verse is parallel in structure to the one before it, but its theme shifts to the expansion so frequent in panegyric and *ritha'*. It is not only his kin who grieve—all men share in this grief. Abu Tammam does this with easy rhetorical felicity as he examines states of affairs. Having gone from "now state S but once non-S" to "S is true of this particular time, but S is true of all times," he now says, "S is true of one particular Arab tribe (the Tayyi'), and S is true of all the Arabs (Bakr and Tamim)." If you assent to the gnomic statement *fa-ma zalati l-ayyamu shimatuha l-ghadru* (and who doesn't?), then you will suspend disbelief and assent, while the ceremony lasts, to the analogous structure *fa-ma 'urriyat minha tamimun wa-la bakru*. This part of the poem ends with a verse that includes both the open temporal horizon and what one might perhaps call the spatial horizon of human group next to human group: "Thus there is no end to our losing the dead for whom settled folk and Bedouin grieve with us."

There are five lines left:

سقى الغيث غيثا وارت الأرض شخصه وإن لم يكن فيه سحاب ولا قطر	26
وكيف احتمالي للسحاب صنيعة بإسقائها قبرا وفي لحده البحر	27
مضى طاهر الأثواب لم تبق روضة غداة ثوى إلا اشتهت أنها قبر	28
ثوى في الثرى من كان يحيا به الثرى ويغمر صرف الدهر نائله الغمر	29
عليك سلام الله وقفا فإنني رأيت الكريم الحر ليس له عمر	30

26   May copious rain water the copious rain [of generosity], rain although without cloud or raindrops, whose form the earth has hidden.

27   But how could I think that the rainclouds would be conferring a benefit by watering a tomb in whose hollow space the very sea has been laid?

28   He departed in unstained clothes; the morning he was buried there was no meadow but it wished it were a tomb.

29   He who had been the life of bounty has been laid in the earth, he whose abundant gifts once overwhelmed the calamities of Time.

30   The peace of God be upon you forever. As for me, I have seen that the noble and magnanimous do not live long.

Verses 26 and 27 are in the usual paradoxical style, neatly constructed. In 26 the *du'a'* contains the assertion that the earth has hidden a "copious rain," and then the poet remarks, in a familiar tactic of Arabic poetry, on the strangeness of his metaphor. In the next verse, he begins by questioning his own thinking, and then uses a second metaphor more hyperbolical than the first.

In verse 27 the phrase *mada tahira l-athwabi* recalls the grand conclusion of the description of battle and death in 13: *taradda thiyaba l-mawti humran fa-ma ata / laha l-laylu illa wa-hya min sundusin khudru*. The clothing motif has been sustained in two intervening verses. In verse 24, *la-in ulbisat fihi l-musibata tayyi'un* is unobtrusive, for the image of someone being clothed in something bad is conventional (as in the Qur'an, 16:112). But in verse 20, the unrolling of the *athwab al-nada* is salient. I don't think such dwelling on the idea of clothing can have gone unnoticed. One may be reminded of al-Sha'bi's remark, cited in Fakhr al-Din al-Razi's commentary to Qur'an 18:12, that "Joseph's story is all in his shirt," *qissat yusuf kulluha fi qamisihi*.[14] In verse 13, the red garments of death became the green silk of paradise. Here, in the *du'a'* section, where the poet speaks of tombs and offers an epitaph, he doesn't want us to cease our mourning over the bloodstained clothes, but does want us to think simultaneously of the unstained ones: the nobility and purity of soul that marked this man's life.

After this there is not much left to say. As verse 26 was to 27, verse 28 is tied to 29 lexically (by the repetition of *thawa*), and by a play on words. The listener would know that the required sense in verse 29 is "He who had been the life of bounty has been laid in the earth." But the other meaning of *thara* (earth or moist earth) must occur to him as well, in a way closing the circle.[15] The *rawda* (land alive with vegetation, here perhaps even 'garden') wishes that it were this man's tomb, and that this man had been the one who gave life to the earth.

Farewell, then, to the dead and, with the gnomic subsumption of this death to some hopeless general truth, bleak comfort to the living.

Notes

1   Abu 'Ali al-Hasan Ibn Rashiq al-Qayrawani, *al-'Umda fi mahasin al-shi'r wa-adabihi wa-naqdihi*, ed. Muhammad Muhyi al-Din 'Abd al-Hamid, 2 vols., 4th printing (Beirut: Dar al-Jil, 1972), 2:137.

2   I am thinking of Ibn al-Rumi's poem *buka'ukuma yashfi . . . .'indi*, which Magda Al-Nowaihi spoke about, along with two other poems, in her memorable last faculty seminar at Columbia.

3   The text is taken from *Diwan Abi Tammam bi-sharh al-Khatib al-Tibrizi*, ed. Muhammad 'Abduh 'Azzam, 4 volumes (Cairo: Dar al-Ma'arif, 1957–65), 4:79–85. I footnote some, but not all, variants given by 'Azzam. The poem is indeed moving, but I should perhaps say at the outset that, as the old critics well knew, Abu Tammam can't long resist being Abu Tammam. For instance, we'd all be better off without *inthaghara l-thaghru* in verse 5.

4   Literally, 'Thus let a matter be grave,' and so on. Al-Tibrizi says voweling with *kasra* is better *(ajwad)*, but the *Diwan* prints *fa-l-yajilla*. The particle *fa-* is used because the adverb is placed before the quasi-imperative (just as word order requires it when the object of an imperative is placed before the imperative, as in several verses at the beginning of Sura 74).

5   'Azzam cites (79n), without further reference, the rebuke by Ibn 'Ammar al-Thaqafi: *iftataha qawlahu bi-abyani khata'in wa-afhashihi min isharatihi ila ma'dumin wa-sti'tafihi ghayra ma'lum.* Ibn 'Ammar's *risala* is not extant (see F. Sezgin, *Geschichte des arabischen Schrifttums*, vol. 2 [Leiden: Brill, 1975], 553).

6   'Azzam is surely right about the inauthenticity of the extra line. He cites an anecdote from al-Suli's *Akhbar Abi Tammam* in which Abu Tammam appears to a man in a dream, is questioned about *kadha fa-l-yajilla*, and reveals that "people have left off a line that stood before it, for I said *haramun li-'aynin an yajiffa laha shafru / wa-an tata'ama l-taghmida ma mtana'a l-dahru // kadha fa-l-yajilla l-khatbu*," and so on. (*Ma amta'a l-dahru* is printed in the Cairo 1937 edition of the *Akhbar Abi Tammam*, 265.) 'Azzam comments: "This verse is an evident interpolation, intended to refute those who censured Abu Tammam for such a beginning, unfamiliar to the ancients." The version with the extra line is patently inferior, and it's impossible to believe that a bold poet like Abu Tammam would have preferred it, alive or dead. It was probably Abu Tammam's innovation that was imitated a generation later in a poem by Ibrahim ibn Ahmad al-Asadi about al-Mutawakkil's murder (al-Husri, *Zahr al-adab wa-thamar al-albab*, ed. 'Ali Muhammad al-Bajawi, vol. 1 [Cairo: Dar ihya' al-kutub al-'arabiya, 1953], 215), beginning with the verse *hakadha fa-l-takun manaya l-kirami / bayna nayin wa-mizharin wa-mudami*. Al-Mutanabbi begins one poem *jalalan kama bi fa-l-yaku l-tabrihu* (rhyme *al-shibu*), but this is of course less strange because the referent of the comparative particle is explicit. He ends another poem with *kadha fa-l-yasir man talaba l-'a'ati / wa-mithla suraka fa-l-yakuni l-tilabu* (incipit *bi-ghayrika ra'iyan 'abatha l-dhi'abu . . . al-dirabu*), but here too there is no problem: the *kadha* refers to all that went before it. Indeed, Ibn 'Ammar

claimed (as cited in 'Azzam's note) that one critic suggested to Abu Tammam that he should have recited his poem over the bones of the dead man, and after having told the man's story, should have pointed to them and said *kadha fa-l-yajilla l-khatbu* . . . .

7 One manuscript reads *man bala yusra kaffihi.*

8 As 'Azzam reports in his note, Ibn 'Ammar pointed out that correct usage would have required *ittaghara* but it would have ruined the play on words.

9 Such concatenation was recognized and admired. See, for example, Ibn Rashiq, *al-'Umda,* 1:129 (in the chapter on natural and artificial poetry), where he speaks of the virtue of *talahum al-kalam ba'dihi 'ala ba'd,* and furnishes two examples of extended passages that show it.

10 For *ata,* one manuscript reads *daja.*

11 *Ma'thur*: decorated with wavy lines, as a damascened sword.

12 On the benefits of a new addressee, see Geert Jan van Gelder, "The Abstracted Self in Arabic Poetry," *Journal of Arabic Literature* 14 (1983): 27, and my *Composition of Mutanabbi's Panegyrics to Sayf al-Dawla* (Leiden: Brill, 1992), 62.

13 I cannot decide whether this means that mourning for this man will go on and on, or that Tayyi' (the tribe from which Abu Tammam claimed to have descended) endlessly produces, and loses, such heroes. The second interpretation would be in tune with an old theme.

14 He means the bloodstained shirt the brothers show to Jacob, the tearing of the shirt by the temptress, and the shirt by which Jacob's vision is restored.

15 The sense of 'good things' (as in the phrase *fulan qarib al-thara* cited in E. W. Lane, An Arabic-English Dictionary, 8 vols., Beirut 1968 (Librairie du Liban) reprint) is presumably itself derived from the basic meaning of *thara.*

4

Dead Garments, Poor Nobles, and a Handsome Youth: Notes on a Poem by al-Sanawbari

Wolfhart Heinrichs

Introduction

The starting point for the following remarks is a poem by al-Sanawbari (d. 945). It is a polythematic poem in three parts; the distribution of topics within it is, however, rather unexpected.[1] It is possible that this seeming strangeness is an impression of the researcher rather than a characteristic of the poetry itself; a simple stocktaking of the topical structures of classical Arabic poems is still needed. However, there is no question that certain arrangements were extremely popular and that the poem at issue here does not exhibit any of these.

Al-Sanawbari was a well-known poet. Unfortunately, he fell through the cracks, as far as the biographical works are concerned, so we know relatively little about his outward life. He hailed from Antioch, but lived mostly in Mosul and Aleppo at the courts of the Hamdanids; he was for a while librarian of Sayf al-Dawla (reigned 944–967). Al-Sanawbari's fame rested first and foremost on his nature poetry: *zahriyat* (flower poems), *rawdiyat* (garden poems), *rabi'iyat* (spring poems), and even *thaljiyat* (snow poems). Adam Mez, in his still admirable book on the 'renaissance' of Islam (that is, the tenth century), finishes his chapter on poetry as follows:

"Thus they stand together in the 4th/10th century, al-Sanawbari and al-Mutanabbi, Ibn al-Hajjaj and [al-Sharif] al-Radi—each one in his field a peak, overlooking all future centuries of Arabic literature."[2]

It is regrettable that only about a third of al-Sanawbari's *Diwan* has been preserved and published. The edition of Ihsan 'Abbas is based on the fragmentary Calcutta manuscript, complemented by a collection of poems and fragments from anthologies and similar works (148 numbers), and a last-minute supplement with poems culled from al-Shimshati's anthology.[3] A further collection of additional poems appeared soon after the 'Abbas edition.[4] I have not seen the new and more comprehensive edition by Mahmud Mustafa al-Halawi (published?).[5] A complete edition of the existing poems and fragments therefore still needs to be produced.

The Poem

The poem appears below in (a) the original Arabic, (b) a literal prose translation, and (c) a poetic translation in unrhymed iambic pentameters, and is followed by commentary.

[First theme: the clothes]

وقال يرثي ثيابه:

Bewailing the death of his clothes, he said (*khafif*):

١   طيلساني على فراقي حريص   قد تولّى كما تولّى القميص

My hooded cloak is bent on leaving me; it has turned its back just as [my] shirt has.

**My hooded cloak is bent on leaving me;
it turned its back on me as did my shirt.**

Commentary: For the meaning of *taylasan* and *qamis* see R.P.A. Dozy, *Dictionnaire détaillé des noms des vêtements chez les Arabes* (Amsterdam: Jean Müller 1845, repr. Beirut: Librairie du Liban n.d.), 278–80, 371–75; and Yedida K. Stillman, *Arab Dress. A Short History From the Dawn of Islam to Modern Times* (Leiden etc.: Brill 2000), index, s.vv. The *taylasan* is described as a hooded cloak (as opposed to the *rida'*), like a monk's cowl, but with the hood going on top of the turban (see Stillman, *Dress*, plates 6 and 7). Due to regional and time differences, the definitions are not always clear and sometimes contradictory (see al-Suyuti, *al-Ahadith al-hisan fi fadl al-taylasan*, ed. Albert Arazi [Jerusalem: The Magnes Press & Hebrew University 1983], 4–8 [Arab.]). According to Mez (*Renaissance*, 368), it was the characteristic garment of the 'theologians' (meaning the *'ulama'*) while the scribes wore the *durra'a*, a low-cut frock, and the military men the *qaba'*, the short Persian jacket. This is probably not the whole truth, as al-Sanawbari is not known to have been a 'man of the cloth,' as it were. But al-Sanawbari's contemporary al-Washsha', in his book about the dandies *(zurafa')* mentions that they wore the *tayalisa* (pl. of *taylasan*) as well *(al-Muwashshah*, ed. Rudolph E. Brünnow [Leiden: Brill 1886], 124). The *qamis* or 'shirt' was worn by merchants and other 'unofficial' people over the trousers and under the *rida'*, according to Adam Mez (*Renaissance,* 369).

أنا بالهجر منهما مخصوص   إن يخصا بالوصل مني فإني   2

If the two of them are meant for union on my part, I am certainly
    meant for avoidance on their part.
For me the two are meant to be with me;
while I am clearly to be shunned by them.

Commentary: For the use of the verb *khassa* in the context of *wasl* and *hajr*, see al-Sanawbari, 233, no. 224 (verse 2): *aqsiri qad khasasti bi-'l-hajri man qad—kana ahra bi-waslikum an yukhassa* [Slow down (woman)! You have singled out for avoidance someone who should rather be singled out for union with you.] The translation takes *minni* and *minhuma* as directional, 'from my (their) point of view.' They can also be understood as the periphrastic device, often used in poetry, for the regular possessive pronoun: *al-wasli minni = wasli, al-hajri minhuma = hajrihima*.

ـه ولا لي أخرى الليالي محيص   آذنا بالبلى فما لهما منـ   3

They announced decay; at the end of the day [lit. nights] there is no
    escaping it either for them or for me.
Decay did they announce; true, neither they
nor I escape from it toward the end.

4 إن نعلي ولت وكانت إذا سرت قلوصي والنعل بئس القلوص

Even my sandal has turned its back [on me]. It used to be my camel
when I traveled; a sandal is the worst of camels.
**My sandal also turned its back on me,
my "camel," when I traveled; there's none worse.**

5 ومتى تقعد الجنيبة بالمركو ب يوما فعمرها مقصوص

When the horse that is led makes the one that is ridden lie down, its
life is going to be cut short.
**The spare horse, when it makes the mount lie down,
its life-span is cut short and over soon.**

Commentary: This is less than clear. The *janiba* is the spare horse that
runs alongside the mounted horse (or, in the olden days, alongside the
camel when the members of a tribe rode into battle; they would change
from the camel to the horse before entering the fray with their lances
[cf. Friedrich Wilhelm Schwarzlose, *Die Waffen der alten Araber, aus ihren
Dichtern dargestellt* (Leipzig: J.C. Hinrichs'sche Buchhandlung 1886), 46,
the term here is *janib*]). We might assume that the foundering horse is left
to die, while the rider continues on the spare horse. But the possessive
suffix -*ha* in *'umruha* clearly refers to the *janiba*. The idea then might be
that even the spare horse will soon be overtaken by death. If we interpret
the preposition *bi-* in *bi-'l-markubi* as a comitative rather than a 'transi-
tivizer,' the first hemistich would read: "When the spare horse lies down
(that is, breaks down) together with the ridden one, . . ." This makes less
sense, but it might be intended as an analogy to the sandal in the previous line, which had already flippantly been turned into a camel. Note, by
the way, that al-Sanawbari has two sandal poems, one in which he gives
thanks for sandals that have been given to him, and another in which he
asks for a *na'l* as a gift (see pp. 14 [no. 5] and 449–501 [no. 8 *takmila*]).

6 ليس يغني العويص عني فتيلا أي شيء أجدى عليّ العويص

Difficult verse does not help me a bit; what has difficult verse
availed me?

**Hermetic verse avails me not one whit,
what profit has it given me to date?**

Commentary *'Awis* (and *mu'tas*) means 'difficult to grasp' and often refers to obscure, mannerist, poetry: *al-'awisu min al-shi'ri ma yas'ubu istikhraju ma'nahu* [*'awis*-poetry is the one whose meaning it is difficult to bring out].[6] This verse is clearly a bitter commentary on the one that precedes it.

٧   ولئن أنشب البلى في ثيابي   مخلبا لا يزيله التخليص

Truly, if decay sinks its claw into my clothes, which cleaning does not remove,
**If fraying sinks its claw into my clothes,
which cleaning cannot afterward remove,**

Commentary: The image of decay "sinking in its claw" is an allusion to Abu Dhu'ayb's (d. ca. 647)[7] famous line: "When Death sinks its claws in, you will find all amulets of no avail."[8]

٨   فثيابي من البلى في أمان   ليس يخشى على ثيابي اللصوص

then my clothes, due to this decay, are under safe conduct; robbers are not feared with regard to them.
**my clothes because of wear and tear are safe,
as robbers are not feared to pilfer them.**

٩   زعم الأصمعي من دون هذا   كان في القر يحفر القرموص

Al-Asma'i says that, for less than this, manholes used to be dug in the cold [(of winter].
**Al-Asma'i has claimed: For less than this
those manholes would be dug for winter's cold.**

Commentary: Our poet here quotes the philologist al-Asma'i (d. 828),[9] in whose writings, as far as they are accessible to me, I have not yet found the *qurmus*. Nor is it listed in the Asma'i dictionary, compiled by Hadi

Hasan Hammudi.[10] The later lexicographer al-Azhari (d. 980), a younger contemporary of al-Sanawbari, reports the following: "I was in the desert [presumably when he was a prisoner of the Qarmatians], and a cold northerly *(ariya)* wind started to blow. I saw those among their servants who had no shelter dig holes *(hufar)* for themselves in the soft earth, crouch [var. spend the night] in them, and throw their garments on top of themselves, thereby repelling the cold of the north wind. They called these holes *qaramis*."[11]

[Second theme: the noble man suffers]

١٠ أي حر رأيته ليس يستو   لي على جل عيشه التنغيص

What noble man have you seen, whose life—most of it—is not
    dominated by bitterness?
What noble man have you descried, whose life
is not preponderantly bitterness?

١١ نفس صبرا فلن يطيق نهوضا   ذو جناح جناحه مقصوص

Patience, my soul! The winged [bird] whose wing has been clipped will
    not be able to rise.
My soul, be calm! A bird will never rise,
who, though bewinged, has found his wings are clipped.

١٢ قد لبست القناعة الآن ثوبا   فاستوى الشري في فمي والخبيص

I have now donned contentedness as a garment; gall [lit. colocynth]
    and sweetmeat are alike in my mouth.
I have now donned contentedness as dress;
alike are gall and sweetmeat in my mouth.

١٣ قذفت بي الخطوب في لجج البحـ   ـر فطورا أطفو وطورا أغوص

The vicissitudes have hurled me into the depths of the sea: sometimes
    I float and sometimes I go under.

Events have hurled me to the ocean's depths;
at times I float and sometimes I go down.

14 كيف يخطو إلي ذل ودوني   سور صبر بنيانه مرصوص

How can any kind of humiliation get to me, as there is, shielding me, a
wall of patience, its structure tightly fit together?
How can humiliation get to me?
A wall of patience, firmly built, my shield.

15 ما جرى ذو الحوافر الصم إلا   خام عن شأوه الوجي ورهيص

The horse with sound hooves runs, while the one with sore hooves
holds back from overtaking him.
The firm-hoofed horse will run ahead, while fear
will hold the sore-hoofed horse from passing him.

16 كم رأى الناس من لئيم بطين   وعلى بابها كريم خميص

How often does one see a mean, potbellied man, on whose door a
decent man [is waiting], his stomach empty.
How often does one see a mean fat man,
and at his door a decent haggard one.

17 غير أن الفرع الشريف إذا هيـ   ـض أبى أن ينهاض منه العيص

However, if the noble offshoot is broken [and powerless], his root will
refuse to be broken.
Yet, if the noble offshoot's strength should break,
his root will certainly refuse to break.

18 قسم الرزق بين حلو ومر   فالذي قد أتيح ليس ينوص

Sustenance has been divided between sweet and bitter; that which has
been ordained does not escape [you].
Your livelihood is either sweet or tart;
that which has been ordained will not pass by.

Commentary: *yanusu*, emendation of the editor for the manuscript variant *fayusu*, which has no meaning.

١٩ كثمار النخل البواسق منها   رطب يانع ومنها شيص

Just like the fruit of the tall date palms: some are fresh and ripe,
    others stoneless and dry.
Just like the fruit of tall and towering palms:
some fresh and ripe, and others without stone.

Commentary: The term *shis* refers to dates that have un(der)developed pits because they have not been pollinated.

[Third theme: the young beloved]

٢٠ يطبيني الكشح الهضيم إذا ما   هزه ساعة القيام البوص

The slender waist entices me, when at the moment of rising up, the
    rear makes it sway;
The slender waist entices me, as soon
as, rising up, the rear has made it sway;

Commentary: The word *bus* is explained as 'buttocks' *('ajuz)* or as 'softness of their fat' *(linu shahmatihi)*.

٢١ وبنان على المفاصل منها   نقر تستقر فيها الفصوص

as do fingers, with pieces of silver on their joints, with cameos
    standing out from them.
and fingers, silver pieces on their joints,
and standing out from them are cameos,

Commentary: The "pieces of silver" and the "cameos" are not real, but metaphorical similes for the white-skinned finger joints (or possibly the entire digits) and the henna-dyed fingertips (cameos are often made of red carnelian [*'aqiq*]).[12]

22 وأثيث مثل الأساود يصبيـ   ـني منه ا لمضفور والمعقوص

and lush [hair] like black snakes, its braids and twists captivate me;
and lush black hair like snakes enraptures me,
the braided part as well as sundry horns;

Commentary: The verbs *dafara* and *'aqasa* are often taken to be near
synonyms in the sense of 'braiding.' But given that *'aqisa 'aqasan* refers to
the horns of the goat that turn backward over the ears, the explanation
that *'aqasa* means twisting the braids back to their roots seems justified.

23 وثنايا لم تعد نور اقحوان   لسقوط الندى عليه وبيص

and [front] teeth that did not abandon chamomile flowers, on which
   there is a gleam because of the fall of dew.
and teeth that are the bloom of chamomile,
on which a gleam betrays the fall of dew.

Commentary: The phrase *lam ta'du nawra uqhuwanin* would in the first
instance mean 'that did not go beyond chamomile flowers.' Since the teeth
of the beloved are, of course, whiter than chamomile petals, that will not
do. If we take the verb to mean 'abandon,' the idea would be that the teeth
never ceased to look like those petals. The gleaming dew is a metaphor for
the saliva glistening on the teeth.

24 وبما قد خلعت فيه عذاري   وعيون الأنام دوني خوص

[I swear] by the fact that I have thrown off all restraints concerning
   him, while the people are too squint-eyed to see me,
I swear by letting go the reins with him,
while people's eyes are squinting, missing me:

Commentary: The translation takes *bi-* as *ba' al-qasam*, introducing the object by which the oath is taken, and the *ma* following it as *ma
al-masdariya* (the fact that). The initial idea is similarly expressed by Abu
Nuwas: *ya man khala'tu l-'idhara fihi wa-man sayyara sitri fi-l-nasi mahtuka*.[13]
In view of this parallel I have rejected the other possible translation,

which has the suffix in *fihi* refer back to *ma*, resulting in the following: "[I swear] by that [that is, the love affair], in which I have thrown off all restraints."

25 فسواء عليّ إن لمت فيه   مهل اللوم فيه والمنقوص

if you blame [me] for him, thinking about [your] censure of me and
    the [real] defect become the same to me
Alike for me, if blame for him you must,
are thinking over blame and fault itself.

Genre: Ritha′ and Ghazal Subtexts

The tripartite structure of the poem is easy to perceive. The first theme, the 'death' of the poet's clothes, in proving that the poet is in dire straits, logically leads to the second theme: in this world the noble suffer and the mean succeed. The final theme, a love song mostly giving a serial description of the beloved, is attached to the poem without any obvious connection.

If we go by the anonymous compiler's introductory note to the *Diwan* ("bewailing the death of his clothes, he said"), the first part of the poem is, so to speak, the *gharad*, the 'purpose,' of the poem—which would also indicate its 'genre.' But what is this genre? There is some ambiguity. First, as the compiler suggests, it is a *ritha′*, a 'dirge.' The term *firaq*, (separation), in verse 1 sets the tone. The verb occurs also in a poetic snippet in his *Diwan* that clearly deals with the 'departure' of the dead:[14]

1 كواكب العيش فارقونا   فما من الحق أن نعيش

2 لما أجدوا الرحيلة عنا   كانت مطاياهم النعوش

1 The stars in [our] life have left us; / it is not right that we live.[15]
2 When they became serious with departing from us, / their mounts were the biers.

In verses 3, 7, and 8, the term *bila* (decay) is repeated; this is the only word referring in any way to the notion of 'death.' Obviously, the poet had to use a term that would be applicable to garments. But he also had to reinforce the 'death' dimension of the dirge, and he finds two solutions for this problem: in verse 3 he posits a parallel between his garments and himself—none will escape decay—while in verse 7 he alludes to one of the most famous dirges in Arabic literature, Abu Dhu'ayb al-Hudhali's elegy on the death of his five sons from the plague in Egypt. This already exhausts the elements pointing to *ritha'*, except maybe for the enigmatic verse 5, which speaks of a life cut short. Already verse 2, however, introduces a new dimension, that of *ghazal* (love poetry). The 'separation' mentioned in verse 1 can also be understood as referring to the lover and the beloved,[16] and the terms used in verse 2, *wasl* (union) and *hajr* (avoidance), are central for love poems: the lover seeks the former, the beloved prefers the latter. But this is already the extent of it. In other words, our poet does not want to get serious; he just flits from one subtext to the next. The only thing he is seriously aiming at is *hazl* (jest).

Before looking more closely at the *hazl* aspect of the poem, let us— if only briefly—expand a bit on al-Sanawbari's connection with the two genres that are involved here: *ritha'* and *ghazal*. His fame as an expert in poetic flower and garden descriptions notwithstanding, he was an important poet also in these two genres.

The *ghazal* dimension of our poem is, of course, not exhausted by the sparse allusions just mentioned; the third part of it is a *ghazal* in its own right and will be treated in due course. It is worth mentioning here that the *ghazal* theme of 'separation' has been used by al-Sanawbari as a subtext in an amusing way elsewhere:

Al-Sanawbari had a baby son, who was breast-feeding. At a certain point he was weaned. Al-Sanawbari entered his house one day, and his son was crying. He said: "What is wrong with my son?" They said: "He has been weaned." So he strode to his cradle and wrote on it:

١   منعوه أحب شيء لديه   من جميع الورى ومن والديه

They denied him the sweetest thing for him / from all mankind and (even) from his parents.

٢   منعوه غذاءه وهو قد كا   ن مباحا له وبين يديه

They denied him his nourishment, which had been / permitted to him and was within reach.

٣ عجبا منه ذا على صغر السـ ـن هوي فاهتدى الفراق إليه

How strange that is on his part! In spite of his young age / he fell in
love and thus Separation found its way to him.[17]

Similarly, there is an extraordinary poem in which al-Sanawbari uses
the subtext of love poetry but with a preponderant elegiac component in
order to invoke a pair of plane trees, one of which had been uprooted by
a gale.[18] Having just been bereaved of a beloved, he presents the remaining plane tree as an image of himself. The personification of the tree and
the sympathy he expresses for it are uncommon and touching, although in
verses 4–6 he hastens to add the differences between himself and the tree
to emphasize his own sorrow:

وقال يذكر دلبتين في بستان غربي قويق كسرت الريح احداهما

He said with regard to two plane trees in a garden west of the river
Quwayq, one of which the wind had broken:

١ أ يا دلبة الغربي أفردك الدهر سقى الدلب دلب الغرب من أجلك القطر

O plane tree of the Western bank, Fate has made you single!
May rain water the plane trees of the West for your sake!

٢ فتاتين عذراوين أختين كنتما قضى الأمر في إحداكما من له الأمر

The two of you were two young women, virgins, sisters;
He who has the commanding power has executed it with regard to
one of you.

٣ كلانا محت آثار و احده النوى فليس له عين تحس ولا أثر

For both of us separation has wiped out the traces of his partner;
there is no substance left of him that could be sensed nor any vestige.[19]

٤ سوى أنني بالوجد والصبر عالم وأنت فلا وجد عليك ولا صبر

Except that I am conscious of emotion and patience,
whereas there is no emotion or patience with you.

5 وتشهد لي عين غزار دموعها   وما لك دمع غزير ولا نزر

My witness is an eye whose tears are abundant,
while you have neither abundant nor scant tears.

6 وعودي قد مص اشتياقي ماءه   وعودك تجري الماء أوراقه الخضر

As for my "wood" [that is, mettle], my yearning has sucked out its
    water,
as for your wood, its green leaves have let the water flow.

7 ألا طال ما سرنا إلى وطنيكما   فسارت إلى أوطان ألبابنا الخمر

Oh, how often did we travel to your realms,
then wine would travel to the realms of our minds —

8 زمان يردينا بظلكما الهوى   رداءين وشى من حواشيهما الزهر

at the time, when love-passion clad us with both your shade
in two mantles, whose hems flowers had embroidered.

9 محب ومحبوب فمن يرنا يقل   سرورا بنا هذا هلال وذا بدر

A lover and a beloved. Whoever saw us said
out of happiness for us: This is a crescent moon and that a full moon.

10 سقى الله ذاك العهد عهدا فقد مضى   وأغلق باب الوصل من بعده الهجر

May God bless [lit. water] that time! It has passed
and separation has locked the door of union after it.

11 ويا ليته إذ مات متنا بموته   ففزنا وهل للموت في تركنا عذر

If only, when he died, we had died from his death!

We would have succeeded then. Does death have any excuse for
sparing us?

12 أليس جميل مات عشقا وعروة   وقيس وغيلان كذا مات والغمر

Did not Jamil die of love and 'Urwa,
and Qays and Ghaylan died that way, so too al-Ghamr.[20]

In this poem verse 3, the one that establishes the parallel fates of the
plane tree and the poet, shows the superimposition of *ritha'* and *ghazal* in
the word *nawa* (being distant, separation). But this is just a quick touch.
After distancing himself from the plane tree in verses 4–6, by enumerating the different reactions of the tree and the human being, memories
flood him of times of love and wine-drinking in the shade of the two plane
trees. Then the trees fade away, and only the poet and his beloved remain.
When he re-enters the present time of the poem in verse 10, he again uses
ghazal terms (*wasl* [union] and *hajr* [separation]) to express the demise of
the beloved. And this leads him to the climactic conclusion, where love
and death coalesce in the martyrs of love. Only, it is all wrong! He, the
lover, should have died, as the precedents prove.

Al-Sanawbari's true *ghazal* poetry constitutes a good part of his output,
both *mudhakkarat* and *mu'annathat*. There is no need here to dwell on this
part of his oeuvre, since Bauer has included his love poetry in the corpus
on which he based his groundbreaking work on love and love poetry in the
ninth and tenth centuries.[21] A few details will be discussed in connection
with the third part of the poem later (this text was not discussed by Bauer).

Al-Sanawbari's production of elegies, though mostly unnoticed in modern studies, was substantial. The following list illustrates the variety he
managed to cultivate in this, on the whole, somewhat monotonous genre:

   A   Religious figures
       (1) the Prophet[22]
       (2) al-Husayn[23]
       (3) the family of the Prophet (*ahl al-bayt*)[24]
   B   Relatives
       (1) mother[25]
       (2) daughter[26]
   C   Friends[27]

D   The pilgrims massacred in Mecca by the Qarmatians[28]
E   The poem under discussion.

Other Dirges on 'Dead' Clothes?

What strikes the reader of the poem first of all is the incongruous-
ness of applying the very serious vocabulary of the dirge, here and there
overlaid with the equally serious language of love poetry, to the rather
ludicrous subject of shabby clothes that are frayed and falling to pieces.
Al-Sanawbari is not the only one who has tried his hand at this. Al-Sudani,
in his book about elegies on non-humans in Abbasid poetry, lists five cases
of a poet—allegedly—lamenting disintegrating pieces of clothing:[29]

   1.   Ibn Abi Karima, contemporary of al-Jahiz (d. 868). The passage
in question is actually the last part (verses 36–47) of a poem of 47 verses,
which Ibn Abi Tahir Tayfur (d. 893) included in a special section of his *K.
al-Manthur wa-l-manzum*, devoted to 'unparalleled' poems.[30] The poem
is indeed without par, since it describes the production of a shirt *(qamis)*
from the selection of a plot for growing the cotton (!) to the finished product, which then falls prey to mice that gnaw holes into it. The humor of
the whole poem is difficult to miss: the description of the very laborious
production process over 35 verses, detailed and sober and serious (though
the sometimes outspoken realism might make the reader smile), leads to
nothing more than the final episode of mice ravishing the shirt and rendering it useless. In our context the first question must be: is this last part
of the poem an elegy?
   Here is van Gelder's translation (with his question marks, but without
his commentary):[31]

(36) I had hardly donned (?) it before a secretly creeping creature was
      given access to it, dainty of snout and ears,[32]
(37) Quick of hearing; listening, then erecting it [sc. its ear, or itself?]
      under cover of darkness, wary of a deft bird,
(38) Looking with a kohl-black eye, not affected (?) by eye-disease,
      with sunken, piercing eyes, exploring the darkness.[33]
(39) Trailing a tail like a leather thong; you would think it was
      something that fell off a winnower's fork on the morning of
      separation when the people departed.[34]

(40) At night [it came]; and it left it [scil. the shirt] full of holes for the wind to blow through: peep-holes like pared coins.

(41) It did not leave out any place but it went over it thoroughly. Such things happen to him whom Fate pursues with hate.

(42) My year (?) announced its [viz. the shirt's] death to me the day I put it on. Time was not to be trusted with it.[35]

(43) Why is it that the hands of Time disregard all people but turn to me, deliberately, in order to kill me?

(44) I have been the prey of cares since I was afflicted because of it; allied to sorrow, showing my secret and outward feelings.

(45) It seems, when night lodges in its dwelling-place, as if I am one that is bitten by a dangerous snake, to whom slumber is forbidden.

(46) From [my] weeping it is evident what I suffer from; for now that it [scil. the shirt] is gone I have no other to protect me.

(47) I say, when misgivings because of it beset my heart: "To you, Ibn 'Ali, I direct my complaints."

The first several verses describe the mice and their nefarious action. In verse 41, Fate *(dahr)* blends in, and in the next line the verb *na'a*, 'to announce the death of,' appears and Fate, now called Time *(zaman)*, appears again. The poet feels singled out by Fate for ill-treatment (v. 43); he is besieged by sorrows due to the shirt catastrophe (v. 44); he is unable to sleep (v. 45); there is no replacement for the loss (v. 46). These are all typical symptoms, which become ubiquitous motifs in elegiacal poetry. Ibn Abi Tahir Tayfur, the compiler of the 'unparalleled' poems, is thus clearly right, when he says in his introduction that the poet "mentioned in it [that is, the *qasida*] a shirt of his that he had bewailed."[36] However, the last line moves beyond the dirge by appealing to one Ibn 'Ali that he listen to the complaint and presumably replace the shirt.

2.   Ibn Hamdawayh (or Hamdoya), also known as al-Hamdawi (d. ca. 884). He was famous, or notorious, for a number of poems (thirty-two, to be exact), in which he made fun of a shabby *taylasan* that had been given to him by Ibn Harb al-Muhallabi; the *taylasan* became proverbial, as the poems became very popular. One of them, a poem of six verses, might conceivably be considered a dirge. I give here my own translation, which takes Josef van Ess's rhymed German rendering into account:[37]

1 Let me bewail my garment, since it has bid farewell.
   I will certainly persist in weeping, as it has persisted [in leaving].
2 O Ibn al-Husayn, don't you see my robe (durra'a)
   in tatters, "gowned" and "robed" with decay?
3 In it are so many tears that, if
   the easterly breeze were to brush past it, it would break up.[38]
4 It is imitating[39] the porousness of my cloak (taylasan), for
   it learned decay from it and so dissolved.
5 May God never give comfort to it [that is, the taylasan]! It has
   infected[40] all my clothes, and so they fell apart!
6 The mountains should praise God, for
   if they were in contact with it, they would cave in and
   break apart.[41]

It looks as if al-Sudani had little reason to include this poem in his collection of sartorial dirges. The weeping and bidding farewell mentioned in verse 1 refer back to the traditional *nasib*, the garment taking the place of the beloved, who departs with her tribe and leaves the inconsolable poet/lover behind.

3.   Ibrahim b. Ishaq al-Hadimi, a little known poet of unknown dates. Since al-Safadi quotes the poetry from the lost part of al-Marzubani's *Dictionary of Poets (Mu'jam al-shu'ara')*, and the latter died in 994, we have a *terminus ante quem*.[42] His *nisba* is unknown; it could also be al-Hudaymi. Neither Hadim nor Hudaym can be found in Yaqut's *Mu'jam al-buldan*. Al-Safadi adduces two poems, which the poet had written about his shirt, the first of which is said to be a *ritha'*. The second is clearly not and will be disregarded here. Unfortunately, the transmission of the text of the alleged *ritha'* is not always well established.

١   قميصي قد أباد أبا وأما   وخالا كان بي برا وعما

My shirt made a father and a mother pass away
and a maternal uncle who was devoted to me and a paternal one.

٢   وأصبح باقيا بفناء جسمي   أرم الدهر منه ما استرم

It became everlasting through the waning of my body,
as I mended away at any part that needed mending.

3 إذا شبرا رممت وها ذراع   فأعلم أن ذلك لن يتم

Whenever I mend a span, a cubit will give way,
and I know that this will never end.

4 أقول له ابغ بي بدلا ودعني   ففعلك قد تنكد واستذم

I say to it: Seek a replacement for me and leave me alone,
for what you do is harsh[45] and deserves blame.

5 فلم يحفل بما حاولت منه   وغناني كيادا لي وظلما

But it did not pay attention to what I wanted to gain from it,
and it sang to me in order to trick me and treat me unfairly:

6 سأصبر صاغرا وأموت غما   وإن جرعت فيك اليوم سما

"I shall persevere in lowliness and die from grief,
even if I were now to be given poison to drink on your behalf."[46]

It strains credulity that al-Safadi, or al-Marzubani, considered this
a dirge. The shirt, in spite of its being aged and moribund, is very much
alive and refuses to quit.

4. Muhammad b. Musa al-Qasani, another obscure poet listed by
al-Marzubani in the existing part of his work.[47] His dates are not mentioned but he is said to be the brother of Abu-l-Ghamr Harun b. Musa,
who is mentioned as a poet elsewhere by al-Marzubani[48] and as a scribe
serving al-Hasan b. Zayd al-ʿAlawi, who is most likely the one who founded
the ʿAlid dynasty in Tabaristan and died there in 884.[49] In the introduction to the poem, al-Marzubani says that it is a long *qasida* in which he
produced a dirge on a tunic *(izar)* of his. At the end he mentions that the
poem consisted of seventy verses, but he quotes only the two *incipit* verses
and then eight verses from elsewhere in the poem. The latter contain a

descriptive praise of the tunic, such as verse 2 of the section: "It was, from among the things of this world, my beauty and my treasure," and so on through the rest of the section. The parts left out by al-Marzubani may, of course, have contained the elegiacal section, but then we might wonder why he used the verb *yarthi* in his introduction without delivering what was promised.

5.   Kushajim's poem on the *mandil*, 'handkerchief,'[50] hardly contains any elements of a dirge and should be disregarded in our context.

A closer look at al-Sudani's collection thus shows that it yields just one unambiguous case of a poem of mourning over a deceased garment, Ibn Abi Karima's murine mini-epic. It is surprising that al-Sudani missed al-Sanawbari's contribution to this "genre," to which we will now return.

Production of Hazl "Jest" in Poetry

First, let us address a general question: since the first part of our poem is obviously meant to be funny, how are funniness and wittiness produced in poetry? There is a certain amount of scholarly literature on *hazl* (jest, joking) but this deals mainly with prose (which mostly means prosimetrum) and focuses on the opposition *jidd wa-hazl* (seriousness and joking) and the social acceptability of the latter.[51] But the internal mechanics of jest in classical Arabic poetry has, as far as I know, not been made the subject of academic inquiry. In the following discussion, examples will be culled exclusively from al-Sanawbari. One possible method to make the reader laugh is to choose an unusual, 'non-poetic' topic. But this approach need not be funny. Compare the following five examples:

1.   On fleas (p. 435, no. 386):

١   حمتني البراغيث طيب الكرى   فليس يطوف الكرى بالمآقي

The fleas have kept me away from pleasant slumber,
so no slumber encircles the corners of my eyes.

٢   طفقن يردن رفاقا دمي   ومن أطول الورد ورد الرفاق

They began to go down in groups to the watering hole of my blood
— the longest watering is the one done in groups,

3 تفوق الحماليج في مشيها   إلي وتقفز قفز العتاق

surpassing the amblers in their march
toward me and jumping like pedigreed horses,

4 ذوات شفار رقاق تفوق   في القطع حد الشفار الرقاق

with fine blades which surpass
in cutting the edge of fine blades,

5 وكالرقباء على العاشقين   فتفسد بالقرص طيب العناق

and [they are] like spies on the lovers
and they spoil the lovely embrace with their biting,

6 تباشر جلد الفتى كالهباء   ويصدرن عن جلده كالزقاق

touching the young man's skin [small] like dust motes,
and returning, thirst quenched, from his skin [big] like water-skins.

Apart from the choice of the itchy topic, there are certain details that enhance the humor of the poem. Verse 1 is still mainly descriptive and does not yield much of what we are seeking. But in verse 2 we have the first of a series of hyperbolic metaphors and similes that inform the whole poem: the idea that the fleas are going down, like camels or other big animals, to the watering hole, which turns out to be the poet's blood. The idea is conveyed by the verb metaphor *yaridna*. Note that the counterpart of this verb, *yasdirna*, is used in the same metaphorical way in the last hemistich, a structural nicety not to be overlooked. Verse 3 contains a 'surpassing' simile: the fleas march faster and jump higher than noble horses. The absurdity of the pesky pests outdoing the noblest of creatures also sets the tone for the next line: fleas' cutting tools are sharper than fine blades. The *tasdir* of *shifarin riqaqin* vs. *al-shifari al-riqaqi* may seem artless, but it can also be seen as iconically representing the relentless biting on all sides. Verse 5 is likely to raise a chuckle, because the fleas are equated with a standard figure in love poetry, the annoying spy *(raqib)* who makes life miserable for the lovers seeking secrecy. The second hemistich is devoid of any imagery, but the picture of the lovers in their passionate embrace warding off and killing the attacking fleas certainly is something of a climax, if not the climax they want. The last verse wraps up the whole process of the fleabite with two expressive similes: the fleas arrive like dust motes and leave like filled water-skins. Ridiculous hyperbolic imagery is the main mechanism for creating humor, but note that the climactic passage of the lovers under siege is entirely image free.

2.   On the river Quwayq, which flows through Aleppo (p. 451, no. 9 [in Supplement]):

١   قويق إذا شم ريح الشتاء   أظهر تيها وكبرا عجيبا

When Quwayq smells the scent of winter [the rainy season],
it displays startling pride and arrogance,

٢   وناسب دجلة والنيل والـ   ـفرات بهاء وحسنا وطيبا

and it equals the Tigris and the Nile and the Euphrates
in splendor and beauty and fragrant smell.

٣   وإن أقبل الصيف أبصرته   ذليلا حقيرا حزينا كئيبا

But when summer approaches, you see it
lowly, despised, sad, and sorrowful.

٤   إذا ما الضفادع نادينه   "قويق قويق" أبى أن يجيب

When the frogs call out to it:
quwayq, quwayq! it refuses to respond.

٥   فيأوين منه بقايا كسين   من طحلب الصيف ثوبا قشيبا

So remnants [of them] take refuge from it, clad
in a new garment made of green summer algae.

6 وتمشي الجرادة فيه فلا تكاد قوائمها أن تغيب

And the locust walks in it
and its legs hardly vanish.

The poem has a scent of *hija'*, invective poetry, about it, especially
in verses 1 and 3 (another little poem addressed to Quwayq is explicitly
called a *hija'*, dealing with the same lack of water as in this poem, see p.
425, no. 372). But the last three verses draw a rather funny scenario of the
summer situation. The croaking of the frogs is reinterpreted as the river's name; they call on it to reappear with ample waters, but no such luck.
So the frogs, covered with the slimy green algae that develop in stagnant
water, decide to look for better ponds. The last line is hilarious: the field
(that is, the riverbed) is left to a small desert animal, the locust, and the
remaining water has become so shallow that the insect's legs do not even
disappear in it. It is not clear whether the last picture painted by the poet
is based on observation, as the frog lines certainly are, or whether he
merely wants to make a poetic point. In any case, it is remarkable that,
apart from the personification of the river and the frogs, there is little
imagery involved here.

3. On scabies *(jarab)* (p. 452–53, no. 11 [in Supplement]):

1 الشيب عنديّ والإفلاس والجرب هذا هلاك وذا شؤم وذا عطب

Being grayhaired and broke and scabby, I think,
are ruin and lucklessness and perdition, respectively.

2 إن دام ذا الحك لا ظفر يدوم ولا يدوم جلد ولا لحم ولا عصب

If this scratching continues, no fingernail will last,
nor any skin, flesh, or tendon.

3 أما تراه على الكفين منتظما كأنه لؤلؤ ما إن له ثقب

Don't you see them[52] lined up on both hands
like pearls without holes?

4 كحبة العنب الصغرى تبين ولا   تزال تعظم ما لا يعظم العنب

Like a tiny grape pip it shows up, and it
does not cease to grow even beyond the grape [in size].

5 ولقبوه بحب الظرف ليتهم   يا نفس ضاعوا كما قد ضاع ذا اللقب

They named them "pustules of elegance." Would that they had
perished, O my soul, just as this name has perished.

The choice of topic is somewhat comical, but not the situation itself;
the poet is not in the mood to display his wit. At most we can point to
the accumulation of terms in verses 1 and 2 that are bound to cause a
smile of sympathy for the poet's misery: In verse 1 he is not only scabby,
but also old and broke, and all three situations are characterized, in a *laff
wa-nashr* figure with three near-synonyms, as ruinous. Verse 2 contains a
suitable hyperbole for the terrible itch, neither the scratcher, the fingernail, nor the scratched, going from skin to flesh to tendon, can withstand
the constant scratching. But the rest is description of the pustules, with
the last line apparently protesting earlier euphemistic nomenclature of
the same.

4. On a cutpurse *(tarrar)* (p. 25, no. 18):

Here we do not need to produce the whole poem, as it has hardly any
comical aspects, apart perhaps from the choice of subject. A summary of
the poem would look as follows:
(1) A cutpurse cut away my cash; my equanimity is gone.
(2) He cut away all the dirhams, shining like little moons.
(3) Rather than my cash, he cut away my mind!
(4) I am entirely beside myself.
(5) I protected them in my tunic; my tunic did not protect them.
(6) The money was removed in the blink of an eye.
(7) It was destiny—praise be to Him who owns all destinies.

The only mildly amusing figurative turn of phrase is the 'correction' in
verse 3: my mind was cut away, not my cash. It is actually a rather elegant

way of making the physical event and the mental reaction to it intersect on the poetic level.

Our last example brings us close to our initial poem about the shabby clothes:

5. On a mantle that caught fire (p. 433, no. 383):

كان ردائي أجل أعلاقي	من جدد كن لي وأخلاقي

My mantle was the most eminent of my treasures,
of new [garments] I had and worn ones.

كان بهائي إذا ارتديت به	وكان نوري وكان أحداقي

It was my splendor, when I donned it;
it was my light and the pupil of my eye.[53]

كنت به أحتبي وكنت به	أعتم في ثروتي وإملاقي

I would wind it around my knees when squatting and I would
wind it around my head, in my period of riches and in my destitution.

كان رفيقي صدر النهار ولي	في الليل منه صنوف أرفاق

It was my companion at the beginning of the day,
and at night I had a variety of uses for it.

مقرمة كان لي ومنشفة	ومئزرا فاضلا عن الساق

A bedspread it was for me, and a towel,
and a waist-cloth, wide around the lower legs.

وكان سترا لباب بيتي أحـ	ـيانا وحينا لحاف طراقي

And sometimes it was a curtain for the door of my house,
and at other times the blanket for my nightly guests.

يكون ذخرا لعقبي الباقي   وكنت أهوى له البقاء لكي   7

I used to wish for it that it survive,
so that it might become a treasure for my surviving progeny.

حماه صوني له وإشفاقي   أصونه مشفقا عليه فما   8

I would protect it, caring for it, but
my protection and care for it did not preserve it.

سيان إحراقه وإحراقي   بل دب منه الإحراق في جسد   9

Rather, burning crept slowly through its body,
whose burning was one and the same with my burning.

وليس دمعي عليه بالراقي   فليس وجدي فيه بمنصرم   10

My sorrow for it has not come to an end,
and my tears over it have not been exhausted.

The poem continues for eight more verses, in which the poet addresses
a noble man called Abu-l-Hasan, suggesting that he replace the burnt mantle. The comical element in the part translated here is the enumeration
of the multiple functions of this garment, which naturally make its loss
all the more painful. There are altogether eight functions: as a wrap around
the legs and the back while sitting on the ground, knees up (this *ihtiba'*
position gives stability); as a turban; as a mantle (this 'regular' use seems
to be intended in the first half of verse 4); as a bedspread; as a towel; as a
waist-cloth; as a curtain for the door; and as a blanket for nightly guests.[54]
To make the situation even more dire, the poet also alleges that he had
intended to leave it to his offspring and later generations.[55]

Among these poems devoted to unusual topics, one (no. 4) is mostly
free of humorous elements; two use the enumeration method for comical
effect (nos. 3 and 5); one draws a funny scenario (no. 2); and one uses ridiculous hyperbolic imagery (no. 1). Clearly, the humorous effect can reside
in a number of different poetic techniques; further study promises less
impressionistic results.

Hazl and Jidd in the Poem

Where does our main poem stand in this respect? So far it is 'unparalleled,' to take up Ibn Abi Tahir Tayfur's principle of selection. In the first place, it is polythematic, which cannot rightly be said of any of the other poems mentioned. But even if we zoom in on the first, humorous part, there are a number of peculiar features. The personification of the hooded cloak and the shirt and their interaction with the poet in both the *ritha'* and the *ghazal* mode is intricate, resulting in melancholy humor. But this is evoked in three verses. Verse 4 adds the sandals ('slippers' might be a better translation) to the worn-out pieces of clothing, but there is no clear allusion to either dirge or love song. There is only a hint of funny *hija'*, the *na'l* is the worst of "camels." Verse 5, if I understand it correctly, describes the fate of the slippers in an enigmatic and abstruse analogy, and verse 6 seems to be the poet's acerbic comment on the fact that his ability to compose such difficult lines has not been honored. Verses 7 and 8 return to the bitter humor of the beginning, but in a straightforward way: the clothes are so frayed that no one would steal them. Verse 9 seems to say that the cold the poet has to endure is considerable and that he might be forced to resort to the old Bedouin custom of digging a whole to crouch in to avoid the cold winds. The learned citation of al-Asma'i and the unusual term *(qurmus)* seem maladroit and thus comical.

The fact is, of course, that underlying the humor is a pretty desperate situation. As mentioned above, al-Sanawbari's life is not well-known; he is said to have been a librarian at the court of Sayf al-Dawla at the end of his life, but he must have had many ups and downs before he got that far. We have already had occasion to mention two poetic requests for gifts by him—one for sandals, the other for a mantle—not likely to have been written by a well-to-do man. We are therefore not surprised to see that the second part of his poem is a complaint about the unfairness of the world, where the cruel succeed and the noble suffer. After a general rhetorical question ('have you ever seen it otherwise?') (vs. 10), he resorts to patience *(sabr)* and contentedness *(qana'a)* (vss. 11–12) as his panacea. In verse 13 he displays desperation and resignation, then in verse 14 hastens back to patience, in a strong metaphor: ". . . a wall of patience, its structure tightly fit together." The next two verses (15–16) present the weak/strong dichotomy of this world—but, it seems, in two different constellations: in the equine analogy of verse 15, strong equals sound and weak equals sick, whereas in verse 16 we have the mean pot belly contrasted with the haggard noble man. Finally, there are certain consolations: a good pedigree cannot be undone (vs. 17), sustenance has been ordained (vs. 18), and even in nature the same 'unfairness' obtains, as the analogy in verse 19 shows.

The love song that forms the third part of our poem is attached to it without any further ado; there is no explicit justification nor any poetic *takhallus*. This *ghazal* itself consists of praise for the beloved in the shape of a list of the attractive body parts: the waist *(kashh)* and buttocks *(bus)*, the fingers *(banan)*, the lush hair *(athith)*, and the (front) teeth *(thanaya)* (vss. 20–23). The last two verses introduce the blamer *('adhil, la'im)*, a standard figure in love poetry, who normally criticizes the love situation per se but also the choice of the object of love.[56] The passage starts with an oath in which the poet swears by his clandestine love affair that merely thinking about the accusations being made against him would be as bad as the original flaw for which he is being accused, that is, the love affair. In other words, the blame is counterproductive: it enhances his passion.

Although it has no major impact on the discussion, we can try to answer the question of the beloved's gender. Is the poem a *mudhakkara* or a *mu'annatha*? Verse 24 contains the prepositional phrase *fihi*, 'with regard to him,' implying the poet is in love with a handsome youth. This is only true, however, if the preferred translation is accepted (see commentary on verse 24). Does the description of the beloved yield any clues? Verse 20 contains the topos of the heavy buttocks, here called *bus*, and the slender waist. Interestingly, of the adjective (as in *imra'atun hawsa'u* [a woman with large buttocks]) it is said that it would not be used of men *(Lisan al-'arab* 7, 8b–9a). This may have been true for the ancient language and literature that is predominantly reflected in the native dictionaries, but in Abbasid love poetry it is quite common also in the *mudhakkarat* (homo-erotic love poems).[57] Verse 22 contains the description of the hair, which is partly braided and the braids curved back; the whole arrangement can thus very aptly be compared to snakes. The simile is old, and the diction of this verse is somewhat old-fashioned. I am uncertain if *madfur* and *manqus* can refer to a male beloved. Bauer does not discuss the coiffures, and the article "Sha'r" in *Encyclopaedia of Islam. New Edition.* 12 vols. to date (Leiden: Brill, 1960-2004) is not much help in this respect. It is thus difficult to decide whether the beloved is male or female, unless we accept the proof of *fihi*.

Why would al-Sanawbari attach this love song to his poem? First, until further notice we should accept that it is part of the poem and not a chance mistake in the transmission. After that, we can only guess. Poetically, the most pleasing interpretation would be to consider this part a *nasib* in reverse: after the bitter humor of the first part and the sheer bitterness of the middle part, it was time to cheer up the listeners and release them from grim reality. The assertive final lines give a fitting finish to the whole poem.[58]

Notes

1   Al-Sanawbari, *Diwan*, ed. Ihsan 'Abbas (Beirut: Dar al-Thaqafa 1970), no. 229, 243–44. All following verses of al-Sanawbari's poetry will be taken from this edition. The poem has been briefly mentioned, but not discussed, by Josef van Ess, *Der Taylasan des Ibn Harb: "Mantelgedichte" in arabischer Sprache*, in *Sitzungsberichte der Heidelberger Akademie der Wissenschaften. Phil.-hist. Kl.* Jahrgang 1979, no. 4. (Heidelberg: Carl Winter, 1979), 43.

2   Adam Mez, *Die Renaissance des Islams* (Heidelberg: Winter, 1922), 264; my translation. Mez has wrongly "Rida" for "Radi."

3   Ali ibn Muhammad al-Shimshati, *K. al-Anwar wa-mahasin al-ash'ar*, ed. Mahdi al-'Azzawi (Baghdad: Wizarat al-I'lam, al-Jumhuriya al-'Iraqiya, 1976); ed. al-Sayyid Muhammad Yusuf, rev. with commentary. 'Abd al-Sattar Ahmad Farraj, vol. 1 (Kuwait: Wizarat al-I'lam, 1977).

4   *Tatimmat diwan al-Sanawbari*, ed. Lutfi al-Saqqal and Durriyah al-Khatib (Aleppo: Dar al-Kitab al-'Arabi, [1972]).

5   Mentioned in Reinhard Weipert, "Literaturkundliche Materialien zur älteren arabischen Poesie," *Oriens* 32 (1990): 328–74, here 363, quoting *Akhbar al-turath al-'arabi* 19 (1985): 20.

6   Ibn Manzur, *Lisan al-'arab*, 15 vols. (Beirut: Dar Sadir—Dar Bayrut 1955–56), 7:58b.

7   Fuat Sezgin, *Geschichte des arabischen Schrifttums*, 12 vols. to date (Leiden: Brill, 1967–84), 1:255.

8   Al-Sukkari: *K. Sharh ash'ar al-Hudhaliyyin*, ed. 'Abd al-Sattar Ahmad Farraj and Mahmud Muhammad Shakir, 3 vols. (Cairo: Maktabat al-'Uruba, n.d.), 1:8.

9   *Geschichte des arabischen Schrifttums* 8 (1982): 71.

10   Hadi Hasan Hammudi, *Mu'jam al-Asma'i* (Beirut: 'Alam al-Kutub, 1998).

11   *Tahdhib al-lugha*, ed. 'Abd al-Salam Harun & Muhammad 'Ali al-Najjar, 15 vols. (Cairo: al-Dar al-Misriya li-l-Ta'lif wa-l-Tarjama, n.d.), 9:386b

12   Thomas Bauer, *Liebe und Liebesdichtung in der arabischen Welt des 9. und 10. Jahrhunderts. Eine literatur- und mentalitätsgeschichtliche Studie des arabischen fiazal* (Wiesbaden: Harrassowitz, 1998), 319–21.

13   Abu Nuwas, *Diwan*, pt. 4, ed. G. Schoeler, 5 parts. (Wiesbaden: Franz Steiner, 1982), 279, no. 196, verse 13.

14 al-Sanawbari, *Diwan*, ed. 'Abbas, p. 216, no. 220.

15 The 'stars' are persons, as the verb agreement in *faraquna* shows.

16 Cf. the title of the work of Ibn al-Marzuban: *K. al-Shawq wa-l-firaq*, ed. Jalil al-'Atiya (Beirut: Dar al-Gharb al-Islami, 1988).

17 512, no. 143 [Supplement]

18 80–81, no. 80.

19 The phrasing of the idea to be conveyed is somewhat obscure, because we are dealing here with two couples: the pair of plane-trees, on the one hand, and the poet and his deceased beloved, on the other. The editor of the *Diwan* suggests that this line might be an allusion to al-Sanawbari's deceased daughter, but lines 7 ff. seem to militate against that. The pronominal suffix in *wahidihi* refers back to *kilana* (*kila* is mostly construed as a masculine singular, see Manfred Ullman: *Wörterbuch der klassischen arabischen Sprache*, 2 vols. in 4 pts to date (Wiesbaden: Harrassowitz, 1970–2007), 1:286–87, which is the best presentation of the grammatical facts), whereas the suffix in *lahu* refers to *wahid*. The pronouns "his" and "him" are "general;" the plane-tree is certainly feminine. The terms *'ayn* and *uthr* form a pair, see Edward William Lane: *An Arabic-English Lexicon*. 8 pts. (Repr. Beirut: Librairie du Liban, 1968), 1:18c, under *athar*.

20 The names are those of famous poets and heroes of love stories, mostly of the tribe of 'Udhra, who died of unfulfilled love: Jamil b. Ma'mar and Buthayna, 'Urwa b. Hizam and 'Afra', Qays b. al-Mulawwah al-Majnun, and Layla (or else Qays b. Dharih and Lubna), and Ghaylan b. 'Uqba Dhu-l-Rumma and Mayy. Only the last name, al-Ghamr, is obscure. The editor of the *Diwan* points to the list of titles of love stories from pre-Islamic and early Islamic times, compiled by Ibn al-Nadim, *al-Fihrist*, ed. Gustav Flügel (repr. Beirut: Khayyat, n.d.), 306, which contains an entry *Kitab al-Ghamr* [in the ed. *'l'mr*] *b. Dirar wa-Juml*. Since the list otherwise contains all the above names, this looks like a good guess. But al-Ghamr and Juml remain just a pair of names.

21 Bauer, *Liebe und Liebesdichtung*, index 2, under as-Sanaubari.

22 No. 100 (*ra'iya*, 56 verses, *munsarih*)

23 No. 140 (*ra'iya*, 20 verses, *sari'*), no. 221 (*shiniya*, 113 verses, *khafif*), no. 256 (*dadiya*, 80 verses, *basit*), no. 140 *takmila* (*ha'iya*, 42 verses, *kamil*). His elegies on al-Husayn and the *ahl al-bayt* show his Shi'ite convictions. The two long ones rhyming in *shin* and *dad* display his poetic prowess, as these are not easy rhyme letters. A fair number of *gharib* words 'needed' to be used, for example, third- and fourth-form quadriliteral verbs in no. 221: verse 16: *ijri'shash* (to be fat and uncouth) verse 79: *ihrinfash* (to get one's dander up) and verse 89: *itrighshash* (to recuperate from illness).

24 No. 357 (*fa'iya*, 54 verses, *wafir*).

25 No. 399 (*qafiya*, 17 verses, *sari'*).

26 No. 103 (*ra'iya*, 30 verses, *sari'*), no. 104 (*ra'iya*, 17 verses, *wafir*), no. 105 (*ra'iya*, 20 verses, *khafif*), no. 106 (*ta'iya*, 9 verses, *wafir*), no. 107 (*ra'iya*, 4 verses, *sari'*), no. 108 (*ra'iya*, 2 verses, *munsarih*), no. 109 (*ra'iya*, 2 verses, *munsarih*), no. 151 (*za'iya*, 17 verses, *tawil*), no. 249 (*dadiya*, 21 verses, *wafir*), no. 250 (*dadiya*, 2 verses, *rajaz*), no.

277 (*za'iya*, 8 verses, *kamil*), no. 304 (*'ayniya*, 5 verses, *sari'*), no. 305 (*'ayniya*, 2 verses, *wafir*), no. 148 *takmila* (6 two-liners written around the cupola of her tomb, rhyme letters: *nun / nun / 'ayn / ha / ta / dal*, meters: *ramal / tawil / wafir / kamil / khafif / kamil muraffal*).

The large number of dirges composed for his daughter Layla, who died an unmarried young woman, has attracted attention for their moving display of heartfelt emotion. They are included in the unpublished MA thesis of Basima bint Ibrahim al-'Isa. "Ritha' al-bint wa-l-ta'ziya fiha fi-l-shi'r al-'arabi min al-qarn al-thani ila nihayat al-qarn al-thamin al-hijriyayn" (MA thesis, King Saud University, Riyadh, 2002), and are separately treated by 'Abd al-Rahman al-Hulayyil in "Ritha' al-ibna fi shi'r al-Sanawbari," in *Majallat Jami'at al-Imam Muhammad ibn Sa'ud*, 26 (Riyadh: Rabi' al-akhar, 2005), 367–425. It is my pleasure to thank my colleague Suaad al-Mana, who was the advisor for the MA thesis, for drawing my attention to these two works.

27 No. 102 (*ra'iya*, 11 verses, *kamil*), no. 110 (*ra'iya*, 3 verses, *kamil*), no. 111 (*ra'iya*, 10 verses, *sari'*), no. 186 (*siniya*, 61 verses, *tawil*), no. 219 (*shiniya*, 7 verses, *khafif*), no. 248 (*dadiya*, 30 verses, *khafif*), no. 251 (*dadiya*, 4 verses, *sari'*), no. 350 (*fa'iya*, 12 verses, *kamil*), no. 397 (*qafiya*, 31 verses, *khafif*)
   While the subjects of the dirges are normally named in the introductory information of the compiler, in this case he is only characterized as a "student of his" (*tilmidh lahu*).

28 No. 101 (*ra'iya*, 39 verses, *tawil*). On this see C. Edmund Bosworth, "Sanawbari's elegy on the pilgrims slain in the Carmathian attack on Mecca (930): a literary-historical study," in *Arabica* 19 (1972): 222–39.

29 'Abd Allah 'Abd al-Rahim al-Sudani, *Ritha' ghayr al-insan fi-l-shi'r al-'abbasi* (Abu Dhabi: al-Majma' al-Thaqafi, 1999), 257–61.

30 Ibn Abi Tahir Tayfur, *al-Manthur wa-l-manzum: al-qasa'id al-mufradat allati la mathal laha*, ed. Muhsin Ghayyad (Beirut: Turath 'Uwaydat, 1977), 97–102. Al-Sudani is obviously unaware of Ghayyad's edition, since he quotes only a few verses (vss. 36–39, 40a, 41b, 44, with variants) and calls these a *maqtu'a*; the quote is second-hand from Muhammad Mustafa Haddara, *Ittijahat al-shi'r al-'arabi fi-l-qarn al-thani al-hijri* ([Cairo:] Dar al-Ma'arif, 1963), 442, who in turn quotes an unidentified manuscript in Dar al-Kutub. Geert Jan van Gelder has offered a transliteration and translation plus commentary of this poem, see, Geert Jan van Gelder, "A Cotton Shirt: An 'Unparalleled' Poem by Ibn Abi Karima (Early 9th Century)," in *Festschrift Ewald Wagner zum 65. Geburtstag*, ed. Wolfhart Heinrichs and Gregor Schoeler, vol. 2: *Studien zur arabischen Dichtung*. (Beirut and Stuttgart: Franz Steiner , 1994), 283–96. Due to its singularity it is at times extremely difficult to understand. Van Gelder rightly observes that in the title of the edition one should read *mithl* (or: *amthal*) instead of *mathal*.

31 Van Gelder, "Cotton Shirt," 291–93.

32 The masculine singular adjectives implicitly refer to *fa'r* which is a generic noun; it seems preferable to translate them as plurals (thus 'creatures'). However, in the next two verses the poet switches to feminine singular adjectives and verbs.

It seems that the poet now focuses on the individual animal, the *fa'ra*, in his description. From verse 39 onward he returns to the masculine singular. In verses 40 and 41 that makes eminent sense, but not in 39, which continues the mouse description. Should the masculine singular in *mustatbi'un* (trailing) be considered poetic license?

33 I agree with the translation 'affected,' but the verb *yarnu*, lit. 'gazes,' does not really yield this meaning. One might suggest *yarbu*, thus: 'eye-disease does not make it swell up.'

34 The 'winnower's fork' is based on a silent emendation *midhra* rather than *midra*, "comb for disentangling hair," as the text has it. The latter seems to fit the context better; the *saqit*, 'something that fell off,' is strands of hair held together by oil, sweat, and dirt, torn out during combing and thrown out of their litters by the ladies (it is probably better to read *zu'un*, pl. of *za'ina* (litter, *howdah*) rather than *za'(a)n*, collective plural of *za'in* (departing one), which is however not impossible either).

35 The text is strange, but the translation seems correct, in the sense of: 'this year that I am in,' that is, death will occur before that year is out.

36 Van Gelder, "Cotton Shirt," 293.

37 Van Ess, *Tailasan*, 33. The text is in Ibn Khallikan, *Wafayat al-a'yan*, ed. Ihsan 'Abbas, vol. 7 (Beirut: Dar al-Thaqafa, n.d. [1971]), 96–97.

38 *Taqashsha'a* refers specifically to the break-up of clouds, which fits in well with the 'breeze' (actually *rih* [wind]).

39 For *tahki* I prefer 'imitate' to van Ess's 'narrate,' as it makes for a clearer idea and a smoother sentence.

40 *A'da* was mistaken by van Ess as an elative of *'aduw*. Taking it as the verb *a'da* (to infect [by contagion]) makes all parts of the line fall into place.

41 Due to the different understanding of verse 5, my interpretation of *qarana* (to be in contact with) also differs from van Ess's, who gives it the meaning of "being of the same age." Note allusion to Sura 59/21.

42 Al-Safadi, *al-Wafi bi-l-wafayat*, ed. Sven Dedering, vol. 5 (Wiesbaden: Franz Steiner, 1970), 319–20.

43 The editor leaves a gap, stating that the manuscript has something like *b'dasy*. In view of *baqiyan* I would like to read this *bi-fana'i*, which seems paleographically close enough.

44 The editor has *dhira'an*.

45 I take the fifth form to be synonymous with the first form *nakida*, although the dictionaries do not seem to list this.

46 The last line, introduced by the "singing" in the preceding line, is a *tadmin*, a quotation from another poem, which in other poems is often put in the mouth of a songstress. Al-Safadi makes the following interesting observation: "If he intended with the rhyme-word (*samm* [poison]) the *samm* of the tailor, that is, the "eye of the needle," then he has produced an excellent *tadmin*. It is probable that he did not intend that, and God knows best. This is a surprising coincidence!" The "eye of the needle" would not, of course, make sense in the context, but it

does seem apropos with all the mending and darning that is going on. One might consider it a *tawriya.*

47 Al-Marzubani, *Mu'jam al-shu 'ara'*, ed. 'Abd al-Sattar Ahmad Farraj ([Cairo:] 'Isa al-Babi al-Halabi, 1960), 412.

48 Ibid., 463–64.

49 See *Encyclopaedia of Islam. New Edition.* 12 vols. to date (Leiden: Brill, 1960-2004), 3:245a, under al-Hasan b. Zayd b. Muhammad.

50 Kushajim, *Diwan*, ed. Khayriya Muhammad Mahfuz (Baghdad: Wizarat al-I'lam, Mudiriyat al-Thaqafa al-'Amma, 1970), 86–88.

51 See Charles Pellat, "al-Djidd wa-l-hazl," in *Encyclopaedia of Islam. New Edition.* 12 vols. to date (Leiden: Brill, 1960-2004), 2:536–37. *idem*, "Seriousness and Humour in Early Islam," *Islamic Studies. Journal of the Central Institute of Islamic Research, Karachi* 2 (1963): 353–62; Joseph Sadan, *al-Adab al-'arabi al-hazil wa-nawadir al-thuqala'* (Tel Aviv: Tel Aviv University Press, 1983); Geert Jan van Gelder, "Mixtures of Jest and Earnest in Classical Arabic Literature," *Journal of Arabic Literature* 23 (1992): 83–108, 169–90; and Ludwig Ammann, *Vorbild und Vernunft: die Regelung von Lachen und Scherzen im mittelalterlichen Islam* (Hildesheim and New York: G. Olms 1993).

52 That is, the *habb* (pustules).

53 Literally, 'my pupils.'

54 Another case of amusing enumeration is found in a poem, in which our poet asks for a gift of sandals (449, no. 8 [in Supplement]). When it comes to the color, he enumerates several possibilities (*sawda'* [black], *safra'* [yellow], *balqa'* [variegated], *dakna'* [dark], *hamra'* [red], and *sahba'* [reddish-brown]) each with an appropriate simile. He then adds the following line: *wa-law kuntu a'rifu khadra'a qultu—ka-l-ma'i dabbajahu al-tuhlubu* [and if I knew green ones, I would say: like water brocaded by green algae.] His poetic talent goes beyond available sandal colors.

55 This reminds me of a light-hearted German poem by Börries Freiherr von Münchhausen (1874–1945), the "Lederhosen-Saga," which tells about the metamorphoses, through several generations, of an indestructible pair of riding-breeches and ends: "Ja, Geschlechter kommen, Geschlechter vergehen— Hirschlederne Reithosen bleiben bestehen." [Yes, generations come, generations go—stag-hide riding-breeches last forever.]

56 Bauer, *Liebe und Liebesdichtung*, 523.

57 Ibid., 310–12.

58 My original intention had been to contribute to this volume, in memory of Magda Al-Nowaihi (who was the first student at Harvard for whom I was the primary PhD advisor and whom I sorely miss), a paper on al-Sanawbari's elegies for his daughter. After learning about the two works mentioned in note 26 I abandoned the idea, although I do think that more can be done on this subject. The present topic arose from an unusual circumstance: in May of 2004, I was invited by the Middle East Studies Center of Ohio State University as a "Visiting Reciter" to take part in a recital of Arabic poetry (including reading of English prose translations). I was responsible for the Abbasid period and chose this unusual

poem. The co-reciters were my local colleagues Michael Zwettler (who chose a poem by ʿAmr b. Qamiʿa, sixth century) and Joseph Zeidan (who read a poem by Badr Shakir al-Sayyab, twentieth century).

5

Loss Written in Stone: Ibn Shuhayd's *Ritha'* for Cordoba and Its Place in the Arabic Elegiac Tradition

Alexander E. Elinson

Introduction

Andalusian poets perfected the art of describing urban settings with the purpose of recalling that which was either lost or was on the verge of being lost, and immortalizing them in poetry. With the numerous losses experienced in al-Andalus beginning in the eleventh century and continuing at an increasing pace until the final fall of Granada in 1492, *ritha' al-mudun* (the city elegy) became a common genre for the Andalusian poet. With the fall of different cities, poets paid homage to homes, plazas, palaces, and entire cities by composing elegies for these places. Collectively, this body of poetry comprised a literary geography of al-Andalus, paradoxically rooted in loss.

By looking at the ways in which poets remembered and expressed al-Andalus, we see that loss is a necessary component in defining place. In fact, the connection between loss, memory, discourse, and location is best encapsulated in the term *topos*, which refers both to a place in discourse and a place in the world. The idea of topography—in both senses of the word—is connected to the ancient Greek art of memory. The art of memory was invented after a catastrophe and began with the collapse of a house.[1]

Bachelard emphasizes the importance of the relationship between place and memory by asserting that physical space is necessary for memory to function, for without it, memory has no depth or duration:

> ... [S]pace is everything.... We are unable to relive duration that has been destroyed. We can only think of it, in the line of an abstract time that is deprived of all thickness. The finest specimens of fossilized duration concretized as a result of long sojourn, are to be found in and through space. The unconscious abides. Memories are motionless, and the more securely they are fixed in space, the sounder they are.[2]

It is this intersection of space, loss, and memory that is of interest in the *ritha' al-mudun*. By looking at the way in which poets used a poetics of loss and nostalgia, I examine the *ritha' al-mudun* in the context of the larger Arabic poetic tradition, as well as within the narrower context of al-Andalus's changing borders, which began to recede in the eleventh century. The Andalus that emerges from these poems is an idealized one that depends on memory and is defined as a series of imaginary reconstructions. As writers work within a clearly defined tradition, each remembered and recreated Andalus is both a unique location defined by individual memory, and a space shared by the larger community, which understands and appreciates the conventions used to define it. On the necessary tension between individual and communal memory, Maurice Halbwachs writes:

> To be sure, everyone has a capacity for memory that is unlike that of anyone else, given the variety of temperaments and life circumstances. But individual memory is nevertheless a part or an aspect of group memory.... One cannot in fact think about the events of one's past without discoursing upon them. But to discourse upon something means to connect within a single system of ideas our opinions as well as those of our circle.[3]

The city elegy is curiously poised between the reality of a tangible loss, acutely felt by the individual, and a highly conventional language that is used to understand and express it. Thus, the object of the *ritha' al-mudun* is a place that is both as solid as stone and as flexible and subjective as individualistic poetic expression.

In this article, I will examine certain conventional techniques of the *ritha' al-mudun* that combine elements of the *ritha'* for a person (repetition, water imagery, hyperbole), as well as elements of the pre-Islamic *qasida* (such as weeping at the abandoned campsite), and place naming. I will conclude with a close reading of Ibn Shuhayd's (d. 1035) elegy for the city of Cordoba, which was besieged and subsequently sacked in 1013 during the Berber *fitna*. By looking at one of the first elegies composed for an Andalusian city, I show that the building blocks of a nostalgic discourse were already in place in the poetic language at this time, and that the Cordoba that the poet remembers is built upon the ruins of previous losses, both human and geographic, and will survive as long as the Arabic poetic discourse used to define it is understood.

Shifting Spaces

In the opening lines of Imru' al-Qays's famous *Mu'allaqa*, the poet stands with his memories in a spot that is fragile and impermanent in the desert sands, yet at the same time curiously fixed, grounded firmly against the blowing winds of time by its poetic weight:

> Halt, my two friends, and let us weep over the memories of a beloved,
>   whose dwelling
> was at the sand dune's rim, between al-Dakhul and Hawmal.
> And Tudih and al-Miqrat, whose traces have not been effaced
> By the weaving of the north and south winds.[4]

Whether this place is real or determinable is of little importance. Even in this early pre-Islamic *qasida*, rather than presenting a description or demarcation of an actual location, the poet uses the emotionally evocative *nasib* and the metaphor of place to express the universally familiar and ineffaceable feelings of desolation, loss, and nostalgia.

The conventional use of the abandoned campsite theme, and the constant evocation of desert place names, locations, and descriptions, confirms the importance of these places, whether real or imaginary, to the poet and to the audience. Jaroslav Stetkevych emphasizes the symbolic nature of these toponyms, and their power to express the nostalgic tone embedded in Arabic poetry. These places may have existed—indeed, many may still be geographically identifiable—but poetically this is no longer important. We do not even know whether the place-names in the most ancient Arabic odes were ever more than evocative moorings for those entirely ethereal effusions of loss and yearning which form the mood of the nasib. With some certainty, albeit poetic certainty, we may thus assume that, at least within the nasib proper, references to places are for the most part of an indirect, symbolic nature, and that particularly in post-Jahiliyah poetry their metaphorization and symbolic saturation become fully consummated.[5]

Yumna al-'Id argues that in pre- and early Islamic Arabic poetry there is an emphasis on the congruity between signifier and signified which requires the use of a poetic language that remains as close as possible to literal meaning. Because, she argues, this poetry is largely concerned with inherited ideals such as valor, steadfastness, bravery, and loyalty, descriptions of physical places are of little concern to the pre-Islamic poets. Thus,

> ... the aesthetic relation with space and place manifested in the
> use of poetic imagery was overlooked. It was seen as an extraneous
> relation void of the intimate and personal associations it actually
> embodied, and the emotional connotations woven into it. The place
> was considered a mere decorative frame . . . . Thus the significance
> of yearning which actually characterized the poetry of the jahiliya
> was not a topic for aesthetic evaluation. Al-wuquf 'ala al-atlal or
> the lamenting of the loss of forsaken grounds was no more than an
> introduction to other ends and goals.[6]

However, al-'Id goes on to explain that later, in the poetry of Abu Nuwas that mocks those who continued to stand weeping at the ruined campsite, there is a "conflict between two forms."[7] These two forms are a poetics based on an ideal, and one "based on actual location not disconnected from social temporality."[8] The lifestyle and poetry of Abu Nuwas challenged the pre-Islamic ideal which András Hámori refers to as the "Poet as Hero."[9] Out of this challenge came a shift in the aesthetics of space:

For the poet, this conflict touches upon an existential question, the relation between life and death, a life that fades away in a stable and fixed time/space situation, and a life that is born in an historical intangibility, generating an aesthetics whose poetic association remains with locality and space.[10]

With the move to the city, poets continued to use the ancient Arabic poetic language in their new urban setting in order to express similar emotions of loss and a yearning for the past. However, it is not the 'reality' of a location that is important, but rather, the effect of its mention. It does not matter whether or not a poet in ninth-century Baghdad or twelfth-century Seville has ever really stood at the ruins of an abandoned campsite. These desert locations and signposts serve the poet and the audience who understand, or at least sense, their symbolic resonance through a familiarity with the language and poetic tradition. The urban poet draws on this tradition and adds new locations to it that, in turn, acquire their own symbolic resonance.

It is not until the Abbasid period, specifically the founding of Baghdad as the imperial capital in 762, that we see a strong attachment to a man-made place and the rise of the *ritha' al-mudun* genre that will eventually mourn its loss. Baghdad quickly became a place known for its splendor, wealth, and culture, and the city provided poets with an entirely different landscape, culture, and aesthetic to use as a poetic palette than did the desert. Poets used this new place and the symbols associated with it, as they did in the pre-Islamic *qasida*, to express loss, nostalgia, sadness, and bliss. The new places were mixed with the old, and an evocative and symbolic space was developed that, by using old poetic language and imagery along with new intellectual developments, expressed the new urban setting.[11]

The urbanization of Arab culture also marked a shift in how Muslim society was to be organized. Although relationships based on kinship, tribe, and lineage would continue to be important, the rise of the city assured that they were no longer the only binding factors. It is now the city that will act as a unifying force, for "[u]rban identity appeals to common memory and a common past but is rooted in a man-made place, not in the soil: in urban coexistence at once alienating and exhilarating, not in the exclusivity of blood."[12]

The city became home to people of different social and economic classes, religions, and origins. The new urban residents were bound not by blood or tribal bonds, but by place. This place served as a well of shared histories, images, associations, and memories. These cities were composed of structures built by and for its citizens—without whom the city would be completely meaningless—and it is in the *ritha' al-mudun* that the focus on people, place, and memory is made clear.

Ritha' al-Mudun al-Andalusi

Poets mourned the loss of kin and loved ones throughout the history of the *qasida*. As well, in this same poetry, there is an attachment to geographical locations (or at least the evocation of these locations), as evidenced in the countless tears shed over abandoned campsites. With the development of the *ritha' al-mudun* genre, these two tendencies were combined. The *ritha' al-mudun* emerged out of the new urban reality in which Arabic poetry thrived. However, the city does not replace or displace the human being in the elegy to the point where the *ritha' al-mudun* is identical to the personal *ritha'*, with the city's name inserted in place of the deceased. In fact, although similar rhetorical devices and images are used in both the personal and city elegies, the latter allows for a new method of altering and blending such themes as *al-atlal* (the abandoned campsite), geographic description, ruminations of the vicissitudes of fate, the inevitability of death, and so on.[13]

With the numerous losses experienced by the Andalusians, starting in 1013 with the fall of Cordoba and ending in 1492 with Granada's surrender to the Catholic monarchs Ferdinand and Isabella, there developed a rich and melancholy tradition of *ritha' al-mudun* in the Islamic west. It is important to point out that the losses incurred in al-Andalus were not all the same: they did not result from the same causes, nor did the cities ultimately fall to the same foes. The past and the place that the poets mourned or longed for was shaped by the present, and by each poet's particular place in that present. They expressed subjective visions of their lost cities, leaving literary documents that, when taken as a whole, drew a very diverse and complex map of al-Andalus.

The remainder of this article will examine the *ritha' al-mudun* in al-Andalus and highlight certain poetic conventions, strategies, and motifs that served to mourn lost cities. I will conclude with an analysis of Ibn Shuhayd's *ritha'* for the city of Cordoba in order to present an illustration of these strategies at work in a relatively early example of *ritha' al-mudun* in al-Andalus. Ibn Shuhayd defines the city by evoking a certain cultural milieu that was lost with its destruction. His Cordoba is based on a nostalgic ideal for some sort of mythical Arab past that consists of the deserts of Arabia and the great architectural and cultural achievements of the eastern and western Islamic world. His monument is built from memory, composed on the heels of its destruction, and is comprised of a conventional poetic language that serves to eulogize and memorialize the lost city of Cordoba, the lost empire of the Umayyads, and the lost status of the Arab littérateur.

Repetition

Discussing the *ritha'* for a person, Ibn Rashiq (d. between 1064 and 1070) dedicates a chapter of his literary treatise, *al-'Umda*, to the rhetorical dimensions of repetition, stating that this device is well suited for expressing sorrow and grief. It is, he says, in the *"ritha'* where repetition is most common, being found where there is calamity and strongly felt pain."[14] By creating a sense of continuity, expectation, and stability through repetition, the poet is able to counter the extreme rupture that comes with death, and ultimately attempt to control it. The repetitious invocation of the deceased's name serves both to preserve his or her memory, and to exorcise the grief that is felt at the loss. Also, the name—like the poem as a whole—acts to replace its bearer. It becomes a tangible object and allows the mourners to shift their attention from the deceased, who is gone, to the name, which can be summoned time and again. As well, the elegist also repeats whole phrases and/or syntactic structures. Taking on a chant-like quality, the poem moves from the realm of words heard aurally or read on a page to an interactive experience not unlike the ritual movements associated with prayer, or the swaying and repetition of God's name in the context of a Sufi *dhikr*.[15]

The use of repetition in the *ritha' al-mudun* fulfills similar functions. By repeating the name of the lost city or cities, and epithets for that city, the poet strives to keep the name, and thus the memory of the place, alive. With the 'real' place gone, all that remains is the poetic one. And it is reference to this poetic space that serves as the city limits within which descriptions of cultural, architectural, intellectual, political, and economic achievements are placed.

The repetitive use of particles such as the vocative *ya*, the enumerative *kam* (many a/so many/how many? and so on), and/or time markers such as *ayyama* (Oh, those were the days when . . .) creates a rhythm and a continuity that allow for a certain comfort and expectation that can act as a counterbalance to the unpredictability and severe rupture that occur with a traumatic loss. As well, this expectation can serve to shorten the distance between the poet and audience: after a rhythm is established, the audience comes to sense what comes next. The line between poet and audience is blurred to the point where all the mourners are standing together, listening and reciting at the same time.

Alternatively, rather than bringing mourners and poet together, repetition can also be used in such a way as to close others out of a very personal loss. For example, in a poem written for his family home destroyed during the Berber *fitna* in Cordoba, Ibn Hazm addresses the home. The direct address, together with the use of the second person singular to refer to the lost dwelling, creates and underlines the intimate relationship between poet and place:

> Oh home, it was not by our choice that you were deserted,
> For if we could have our way, you would be our burial place.
>
> . . . . .
>
> Oh best of dwellings, the praiseworthy have left
> And the rain-clouds have watered you, how splendid you were, how
> > content.
>
> Oh unveiled gardens, surrounded by
> Riyads with cool water. After we left, they became dust.
>
> Oh fate, deliver my greetings to its inhabitants
> Even if they live in Marwin, or have crossed the river.[16]

Toward the end of the poem, the poet turns away from the house as intimate interlocutor. The vocative calls increase feverishly, and he directs his attention outward and all around him. At first, this appears to be a desperate attempt to reach out and find consolation in companionship and shared suffering, but in fact the poet addresses his own emotions and thus remains standing alone. The grief he feels is a personal one, not to be shared with others:

Alas, my body is sick, and Oh how my heart beats restlessly,
And Oh my soul is bereaved, and Oh my liver burns.

Oh worry, do not leave, and Oh grief, do not become exhausted,
Oh passion, do not become anxious, and Oh separation, do not
    take flight.

Oh Fate, do not be distant, Oh covenant, do not come undone
Oh tears, do not harden, Oh illness, do not get better.

In the following short example, the unknown poet of this *ritha'* for Toledo following its fall to the Christians in 1085 produces a multi-layered repetition which, through its syntactic pattern and explicit language, expresses the overwhelming and uncompromising power of Fate, and humankind's inability to counter it. A pattern is established in the first hemistich that is then explained, repetitively, in the second. It is as if the poet does not want the audience to miss the significance of the repetition, but knows that it will, for history repeats itself and lessons are rarely learned:

Oh sorrow, Oh sorrow, sadness,
Fate repeats that which is repeated.[17]

Another rich example comes in a short poem by Abu al-Mutarrif b. 'Umayra (1186–1259) in which the poet longs for his birthplace Shaqr (Júcar), located in eastern Andalus just south of Valencia. He combines *jinas* (paronomasia) with repetition in the first and last lines to draw attention to the place that is the focus of the poem. In the poem's very first word, Ibn 'Umayra commands his audience to "remember," and repeats the root *(dh-k-r)* in the second line. Also, the sounds *qaf* and *ra'* are repeated throughout. A tension is thus created in that, although this short piece displays quite a density of *badi'* that draws a fair bit of attention to the poet and his skill, it is remembrance of the lost city that is central to the genre's goals. If we view this rhetorical flair as a poetic display of the literary taste of the time that celebrates both the city and the literary prowess it fostered, the poem succeeds. The compactness of the poem combined with these displays of poetic skill results in a well-crafted literary monument to a place and time that no longer exist:

> Remember the time in the east, for the east is quite far away.
> It melted away sadly in a flash, and the lightning was sparkling.
> . . . .
>
> Oh how I long to be in Shaqr, or in the blueness of its waters,
> And in it, in Shaqr, shining blue wells.[18]

Finally, in this example from a poem by Abu Musa Harun b. Harun mourning the loss of Seville, which fell in 1248, the poet combines repetition of the vocative *ya* (Oh), and the particle *kam* (How many?). The result is that the audience is unable to turn away, thus making the grief unrelenting and all the more unbearable:

> Oh Seville, is this the sentence that Fate has passed for you?
>
> . . . .
>
> Oh paradise, our sins tore us from your beauties.
> We now must experience sorrow and regret.
>
> Oh you who inquires about the plight of the Muslims,
> Shout out so that even the deaf will hear about it.
>
> . . . .
>
> How many prisoners went off in strong shackles,
> Their broken feet complaining of the disgrace?
>
> And how many nursing babies were snatched from their mothers and
>   became
> victims,
> Having been weaned by the tumult?

. . . .

How many in Triana remained mourning
In their hearts, sending forth deep emotions more and more?
Oh its beauty, everyone knows its beauty.
Only grace and goodness in abundance betook themselves toward it.[19]

Joining of East and West/The Desert and the City

For the Andalusian poet, the evocation of eastern place names, real or imagined, was common practice. Poets in the pre-Islamic and early Islamic periods made use of toponyms for purposes beyond that of locating the poem's events. By using place names, the poets drew upon a poetic language and tradition rich in literary references and semantic potential. The Andalusian poets, like their eastern peers and predecessors, exploited the rich symbolism of natural locations such as the Najd highlands, the Nile, Euphrates, and Tigris rivers, as well as contemporary man-made urban centers such as Mecca, Medina, Baghdad, and Damascus. These places are imbued with broadly understood and appreciated historical, cultural, and spiritual importance, and their mere mention conjures up a host of images and emotional responses that carry the audience far beyond the boundaries of the actual words.

Generally speaking, Bedouin style and imagery were quite popular among Andalusians who emulated poets such as al-Mutanabbi (d. 965), al-Sharif al-Radi (d. 1015), and Mihyar al-Daylami (d. 1036). These urbane eastern poets, like the Andalusians who followed, did not claim that they were describing a desert reality based on firsthand experience. Rather, they worked within a poetic framework that utilized the traditional themes, images, and locations both out of nostalgia for the 'golden age' of pre-Islamic poetry and in order to respond to and engage in a dialogue with that tradition.[20] According to Magda Al-Nowaihi, evocations of Bedouin imagery and motifs "were part of a poetic technique which developed out of admiration and nostalgia for older times and Arabian things."[21] However, this nostalgia did not strictly relegate poetry to the past, for the neoclassical style that Andalusian poets so admired was "a combination of bedouin subjects, language and spirit with the *muhdath* (modern) rhetorical style, and the general inclination of the *muhdathun* to search for new and innovative images and concepts."[22]

In the Andalusian *ritha' al-mudun*, poets made use of eastern place names, but added to their evocative potential by mentioning locations in al-Andalus as well. Using the rich symbolism of an eastern place such as Najd, Mecca, or Baghdad served to draw upon the audience's collective poetic and cultural sensibilities, and placed them in the elegiac world of the classical Arabic poetic language. Then, the poet could add local (Andalusian) place name references that, although not having the benefit of as long a tradition in the poetic consciousness as did their eastern counterparts, carried with them a local emotional importance that hit quite a bit closer to home. Eastern and Andalusian places are taken out of their respective locations (east and west) and each is infused with the other's historical, emotional, and symbolic importance. The eastern places are made local, and the Andalusian places are made distant and exotic. The result is a poetic palimpsest of west and east, urban and desert, present and past.

Ibn 'Umayra's work displays a penchant for using Arabian or Bedouin themes that well serve his nostalgic tone. In a letter written to his friend Ibn al-Abbar (d. 1260) on the fall of Valencia, Ibn 'Umayra includes a poem that implicitly mourns the loss of his homeland through the use of Arabian place and Bedouin references. He refers to archetypal locales that, according to Yaqut al-Hamawi,[23] were popular stopping points (real and metaphoric) for pre-Islamic poets.

He weeps for the time spent in Mushaqqar and al-Liwa,
But where is al-Liwa now? And where is Mushaqqar?[24]

These names are not chosen for their symbolic and canonical weight only. Note that Ibn 'Umayra's birthplace, Shaqr, is referred to in the Arabian place Mushaqqar through the shared root letters of their names *(sh-q-r)*. In the context of the poem, they are one and the same place, both physically gone, but textually remembered. The poem is replete with symbols from the Bedouin *qasida*, and because he does not actually name Valencia or Shaqr, it sets and sustains the elegiac tone of the larger letter that contains it, rather than act as a direct *ritha'* for the lost city.

In another short piece, Ibn 'Umayra pays homage to the rich highlands of Najd before feeling justified to weep over his own city. Jaroslav Stetkevych has this to say about the poem:

Thus Ibn 'Umayrah al-Makhzumi, a seventh/thirteenth-century poet from al-Andalus, will talk of his sorrow over the loss of Valencia by first invoking ancient Bedouin passions of the heart (vv. 1–2) and that heart's yearning for its autochthonous place of repose, the distant Najd of Arabia (v. 3). Only then may he give himself the poetic license to elicit the concrete place-name of Valencia (v. 7), for such a Valencia will now be endowed with the poetically validated, elegiac quality of a "lost paradise" (v. 10).[25]

While it is not completely surprising that the poet refers metaphorically to his lost city as a "paradise," and the uprooting of himself and his fellow Valencians as an "expulsion" of epic proportions, the expression does resonate at multiple levels. The immediate reference is to Valencia, but the Qur'anic usage is also recognizable.[26] *Jannat al-khuld* was also the epithet given to Baghdad by al-Khuraymi, itself an allusion to the name of a Baghdadi palace.[27] Ibn 'Umayra's Valencia lies somewhere between east and west, heaven and earth:

Oh heart, you who proclaim this ardent passion,
Must love's intemperance be so manifest?

But can a lovelorn one hope to forget
Love's agony of thirst, rejection's awesome jolt?

He yearns for Najd, but all in vain!
The adverse turns of time have doomed him never to return.

Oh mountain of water-sated verdure, like none I knew,
How time's ill turns of fortune slighted your spring.

And Oh you people that I love—but events now exact
That I stand alone, apart from those who merit love—
Will pleasure one day be bared of desire,
When to us it bodes denial at all times?
After the woe that befell Valencia,
Will beacons in the heart still shine with secret candescence?

People hope for shields against afflictions
That transfix them with their pliant spears.
Yet would that I knew, will she once more rise,
Will her star return as it once was?

Or did the sons sin their fathers' sins
And bring upon themselves expulsion from paradise (jannati
l-khuldi)?[28]

Taking a short trip across the straits to North Africa, we find Malik b.
al-Murahhal (born 1207 in Ceuta, died 1299 in Fez)[29] calling on his com-
patriots to take up arms and join the *jihad* to restore Islam to its former
glory in the Iberian Peninsula. Because his goal is for Muslims to band
together against the Christian enemy, Ibn al-Murahhal does his best to
foster unity and bring the edges of the Muslim world together. He speaks
to his North African brethren, and pointing toward the Andalusian shore,
reminds them that,

It is nothing but a piece of your own land,
Its people are from you, and you from them.[30]

After rhetorically bridging this relatively short distance between the
shores of North Africa and al-Andalus, the poet goes on to join west to
east. Western Islam as symbolized by Cordoba and its great mosque is
placed on the same symbolic level as the holy sites of Mecca, and Seville's
cultural achievements are like those of Baghdad. The Islamic world—
its north, south, east and west—is brought together, at least within the
boundaries of this poem:

Cordoba, it is she for whom Mecca weeps
Sadly, as well as al-Safa' and Zamzam.

And Seville is Baghdad's sister, but
Its days were of youth and dreams.

Sometimes, poetic references to eastern places are less explicit than the
ones cited above. Instead of naming well-known cities or places, poets make

veiled references to eastern locations that rely on an audience's familiarity with the poetic tradition. Elías Terés examines several instances of the pairing of the words *jisr* (bridge usually made of wood) and *rusafa* (bridge usually made of arched stone) in the works of Andalusian poets.[31] In a nostalgic piece on his birthplace, rich with Bedouin imagery, al-Rusafi (d. 1177) says:

Order the rain to the jisr and the rusafa,
I am sure that the rain will water the rusafa and the jisr.[32]

Ibn al-Abbar, who wrote extensively on the fall of Valencia, mixes this phrase with Qur'anic allusions to paradise in the following example:

Nobody yearns more than I
For a life passed between the rusafa and the jisr.

Paradise on earth, without equal in beauty
By which rivers run in all directions.[33]

In a rhymed prose epistle, he also writes: "Where are Valencia and its houses, and the rustling of its leaves and its cooing doves? Where are the adornments of its *rusafa* and its *jisr*?"[34] Terés cites other such mention of the *rusafa* and *jisr*, and shows that, in fact, they allude to a line first attributed to 'Ali b. al-Jahm who wrote in the ninth century about Baghdad's *rusafa* and *jisr*:

Wild cows' eyes between al-rusafa and al-jisr,
Attract love where I know, and where I do not.[35]

Like the references to Arabian locations cited above, which are either real or mythical, but whose literary importance is indisputable, these poets, with their subtle nod toward Baghdad at the height of its glory, link their stylized memories and expressions of Valencia to the Abbasid imperial city. It is both a nod of deference to the old world capital, and a claim of comparability to the recently lost Valencia. It is worth noting that Jaroslav Stetkevych traces the reference back one step further. Through an etymological examination of *al-rusafa* and *al-jisr* that takes us back to the desert of the pre-Islamic Bedouin *nasib*, Stetkevych concludes that

[w]hat we thus obtain in the two nasib lines by 'Ali Ibn al-Jahm is not so much a landscape or a topography of caliphal Baghdad as a complex metaphor built out of internalized loci where yearning occurs, or where it is possible.[36]

Even Ibn al-Jahm is drawing upon a vocabulary infused with nostalgic resonance. Each subsequent re-contextualization of *al-rusafa* and *al-jisr*, adds additional layers of meaning and referents.

Water and the City

As was the case in the pre-Islamic *ritha'* where poets used liquid imagery, such as calling upon their eyes, the sky, or the gods to send forth rain to water the deceased's grave and thus renew the life that was lost, the poets of later periods continued to employ this theme.[37] In the Andalusian *ritha' al-mudun*, poets used imagery drawn from the abundant flowing streams that watered gardens, orchards, and fields in al-Andalus. To the poet who stands in the ruined city, life as he has knows it has dried up. The description of the verdant and fertile past is contrasted with the desolate present. For example, Ibn Shuhayd extends the reach of distant rivers to al-Andalus, and addresses his lost Cordoba saying:

> The Euphrates flowed plentiful through your two shores,
> > as did the Tigris.
> So too the Nile and the River Kawthar.

> You were watered by the life-giving waters of a cloud.
> Your gardens were given life and flourished from these waters.[38]

Ibn Hazm, in the *ritha'* for his boyhood home cited above, is even more explicit in his comparison of past and present, juxtaposing the well-watered and life-giving past to the barren present.

> Oh best of dwellings, the praiseworthy have left
> And the rain clouds have watered you, how splendid you were,
> > how content.
> Oh unveiled gardens, surrounded by
> Riyads, cool water. After we left, they became dust.

In contrast to the above examples that provide no solution or alternative to the state of affairs the poets find themselves in, the following examples present different ways poets manipulated the metaphor of water or liquid with different effects. According to the inscription in his *diwan*, Ibn Sahl al-Ishbili (d. 1245 in Ceuta) composed a poem at the request of Seville's governor al-Sayyid Abu 'Abd Allah b. al-Sayyid ibn 'Umran in 1242 calling for Muslim support against the Christian threat to the city. Ibn Sahl manipulates the dual nature of water imagery and shows that water can bring death (tears, salt water), while also being a necessity for renewing and perpetuating life (fresh water). The brackish, muddy, and thus useless water of this world can be exchanged for the pure life-spring of the next, but this exchange can only occur through *jihad*. Through action, tears can be turned into fresh water, and death into life:

Leave your houses for the House of Greatness, and ride
The swirling dust[39] to verdant tranquility.

Drink from the muddy springs to regain your peace of mind.
They are watered by the water of a basin that is anything but muddy.

Take upon yourselves the brackish water of the sea
For by it, you will drink from the Kawthar River.

. . . .

The right path has shown itself. The thirsty one complains, but you[40]
Are shade and watercourses like the rain watered springtime.[41]

In an example from a Hebrew elegy mourning the destruction of the Jewish communities in al-Andalus (Heb., *Sefarad*) and North Africa, Abraham Ibn Ezra (1089–1164) emphasizes water's ability both to destroy and to revive. The poem (*ahah yarad / 'al sefarad / ra' min ha-shamayim* [Alas! Calamities have come down from the heavens upon Sefarad])[42] is composed in strophic form, and includes a *matla'* (introductory strophe), the second line of which ends with the word 'water' *(mayim)*. Each strophe of the poem has nine lines that share a rhyme syllable, and a tenth line whose rhyme, like that of the *matla'*, is 'water.' Assuming the choral recitation of this strophic poem *(muwashsha)* that follows the pattern as posited by Samuel Stern,[43] the *matla'* is repeated by the audience or chorus after each strophe, which emphasizes the calamity that pours forth from the sky. The *matla'* goes as follows:

> Alas! Calamities have rained down upon Sefarad from the heavens
> (min ha-shamayim)
> My eye! My eye! Water falls from it (yordah mayim).

The second line is taken from the biblical chapter Lamentations 1:16, and the broader tone and theme of this chapter would not be lost on an audience familiar with this context. The very first verse of Lamentations begins thus: "How does the city sit alone, who once contained so many people? She is like a widow that was great among nations" (Lamentations 1:1). It is striking how similar this biblical chapter is to the *ritha' al-mudun* in imagery and tone. The effect is that the words, references, and meaning of the poem cannot be separated from those of Lamentations, a chapter that recalls Zion's past beauties and charms and laments the current lot of the Jewish community, a result of its sins. The underlying theme of the poem is the sinfulness of the Jews of Ibn Ezra's own time, which brought about the calamities, both immediate (that is, in al-Andalus and North Africa), and of the larger Jewish exile.[44] After enumerating the losses of important Jewish communities in Andalusian cities such as Lucena, Seville, Cordoba, Jaen, Almeria, and across the water in the North African cities of Fez, Meknes, Ceuta, Sijilmassa, Tlemcen, and Dra'a, the poet blurs the line between these local losses and Jewish exile from Israel. The poet speaks for the sinner that is the Jewish people, asking:

> For whom can I wait? And what can I say, when everything, my own
> hand has done?

Indeed, help can only come from God, and although passive in waiting, Israel raises her head seeking deliverance:

> She remains, tears on her cheeks, in the hand of Hagar who
> Rains arrows down upon her; Until my Lord looks down from Heaven
> (mi-shamayim).

In effect, the poet combines biblical allusion and contemporary events to form a single symbolic-realistic loss.[45] Imagery and form work together, and the deluge that comes in the repetition of the *matla'* emphasizes God's omnipotent power both to destroy and to save.

Ibn Shuhayd's Ritha' for Cordoba

In Ibn Shuhayd's *ritha'* for Cordoba,[46] the poet delineates the city's boundaries in a highly stylized fashion, defining what it is and what it is not, and mourning the loss of an Arabic literary culture as he himself defines it. The destruction of Cordoba at the hands of Berber factions not only marked the effective end of the Umayyad dynasty in al-Andalus, but also the end of a perceived 'pure' Arabic culture and political unity upon which the Umayyads and their supporters based their claims of caliphal legitimacy.[47]

Ibn Shuhayd was born into an aristocratic family of high standing that was "one of the families holding a virtual monopoly of the posts in the administration. The power of these families, closely linked as they were to the royal house and later to the 'Amiris, continued unimpaired throughout the decline of the Arab aristocracy. . . ."[48] This aristocratic background is reflected in Ibn Shuhayd's writing, which expresses the importance of striving for and defending the purity of Arabic language and literature. Ibn Shuhayd took issue with the modernist *(muhdath)* school that originated in the east and was so popular in al-Andalus during his lifetime. In fact, he saw this style as detrimental to poetry and unsuitable to the Andalusian cultural environment. He asserts that

> [j]ust as every place has its own dialect so every age has its proper style, every period its manner and each group of nations its own kind of oratory and manner of rhetoric. . . . Nowadays every poem which does not employ jinas or something similar is abhorred by the ears, but moderation in this matter is to be recommended.[49]

A proponent of a specifically Andalusian literature, Ibn Shuhayd attempts to distance himself from the *muhdath* poet in a quest for something that he considered unique and exceptional, based on a nostalgic and idealized conception of Arabic linguistic and literary purity. He derides Andalusian grammarians and other littérateurs for allowing the language to deteriorate to the point where it "is simply incorrect

stammering *(lukna a'jamiya)* [used] to convey the meaning. . . .The Arabs
and their language are gone."[50] What is ironic is that Ibn Shuhayd's poetry
does exhibit a number of 'modern' literary features, as we will see.

Ibn Shuhayd seems intent on creating and promoting a distinct
Andalusian literature, but where is this Andalus? In his *ritha'* for Cordoba,
he locates al-Andalus in a literary space very much connected to the larger
Arabic culture that he mourns, as well as part of an ideal cultural space
that he simultaneously remembers and defines. What follows is a close
reading of this poem that focuses on the themes and strategies of the
city elegy as discussed above. I have divided the poem into thematically
defined units that have been subtitled accordingly.

Alone at the Ruins[51]

1   There is no one in the abandoned campsite to tell us about the
loved ones
So whom can we ask about their situation?

2   Do not ask anyone except for Separation
For it is what distances you from them, wherever they may have
gone.

3   Time oppressed them and they were scattered
In all directions, and most of them perished.

4   Calamities flowed over their homes
And them; and both they and [their homes] were [permanently]
transformed.

5   Call upon Time to embellish their courtyards with flowers
That nearly make their hearts glow.

Standing on the ruins of the abandoned campsite *(al-tulul)*, Ibn Shuhayd
begins his poem searching for "loved ones," both for the sake of curing
his loneliness and also to question them about these ruins and what has
produced them. Unfortunately, the poet receives no answer. The pair of
companions that often stands with the poet in the *nasib* is absent. In fact,
we learn in the second verse that the poet is alone with a single listener (signified by the second person singular *la tas'alanna*, and referring to the poet
himself), whose response is ensured through the use of the energetic form
of the negative command.[52] The imagery of the ruins and the absence of
any sort of interlocutor create a scene of isolation, desolation, and despair.

In the second verse, we remain within the lexical field of the desert with Ibn Shuhayd's references to the symbolically rich Najd and al-Ghawr. Yaqut al-Hamawi cites various sources that place al-Ghawr on the southern Arabian coast in Yemen or on the plain between Jerusalem and Damascus. The more general meaning of the word, *al-ghawr*, is lowland. Idiomatically, when used in conjunction with Najd, or the verbal form *anjada*, the expression *anjadu wa-agharu* means 'whether they have gone upland or down,' or 'wherever they may have gone.'[53] This expression, used to describe the expulsion of the Cordoban citizenry and the poet's own sense of bewilderment and isolation in having been left behind, places them somewhere between al-Andalus and the Arabian Peninsula, wandering in poetic limbo.

Verses 3 and 4 are linked by a syntactic parallelism in each of their first hemistichs, as well as by the *jinas* of the first verbs of each, *jara* (جار) and *jara* (جرى). The final words of each hemistich (verse 3—*jara l-zamanu 'alayhim fa-tafarraqu* [Time oppressed them and they were scattered . . .], verse 4—*jarati l-khutubu 'ala mahalli diyarihim* [Calamities flowed over their homes . . .]) underline an opposition where in verse 3, the focus is on the people of Cordoba ("they"), and in verse 4, it is the place ("their homes"). This is more clearly articulated at the end of the fourth verse, and we see it again in verse 18:

4 Calamities visited their homes
   And them, and both they and [their homes] were [permanently]
   transformed *(taghayyarat wa-taghayyaru)*
18 Oh paradise, the wind of death has blown
   Over it and its people, both it and they were destroyed
   (tadammarat wa-tadammaru).

It is here that Ibn Shuhayd emphasizes the shared fate of Cordoba, the place, and Cordoba, the people. This pattern is repeated twice, but the poet makes use of other strategies to convey the same relationship between place and people throughout the poem, as will be seen below.

Verse 5 serves as a transition *(takhallus)* between the *nasib* imagery and vocabulary of the preceding four verses and the *ritha'* proper that occupies the remainder of the poem. Ibn Shuhayd's repetitious invocation of Fate in verses 3, 4, and 5 *(al-zaman, al-khutub, al-zaman* respectively) underlines his recognition of its capricious ability to give life, and to take it away. It has destroyed Cordoba and scattered its inhabitants, but it can also be called upon to bring light and life once again to the ruined city, albeit in the form of flowers that will grow over the ruins. This is interesting considering Ibn Rashiq's assertion that "there is no difference between the *ritha'* and the *madh*, except for the fact that the *ritha'* contains some sort of indicator that the object of the poem is dead, such as 'he was' or 'this and that have been lost to us,' and other devices of this sort."[54] Stefan Sperl, in his examination of the panegyric, points to a structural balance between the *nasib* and *madih*, where Fate in the *nasib* is all-powerful, thus leaving destruction and barrenness in its wake. However, in the panegyric section, the *mamduh* holds the power to counter Fate by reviving and offering protection. Applying this antithetical structure, which Sperl calls the 'strophe' and 'antistrophe,'[55] to our current poem, we notice that Cordoba does not have the power to counter Fate. This stresses a major difference between the *ritha'* and *madih*, that being the finality of the loss in the *ritha'* and the overwhelming power of Fate, as opposed to the *mamduh*'s power in the panegyric. It emphasizes the fact that the Cordoba Ibn Shuhayd mourns can never be revived, except in verse.

Defining the Boundaries of Cordoba

6 For the likes of Cordoba, the weeping of one
   Who cries with an overflowing eye is trite.

7 A dwelling, may God forgive the faults of its people;
   They were Berberized, Westernized, and Egyptianized.

8 Everywhere there are groups of them
   Weakened from separation, bewildered.

The actual *ritha'* begins in verse 6, and in verse 7, following the pattern established earlier that accords equal attention to place and people, the line starts with mention of the former, and ends with a description of the 'transgressions' of the latter. Having formally begun the *ritha'*, Ibn Shuhayd proceeds to define, and obscure, Cordoba's cultural and political borders. As James Monroe points out in the notes to his translation of the second hemistich *(fa-tabarbaru wa-tagharrabu wa-tamassaru)*, the word *tabarbaru* refers to the Berber Hammudis who, taking advantage of growing Berber discontent in Cordoba, established themselves as a rival power to the Caliph Sulayman, which ultimately led to the fall of the Umayyad Caliphate. The reference to 'Egyptianization' points to a lineage the Hammudis traced back to 'Ali b. Abi Talib, the Prophet's son-in-law and spiritual and political leader of the Shi'ites, whose adherents, the Fatimids (named for Fatima, the Prophet's daughter and 'Ali's wife), ruled Egypt at the time and challenged the Andalusian Umayyads' claim to the Caliphate.[56]

The verb *tabarbara* is not neutral and the English translation 'to Berberize' does not express the full meaning of the Arabic in its cultural context. The word carries with it a sense of backwardness, ignorance, and, quite literally, barbarity (originally a Greek term used to describe any non-Greek who spoke an incomprehensible language that, to the Greeks, sounded like babbling). To say that someone has been 'Berberized' is an assertion of superiority that marks a clear line between 'us' and 'them.' Standing in al-Andalus, and acting as the defender of the Caliphate and Arabic language and letters that he was, Ibn Shuhayd saw these Berbers as a political, racial, and cultural threat. They were a foreign element, hailing from 'over there' (North Africa), and thus did not belong in Ibn Shuhyad's conception of Arab Cordoba.[57] Understood alongside his criticism of the state of Arabic in al-Andalus, which he refers to as "incorrect stammer-ing" *(lukna a'jamiya)*, *a'jami* being a word used by the Arabs to describe the local Spanish Romance language,[58] Ibn Shuhayd is vaunting a pure Arab Andalusian culture that is delocalized. He guards al-Andalus from Romance-speaking Spain *(al-'ajamiya)*, and Berber-speaking North Africa *(al-barbariya)*, seeking to preserve its Arabism *(al-'arabiya)*.

The verb *tagharraba* is richly problematic in that, geographically, it can be understood to specify the area of modern day Morocco (in Ibn Shuhayd's time, *al-Maghrib al-Aqsa*), or the Islamic west in general *(al-gharb al-Islami)* which would include al-Andalus and al-Maghrib al-Aqsa. The verb's root, *gh-r-b*, also carries with it the meaning of feeling isolated, for-eign, or alienated. As mentioned above, Ibn Shuhayd's criticism of the state of Arabic in al-Andalus points to a desire to return to a time and place in which the language (and culture) was unadulterated. There is a nostalgic look to a mythical state of linguistic purity that is neither wholly in the west, nor specifically in the present. The poet, standing on the ruins of Cordoba, feels isolated, alone, and out of place, and speaks for the lost Cordobans, of whom he is one.

The Architecture of the Past

9　In my time there, its people were unified,
And life in it was green.

10　And the winds of its splendor were shining over them,
With scents emanating ambergris.

11　And the abode—perfection had pitched its tent there,
While it was beyond any decrease.

12　And the people felt secure that its beauty would never change
Wearing it as a turban and a cloak.

13　Oh how I long for their nobility in its palaces and its ladies'
quarters
When its full moons were concealed in its palaces.

14　And the palace—that of Banu Umayyad—so abundant
With everything, but the Caliphate was even more abundant.

15　And the Zahiriyya with its boats that shined brightly
And the 'Amiriyya that was filled with stars.

16　And the Grand Mosque that was jammed with all who
Recite, hear, and study anything they wished to.

17　And you would see that the alleys of the markets
Were never empty of shopping throngs.

18　Oh paradise, the wind of distance has blown
Over it and its people, both it and they were destroyed.

After a brief description of the expulsion and exile of Cordoba's population (verses 7 and 8), verse 9 makes the transition from the present ruined state of Cordoba, where we stand with Ibn Shuhayd, to a nostalgic rumination of Cordoba's past. The section is notable for the overflowing emotion that each conjunctive *waw* (and) extends. Each verse begins with a *waw* and is followed by a noun, creating a syntactic unit. This larger section can be divided into two smaller sections that are thematically distinct, punctuated by the vocative *ya* in each of verses 13 and 18.

In the first of the two sections (running from verse 10 to verse 13), rather than relying on a descriptive poetics set in stone, Ibn Shuhayd paints using an impressionist's brush, setting the mood by evoking the scent of flower blossoms, the exquisite perfection of the dwelling *(dar)* that once was, and a beauty Cordoba's inhabitants never imagined could be effaced. Without retreating from the assertion that Cordoba is just as much about place as it is about the people who inhabit(ed) it, verse 13 (the transitional verse between the two subsections) leans heavily on the importance of place. This is emphasized by repeating the possessive pronoun "its" *(-ha)*, referring to Cordoba—a name, it is important to note, heard for the first and last time in verse 6 of the poem. In fact, since its mention, Cordoba is both absent and present in this possessive pronoun that appears at least once in each verse up to this point. The insistent, almost obsessive repetition of "its" (that is, Cordoba's) in verse 13 betrays a need for Ibn Shuhayd to reassert the presence of Cordoba, if only poetically, and literally to re-inscribe it onto the landscape.

A tangible re-mapping begins in the following verse (verse 14) and although the pattern established above continues *(waw* + noun), the references are much more concrete: buildings, palaces, streets, and so on. Ibn Shuhayd is now referring to 'real' places, but instead of realistic and detailed description, he draws upon Arabic poetry's symbolic use of toponyms. Brief mention of the Umayyad palace and the great mosque of Cordoba is sufficient to resonate with meaning in much the same way as mention of symbolic eastern locations such as Najd, Siqt al-Liwa, or Baghdad. The evocative power of these place names for Ibn Shuhayd's audience would have been so great that the mere sounds of their names would have prompted an emotional response without the poet having to provide detailed descriptions.

There is a clear hierarchy that Ibn Shuhayd respects, beginning with the Umayyad palace, the symbolic center of the Caliphate at the height of its power. The Banu Shuhayd came to al-Andalus from Syria during the reign of 'Abd al-Rahman I (756–88) following the rise of the Abbasids in the east, and remained loyal to the Umayyads until their fall in 1031.[59] For Ibn Shuhayd, the Umayyads symbolized political strength, vitality, and legitimacy, as well as a more personal reminder of a privileged youth spent within the walls of palaces, courtyards, gardens, and villas. It is likely that Ibn Shuhayd was raised on a steady diet of lore about Umayyad and Arab greatness, as well as a linguistic and literary education that would befit his noble standing. But it is also likely that he had heard talk and sensed the dissolution of this ideal world of the Umayyads, whose power, by the time of Ibn Shuhayd's birth in 992, was already waning.[60] A nod to the Umayyads is expected, but it is one tinged with irony and sadness, and a knowledge that their days are over.

From here, the poet shifts his focus to palaces built by Muhammad b. Abi 'Amir (who later took the title, "al-Mansur"), a high official in the Umayyad court who took advantage of the power struggle that emerged upon the fourteen-year-old Hisham's ascension to the Caliphate in 976. Ibn Shuhayd's father was given his first administrative post under al-Mansur,[61] and it was during al-Mansur's time that Ibn Shuhayd was born. If verse 14 is read as an obligatory affirmation of loyalty to the Umayyad Caliphate, verse fifteen draws attention to itself in such a way as to invite the audience to linger for a moment in the palaces contained therein. There is a symmetry between the two hemistichs, which are syntactically identical, and both have parallel *jinas* on the names of two of al-Mansur's palaces (*al-Zahiriya / tuzhiru* and *al-'Amiriya / tu'maru*). The names of the palaces themselves are not 'original,' but rather they allude to a specific place and person respectively. The former is a clear nod, and challenge, to the older *Madinat al-Zahra'*, the palace-city established by 'Abd al-Rahman III al-Nasir (d. 961), and also destroyed by Berbers around the same time as the sacking of Cordoba. *Al-'Amiriya* takes its name from al-Mansur (Muhammad b. Abi 'Amir) himself. No trace remains of it except for literary references such as the one we have in front of us, as well as descriptions of the contents of its gardens.[62] Finally, the root *'-m-r* that forms both the palace's name and that of its builder, signifies a flourishing civilization that once teemed with life. Through the manipulation of al-Mansur's name, as well as the names of his two main palaces, Ibn Shuhayd emphasizes *his* lost world, which is grand, alive, and personal.

Continuing outward from the regal and fixed symbols of the ruling elite, Ibn Shuhayd takes us to the great mosque of Cordoba, a public space symbolic of Cordoba's grandeur. From there, it is on to the bustling markets. The section is brought to a resounding close in verse 18 where all of the aforementioned components of Cordoba are collected under the all-encompassing paradise (*janna*), but as quickly as the city is contained in this word, which signifies the uncontainable, it is destroyed completely (*fa-tadammarat wa-tadammaru*). We expect that this total destruction is indeed final, and thus, the end. However, the job of the poet is not finished yet.

The Conflation and Immortalization of Space

19 I am afflicted by you, in death. As was only right
    As long as you live, we do not cease to sing your praises.
20 Your courtyards were a Mecca to pilgrims
    The frightened taking refuge in them, and being saved.
21 Oh abode, in which the bird of separation alighted, and in its people
    So that they were transformed and became unrecognizable.
22 The Euphrates flowed plentiful through your two shores, as did the Tigris.
    So too the Nile and the River Kawthar.
23 You were watered by the life-giving waters of a cloud.
    Your gardens were given life and flourished from these waters.

In verse 19, in a last-ditch effort to save his city, Ibn Shuhayd emphasizes the fact that it is his job as poet, and the audience's job as mourners,
to perpetuate Cordoba's life in the only possible way available to them—
through "sing[ing its] praises *(nafkharu)*." Revivification is further
achieved by emphasizing that the city was once given life by the waters
of the Euphrates, Tigris, Nile, and the river Kawthar of paradise. The
meeting of these waters in Cordoba once allowed it to exist everywhere,
straddling the boundaries between east and west, this world and the next.
The comparison between a city and paradise is a common one. We saw
it in al-Khuraymi's elegy for Baghdad, as well in numerous examples of
Ibn 'Umayra's work. It is, of course, a convenient metaphor that draws
upon already established images of the heavenly ideal.[63] However, it also
removes the city from the realm of reality and bestows upon it a transcendent quality that emphasizes its worldly death, but guarantees it an
eternal life in the hereafter.

The Poet Speaks

24 My sorrow is for the house whose familiar pleasures I knew
    And for its gazelles, who pranced and swaggered in its courtyard.
25 Oh for the days when the eye of every kindness
    Everywhere, gazed upon it.
26 Oh for the days when the command in it was but one;
    That of its 'Amir, and the 'Amir was the one who issued commands.

27 Oh for the days when the palm of every hand of peace and security
   Rose to it in peaceful greetings and rushed toward it.
28 My sadness for its generous leaders and narrators,
   Its honest ones and protectors, repeats itself.
29 My soul, for its blessing and pureness,
   And splendor and glory, is grieving.
30 My heart, for its mild-mannered scholars,
   And its refined littérateurs, is weakened.

Verse 24 begins the poem's finale. Here, the poet steps out of the shadows and reluctantly asserts his presence with the possessive "my" in *asafi*, and as the subject of the verb *'ahadtu* (I was bound to/I knew), a role which, up to this point, has been entirely absent. There are three other instances where the poet appears as a verbal subject, hinting at his active presence within the text, but even in these examples, his personal voice is subsumed by the plural "we" (*nastakhbiru* verse 1, *lam nazal . . . nafkharu* verse 19). The focus of the *ritha'* is, of course, the destroyed Cordoba. Therefore it is natural for the poet to cede attention to the city. Nonetheless, the poet's importance as spokesperson and elegist is undeniable. Without the poet, there is no poem, and without the poem, Cordoba ceases to exist. So it is from this verse on that Ibn Shuhayd cautiously shares a little space with Cordoba. I say cautiously because the verbal agency of the poet fades as quickly as it came, and all we have left of him is the possessive "my" once again (*asafi, hazani, nafsi, kabidi*).

In this final section, there is a negotiation between past and present in which two syntactic patterns battle for dominance, with the present getting the final word. The obsessive syntactic repetition in the last three verses (the same as that of verse 24) expresses the complete and utter despair of the poet's physical and emotional being (*asafi . . . tatabakhtaru, hazani . . . yatakarraru, nafsi . . . tatahassaru, kabidi . . . tatafattaru*).

In the end, the loss expressed by Ibn Shuhayd is distinctly personal and human. The city of Cordoba that the poet mourns was a physical reality that could be mapped upon the landscape, but equally, it was the people who populated the landscape and who sung its praises that Ibn Shuhayd considered to be Cordoba. More precisely, it was the lettered Arab elite who remembered and wrote about Cordoba using poetic strategies that combined concrete realities and imaginative poetic discourse.

The *ritha' al-mudun* genre that developed with the urbanization of Arab-Muslim society in the eighth and ninth centuries shared themes, images, and rhetorical strategies with the *ritha'* for a person that preceded it. With the move to the city, however, and new types of loss which accompanied that move, the elegist employed these inherited aspects of the *ritha'* while incorporating more modern rhetorical devices, urban images, and conceptions of place. In Ibn Shuhayd's elegy for the city of Cordoba, he defines place geographically, architecturally, racially, symbolically, and literarily. Even in this relatively early example, the poet clearly defines what al-Andalus was, and what it has become, in his choice of classical literary motifs and references. The fall of Cordoba marked not only the end of the Umayyad Caliphate in al-Andalus but also the imagined Arab past that it represented to Ibn Shuhayd.

Appendix

رثاء قرطبة لابن شهيد

١ ما في الطُّلولِ مِن الأَحبّةِ مُخبِرُ — فَمَن الّذي عن حالها نَسْتَخْبِرُ

٢ لا تَسْأَلَنَّ سِوى الفراقِ فإنّهُ — يُنْبِيكَ عنهم أَنْجدوا أَم أَغْوَروا

٣ جارَ الزَّمانُ عليْهم فَتفرّقوا — في كُلِّ ناحيّةٍ و بادَ الأَكْثُرُ

٤ جَرَتِ الخُطوبُ على محلِّ ديارهم — و عليْهِم فتغيرَّتْ و تغيرّوا

٥ فدَع الزَّمانَ يصوغُ في عرصاتِهم — نوراً تكادُ له القُلوبُ تُنوِّرُ

٦ فلمِثْلِ قرطبةَ يقِلُّ بُكاءُ مَن — يَبْكي بعَينٍ دمعُها متفجِّرُ

٧ دارٌ أقالَ اللهُ عَثرةَ أَهْلها — فتبربروا و تغرّبوا و تَمصّروا

٨ في كُلِّ ناحيةٍ فريقٌ منهم — متفطِّرٌ لفراقِها متحيِّرُ

٩ عَهْدي بها و الشملُ فيها جامعٌ — مِن أهلِها و العيْشُ فيها أخضرُ

١٠ و رياحُ زَهْرَتِها تلوحُ عليْهِم — بِرَوائحٍ يَفْتَرُّ منها العَنْبرُ

١١ و الدارُ قد ضَربَ الكَمالُ رِواقَهُ — فيها و باعُ النقص فيها يقصُرُ

١٢ و القَوْمُ قد أمنوا تَغَيرَّ حُسْنِها — فتعمَّموا بِجَمالِها و تأزَّروا

١٣ يا طِيبَهُمْ بِقُصورِها و خُدورِها — و بُدورِها بِقُصورِها تتخدَّرُ

١٤ و القصرُ قصرُ بَني أمِيَّةَ وافرٌ — من كلِّ أمرٍ والخلافةُ أَوْفَرُ

١٥ و الزاهريّةُ بالمراكب تُزْهِرُ — و العامِريّةُ بالكواكب تُعْمَرُ

١٦ و الجامعُ الأَعْلى يغصُّ بكلِّ مَن — يَتْلو و يَسْمَعُ ما يَشاءُ و يَنْظُرُ

١٧ و مسالكُ الأسواقِ تشهد أنّها — لا يَسْتَقِلُّ بِسالكيها المَحْشَرُ

١٨	يا جنَّةً عَصفتْ بِها و بِأَهْلِها	ريحُ النّوى فتدمّرتْ و تدمّروا
١٩	آسى عليْكِ مِن المماتِ و حَقّ لي	إذ لم نَزَلْ بكِ في حياتك نَفْخَرُ
٢٠	كانت عِراصُك للمُيَمِّم مَكَّةً	يأوي إليْها الخائفونَ فيُنْصَروا
٢١	يا مَنْزلاً نزلتْ به و بِأَهْلِه	طيرُ النّوى فتغيّروا و تنكّروا
٢٢	جادَ الفُراتُ بِساحَتيْكِ و دِجْلَةٍ	و النّيلُ جادَ بها و جادَ الكَوْثَرُ
٢٣	و سُقيتَ مِن ماءِ الحياةِ غَمامَةً	تحيا بِها منكَ الرّياضُ و تُزْهِرُ
٢٤	أَسفي على دارٍ عهدْتُ ربوعَها	و ظباؤُها بِفنائها تتبختَرُ
٢٥	أيّامَ كانت عينُ كلِّ كرامةٍ	من كلِّ ناحيةٍ إليْها تَنْظُرُ
٢٦	أيّامَ كان الأمرُ فيها واحدا	لأميرها و أميرٍ من يتأمَّرُ
٢٧	أيّامَ كانت كفُّ كلِّ سلامةٍ	تسمو إليْها بالسّلامِ و تَبْدُرُ
٢٨	حَزَني على سَرَواتِها و رُواتِها	و ثِقاتِها و حُماتِها يتكرّروا
٢٩	نَفْسي على آلائها و صفائها	و بَهائها و سَنائها تتحسرُ
٣٠	كَبِدي على عُلمائها حُلمائها	أدبائها ظرفائها تتفطّرُ

Notes

1   Svetlana Boym, *The Future of Nostalgia* (New York: Basic Books, 2001), 77.
2   Gaston Bachelard, *The Poetics of Space: the Classic Look at How We Experience Intimate Places*, trans. Maria Jolas (Boston: Beacon Press, 1994), 9.
3   Maurice Halbwachs, *On Collective Memory*, trans. Lewis A. Coser (Chicago and London: The University of Chicago Press, 1992), 53.
4   al-Khatib al-Tabrizi, ed., *al-Qasa'id al-'ashr*, ed. Fakhr al-Din Qabawa (Beirut: Dar al-Afaq al-Jadida, 1980), 20. All translations are mine unless otherwise noted.
5   Jaroslav Stetkevych, *The Zephyrs of Najd: The Poetics of Nostalgia in the Classical Arabic Nasib* (Chicago and London: The University of Chicago Press, 1993), 107.
6   Yumna al-'Id, "The Aesthetics of Space and the Longing for the Lost City," trans. from Arabic by Samira Aghacy, in *Myths, Historical Archetypes and Symbolic Figures in Arabic Literature: Toward a New Hermeneutic Approach, Proceedings of the International Symposium in Beirut, June 25th –June 30th, 1996*, ed. Angelika Neuwirth, Birgit Embaló, Sebastian Günther, and Maher Jarrar (Beirut: In Kommission bei Franz Steiner Verlag Stuttgart, 1999), 72.
7   Ibid, 73.
8   Ibid.
9   András Hámori, *On the Art of Medieval Arabic Literature* (Princeton: Princeton University Press, 1974), 3.
10 Al-'Id, "The Aesthetics of Space," 73.
11 One of the earliest *ritha' al-mudun* was for the city of Baghdad, composed by Abu Ya'qub Ishaq al-Khuraymi (d. 829) following the civil war of succession between Harun al-Rashid's sons, al-Amin and al-Ma'mun (809–813). See 'Ali Jawad al-Tahir and Muhammad Jabbar al-Mu'aybid, eds., *Diwan al-Khuraymi* (Beirut: Dar al-Kitab al-Jadid, 1971), 27. See also Michael Fishbein, *The History of al-Tabari*, vol. 31: *The War between Brothers* (Albany: State University of New York Press, 1985), 139.
12 Boym, *The Future of Nostalgia*, 76.
13 This point is discussed in Ibrahim al-Sinjilawi's useful survey on *ritha' al-mudun*. See *idem, The atlal-nasib in Early Arabic Poetry: A Study of the Development of the Elegiac Genre in Classical Arabic Poetry*, ed. Nasser al-Hasan 'Athamneh (Irbid, Jordan: Yarmouk University Publication, Deanship of Research and Graduate Studies, 1999) [in English].
14 Abu 'Ali al-Hasan Ibn Rashiq al-Qayrawani, *al-'Umda fi mahasin al-shi'r wa-adabihi wa-naqdihi*, ed. Muhammad Muhyi al-Din 'Abd al-Hamid, vol. 2 (Cairo: Matba'at al-Sa'ada, 1964), 76.
15 Suzanne Pinckney Stetkevych, *The Mute Immortals Speak: Pre-Islamic Poetry and the Poetics of Ritual* (Ithaca, NY: Cornell University Press, 1993), 163. For a discussion of repetition and other rhetorical strategies utilized in the English elegy, see Peter M. Sacks, *The English Elegy: Studies in the Genre from Spenser to Yeats* (Baltimore and London: The Johns Hopkins University Press, 1985).

16 Lisan al-Din ibn al-Khatib, *A'mal al-a'lam*, 2nd ed., ed. E. Levi Provençal (Beirut: Dar al-Makshuf, 1956), 107–08. Also in 'Abdullah Muhammad al-Zayyat, *Ritha' al-mudun fi-l-shi'r al-Andalusi* (Benghazi: Jami'at Qaryunis, 1990), 658.

17 Ahmad b. Muhammad al-Maqqari al-Tilimsani. *Nafh al-tib min ghusn al-Andalus al-ratib*, ed. Ihsan Abbas, 8 vols. (Beirut: Dar Sadir, 1968), 4:484. Also in al-Zayyat, *Ritha' al-mudun fi-l-shi'r al-Andalusi*, 671.

18 Muhammad b. 'Abd al-Malik al-Marrakushi, *al-Dhayl wa-l-takmila*, vol. 1, pt. 1, ed. Muhammad Bin Sherifa (Beirut: Dar al-Thaqafa, n.d.), 17. Also in al-Zayyat, *Ritha' al-mudun fi-l-shi'r al-Andalusi*, 688; Muhammad Bin Sherifa. *Abu al-Mutarrif Ahmad b. 'Umayra al-Makhzumi: hayatuhu wa-atharuhu* (Rabat: Manshurat al-Markaz al-Jami'i li-l-Bahth al-'Imi, n.d.), 232.

    tadhakkar 'ahda l-sharqi wa-l-sharqu shasi'un
    wa-dhaba asa li-l-barqi wa-l-barqu lami'un

    ......

    wa-kayfa bi-shaqrin aw bi-zurqati ma'ihi
    wa-fihi li-shaqrin aw li-zurqi mashari'in

19 Ibn 'Adhari al-Marrakushi, *al-Bayan al-mughrib fi akhbar al-Andalus wa-l-Maghrib*, pt. 3, ed. Ambrose Huswais Mirenda and Muhammad Ibn Tawit (Tetouan: Dar Krimadis li-l-Tiba'a, 1960), 382. Also in al-Zayyat, *Ritha' al-mudun fi-l-shi'r al-Andalusi*, 698.

20 For a discussion of Mihyar's use of desert imagery see Stefan Sperl, *Mannerism in Arabic Poetry: A Structural Analysis of Selected Texts (3rd century AH/9th century AD–5th century AH/11th century AD)* (Cambridge: Cambridge University Press, 1989), 58–59. For a discussion of how Ibn Khafaja utilized Bedouin motifs, see Magda Al-Nowaihi, *The Poetry of Ibn Khafajah: A Literary Analysis* (Leiden, New York, and Köln: E. J. Brill, 1993), 4–5 and 11–13. Ihsan Abbas treats the Andalusian use of "Arabian" themes in general in *idem, Tarikh al-adab al-Andalusi: 'asr al-tawa'if wa-l-murabitin* (Amman: Dar El Shorouk, 1997), 108–17.

21 Al-Nowaihi, *The Poetry of Ibn Khafajah*, 13.

22 Ibid., 5. For a more detailed discussion of these issues, see Ahmad Haykal, *al-Adab al-Andalusi: min al-fath ila suqut al-khilafa* (Cairo: Maktabat al-Shabab, 1962), 217–32.

23 See Yaqut al-Hamawi, *Mu'jam al-buldan*, 5 vols. (Beirut: Dar Sadir, 1984), vols. 3 and 5 respectively.

24 Al-Zayyat, *Ritha' al-mudun fi-l-shi'r al-andalusi*, p. 678. See also al-Maqqari, *Nafh al-tib min ghusn al-Andalus al-ratib*, 4:493.

25 J. Stetkevych, *The Zephyrs of Najd*, 106.

26 "Say: 'Is that better or the eternal garden (*jannat al-khuld*) that was promised to the righteous?'" *Al-Furqan*, 25:15.

27 See note 11 above.

28 J. Stetkevych's translation. See also Ibn Sa'id al-Andalusi, *Ikhtisar al-qidh al-mu'alla ikhtasarahu Abu 'Abd Allah b. Khalil*), ed. Ibrahim al-Abyari (Cairo: al-Hay'a al-'Ama li-Shu'un al-Matabi' al-Amiriya, 1959), 48; al-Maqqari, *Nafh al-tib min ghusn al-Andalus al-ratib*, 1:305; al-Zayyat, *Ritha' al-mudun fi-l-shi'r al-Andalusi*, 682.

29 'Abdullah Gannun, *al-Nubugh al-Maghribi fi-l-adab al-'arabi*, 3rd ed., vol. 1 (Beirut:

Maktabat al-Madrasa wa-Dar al-Kitab al-Lubnani li-l-Tiba'a wa-l-Nashr, 1975), 237.

30 Muhammad Bin Tawit, *al-Wafi fi-l-adab al-'arabi fi-l-Maghrib al-aqsa*, 2nd ed., vol. 1 (Casablanca: Dar al-Thaqafa li-l-Nashr wa-l-Tawzi', 1998), 343

31 Elías Terés, "Textos Poeticos sobre Valencia," *Al-Andalus: Revista de las Escuelas de Estudios Árabes de Madrid y Granada* 30 (1965): 291–307.

32 Abu 'Abd Allah Muhammad b. Ghalib al-Rusafi, *Diwan al-Rusafi-l-Balansi*, ed. Ihsan Abbas (Beirut: Dar al-Thaqafa, 1960), 69.

33 Terés, "Textos Poeticos sobre Valencia," 295. For the Arabic text see Ibn Said, *al-Mughrib fi hula al-Maghrib*, vol. 2/2. ed. Shawqi Dayf. (Cairo: Dar al-Ma'arif bi-Misr, 1955–64), 311.

34 Muhammad b. 'Abd al-Mun'im Al-Himyari, *Kitab al-rawd al-mi'tar fi khabar al-aqtar*, ed. Ihsan Abbas (Beirut: Maktabat Lubnan, 1975), 100.

35 Khalil Mardam, ed., *Diwan 'Ali b. al-Jahm* (Beirut: Dar Sadir, 1996), 135. This verse survives into the twentieth century, in Badr Shakir al-Sayyab's poem "al-Mabgha" (The Whorehouse) where the line signifies something quite different. Al-Sayyab says: "Baghdad is a nightmare (a disgusting carnage / Swallowed by the sleeper / Whose hours are days, whose days are years, with the year a yoke: / The year is a wound smoldering in the soul). / The wild cow's eyes between Rusafa and the bridge / Are bullet holes that embellish [like the dots of letters] the flat white surface of the full moon . . ." Quoted in Terri DeYoung, *Placing the Poet: Badr Shakir al-Sayyab and Postcolonial Iraq* (Albany: State University of New York Press, 1998), vii.

36 J. Stetkevych, *The Zephyrs of Najd*, 109.

37 For a fascinating discussion of the *ritha'* in general, and of the importance and gendered determination of the symbolic use of liquid flow in the *ritha'* and associated *tahrid*, see S. P. Stetkevych, *The Mute Immortals Speak*, 161–205.

38 The full poem will be analyzed below.

39 I have translated the second hemistich as I did in an attempt to preserve the parallelism I perceive in these verses. In each hemistich, there is an opposition made that can be illustrated as *al-dunya*: *al-akhira* // dryness/fertility. However, *ghamrat al-'ajaj* can also mean 'the tumultuous waves/sea,' which would also make sense, considering the fact that many Andalusian poets during this period directed their calls to Muslims across the Straits of Gibraltar in North Africa. This reading would also enhance the juxtaposition of fresh and salt water.

40 That is, the *mujahidun*.

41 Muhammad Faraj Dughaym ed. *Diwan Ibrahim b. Sahl al-Ishbili* (Beirut: Dar al-Gharb al-Islami, 1998), 157.

42 Israel Levin, ed., *Yalkut Avraham Ibn Ezra* (New York and Tel Aviv: Israel Matz Hebrew Classics and Edward I. Kiev Library, 1985), 101–103.

43 For a detailed description of the *muwashshah* form, see Samuel Miklos Stern, *Hispano-Arabic Strophic Poetry*, ed. L. P. Harvey (Oxford: Clarendon Press, 1974), 12–41.

44 Ross Brann provides a more in-depth discussion of these issues in "Structures of Exile in the Hebrew and Arabic Laments of Sefarad/al-Andalus," [Hebrew] in

Sefer Israel Levin, ed. Reuben Tsor and Tova Rosen (Tel Aviv: University of Tel Aviv, 1994), 45–61.

45 It is interesting to consider that the allusion to the Hebrew biblical tradition can be compared to the Arab poets' use of the pre-Islamic and Eastern poetic traditions for inspiration and poetic emphasis. I thank Raymond Scheindlin for bringing this analogous usage of tradition to my attention.

46 Fatima Tahtah briefly discusses this poem in *al-Ghurba wa-l-hanin fi-l-shi'r al-Andalusi* (Rabat: Manshurat Kulliyat al-Adab, 1991), 70–71. Cynthia Robinson also provides a stimulating analysis in "Ubi Sunt: Memory and Nostalgia in Taifa Court Culture," *Muqarnas* 15 (1998): 20–31.
    Another treatment of this poem is contained in Muhammad Sa'id Muhammad, *al-Shi'r fi Qurtuba* (Abu Dhabi: al-Majma' al-Thaqafi, 2003) which, unfortunately, I have been unable to refer to as of this writing. However, I thank Muhsin al-Musawi for the reference.

47 For more details surrounding the events of this period, see Hugh Kennedy, *Muslim Spain and Portugal: A Political History of al-Andalus* (London and New York: Longman, 1996), 109–30.

48 James Dickie, "Ibn Šuhayd: A Biographical and Critical Study," *Al-Andalus: Revista de las Escuelas de Estudios Árabes de Madrid y Granada* 29 (1964): 250.

49 Quoted in Ibid. For Arabic text, see Ibn Bassam al-Shantarini, *al-Dhakhira fi mahasin ahl al-jazira*, vol. 1, pt. 1 (Cairo: Matba'at Lajnat al-Ta'lif wa-l-Tarjama wa-l-Nashr, 1939), 202–203.

50 Al-Shantarini, *al-Dhakhira*, vol. 1, pt. 1, 229.

51 *Diwan Ibn Shuhayd al-Andalusi*, ed. Ya'qub Zaki (Cairo: Dar al-Katib al-'Arabi li-l-Tiba'a wa-l-Nashr, 1969), 109–11. See appendix for Arabic text.

52 See William Wright, *A Grammar of the Arabic Language*, vol. 2, rev. W. Robertson Smith and M. J. de Goeje (Beirut: Librairie du Liban, 1974), 44.

53 See al-Hamawi, *Mu'jam al-buldan*, vol. 4, 217.

54 Ibn Rashiq, *al-'Umda*, v. 2, 147.

55 Sperl, *Mannerism in Arabic Poetry*, 25.

56 James T. Monroe. *Hispano-Arabic Poetry: A Student Anthology* (Berkeley, Los Angeles, and London: University of California Press, 1974), 160.

57 Maya Shatzmiller discusses the rise of 'Berberism' in al-Andalus and the literary genre that expressed it (*mafakhir al-barbar, mafadil al-barbar*, or *mahasin ahl al-Maghrib*). See Maya Shatzmiller, *The Berbers and the Islamic State: The Marinid Experience in Pre-Protectorate Morocco* (Princeton, NJ: Marcus Wiener, 2000), 29–39. For their part, the Andalusis also composed treatises that celebrated the superiority of al-Andalus over that of al-Maghrib. However, one must avoid taking these writings too literally as treatises vaunting real notions of cultural superiority of one group over another. Not only are the definitions of place, ethnicity, race, and culture somewhat slippery, but the genre itself stems from the earlier genre of debate literature, and thus conforms to, and depends on, certain literary conventions. For a discussion of this genre (*fadl al-Andalus*) see the author's "Singing the Praises of al-Andalus, Silencing its Critics," in "Looking Back:

The Poetics of Loss and Nostalgia and the Literary Definition of al-Andalus in Arabic and Hebrew Literature" (PhD dissertation, Columbia University, 2004). See also Emilio García Gómez, *Andalucía contra Berbería: Reedición de Traducciones de Ben Hayyan, Šaqundi y Ben al-Jatib* (Barcelona: Publicaciones del Departamento de Lengua y Literatura Árabes, 1976).

58 Consuelo López-Morillas, "Language," in *The Literature of al-Andalus*, ed. María Rosa Menocal, Raymond P. Scheindlin, and Michael Sells (Cambridge: Cambridge University Press, 2000), 36.

59 Dickie, "Ibn Šuhayd: A Biographical and Critical Study," 243.

60 Kennedy, *Muslim Spain and Portugal*, 82–129.

61 Dickie, "Ibn Šuhayd: A Biographical and Critical Study," 247.

62 María Jesús Rubiera, *La arquitectura en la literature árabe* (Madrid: Ediciones Hiperión, 1988), 134.

63 For a discussion of the imagery used and dimensions covered by the paradise motif, see Aziz al-Azmeh, "Rhetoric for the Senses: A Consideration of Muslim paradise Narratives," *Journal of Arabic Literature* 26, no. 3 (1995): 215–31.

6

Arabic Poetics and Representations of Women in the Andalusian Hebrew Lament

Jonathan P. Decter

Introduction

Like their Muslim contemporaries, the Arabic-speaking Jews of al-Andalus commemorated death with a specific set of rituals, including the recitation of poems of lamentation. From the pens of most of the major Hebrew poets survive panegyric laments over patrons and friends, intimate familial laments, laments that focus on comforting the anguish of surviving relatives, and even occasional examples of laments over oneself (written when one's death was impending). Andalusian Hebrew laments exhibit significant variation, sometimes adhering to the structure and style of Arabic poetry but sometimes following different patterns. In the Arabic-influenced examples, we find metered verses that follow monorhyme or *muwashshah* form. Some examples even make use of a multithematic *qasida* structure, beginning with themes such as complaint against Time *(zaman)* or the World *(tevel* [Ar. *dunya*]) and then making a transition to the panegyric proper. Other laments abandon Arabic prosody and introduce original structural elements such as a dialogue between the deceased speaking from the grave and a surviving parent.[1]

Laments over women—including mothers, wives, sisters, and daughters—form a small but significant subgenre within the Hebrew poetry of lamentation.[2] This article treats aspects of Andalusian Hebrew laments over women from the perspective of gender, focusing on the ideal female characteristics included in panegyric sections, the use of female speakers within poems, and the curious practice of not identifying deceased women by name. Composing laments over women presented considerable challenges for poets whose literary sensibilities were informed by Arabic poetics. Because much lamentation poetry was a variation on the traditional panegyric genre, it was awkward to lament women, who generally did not serve as the subject of praise, the *mamduh*, in panegyric. Women were therefore praised for a strictly delimited set of personal characteristics that were distinct from the traits for which men were extolled. In many instances, Hebrew poets sought alternative strategies for lamenting the death of women that obviated the need for panegyric altogether. Also, poets sometimes introduce women as speakers within poems—either as the deceased speaking from beyond or as a surviving relative; such discursive practices may have grown from written and oral traditions of women lamenting in Arab society from pre-Islamic times to the Andalusian period.

Lamenting the Dead in Judaism

Jewish lamentation over the dead did not originate in Islamic Iberia. The Bible preserves numerous laments such as David's lament over Saul and Jonathan (2 Samuel 1:17–24) and his lament over Abner (2 Samuel 3:33–34). These laments are extremely secular in nature and are without any reference to God or divine justice. Although no text of a lament over a woman is preserved, the tragic death of Jephthah's daughter was lamented annually: "So it became a custom in Israel to go every year, for four days in the year, and chant dirges for the daughter of Jephthah the Gileadite" (Judges 11:40). Prophetic writings and the book of Lamentations include dirges—spoken in the voices of men and women—over Jerusalem as a deceased woman.[3]

The Talmud preserves a number of Hebrew and Aramaic laments appropriate for men to recite upon the death of great rabbis (Moʻed Katan 25b) as well as Aramaic (that is, vernacular) couplets that 'female mourners' (*meqonenot*) were reported to have uttered, also over men (Moʻed

Katan 28b).[4] Although we do not have laments composed for women from the Rabbinic period, the employment of professional female mourners for women's funerals is well documented, at least for the Mishnaic period (before 200 CE) since Rabbi Judah suggests "[For his wife's funeral], even a poor man in Israel cannot employ fewer than two flute players and female mourners *(meqonenot)*" (Ketubbot 4:4).[5]

Maimonides's (b. Cordoba 1135–d. Fustat 1204) exhaustive compendium of Jewish law, the *Mishneh Torah*, outlines the requirements for a wife's funeral following the opinion of Rabbi Judah in the Mishnah with specific reference to laments:

> If a man's wife dies, he is required to pay for her funeral and to arrange for her a eulogy and poems of lamentation according to the custom of every country; even the poor man in Israel cannot employ fewer than two flute players and female mourners. If he is a rich man, all [of the arrangements] should be executed according to his status. If her status is superior to his, she is to be buried according to her status, for a woman can ascend [in status by marrying her] husband but not descend, even after death.[6]

The documents of the Cairo Geniza, which reflect the social reality of Jews in the medieval Islamic world (especially in Fatimid Egypt), contain numerous references to the employment of 'mourning women' at the funerals of men and of women.[7] Many Hebrew poems from al-Andalus contain references to lamenting and wailing women.[8] In one fascinating Geniza document from the twelfth century, the judge Nathan ha-Kohen ben Solomon directs a query in Judeo-Arabic to Nathan ben Samuel he-Haver whose female relative had recently died. Apparently, the judge was expected to deliver a learned and honorary oration in poetic form at the woman's funeral:

> My mind has become rusty, I am no longer what I used to be and I have no ideas. Tomorrow they will ask me to speak. Kindly write a short alphabetical [eulogy] on the reverse side of this note, giving the essence of the story of Naomi adapted to the case of this lady. Proceed in this composition according to your own taste and send it over immediately.[9]

The text to be recited was expected to be in Hebrew, to follow a specific literary form (alphabetical acrostic), and to draw upon learned references, in this case the biblical story of Naomi and her daughter-in-law Ruth. Notably, it is not clear that all surviving laments were intended to be read during the funeral ceremony proper. Jefim Schirmann published a series of seven poems by this same Nathan ben Samuel on the death of a certain woman, apparently designating one poem for each of the seven days of mourning (*shiv'a*).[10]

Most poems were addressed to surviving relatives of the deceased. When men died, poems were addressed to their sons and occasionally to their wives. Poems addressed to women raise the question of whether these women would be able to understand what they were given. Although some women, a great minority, had basic education in Hebrew, it is also possible that they could appreciate the sentiment of receiving a poem of consolation without fully understanding its contents; also, male relatives could have explained the meaning to them. When poems were composed on the deaths of illustrious men such as Hai Gaon (a dean of Jewish learning in Baghdad, who was eulogized by Samuel the Nagid and Solomon Ibn Gabirol) or Yequtiel (Ibn Gabirol's patron), the intended audience was the community at large.[11] Not surprisingly, we have no known laments for women that were intended for the community.[12] All of the laments over women or girls are addressed to their husbands, sons, brothers, or fathers.

Praising Women

Like their Arabic counterparts, Hebrew laments often read like panegyric poems with the modification that the magnificent qualities of the *mamduh* are set in the past tense; Ibn Rashiq writes in his *Kitab al-'umda*: "There is no difference between lament and praise except that lament includes something that indicates that the one intended is dead such as 'was' (that is, use of the past tense), or 'we have lost so and so' or other things similar to this to inform that he is dead."[13] The qualities for which deceased men are praised are hardly distinguishable from the qualities of living men. They possess(ed) intelligence, vast learning, wealth, generosity, fine lineage, sophisticated manners, eloquent speech, physical prowess, the respect of their contemporaries, and so on.

Books of Arabic literary criticism, with which Hebrew poets were abundantly familiar, exhibit an acute awareness of the difficulties with praising women in laments.[14] Ibn Rashiq writes: "The most difficult lament for a poet [to compose] is over a child or a woman due to the few things that can be said about them and the scarcity of descriptive traits."[15] In an article treating the theory and practice of eulogizing women in Arabic poetry, Suaad al-Mana calls attention to the opinion of al-Husri in his *Zahr al-adab wa thamar al-albab*:[16]

> The practice concerning women is narrow in scope and extremely restricted. Most of that used to praise men is disparaging to [women] and a mark of disgrace . . . Do you not see that generosity, faithfulness in pledges, bravery, sagacity, and similar terms that are praiseworthy qualities in men would be a blemish and a disgrace were [the poet] to praise women with them?[17]

The panegyric section of the female lament, then, must be a variation on a male panegyric form that emphasizes ideal 'feminine' qualities (such as modesty, humility, honesty, etc.) but is reticent about other character traits. Although some Andalusian Arabic poets extol the former beauty of their deceased wives, the use of beauty imagery is generally considered unsuitable for the poetry of lamentation.[18] As al-Mana shows, the prescriptions of critics are not entirely consistent with the practices of poets, for numerous Arabic poems from the pre-Islamic period through the twelfth century also praise women for generosity and intelligence. Still, the opinions of critics probably had significant value for Hebrew poets seeking to emulate the norms of Arabic verse.

Hebrew panegyrics in honor of women are extremely rare. Unidentifiable women are 'praised' as love objects in Hebrew *ghazal*—with mention made of their devastating physical beauty, coy behavior, powerful glances, and ornamentations of dress—but these are hardly directed toward real or specific women.[19] Even Hebrew wedding poems, which are largely panegyrics in honor of the bridegroom and his family, generally present women in a manner similar to their counterparts in *ghazal* except with the expectation that sexual consummation is presented as possible:

> Rejoice, O youth, in a fawn of love and you will both ring out joyously!
> Take pleasure in her lovely form, like a palm tree in stature yet
>   quivering like branches of myrtle.

Do not fear the sound of jewels on her neck nor the clank of finery at
   the hour of twilight!
And do not fear her dove-like eyes, drunk with the wine of passion!
Be courageous in embracing arms adorned in bracelets and the beauty
   of bangles.
Do not flee from the asps of locks upon the face bathed in blushes!
They have come out to greet you in peace although they veil and hide
   the glory of her face.
The pomegranates in the rose garden are encased with tips of spiced
   studs;
When your hands pass over their surface, they slowly squeeze and
   caress them.[20]

The bride possesses all of the characteristics of a conventional beloved
in love poetry.

The poem is distinguishable from a love poem only in that the reader
expects sexual union between the suitor/groom and his beloved/bride,
whereas most love poems end with the lover in a state of frustration.[21]
Even though we are reading about a specific bride, we still do not feel
that we are reading about a 'real' woman.[22] It is rare to find examples of
Hebrew wedding poems praising women for wisdom or moral qualities,
though some exceptions do exist.[23]

Lamenting Women

The ideal characteristics of women presented in Hebrew laments combine
conventions of the social environment of Islamic Iberia and the Hebrew
literary tradition. One source that is frequently evoked by the Hebrew
poets, especially when lamenting wives and mothers (in poems addressed
to husbands or sons), is the famous biblical passage on the idealized 'wife of
valor' in Proverbs 31: she is diligent, capable, vigorous, generous toward the
poor, and kind with her tongue. Of these, it is only a woman's generosity
and kind speech that are evoked with any frequency in Andalusian Hebrew
laments. Like their Arabic counterparts, Hebrew poets also praise wom-
en's discretion, aversion to gossip and falsehood, and humility. As in much
Arabic-inspired Hebrew verse, especially love poems, women are likened to
rare gems and constellations. A typical example of a lament over a woman is
the following by Moses Ibn Ezra concerning the death of a friend's sister:

He shouted, "Alas!" for his sister. Who could not lament the topaz
    that has been lost?
She wandered like a bird from its nest, therefore [his soul] wishes it
    could wander after her.
The ground she trod upon is her dwelling place today, when yesterday
    she trod upon Orion!
She spreads her couch in the bottom of a pit, when yesterday she
    spread out on the Pleiades and the Great Bear!
How [these constellations] wished to hide their beautiful faces in
    obscurity, [when previously] the moon envied their splendor!
My soul has known no other day when the earth was a snare for the
    stars above.
Kindly teaching was on her tongue; she always came early to the gates
    of truth.[24]
Her sister the sun withheld her light and stood fixed on its circuit
    without running.
She was the moon's rival wife but still [the moon] wished her grave to
    be set beside her.
Every noble woman rushed to lament her; every well-bred princess
    grieved after her.[25]

The references to gems and heavenly bodies are most general; it is left
somewhat ambiguous whether her superlative qualities relate to physical beauty or moral qualities, though the reference to the constellations
hiding their beautiful faces suggests the former. The character traits of
"kindly teaching" and alacrity for truth derive from the Bible. Some elements are drawn from the social world of women such as the idea of a
"rival wife" beside whom one might be buried and the role of mourning
women including women of high rank.

    Only in rare instances is a woman remembered for her intellect. One
exception is preserved in a Geniza document wherein a father laments a
daughter who had died at a mature age. He recalls the days when he taught
her as a young girl: "When I remember how intelligent, how knowledge-
able, how graceful of diction you had been . . . Would that I could listen to
you again while I taught you the Bible or quested you in its knowledge by
heart, 'let me see your face, let me hear your voice' (Song of Songs 2:14)."[26]
The reservation with which a poet praised a woman for her wisdom is

illustrated well by the following hyperbolic flourish by Moses Ibn Ezra in a lament dedicated to two sons on the death of their mother:

> It is difficult for me to call she who makes fools wise 'woman.'
> She was created female but was given the name 'wise' for she makes all fools clever.[27]

This woman is praised with the widest range of traits encountered in the Hebrew corpus; she is described as wise, generous, truthful, and full of humility. The poet praises her lineage (mentioning both parents) and ultimately turns to the two sons (called "two tendrils") who become the subject of a lengthy panegyric themselves:

> [She was] a word of truth in the Earth's mouth, but since the day God took her, it has been unable to speak.
> She was laughter on the Earth's face; without her, its face glowers for "a hidden word is a glowering face."[28]
> She spoke words sweeter than honey to the downtrodden, healing for all the sick.
> She had a spirit of generosity that bestowed to beggars and a hand [so generous] that the clouds stopped up when she gave forth rain.
> She was a necklace on the neck of Uprightness, a bracelet on the right hand of Preciousness, and signet ring on the left hand of Truth.
> A veil of humility covered her face until the day she became hidden in the ground.
> With her mind's eye she saw future events and she kept her body's eye from seeing evil.
> How can one measure the might of her parents? Who can measure the ocean with the palm of the hand or with a water skin?
> She was a tree whose top reached the heavens; she was comparable to every tree in the Garden of God.
> Her two tendrils produced gracious fruit, sweet to the mouth of its tasters . . . .

Although characteristics of the 'wife of valor' in Proverbs 31 inform some of the ideal qualities listed (kind speech, charitableness), others such as diligence, vigor, and capability play no role. Ideal female characteristics thus follow the conventions of Arabic poetry more than the Bible; the women of Ibn Ezra's laments remind one of the mother of Sayf al-Dawla—eulogized by al-Mutanabbi as "eager to be bountiful" to the beggar, "concealing the secret," and "truthful in speech"—more than the 'wife of valor.'[29] Beneath the surface of some traits for which the deceased woman is praised is the implication of typical blameworthy female characteristics. Her truthful speech implies a stereotype of the deceptive woman. The deceased's 'sweet words' betray the conception that women used their tongues for ill-purposes such as gossip. Beneath the compliment of humility is the perception of women being vainglorious and haughty. The deceased is thus an exception to her lying, gossiping, and prideful counterparts, who are often subjects portrayed and satirized in medieval Hebrew literature.[30]

Lamenting Daughters

Like laments over women, laments over young children posed difficulties for poets since children possessed few character traits poets thought appropriate to mention.[31] It is useful to compare poems on deceased sons and daughters to understand the relative values assigned to children of different sexes, parent's hopes for their children's futures, and the construction of gender in medieval Judaism more generally. The earliest Hebrew lament, if it may even be called such, over a daughter (and the earliest over a female altogether) is by Samuel the Nagid who heard the news of his daughter's death from the battlefield. Like many of his poems, this poem is addressed to the poet's son, Joseph, who compiled his father's *diwan* at a young age:

> Wrap my head in turbans and mantles! Rend my clothes by cubits and handbreadths!
> Break musical instruments, lyre and drum, and pour out the wine of grapes, either fresh or dry!
> Erase joys from my heart! Rise up and write a writ of divorce for joys and pleasures!
> And call out: "'Alas!' Joseph cries out from a house of mourning, sitting by the corpse and shouting 'Alas, my sister!'"
> Lament her loss and be concerned for her death, the day she was taken from among pampered maidens.

When [Joseph] was crushed, the hearts of mothers and concubines
were crushed; when he wept the eyes of maidservants and families
wept.

[Joseph's] heart burned down the house of mourning for he was not
accustomed to the flames of burning hearts.

If you refuse to be consoled, raise up your voice in the street and at
home with shouts and cries.

Pay attention to my words, and take eloquent speech from my mouth,
and like me [you] will speak eloquently.

Pay close attention and consider this letter I have sent you from a
house of battle full of disputes and rebukes . . . .[32]

In the first three verses, the poet evokes conventional rituals of mourning. In the fourth line, he turns to the subject of his son's suffering, and
from there offers his son the advice he offers in so many other poems: to
learn from his father to speak and write eloquently. The final verse translated here introduces the theme of war, which becomes the subject of the
rest of the poem for another fourteen lines. Thus, the initial references
to lamentation quickly give way in the prelude to the father's advice to
his son and then to war poetry, the genre to which the poem most fully
belongs. We notably learn nothing about the girl (age, characteristics,
etc.) except that Joseph had a bond with her. Within the lament, the poet
is more concerned for the suffering of the surviving brother than the
loss of his daughter or his own bereavement. Following the conventions
of Arabic poetics, the father did not portray himself as overly emotional
concerning the death of his daughter. A poem by al-Buhturi on the death
of "one of the daughters of the Banu Hamid" stresses to the father that it
is not fitting for a man, especially a warrior, to weep over a daughter: "Do
you weep for one who does not fight with a sword that protects what is
behind the back and who does not brandish a standard?"[33]

Laments on the deaths of young children focus on the loss of potential
accomplishments rather than on actual traits. In a moving poem by Judah
Halevi, a father's voice laments the death of his young son:

How am I suddenly bereft of the son I reared and brought up?
I put my horn in the dust[34] for my splendor is struck down,
I hoped to boast over him, one day to sing his praises,

But I did not know what the day had born.[35]
My friends, have compassion for me, for God took from between
 my arms
The light of my eyes, the child of my delight. I ritually washed [his
 corpse] with my tears,
I buried him between my ribs so that I might speak with him at times.
My heart, my heart! My suffering, my suffering! My heart has died
 because the boy has died.[36]

A useful comparison can be made with another poem by Halevi spoken in the voice of a mother over a daughter:

Daughter taken from her mother's chamber
How can I live when she is formed from my soul?
I split rocks when I see her form.
How can the moon's glory fade?
There in Sheol I will see the day of her wedding,
How she will make a lump of earth her wedding canopy,[37]
How a clod from her grave will be sweet to her.
It has become very bitter for me, my daughter, because you are absent,
For death separates you and me.[38]

The future did not hold hopes of boasting over the child's achievements but rather of rejoicing in the girl's marriage. The boy held promise of accomplishment in the public sphere while prospects for the girl resided in entering maturity in family life.

A telling example of the idealized values of sons and daughters comes from a rhetorical episode in a collection of Hebrew *maqamat*, the *Taḥkemoni* by Judah al-Harizi (ca. 1166–1225). As is typical of the *maqama* genre, the protagonist Hever the Kenite overcomes seemingly impossible literary feats with a clever wit and mastery of language (in this case the Hebrew of the Bible). In the twenty-third episode, he displays his virtuosity in eloquence by composing an epistle for an aristocrat "whose daughter died yesterday but whose wife gave birth to a son today," a task of mixing "consolation with joyful tidings" that had stumped the aristocrat's confidants. Of course, Hever composes the epistle without batting an eyelash, making use of many biblical phrases:

After the clouds of tears broke open and the groaning and crying reached the heavens, God renounced the punishment. The cloud of weeping that had broken through the breach was stopped up and water was withheld from the land. The water is dried off the cheeks. Destruction is rebuilt; the hook is fastened. Instead of the light of the moon, the light of the sun has risen. After our shade has departed and our standard fallen, and our dancing turned to mourning, God's countenance shone upon us so that He removed our gloom and made the fallen stand. He exchanged our mourning for joy and turned our anguish to dancing. After our hands were weakened and our eyes were dimmed, evening turned to noon and the sun stood at midday. Suddenly, injury was bandaged; in an instant the illness was cured. Lament turned to melody, sighing to joy, and bitter cries to the sound of song. Tragedy became rejoicing; anger became happiness and song. We stripped off sackcloth and fastened on necklaces. If a treetop has been hewn off, now a precious cedar grows for greatness and majesty. If yesterday the moon set, today the sun rises. The daughter rests in peace and the father is comforted. The son will flourish and his light will shine forth. Through him, you will rule over and storm against Time. Your heart has produced that which it desired. It has replaced brass with gold. Instead of coal, it has raised a torch. It replaced cedar with acacia,[39] a seat with a bed, a veil with a turban, a [priest's] headgear with a [king's] signet ring ... an inkwell with a scribe's quill ... a sheath with a sword, a target with an arrow, women's quarters with a house of study .... [40]

The birth of the boy serves more than adequately to reverse mourning into rejoicing. The series of exchanges of lesser for greater are not all as banal as trading brass for gold. Several phrases are obvious metaphors for the exchange of female genitalia for male (sheath for sword, inkwell for quill) and several metonymically refer to the separate social worlds of men and women. Rather than raising a girl to wear a veil, at best to succeed in guarding her reputation and humility, a father might expect his son to become a respected turban-wearing dignitary.[41] Whereas a daughter might grow to live secluded in the women's quarter of the home, for aristocratic women would be expected to stay indoors, a son might become a learned scholar in the house of study, truly a man's domain. In the end, the epistle is not a lament at all. The birth of the boy is a cause for celebration that far outweighs the 'loss' of the daughter. One imagines that had the fictional scenario been reversed such that the man lost a son but gained a daughter, the epistle would have been an actual lament, perhaps even intensified, for every praiseworthy quality the girl might offer would be a bitter reminder of the superior potential that had been lost with the son.[42] Perhaps the hardest poem to write, at least one that would not offer an obvious literary structure for juxtaposing losses and gains, would be one dedicated to a man who lost a son yesterday but whose wife gave birth to another son today.

The Absence of Women's Names

One detail that consistently distinguishes the Hebrew laments about men from the laments about women concerns naming the deceased within the poem.[43] Whereas laments about men—patrons or friends, mature men or children—frequently include the Hebrew name of the deceased, there is not one known example of a deceased woman or girl named within a poem. In fact, laments over men often make the name a point of focus. In a twenty-two stanza lament by Judah Halevi over a respected man named Joseph, every stanza concludes with the deceased's name, often drawing on biblical verses:

> Today is not a day for exultation. Get yourself a large sheet, intone a
>   dirge, and write upon [the sheet] "for Joseph."
> Mourn through the night[44] for only to mourn and to shout bitterly
>   came the brothers of Joseph.
> The Shining One, the Son of Dawn is erased! How did you fall from
>   the heavens? Thus shall you speak to Joseph. . . .[45]

Names were also included in poems over sons. In a famous lament written by Abraham Ibn Ezra over the death of his son Isaac, the poet fully exploits his and his son's names by concluding every stanza with the word 'Isaac' and drawing on verses from the Abraham–Isaac story in Genesis: "Father of the child, come forth and eulogize, for God has separated from you *your son, your only one, the one that you love, Isaac*" (Genesis 22:2).

Yet not one Hebrew lament from al-Andalus includes the name of a deceased woman or girl, which may be related to the Arabic environment in which the poetry was written. The naming of women within Arabic poems is a complex issue. Poets refrain from explicitly naming women of high status, especially the relatives of powerful men, for the sake of etiquette. Al-Mutanabbi never refers to the mother of Sayf al-Dawla by name in his lament over her though he explicitly refers to the illustrious son twice.[46] Similarly, al-Mutanabbi's lament over Sayf al-Dawla's sister toys with the convention of referring to the deceased woman without naming her explicitly, arguing that it is better to describe than to name:

> O sister of the greatest brother! O daughter of the greatest father! You
>   carry these two nicknames because of your most noble lineage.
> I honor your greatness by calling you "wept for;"[47] whoever has
>   described you has named you for the Arabs.[48]

Some anecdotes praise the practice of avoiding illustrious women's names in public discourse, especially after their deaths. Al-Mas'udi relates an anecdote in which 'Abd Allah Ibn Salih is praised for showing tact by not evoking the name of the deceased mother of Harun al-Rashid, Khayzuran (whose name means 'bamboo'). Ibn Salih had sent the Caliph a gift of fruit and nuts stacked upon *bamboo* trays including a note stating "I have gathered some of each species [of fruit and nut], placed them in *reed* trays and sent them to the Commander of the Faithful . . . ." What was praiseworthy was that he used the word 'reed' *(qudban)* instead of 'bamboo' *(khayzuran)* out of respect for the deceased mother.[49]

However, we also find that (even powerful) women's names were mentioned in poems, even during the Abbasid period. Ibn Rashiq cites (with condemnation) a verse by an unnamed poet in which Zubaydah, wife of Harun al-Rashid, is explicitly named.[50] Al-Mana has shown that panegyrics for great men between the pre-Islamic and the Abbasid periods often name mothers when extolling the *mamduh*'s lineage despite the proscriptions of the critics.[51] Arabic laments occasionally include the name of a deceased woman or girl, as in the following verse by the Andalusian poet Abu 'Amar Ibn al-Hamara over his wife: "O Zaynab, You have departed! On [animal] back the living rides your burden . . . ." (that is, I, your surviving husband, nearly ride the funerary bier that brings you into the grave).[52] Similarly, the Abbasid poet al-Sanawbari evokes the name of his daughter Layla in several laments over her.[53]

This article is not the place to treat fully the practices of evoking and concealing women's names in Arabic verse.[54] From the perspective of the Arabic literary critics and the practices of poets, it seems that socially superior men could evoke the names of socially inferior women, but that male subordinates were dissuaded from evoking the names of women of high rank. Suppressing names may have been a way of guaranteeing the greatest respect for the female deceased in a society that fiercely safeguarded women's reputations and dignity. The prescription to refrain from naming women might have been sufficient to prevent the Hebrew poets from doing so in their laments.

On the other hand, women's names might have been omitted from Hebrew laments for a far more pedestrian reason. The documents of the Cairo Geniza may provide a clue. Whereas men generally held biblical names with Arabic and Hebrew equivalents (Yusuf/Yosef, Ibrahim/Avraham, Sulayman/Shelomo, etc.), it was rare (at least in medieval Egypt) for women to hold biblical or Hebrew names at all. With great infrequency is a woman referred to as Sara or Maryam, and these names surface among Muslim women as well. Goitein suggests that this "startling deficiency would seem to demonstrate a chasm between the popular local subculture of the women and the worldwide Hebrew book culture of the men."[55] Extolling the preeminence of biblical Hebrew, the Hebrew poets of al-Andalus almost never made use of words without precedent in the Hebrew Bible. Thus authors may have been reluctant to transliterate foreign names for the *aesthetic* purpose of preserving the purity of the Hebrew text.[56] The lack of Hebrew names for women might be sufficient in explaining the absence of their names in a poetic corpus fixated on emulating a pure biblical style, though the issue of etiquette was a likely contributing factor.

In contrast with the Andalusian examples, Hebrew literature written in the wake of the Crusades in the Rhineland does include the names of women, as in the moving poem by Eliezer bar Judah of Worms (ca. 1165–1230), who saw his daughters Bellet and Hannah murdered before his eyes:

Let me tell the story of my eldest daughter Bellet: She was thirteen
years old, and as chaste as a bride. She had learnt all the prayers and
songs from her mother, who was modest and kind, sweet and wise.
The girl took after her beautiful mother and every night she would

make my bed and take off my shoes. She did her housework quickly, and always spoke the truth. She worshipped her Maker, she weaved and sewed and embroidered, she was filled with reverence and pure love for her Creator. For the sake of Heaven, she sat down by me to hear my teaching. And that is when she and her mother and her sister were killed, on the night of the twenty-second of Kislev . . . . [57]

The Hebrew literature of the Crusades often mentions women with biblical names such as Rachel (whether or not these were the real names of women is open to debate), but in this poem even the non-Hebrew name Bellet is simply transliterated into Hebrew characters.[58] The Hebrew authors of Christian Europe did not subscribe to the purist aesthetic of their counterparts in al-Andalus.

Women's Voices

It is well known that some women became famous for their ability to craft Arabic verse; poets such as al-Khansa' and Layla al-Akhyaliya were perhaps best recognized for their poetry of lamentation.[59] The only pre-Islamic verse preserved by the Jewish poet Sara al-Qurayziyya is a lament over her fallen kinsmen of Yathrib.[60] Medieval critics express great appreciation for the unbridled emotion of female lamentation; anguished outpourings of grief were apparently disfavored for male poets. In the chapter on lamentation in his *Kitab al-'umda*, Ibn Rashiq praises women's lamentation and writes that "women are the most grief-stricken of people when calamity [strikes] and the most severe in mourning upon death."[61] The vast corpus of Andalusian Hebrew verse possesses only one poem that might be attributable to a woman, and this is not a lament.[62] Nevertheless, Hebrew poets often found opportunities to include the voices of female speakers within their laments. The Arabic precedents of laments by women, the evidence for female mourners in the Talmud, and the everyday practices of female mourners may have created a poetic need for female voices. Whereas women's voices are neglected (or at least circumscribed) in other Hebrew genres, omitting them from laments might have seemed at odds with the actual practices of lamentation. Women speak in laments both as grief-stricken surviving relatives and as deceased speakers pronouncing their anguish from beyond the grave.[63]

The idea of a voice speaking from beyond the grave may derive from the practice of Arabic poets to compose short verses to be inscribed on tombstones in the voice of the deceased. For example, al-Sanawbari composed six couplets to be inscribed on each face of his daughter's memorial shrine. In the first three and in the last two, the father addresses the daughter, but in the fourth the daughter's voice speaks to her parents: "O my parents! May God protect you both! Do not abandon my grave but visit it! My face has lost its freshness; the grave has effaced it and wiped it out."[64] Some Hebrew samples bring together the voices of multiple poetic speakers more elaborately, engaging the living and the dead in a sort of dialogue.

In one poem by Judah Halevi, the first several stanzas are spoken in the voice of the bereaved mother who weeps bitterly over her lost daughter, who died before marrying. The refrain verse "for death separates you and me" evokes Ruth's promise to her mother-in-law Naomi (Ruth 1:17) to follow her loyally unto death:

Woe my daughter, have you forgotten where you live,
For your pallbearers have journeyed to Sheol?
I have nothing left of you[65] except your memory.
I cherish the dust of your gravestone.
Now it is prohibited to ask after your welfare. You are naught,
For death separates you and me.
Daughter taken from her mother's chamber
How can I live when she is formed from my soul.
I split rocks when I see her form.
How can the moon's glory fade?
There in Sheol I will see the day of her wedding,
How she will make a lump of earth her wedding canopy,
How a clod from her grave will be sweet to her.
It has become very bitter for me, my daughter, because you
    are absent,
For death separates you and me.
A rose picked before her time.
Her image is a perpetual symbol between my eyes.
How tears overflow like a river,
How the daughter of the Great Bear is gathered in the bosom of dust,
How the sun is enwrapped in wormwood,

The cords of Sheol are a turban upon her head!
Woe, my daughter, no one pleads for your revival,
For death separates you and me. . . . [66]

The final stanza also begins with the continuation of the mother's speech, quoting the famous words of Jephthah when he realizes his obligation to put his daughter to death to fulfill the vow he had made to God: "Woe, daughter! You have brought me low."[67] Immediately following this line, the daughter's voice speaks from the grave:

Alas for my mother for she gave birth to me![68]
Today you have truly rejected me,
For you raised me for Death's firstborn.[69]
When my turn came you cast me out.
You crowned me with a crown of dust,
And married me[70] under a wedding canopy of naught.
Truly against your will, for it was not your desire,
For death separates you and me.

Israel Levin has suggested that such poems with multiple speakers may represent an otherwise lost folk tradition wherein mothers offered laments over children.[71] Tova Rosen notes that poems wherein women's voices lament are among the rare examples of Hebrew poems in which women's speech is represented at all and agrees that they might derive from actual practices of mourning:

The song form, the simplified rhetoric, the folkloric elements, and
the intense emotionality of these poems written in the woman's voice
suggest that the poets who put them to writing may have followed an
oral female tradition of lamentations. The woman's voice here might
be representative of the women keeners who, in traditional societies,
are burdened with the task of expressing the grief of the community.
It is this social task which grants women the right of speech in
lamentation poems.[72]

The representation of women's speech in these poems may indeed be intended to imitate in Hebrew the vernacular dirges recited by bereaved women. If this is the case, then we have a poet's attempt to represent vernacular speech in a language that was not actually spoken.[73] Also, the employment of female speakers may have been appealing because of the written tradition of Arabic female laments. Given the social restrictions placed on men concerning the display of unbridled emotion, especially when it came to lamenting daughters, poets may have found it advantageous to create a female speaker within the poem for the expression of anguish.

A more rhetorically sophisticated poem featuring a female speaker from beyond the grave was written by the Talmudist of Toledo Meir ben Todros Halevi Abulafia (1170–1244). Although the author lived in Christian Iberia, he remained strongly informed by the Arabic literary tradition. After the death of his sister, Abulafia wrote the poem to console his father:[74]

> Clouds! Bear greetings of my grave to my father, not from my mouth
> but from my writing,
> Call him with the lips of what has befallen me, what befell my lips and
> speech.
> Go to him, lest my distress become his and he will grow sad for my
> misfortune.
> What benefit would there be in his grieving for my misfortune?
> Would my pain be alleviated by his pain?
> Would it be good that they tear his pericardium on my account? I
> sinned against my father,
> Who appointed my bed his wings of kindness and made my chariot
> the neck of his compassion.
> I rose like the sun out of its dwelling but behold, I set in a place of
> Ruin!
> Today Sheol has led me to its chambers and twisted my path from [my
> father's] chambers.
> Its stones have embraced my limbs for I am hewn from what they are
> hewn.
> The clods of earth from its rivers are sweet to me like honey and now
> I loathe my wine and my milk.
> I have chosen stores of dirt as my treasure so now I despise stores of
> gold.

My flame has gone out, extinguished like a wick; I have darkened, my
 flame does not shine.

With Time's mouth I send the greetings of my grave to those who
 inquire after me and encamp around me.

Desist from me! Why do you call me? Know that the hand of the Lord
 has struck me,

And Death, from the chamber of the Companion of my youth,[75] has
 suddenly preyed upon me like a lion.

He removed me from security and cast my burden on my grave.

The gravediggers covered my face with dust, which yesterday was
 treading for my feet!

I draw every man after me; my friends and foes come to me alike.

God appoints this house for all the living. Sinner and prophet will
 perish together

Until souls will return to their corpses. Then, when I return [to life], I
 will see their faces again.

He sets my pain in your hearts (within which my heart found care).

He causes a sea of tears to flow on your faces, and commands a
 weeping deluge.

May He water my grave with the dew of fresh growth[76] and command
 the deep of your tears: "Be dry!"[77]

The opening verses urge the father to accept his daughter's death and
praise him for the kindness he showed her while she lived. The daughter's
voice then describes the horrid conditions of existence in the grave and
concludes with the hopeful promise of reunification with loved ones with
the resurrection of the dead. The man's social role as a kind and compas-
sionate guardian of women, a role of which the father has been stripped
by Death's decree, is emphasized through the female speaker's voice:
"[Death] removed me from security." Again, this poem contains no section resembling a panegyric with a description of the daughter's qualities
or characteristics. Most of the poems that feature a voice speaking from
the grave treat women or children.[78] These laments focus on the emotional aspects of loss—the imagined tragic experience of the deceased
and the suffering of the survivors—rather than on the praiseworthy characteristics of the deceased. Because of the restrictions surrounding the
composition of panegyrics for these classes of people, poets may have

found it expedient to circumvent the need for panegyric by making the deceased the speaker within the poem.

Conclusion

Only recently has gender been considered a significant topic of inquiry for treating the Hebrew poetry of the Middle Ages; studies have generally focused on the poetry of desire, misogynistic literature, and the place of women and feminine imagery in aphoristic and philosophical poetry.[79] Laments over women are rare in the Hebrew corpus in that they treat actual women who lived and breathed, however anonymous these women might be to us. Despite their 'realness,' the character traits of these women are greatly obscured behind the conventional discursive practices of the Andalusian Hebrew poets; when poems do include panegyric sections, we sense the poets' acute awareness of Arabic poetry and criticism, which often set strict boundaries for female panegyric. More than these laments by male authors reflect the social reality of women in medieval Jewish society, they served to construct ideal female roles within that society. The poems are therefore most valuable in our attempt to read the values of life through the literature of death. Male authors employed women as speakers within poems to allow for an emotional register otherwise unavailable to them and also, in all likelihood, to represent in Hebrew writing a form of sanctioned women's vernacular speech in the public domain. It also seems that poets were most comfortable composing laments for women that circumvented panegyric. By saying as little about women as possible, the poets may have aimed to display proper etiquette, though this also yielded the unfortunate result of erasing these women's marks on history.

Notes

*   I wish to thank Alexander Elinson, Marlé Hammond, Dana Sajdi, Raymond Scheindlin, and Tova Rosen for their valuable comments on this article.

1   The most thorough treatment of the Hebrew poetry of Lamentation in the context of Arabic literature is Israel Levin, *The Lamentation over the Dead: A Comparative Study of a Genre in Spanish-Hebrew and Arabic Poetry* (Tel Aviv: University of Tel Aviv, 1973) [Hebrew]. See also Varda Padva, "The Voice of the Dead in Elegy," *Jerusalem Studies in Hebrew Literature* 10 (1988): 629–81 [Hebrew]. On Arabic lamentation poetry *(ritha')* in al-Andalus, see the discussions by Ihsan Abbas, *Tarikh al-shi'r al-andalusi: 'asr al-tawa'if wa-l-murabitin* (Amman: Dar El Shorouk, 1997), 95–101; Shawqi Dayf, *Tarikh al-adab al-'arabi: 'asr al-duwal wa-l-imarat: al-Andalus* (Cairo: Dar al-Ma'arif, 1994), 323–38.

2   The subject is treated briefly in Levin, *The Lamentation over the Dead*, 88–94.

3   Jeremiah 9:16–17, 19:3; Joel 1:8; Lamentations 2:18–19.

4   See E. Feldman, "The Rabbinic Lament," *Jewish Quarterly Review* 63 (1972–73): 51–75.

5   The practice seems more limited during the Talmudic period, since the rabbinic discussions connected with this Mishnah delineate between cases where the employment of female mourners is or is not customary for the woman's family.

6   Mishneh Torah, Women: Laws of Matrimony, 14:23. See also Maimonides's gloss to Mishnah Ketubbot 4:4, where he declares that the law conforms to the opinion of Rabbi Judah.

7   S.D. Goitein, *A Mediterranean Society: The Jewish Communities of the Arab World as Portrayed in the Documents of the Cairo Geniza*, 6 vols. (Berkeley: University of California Press, 1967–93), 5:163.

8   For example, Moses Ibn Ezra, *Secular Poetry*, ed. Heinrich Brody (Berlin: Schocken Press, 1935), 51, lines 17–19 [Hebrew].

9   Goitein, *A Mediterranean Society*, 5:164. Nathan responded (on the other side of the folio) that he was too grief-stricken to compose the poem at the moment but that he would attend to the matter later that night.

10   Jefim Schirmann, "Poets Contemporary with Moses Ibn Ezra and Judah Halevi," *Studies of the Research Institute for Hebrew Poetry* 6 (1945): 291–96 [Hebrew]. It was not uncommon for Arabic poets to compose series of laments over an individual; see Alan Jones, ed., *Early Arabic Poetry*, vol. 1: *Marathi and Su'luk Poems*, Oxford Oriental Institute Monographs, No. 14 (Reading: Ithaca Press, 1992), 26.

11   Samuel Ha-Nagid, *Diwan Samuel the Nagid*, ed. Dov Jarden (Jerusalem: Hebrew Union College Press, 1966), 231–36 [Hebrew]; Solomon Ibn Gabirol, *The Secular Poetry of Solomon Ibn Gabirol*, ed. Dov Jarden (Jerusalem: Dov Jarden, 1975), 301–302 [Hebrew] is addressed to the "Children of Exile." Ibn Gabirol wrote several laments over his patron Yequtiel, some of which have a very public feel (for example, his *Secular Poetry*, 290–300).

12   In an epistle to his patron Hasdai Ibn Shaprut, Menahem Ben Saruq mentions laments that he had composed about the patron's mother and father. Only

regarding the laments for the father did the author add "that all Israel lamented each day of mourning." See Jefim Schirmann, *The Hebrew Poetry of Spain and Provence*, 2 vols. (Jerusalem and Tel Aviv: Bialik Institute and Dvir Publishing, 1954), 1:23–24, lines 281–92 [Hebrew].

13   Abu ʻAli al-Hasan Ibn Rashiq al-Qayrawani, *al-ʻUmda fi mahasin al-shiʻr wa-adabihi wa-naqdihi,* ed. Muhammad Muhyi al-Din ʻAbd al-Hamid, 2 vols. (Cairo: Matbaʻat Hijazi, 1934), 2:139.

14   On the subject of Jewish knowledge of works of Arabic literary criticism, see Joseph Danah, *Poetics in* Kitab al-muhadara wa-l-mudhakara *by Moses Ibn Ezra, and Its Sources in Arabic Books of Poetry and Criticism* (Tel Aviv: University of Tel Aviv, 1977) [Hebrew].

15   Ibn Rashiq, *al-ʻUmda,* 2:146–47. Discussed also in Levin, *The Lamentation over the Dead,* 88.

16   Suaad al-Mana, "Al-shiʻr wa-l-naqd wa-l-marʼa: dirasat li-simat al-marʼa al-maʻnawiya fi-l-shiʻr al-ʻarabi al-qadim wa fi-l-tanzirat al-naqdiya," *Qiraʼat turathiya* 13 (1994): 317–38.

17   Ibid., 319. The quotation is taken from a section on "panegyric for women" *(madih al-nisaʼ)* in al-Husri's *Zahr al-adab wa thamr al-albab,* vol. 2 (Cairo: Dar al-Khaya al-Kutub al-ʻArabiya, 1953), 348–49. It does not refer specifically to laments.

18   On the Andalusian examples, see ʻAbbas, *Tarikh al-shiʻr al-andalusi,* 95–101. Al-Mutanabbi was critiqued by literary critics for mentioning the beauty of Sayf al-Dawla's mother, especially since she died in old age; see Ibn Rashiq, *al-ʻUmda,* 2:147: "What is the matter with him that he describes the beauty of this old woman?"

19   See Tova Rosen, *Unveiling Eve: Reading Gender in Medieval Hebrew Literature* (Philadelphia: University of Pennsylvania Press, 2003), 30–63; Raymond Scheindlin, *Wine, Women, and Death: Medieval Hebrew Poems on the Good Life* (Philadelphia: Jewish Publication Society, 1986), 77–134.

20   Ibn Ezra, *Secular Poetry,* 160, lines 28–36. The Arabic superscription of the poem reads *wa-lahu ila abi al-Hasan Ibn Matar ʻinda ʼibtinaʼihi fa-qala* (by him to Abu al-Hasan Ben Matar on the occasion of the consummation of his wedding, he said).

21   See also Tova Rosen, *Unveiling Eve,* 9.

22   This is not to say that we learn true personal characteristics in panegyrics for men; all panegyric poetry in this period is stylized and conventional.

23   For example, Judah Halevi, *Diwan des Abu al-Hasan Jehuda ha-Levi,* ed. Heinrich Brody, 4 vols. (Berlin: Mekize Nirdamim, 1894–1930), 2:60, line 22, where a bride is praised for her beauty and intelligence. The *diwan* is hereafter referred to as *Diwan Judah Halevi.*

24   Proverbs 31:26; 8:34.

25   Ibn Ezra, *Secular Poetry,* 50–51, lines 8–17. According to the Arabic superscription to the poem, it was dedicated to Abu al-Faraj Yoshiya ben Bazzaz concerning the death of his sister.

26   Elkan Nathan Adler collection, Jewish Theological Seminary of America, 2935, f.17. Goitein discusses this line as evidence for the (rare) education of girls, *A Mediterranean Society,* 2:184.

27 Ibn Ezra, *Secular Poetry,* 140, lines 8–9.

28 Proverbs 25:23.

29 For al-Mutanabbi's famous lament over the mother of Sayf al-Dawla, see al-Mutanabbi, *Poems of al-Mutanabbi,* trans. and ed. A. J. Arberry (Cambridge: Cambridge University Press, 1967), 57–63, esp. lines 21 and 26.

30 Rosen, *Unveiling Eve,* 7–18; 103–23.

31 See the quote of Ibn Rashiq above. On the Arabic tradition of lamenting children, see 'Abd al-Mu'in al-Malluhi, *Marathi al-aba' wa-l-umahhat li-l-banin wa-l-banat* (Beirut: Dar al-Kunuz al-Adabiya, 1996).

32 Ha-Nagid, *Diwan Samuel the Nagid,* 50.

33 Text in Abu 'Amr Ahmad Ibn Muhammad 'Abd Rabihi al-Andalusi, *Kitab al-'Iqd al-Farid,* ed. Ahmad Amin, Ahmad al-Zayn, and Ibrahim al-Ibyari, vol. 3. (Cairo: Matba'at Lajnat al-Ta'lif wa-al-Tarjamah wa-al-Nashr, 1953), 283, line 6. The poem is the only lament over a daughter included in the wide sample of laments in *al-'Iqd al-Farid,* 282–84. See also Levin, *The Lamentation over the Dead,* 89.

34 A sign of mourning in Job 16:15.

35 Cf. Proverbs 27:1.

36 *Diwan Judah Halevi,* 2:149, lines 4–11.

37 The idea of marrying a daughter in the grave or to the grave is found in Arabic examples from al-Andalus; see, for example, the short poem by Ibn Sara al-Andalusi in al-Malluhi, *Marathi al-aba' wa-l-umahhat,* 243, line 3: "Wrongfully we have married her to the tomb."

38 Ibid., 2:136, lines 7–15. This poem is discussed further below.

39 Used to build the ark in the tabernacle (Deuteronomy 10:3, etc.)

40 Judah al-Harizi, *Sefer Tahkemoni,* ed. Y. Toporovsky (Tel Aviv: Mosad HaRav Kook, 1952), 220–22.

41 On veiling practices among Jewish women in the Middle Ages, see Yedida Stillman, "'Cover Her Face': Jewish Women and Veiling in Islamic Civilization," in *Israel and Ishmael: Studies in Muslim-Jewish Relations*, ed. Tudor Parfitt (New York: St. Martin's Press, 2000), 13–31. On the veil in medieval Hebrew rhymed prose narratives, see Rosen, *Unveiling Eve,* 149–67.

42 Consider the single verse by an unknown Arabic poet who lost five sons and gained five daughters: "Five, because of whom my face was the East, are taken away by five, because of whom my face is scorched black." Arabic text in al-Malluhi, *Marathi al-aba' wa-l-ummahat,* 161.

43 By 'name' I mean 'given name,' although the issues discussed also have relevance for the use of *kunyas*, which are somewhat more common in the Arabic corpus; *kunyas* are not used in the Hebrew texts.

44 Literally 'late' or 'on the watch.'

45 *Diwan Judah Halevi,* 2:87, lines 1–6.

46 See the poem in al-Mutanabbi, *Poems of al-Mutanabbi,* 57–63. Of related significance is the verse by the Andalusian Jewish poet Qasmuna bat Isma'il in which the poet laments her own virginity while refraining from calling herself by name: "I see a garden, ripe for the picking, who will extend a hand a pluck it? /

Alas, youth passes by, wasted, and the one *I dare not name* remains alone" (English trans. M. J. Viguera). The Arabic verse can be found in A. al-Maqqari, *Nafh al-tib min ghusn al-Andalus al-ratib,* ed. Ihsan 'Abbas, vol. 3 (Beirut: Dar al-Sadir, 1968), 530. On Qasmuna in general, see J. A. Bellamy, "Qasmuna the Poetess: Who Was She?" *Journal of the American Oriental Society* 103 (1983): 423–24; María Ángeles Gallego, "Approaches to the Study of Muslim and Jewish Women in Medieval Iberian Peninsula: The Poetess Qasmuna bat Isma'il," *Miscelánea de estudios Árabes y Hebraicos: Sección Hebreo* 48 (1999): 63–75.

47 *Mu'abbanatan,* 'eulogized.'

48 *Diwan al-Mutanabbi,* ed. Nasif al-Yaziji (Beirut: Dar al-Sader, 1964), 280–81, lines 1–2.

49 Al-Mas'udi, *Muruj al-dhahab wa-ma'adin al-jawhar* (*Les prairies d'or*), ed. C. Barbier de Meynard, vol. 6 (Paris: Imprimerie impériale, 1861), 353–54.

50 Ibn Rashiq, *al-'Umda,* 2: 349. See also the poem by the Andalusian Sara al-Halabiya over Safiya bint Muhammad al-'Azafi in which the *mamduha*'s name is suggested in the poem's opening stanza and is mentioned explicitly later on. See Ahmad Ibn al-Qadi, *Jadhwat al-iqtibas fi dhikr man halla min al-a'lam madinat fas* (Rabat: Dar al-Mansur, 1973), 527, verses 1, 6; Teresa Garulo, "Una poetisa oriental en al-Andalus: Sara al-Halabiyya," *Al-Qantara* 6 (1985): 168–69; Beatrice Gruendler, "Lightning and Memory in Poetic Fragments from the Muslim West: Hafsah Bint al-Hajj (d. 1191) and Sara al-Halabiyyah (d.c. 1300)," in A. Neuwirth and A. Pflitsch, eds., *Crisis and Memory: Dimensions of Their Relationship in Islam and Adjacent Cultures* (Würzburg: Ergon Verlag in Kommission, 2001), 435–52.

51 Al-Mana, "Al-shi'r wa-l-naqd wa-l-mara'a," 324–26.

52 Arabic text in Dayf, *Tarikh al-adab al-'arabi: 'asr al-duwal wa-l-imarat al-andalus,* 326: *a zaynabu inna za'anti fa-inna zahran / aqallaki sawfa yarkabuhu al-muqimu.* None of the Hebrew poets wrote laments over their own wives.

53 Ahmad Ibn Muhammad al-Sanawbari, *Diwan al-Sanawbari,* ed. Ihsan 'Abbas (Beirut: Dar al-Thaqafa, 1970), 100, 104, 264. I wish to thank Ghada H. Qaddumi for directing me to this poet. The naming of sons in Arabic poems is much more common; see examples in al-Malluhi, *Marathi al-aba' wa-l-ummahat,* 87, 128, and elsewhere.

54 Although she does not discuss the discursive practices of concealing names, see the useful chapter on women's names in al-Andalus by Manuela Marín, *Mujeres en al-Ándalus,* Estudios onomástico-biográficos de al-Ándalus, 11 (Madrid: Consejo Superior de Investigaciones Científicas, 2000), 33–78.

55 Goitein, *A Mediterranean Society,* 3:315. Also, the evidence from Christian Toledo after the thirteenth century suggests that women did not have Hebrew names; see Nina Melechen, "Calling Names: the Identification of Jews in Christian Documents from Medieval Toledo," in *On the Social Origin of Medieval Institutions: Essays in Honor of Joseph F. O'Callaghan,* ed. Donald Kagay and Theresa M. Vann (Leiden: E. J. Brill, 1988), 21–34.

56 Similarly, although we find biblical place-names mentioned frequently in the corpus, we seldom find names of cities transliterated into Hebrew. City names

are sometimes rendered into biblical language such as *beit rimon* (House of Pomegranate) for Granada. On the ideal of biblical Hebrew in Andalusian Hebrew poetry, see Ross Brann, *The Compunctious Poet: Cultural Ambiguity and Hebrew Poetry in Muslim Spain* (Baltimore: The Johns Hopkins University Press, 1991), 23–58.

57   Trans. T. Carmi, *The Penguin Book of Hebrew Verse* (New York: Penguin, 1981), 387–88.

58   Further on the Hebrew literature of the Crusades, see Susan Einbeinder, *Beautiful Death: Jewish Poetry and Martyrdom in Medieval France* (Princeton: Princeton University Press, 2002).

59   See, for example, A. F. L. Beeston, ed., *Arabic Literature to the End of the Umayyad Period* (Cambridge: Cambridge University Press, 1983), 85–89.

60   For her verse and the circumstances surrounding it, see Abu al-Faraj al-Isbahani, *Kitab al-aghani*, ed. Ibrahim al-Ibyari (Cairo: Dar al-Sha'b, 1974), 8808–09.

61   Ibn Rashiq, *al-'Umda*, 2:145.

62   On the sole poem attributed to a female author, see Rosen, *Unveiling Eve*, 1.

63   On the theme of the dead speaking from the grave, see Padva, "The Voice of the Dead in Elegy." Padva argues that the origins of the theme are to be found in the Hebrew poetry of the Islamic East, adducing several examples from Geniza manuscripts, and that Jews may have been influenced by Greek laments and epitaphs.

64   Al-Sanawbari, *Diwan al-Sanawbari*, 514.

65   Literally, 'I have no portion of you.'

66   *Diwan Judah Halevi*, 2:136.

67   Judges 11:34. Jephthah had tragically vowed to God to kill "whatever comes out the door of my house" for being granted victory in battle against the Ammonites; upon returning home, his nameless daughter came out to greet him and Jephthah uttered: "Woe, daughter, for you have brought me low." It is most interesting that the female speaker quotes a male character.

68   Cf. Jeremiah 15:10.

69   Cf. Job 18:13.

70   Literally, 'caused me to dwell,' used in the sense of marriage in Ezra 10:2 and elsewhere.

71   Levin, *The Lamentation over the Dead*, 216–25. See there also the discussion of a similar poem by Halevi.

72   Rosen, *Unveiling Eve*, 16–17.

73   On this phenomenon in modern Hebrew literature, see Itamar Even-Zohar, "Authentic Language and Authentic Reported Speech: Hebrew vs. Yiddish," *Poetics Today* 11, no. 1 (1990): 155–63.

74   Hebrew text in Schirmann, *Hebrew Poetry*, 2:272–73. Another example by the same poet may be found in Hayyim Brody, "Poems and Letters by Rabbi Meir Halevi Abulafia," *Studies of the Research Institute for Hebrew Poetry* 2 (1936): 44–46 [Hebrew]; discussed in Padva, "The Voice of the Dead in Elegy," 640.

75   Jeremiah 3:4, referring now to her husband.

76　Cf. Isaiah 26:19 where the context is resurrection: "O, let your dead revive! Let corpses arise! Awake and shout for joy, You who dwell in the dust! For your dew is like the dew on fresh growth. You make the land of the shades come to life."

77　Cf. Isaiah 44:27: "I, who said to the deep, 'Be dry;' I will dry up your floods."

78　One example of a male voice speaking from the grave derives from a poem dedicated to a woman on the death of her husband. The poem begins with a description of the suffering of the bereaved widow and her orphaned children. The children beg their father to remember them and he responds from the grave: "Go, turn back, my daughters / For my lips have become too heavy to speak / A voice from my fathers' calls me / To go to them, to go to my grave. / What can I do when the taskmasters surround me / And the earth calls me to lie with her?" *Diwan Judah Halevi*, 2:148. The poem contains no panegyric.

79　Rosen, *Unveiling Eve*.

7

Qasida, Marthiya, and Différance[1]

Marlé Hammond

Introduction

The *qasida* and the *marthiya* both originate from the depths of Arabic literary pre-history—on this most scholars would concur. They would also agree that, at some point in their evolution, they came to resemble each other in many important respects. Thematically, they both celebrate the exploits of tribal heroes, record individual contributions to communal history, and reflect an ethos of chivalry. They also exhibit structural similarities: Pellat concedes that the *marthiya* is, in effect, a bipartite *qasida* in which an encomium for the deceased is preceded by what he describes as a replacement for the *nasib*, namely an exhortation of the eyes to cry.[2] In discussions of the *qasida*'s origins, scholars tend to focus on its modular structure and how the different sections and the transitions between them come together over time to form a poetic model.[3] In other words, they focus on the development of its polythematic nature. Discussions of the *marthiya*'s origins, on the other hand, usually refer, either straightforwardly or obliquely, to a kind of primordial female lament *(niyaha)* expressive of feminine sentimentality.[4] In those instances when scholars acknowledge the modular potential of the *marthiya*, they often do so by disassociating the complex structural form of the polythematic *marthiya* with the simpler female-authored elegiac *qit'a*. Hence al-Hufi generalizes that women's elegies, unlike men's,

143

are monothematic since, according to him, they rarely contain *ḥikma* and never feature an amatory prelude.[5] In a similar vein, Bellamy distinguishes between the 'short' *marthiya*s, which he associates with women and believes to be derived from the *niyaḥa*,[6] and the 'long' *marthiya*s, which he states are predominantly male-authored and the existence of which he attributes to "the difficulty male poets had in divorcing themselves from the tripartite *qasida*."[7]

Despite their similarities, the 'polythematic' ode is viewed, either explicitly or by default, as male territory, while the *marthiya* is understood to be a ritually sanctioned outlet for feminine sentimentality. Men express; women emote. Scholars and historians of Arabic poetry have attributed this poetic division of labor, or women's 'confinement' to the genre of elegy, either to a kind of psychological natural law (that is, women weep) or to socio-cultural factors that circumscribed women's expression (that is, women composed laments because it was historically plausible for them to do so while it was implausible for them to compose *ghazal*, for example). While some of these arguments, especially those of the second category, are enlightening and convincing, they tend to emphasize and often exaggerate the societal limitations placed on women's poetic expression.[8] They further the view that women composed what they could or what they were allowed. Here, through my analysis of women's exploitation of poetic codes, I hope to demonstrate that women composed not *what they could*, but rather *what they would,* in other words what they desired to write. That they excelled in the *marthiya*, in particular, is a result of a convergence of factors, not the least of which is that the form/genre, as it coalesced in the late Jahiliyya and early Islam, is symbolically driven by female sexuality in much the same way as the *qasida* exhibits a form of masculine carnality. Incest taboos often prevent us from reading women's *marathi* erotically, since many of them are composed about the poets' blood relatives rather than husbands or lovers, but this does not preclude sexual interpretations, if we understand sexuality as an economy of desire which is not necessarily carnal. Such an economy could be constructed around the eye and its tears; after all, the trope of the beloved's eye, and particularly her (or his) glance—the return gaze, as a source of sexual seduction in Arabic love poetry is common enough to confirm the sexualization of this particular organ.[9] The eye of the nostalgic poet, be it in the context of the *marthiya* or in the context of the amatory prelude of the polythematic ode, does not incite desire but rather contains it: building it up through its gaze, over the abandoned campsite or over the grave, and releasing it through tears.

The Qasida

The *qasida* paradigm is well known and the subject of many important studies.[10] The manifestation of that paradigm which concerns us here, both because it is contemporaneous with the golden age of women's *marathi* and because in many ways it has been the standard against which most other valued paradigms in the classical Arabic tradition are held, is that of the so-called polythematic or tripartite (as opposed to 'bipartite') ode. Although it is true that this categorization is by and large a conceit of modern scholarship, and that in classical Arabic poetics the term *qasida* would be applied to any poem in an acceptable meter and of a certain length, it represents an apt encapsulation of a literary paradigm that had circulated throughout Arabic-speaking lands since pre-Islamic times. It describes a composite poem of approximately thirty to one hundred lines that may be divided into a sequence of sections dominated by different themes or motifs. It frequently opens with a *nasib*, or what is often translated as an erotic or nostalgic prelude. Typically, in this section, the male poet bemoans the loss of a female beloved, who has departed from a campsite upon whose 'traces' the poet now gazes. From the *nasib*, the poet moves on to describe a journey, usually astride a *naqa* or she-camel; this is called the *rahil*. At journey's end the poet engages in what is presumably his ultimate purpose, which tends to be either *fakhr* (boasting) or *madh* (panegyric), where the poet celebrates the virtues of either his tribe or his leader. Hence the terms 'polythematic' and 'tripartite' reflect this triad of *nasib–rahil–fakhr/madh*. Although certain aspects of the *qasida* paradigm draw upon or allude to female sexuality, the dominant current in its typical enactment is overwhelmingly 'male.' A male poet, or poetic persona, if you will, weeps in a grammatically masculine voice, addressing other (often two) presumably masculine presences. At the outset, he contemplates the departure of a female other and mourns her recession into his past. As consolation, he 'mounts' a female camel and lauds its speed, grace, endurance, and trustiness as it leads him toward a loftier, if less romantic, purpose of glorifying in oneself, one's people, or one's leader. It is this transition away from a female beloved and the transfer of desire from her toward a riding beast that conveys the poet toward a primarily masculine homo-social environment that I believe marks it as a masculine paradigm with carnal dimensions.[11] Few if any 'polythematic' *qasida*s fit this model to a tee, but many adhere to its general blueprint and many more seem to transgress its boundaries in a rather deliberate fashion, thereby suggesting that they are maintaining a kind of healthy dialogue with, and respectful homage to, the very paradigm they subvert.

The Marthiya

Compared to the *qasida*, the *marthiya* has not garnered as much scholarly criticism and debate as its complexity and historical literary significance merit.[12] Nevertheless, certain points of comparison and contrast between the two paradigms have been noticed by scholars, in particular the many parallels between the poems' introductory sections. Mayy Khulayyif describes these similarities thus:

> The opening of the woman poet's ritha' frequently begs comparison with the openings of the panegyrists' qasidas; for in the latter case there is talk of ruins whose source is woman, and there is the poet, weeping, and memories of a place, and in the former there is elegiac talk in which the poet calls on her tears to assist her. It is an anxious, mournful talk, at whose outset appears the weeping "I" as well as the elegiac subject "you," and, in many poems, the name of the elegized [marthi] appears in the opening line. And, instead of addressing companions, the [f.] poet addresses the eye or eyes, in either the singular or dual, in the form of a command beseeching one or both of them to cry.[13]

Here, in the *marthiya*, a woman speaks about her grief at the loss of a beloved, usually a father, brother, or son, who has departed—this time into the next world rather than on to the next campsite. The gender of the beloved is usually male: hence the sexual polarization between poet and beloved carries over from the *qasida* to the *marthiya*. Likewise, the opening of the *marthiya* contains many parallels with the *nasib*. Instead of addressing outward companions, the poet often looks inward, bidding her eyes (singular or dual) to cry. Moreover, the poet sometimes stands over the deceased's grave *(qabr)*—his new resting place, which in some sense substitutes for the abandoned dwelling (*dar* or *manzil*) of the *nasib*. It is apparently at the end of the *nasib* where the (thus far acknowledged) symbolic and thematic parallels between the *marthiya* and the *qasida* end. While some people highlight the existence of what might be termed 'sections' of the *marthiya*, such as the announcement of the beloved's death, a description of the death scene, and a call for vengeance, no generalized pattern has been perceived; hence the modularity of the *marthiya*—its polythematic-ness—has been, for the most part, ignored.[14] Many read the *marthiya*, and the woman's *marthiya* in particular, as a binary structure with a sentimental opening section followed by a texturally monotonous enumeration of the deceased's praiseworthy characteristics, which I will label for the sake of convenience the *ta'bin*. What the *marthiya*—at least the woman's *marthiya*—most definitively lacks is the *rahil*.[15] However, one may observe that the *ta'bin* section in many ways corresponds to the *rahil* of the tripartite ode: like the *rahil*, the *ta'bin* often reads as a journey, albeit a metaphorical and metaphysical one. Also, much like the *rahil*'s role in the *qasida*, the *ta'bin* serves as a kind of spatial and temporal axis for the entire *marthiya*. Furthermore, on a formal level, the *ta'bin* section is often rife with epithets, not only for the deceased but also for animals, a phenomenon that tends to characterize the *rahil* of the *qasida*.[16] Naturally, the epithets for the elegized in the *ta'bin* have many characteristics that distinguish them from the animal epithets of the *rahil*; perhaps the most important of these is the prevalence in the former context of denotants formed on active participle and intensive adjective patterns.

In order to examine the modularity of the woman's *marthiya*, to substantiate the alleged parallels between the *rahil* and the *ta'bin*, and to unravel the complex web of differences between the *qasida* and the *marthiya*, I have selected three sample elegies for analysis. They were, in a sense, 'cherry-picked,' in that they were chosen for their artistry, their length, their relatively complex thematic structures, and their celebrated reception in the canon. One should not, however, take this to mean that they are exceptional or even unsual. The first, Su'da bt. al-Shamardal's elegy for her brother As'ad appears in the *Asma'iyat*, and it therefore has a unique status at the heart of the Arabic poetic canon. The other poems, the *ra'iya* by al-Khansa' for her brother, Sakhr, and the *ra'iya* by Layla al-Akhyaliya's for her lover, Tawba, are 'canonical' by virtue of their composers' fame and reputations.

The poems should not necessarily be considered 'representative' of the elegiac genre in the typical sense. Rather, each poem, in the paradigmatic considerations that inform its content, structure, and meaning, demonstrates that the *marthiya* offered women the means to express poetic sentiment and display poetic virtuosity in numerous and complex ways. Through the *marthiya*, women exploited a poetic code that differed from that of men only insofar as individual poets situated themselves, as gendered beings and personas, within the overall framework of a poetic system in which gender plays an important role—grammatically, symbolically, and metaphorically. Since the womanliness or manliness of the author is not a chromosomally determined phenomenon, I like to perceive the gender of the author as a stance: a woman may write as a man and a man may write as a woman. But how do we as readers interpret and weigh the signs of the author's sexuality? Stance implies a position that an author adopts which is defined both by his or her history and background (either real or imaginary) and by a project proposal of aims and intentions (to be accomplished or foiled). 'Abd al-Majid Juhfa expresses a similar view when he implies that sex figures into authorship as part of a *huwiya mawqifiya* or 'positional identity' formed by and defined against the complex power relationships that inform literary discourse. For him, women's writing differs from men's not through its nature *(tabi'a)* but rather through its consequence *(natija)*.[17] For our purposes here, however, Juhfa's theoretical framework is flawed at its very base: he sees all writing, including women's writing, as inherently masculine, which leads him to conclude, for example, that when women speak Arabic in the first person (singular or plural), they do so via a masculine pronoun/consciousness *(damir)*.[18] I could not disagree more. For me the writer's baseline is either neuter or, if you will, trans-gendered. Every writer, male or female, assumes his or her own particular sexual posture based upon his or her exploitation of countless tropes, both sexed and unsexed, at his or her disposal. Furthermore, the writer must work to maintain that authorial sexual persona. In other words, the stance cannot be maintained or it results in stagnation; the author must continuously reposition himself or herself, reassess what has been written and regroup for the text ahead. At every step in the process, there are choices to be made and all of these choices potentially affect the sexual content of the text as well as the perceived sexuality of the writer. In sum, the female writer *differs* from the male writer *in conse-quence* in that, as a result of a number of external factors imposed upon her, be they socio-cultural or biological, she tends to favor certain topics over others; she *defers* from the male writer *in essence* in that she willfully exploits the same referential codes of meaning, albeit to different effect. The 'difference' between men's and women's writing, here, that is to say between the woman's *marthiya* and the man's *qasida*, involves points of contrast between them. 'Deferral,' as I conceive it, would, on the other hand, relate to points of similarity that the two forms share but that are expressed on dissimilar spatial or temporal planes.

A Note on the Man's *Marthiya*

Men also composed elegies for the dead, from pre-Islamic times onward. Their contributions to the genre, especially the lengthier and more cel-ebrated specimens, have been recognized as polythematic and are often read as tripartite *qasida*s composed in the *gharad* of *ritha'*. To the extent that men's long *marathi*, as Bellamy asserts, resemble *qasida*s, they would tend to fall under that rubric in the context of this chapter. There are, however, some poignant images that are developed in women's *marathi* that have interesting parallels in men's *marathi*, and in some cases I draw attention to those parallels in my textual analyses below, especially when these images relate to human sexuality. But while it is important to acknowledge the ways in which the man's elegy resembles both the man's *qasida* and the woman's elegy, it is equally incumbent upon us to recog-nize that there are other ways in which the man's elegy sets itself apart from each of those categories. There are three *topoi*, in particular, that appear to be the exclusive domain of men's *ritha'*. These narrative themes are listed by al-Khatib, under the heading "Pre-Islamic Man's Special Grief," who points out that male poets refer to the following activities to express their emotions: 1) the slaughtering of a she-camel over the grave of the elegized; 2) the harnessing of a live she-camel to the grave, where the animal, deprived of food and water, is left to die; and 3) the pour-ing of wine over the grave.[19] It is curious and, I believe, revealing, that two out of three of the themes treated by male as opposed to female ele-gists involve the she-camel or *naqa*, or in other words, the very animal that dominates the *rahil* of the tripartite ode and thus helps to define the form itself.

Différance

What is written as différance, then, will be the playing movement
that "produces"—by means of something that is not simply an
activity—these differences, these effects of difference.[20]

The question may arise in the minds of some readers as to what the
study of these two pre-Islamic Arabic poetic forms and their structural and symbolic similarities and dissimilarities has to do with Jacques
Derrida,[21] a 'Western' deconstructionist, and his 'non-concept' of *différance*, to which the title of this chapter so boldly alludes? The term
différance, a pun based on the French verb *différer*, connotes both deferral
and difference. Derrida coined it in an attempt to broaden the scope of
Saussurian theory of language as a system of meaning operating on principles of differentiation.[22] By adding notions of deferral and delay to that
of differentiation, Derrida destabilizes the relationships between sign,
signifier, and signified such that they actively produce differences in the
process of meaning creation. While *différance* applies first and foremost
to linguistics, a fact to which its very orthography attests,[23] it describes
an active production of differences in any semiotic system. Derrida himself finds versions of *différance* operating under other names in the works
of his philosophical forerunners, such as Nietzsche, Heidegger, and
Freud.[24] Derrida may have coined the term, but the idea it conveys seems
almost universal.

In the context of this chapter, and of classical Arabic poetics more
generally, this notion enables us to open up texts and vastly improve
our understanding of the poetry we study on two fronts. First, since by
its dictates it precludes the possibility of closed or fixed sign systems, it
helps to debunk the notion that Arabic poetry is a craft styled upon hackneyed conventions, endlessly reconfigured. Second, it could loosen the
grip of philology on our textual interpretations. If we acknowledge the
contingency of meaning in each semantic unit—its spatial and temporal
boundlessness—then we will be forced to rely less on the precise definitions of words and their meanings within certain grammatical phrases and
focus instead on the imprecision of meaning and the 'ungrammaticality'[25]
of poetics.

On the level of gender, which clearly has bearing on the matter at
hand, that is the *marthiya* and the nature of its relationship to the *qasida*,

thinking about apparent discrepancy as a kind of 'sexual *différance*' has certain advantages. First, one cannot think about sexual *différance* as sexual *difference*, since the former refers to an action rather than an accident. Binary oppositions such as x/y, male/female and he/she, which have become analytically barren and stultifying, are cast aside. Second, since *différance* implies a common activity or force governing apparent disparities or polarities, it reminds us that manifestations of gender difference are born from the same system of meanings driven by differentiation and deferral. We are not speaking of a masculine poetics and a feminine poetics but rather of a unified poetics whose signifiers exploit gender as one line of difference-production, hence meaning-production. The *marthiya* defers from the *qasida,* and the *qasida* defers from the *marthiya*. It is the point from or to which a particular poet defers meaning, either consciously or unconsciously, which I call 'stance,' and it is here that historical specificity enters the equation and that social, cultural, political, and religious constructs of gender meet grammatical and poetic ones to express a point of view associated with either man or woman.

Another advantage of *différance* is that, through its connotations of deferral and differentiation, it carries within it both temporal and spatial dimensions. Space and time, or spacing *(espacement)* and temporization, are key components of the non-concept, and together they help to tease out the differences between the *qasida* and the *marthiya*.[26] Their thematic delineation depends in large measure not only on the prescriptions of genre and form but also on the stance and postural sexuality of the poet-persona. The poet opens his or her poem at a specific point of time at a specific point in space,[27] and from there the narrative element of the poem moves forward, backward, aside, and in and out of each dimension, in ways that have some bearing on gender.

The Sample Poems

1. *'Ayniya: Amin al-hawadithi wa-l-manuni urawwa'u?*

The following poem is attributed to one Su'da bt. al-Shamardal[28] and is said to be an elegy for her brother, As'ad, who is named in the poem. Her dates, as well as that of the poem, are unknown, but she probably lived during the late Jahiliyya or early Islam.[29] Little is clear about the circumstances of her brother's death, in part because, perhaps unusually for a poem of its length, it contains only one place name (al-Risaf) and few personal ones. The reference to the deceased in verse 12 as Ibn Majda'a would suggest that he and the poet were half-siblings with the same mother, but some have rendered her name as Bint Majda'a, so this, too, is unclear. All we can presume is that the deceased was a warrior struck down in battle, as were the elegized in the other two poems under discussion. This is the case for the majority of extant *marathi*, be they female- or male-authored, from pre- and early Islamic times.

'Ayniya[30]

١	أمن الحوادث والمنون أروع	وأبيت ليلي كله لا أهجع
٢	وأبيت مخلية أبكي أسعدا	ولمثله تبكي العيون وتهمع
٣	وتبين العين الطليحة أنها	تبكي من الجزع الدخيل وتدمع
٤	ولقد بدا لي قبل فيما قد مضى	وعلمت ذاك لو أن علما ينفع
٥	أن الحوادث والمنون كليهما	لا يعتبان ولو بكى من يجزع
٦	ولقد علمت بأن كل مؤخر	يوما سبيل الأولين سيتبع
٧	ولقد علمت لو أن علما نافع	أن كل حي ذاهب فمودع
٨	أفليس فيمن قد مضى لي عبرة	هلكوا وقد أيقنت أن لن يرجعوا
٩	ويل م قتلى بالرصاف لو أنهم	بلغوا الرجاء لقومهم أو متعوا
١٠	كم من جميع الشمل ملتئم الهوى	كانوا كذلك قبلهم فتصدعوا
١١	فلتبك أسعد فتية بسباسب	أقووا وأصبح زادهم يتمزع
١٢	جاد ابن مجدعة الكمي بنفسه	ولقد يرى أن المكر لأشنع
١٣	ويلمه رجلا يليذ بظهره	ابلا ونسال الفيافي أروع
١٤	يرد المياه حضيرة ونفيضة	ورد القطاة اذا اسمأل التبع

١٥	وبه الى أخرى الصحاب تلفت	وبه الى المكروب جري زعزع
١٦	ويكبر القدح العنود ويعتلي	وبألى الصحاب اذا أصات الوعوع
١٧	سباق عادية وهادي سرية	ومقاتل بطل وداع مسقع
١٨	ذهبت به بهز فأصبح جدها	يعلو وأصبح جد قومي يخشع
١٩	أجعلت أسعد للرماح دريئة	هبلتك أمك أي جرد ترقع
٢٠	يا مطعم الركب الجياع اذا هم	حثوا المطي الى العلى وتسرعوا
٢١	وتجاهدوا سيرا فبعض مطيهم	حسرى مخلفة وبعض ظلع
٢٢	جواب أودية بغير صحابة	كشاف داوي الظلام مشيع
٢٣	هذا على اثر الذي هو قبله	وهي المنايا والسبيل المهيع
٢٤	هذا اليقين فكيف أنسى فقده	ان راب دهر أو نبا بي مضجع
٢٥	ان تأته بعد الهدو لحاجة	تدعو يجبك لها نجيب أروع
٢٦	متحلب الكفين أميث بارع	أنف طوال الساعدين سميدع
٢٧	سمح اذا ما الشول حارد رسلها	واستروح المرق النساء الجوع
٢٨	من بعد أسعد اذ فجعت بيومه	والموت مما قد يريب ويفجع
٢٩	فوددت لو قبلت بأسعد فدية	مما يضن به المصاب الموجع
٣٠	غادرته يوم الرصاف مجدلا	خبر لعمرك يوم ذلك أشنع

1 Is it due to the accidents of fortune and the fates that I feel frightened
   and that I spend all night without slumber?
2 I spend the night withdrawn, weeping for As'ad
   for eyes cry and shed tears for one such as him

3   The bleary eye discerns
    that it weeps and tears up from violent, internal grief
4   It has occurred to me before, in what has passed
    I have come to know—if only knowledge were of use
5   that neither Fortune nor Fate shows mercy
    not even when the aggrieved weeps
6   I have come to know that those who are the last to remain
    will follow in the path of the first to leave
7   I have come to know—if only knowledge were of use—
    that every living creature passes on and is bid farewell
8   Have I not learned the lesson from those who have already
        departed
    they vanished and I knew for certain that they would not return
9   Woe to the mothers[31] of those killed at al-Risaf, if only they
    had reached their tribe's expectations or been granted a long life
10 How many, before them, were united, cemented by affection,
    but then went their separate ways
11 Let the youths who inhabited the deserts weep over As'ad,
    They have left and their provisions have been divided up
12 The brave son of Majda'a offered himself to Death
    for he did see that retreating would be more hideous
13 Woe to the mother of a man [in whose shadow camels would find
        shelter],
    a swift runner through waterless deserts, a formidable figure
14 He would lead rank and file to water
    like a sandgrouse when shadows contract[32]
15 He would look after the tail-draggers
    and attend urgently to the despondent
16 He would extol the lone arrow and advance
    to the head of the group when the jackals yelped
17 Winner of horse-races, guide of night-travelers
    Valiant fighter, eloquent caller, quick to respond
18 The Bahz[33] took him away, so their ancestor looms larger
    while my people's ancestor has become fearful
19 [You] have made As'ad the target of spears,
    May your mother grieve your death, what patch can mend that
        tear

20 O you who would feed hungry riders when
they urged their mounts quickly uphill
21 They struggled on their night journey, some of their mounts
tired out, others left behind, others limping
22 Traveler across valleys without companions
Intrepid explorer of the desert of darkness
23 This in the footstep of [the one] who preceded him
[Indeed] the path to Fate is well trodden
24 This is [a] certainty, so how can I forget his loss
if Time churns or the bed unfits me
25 If you came to him after a short rest [part of the night] with a need
calling
he would fulfil it with utmost generosity
26 Milky-palmed, distinctly soft-hearted,
First, high-forearmed, bountiful
27 Selfless when the she-camel, seven months pregnant, yields little
milk
and when hungry women smell the broth
28 After As'ad, ever since I was distressed by his [battle] day
— for Death is one of those things that disturbs and distresses —
29 I wish I could accept for As'ad a ransom
that the aggrieved and pained would be loathe to give as
compensation
30 You left him, knocked down, on the Day of al-Risaf
a hideous piece of news, on your life, about that day

2. Ra'iya: Ya 'Aynu judi bi-dam'in minki mighzari

This is one of many poems by the *mukhadrama* al-Khansa' elegizing
her brother Sakhr. He is believed to have died at about the age of fifty
in approximately the year AD 651 of wounds sustained in the battle of
Yawm Dhat al-Athl.[34] According to Bint al-Shati', Sakhr suffered ago-
nizingly from those wounds for more than a year before he finally died.[35]
Al-Khansa' wrote elegies for her brother Mu'awiya as well, but Sakhr is
generally considered to have been the favoured of the two, hence a more
inspirational figure.

Ra'iya[36]

وابكي لصخر بدمع منك مدرار	يا عين جودي بدمع منك مغزار	١
كأنما كحلت عيني بعوار	اني أرقت فبت الليل ساهرة	٢
وتارة أتغشى فضل أطماري	أرعى النجوم وما كلفت رعيتها	٣
محدثا جاء ينمي رجع أخباري	وقد سمعت ولم أبجح به خبرا	٤
لدى الضريح صريع بين أحجار	يقول صخر مقيم ثم في جدث	٥
دراك ضيم وطلاب بأوتار	فاذهب فلا يبعدنك الله من رجل	٦
مركبا في نصاب غير خوار	قد كنت تحمل قلبا غير مهتضم	٧
مر المرارة حر وابن أحرار	مثل السنان تضيئ الليل صورته	٨
وما أضاءت نجوم الليل للساري	وسوف أبكيك ما ناحت مطوقة	٩
حتى تعود بياضا جؤنة القار	ولن أسالم قوما كنت حربهم	١٠
عميمة سوف يبدو كل أسراري	أبلغ خفافا وعوفا غير مقصرة	١١
حلت على طبق من ظهرها عار	والحرب قد ركبت جرباء باقرة	١٢
وشمروا انها أيام تشمار	شدوا المازر حتى يستذف لكم	١٣
في يوم نائبة نابت وأقدار	وابكوا فتى الحي وافته منيته	١٤
راموا الشكيمة من ذي لبدة ضار	كأنهم يوم راموه بأجمعهم	١٥
ملحب غادروه غير محيار	حتى تفرقت الأبطال عن رجل	١٦
تتابعا من نياط الجوف فوار	تجيش منه فويق الثدي مزبدة	١٧
في جارة الموت مطلوبا بأوتار	تجللته الرماح القوم عن عرض	١٨

١٩ كان ابن عمكم منكم وضيفكم   فيكم فلم تدفعوا عنه باخفار

٢٠ لو منكم كان فينا لم ينل أبدا   حتى تلاقى أمور ذات اثار

٢١ أعني الذين اليهم كان منزله   هل تعلمون ذمام الضيف والجار

٢٢ لا نوم حتى تعود الخيل عابسة   ينبذن طرحا بمهرات وأمهار

٢٣ أو تحفزوا حفزة والموت مكتنع   عند البيوت حصينا وابن سيار

٢٤ فتغسلوا عنكم عار تجللكم   غسل العوارك حيضا بعد أطهار

٢٥ حامي العريق لدى الهيجاء مضطلع   بذي سلاح وأنياب وأظفار

٢٦ بفيلق الخيل تنزو في أعنتها   مثل الأسود توافت عند جرجار

1 O eye, well up with copious tears
   Make the tears for Sakhr stream from you

2 For I could not sleep, and spent the night awake
   as if my eye had been lined with mote

3 Watching over the stars, although no one made me their shepherd
   at times I would cover myself with my ragged nightclothes

4 and I had heard a report in which I certainly did not delight
   from a reporter who kept repeating the news

5 saying, "Sakhr resides over there, in a grave
   at the tomb lying amongst the rocks"

6 Go, then.[37] May God not keep you far, a man such as you
   One who prosecutes injustice and exacts retaliations

7 You bore a non-oppressive heart
   upright, unbending

8 Like a spearhead whose blade illuminates the night
   Firm and resolute, free and noble

9 and I shall weep for you as long as the dove coos
   and as long as the stars light up the dark for the night traveler

10 and I shall not make peace with a people with whom you made war
   until the tar-smeared jar turns to white

11 Tell the Khufaf and the 'Awf that my secrets
   will appear, unabridged and in public

12 War had mounted a scabby [splitting/trampling] camel
   and alighted in a land from its bare back

13 Fasten your waist-wrappers in order that you be ready and able
   and tuck them up for these are days for war

14 Weep for the young man of the tribe whose Death came upon him
   on a day when Misfortune and the Fates prevailed

15 as if they, on the day they all engaged in a shooting match with
   him
   shot at an intractable, carnivorous lion

16 such that the heroes dispersed, leaving a man alone
   cut by swords but not disoriented

17 Just above the breast, a foam boils over from him
   followed by the belly's blood vessel bubbling up

18 The raised spears rained down on him, sidelong
   in the neighboring land of Death, a cause for blood-vengeance

19 He was your cousin, one of you, and your guest
   amongst you, yet you did not protect him with an escort

20 Had one of yours been amongst us, he would not have been taken
   at all
   until matters of the utmost consequence presented themselves

21 I mean those with whom he found shelter
   do you not know what is due to the guest and protected neighbor

22 There will be no sleep until the horses return, stern-faced,
   flinging and miscarrying fillies and colts

23 or until you dig a ditch, for death draws nigh
   to the clans of the Husayn and the Ibn Sayyar[38]

24 then you wash away a shame that has en-clothed you
   the way menstruating women wash in the wake of the pure

25 Defender of the noble, taking on in battle
   those armed with weapons, fangs, and claws

26 with an army of horses leaping in their reins
   like lions assembling for the kill

3. Ra'iya: Nazartu wa-duni min 'Amayata mankibun

This is an elegy by the Umayyad poet Layla al-Akhyaliya (d. ca. 704) for her slain beloved Tawba. In the previous two poems, Su'da and al-Khansa' bemoan the loss of their brothers. Here, the poet elegizes a lover, who was also a poet, and who dedicated much of his verse to her. Layla al-Akhyaliya stands out among other women poets for her generic versatility. While it is true that she is known primarily for her *marathi*, she also composed a fair amount of invective and authored the only poem by a woman to be acknowledged as a polythematic *qasida*.[39] The circumstances behind Tawba's death are crucial to the interpretation of certain lines of this poem. According to various *akhbar*, Tawba was killed in retaliation for his slaying of a man called al-Salil, who figures in verse 13, a member of the Banu 'Awf clan (mentioned in verse 5) with whom Tawba often argued. Tawba and a small band of companions were ambushed near an oasis. All of the companions fled, except Tawba's brother 'Abdullah, named in verse 38, who was injured and made lame in the attack. Toward the end of the poem a second figure, one called Hammam b. Mutarraf, who was somehow caught up in the row between Tawba and al-Salil, is mentioned.

Ra'iya[40]

١	نظرت ودوني من عماية منكب	وبطن الركاء أي نظرة ناظر
٢	لأونس ان لم يقصر الطرف دونهم	فلم تقصر الأخبار والطرف قاصري
٣	فوارس أجلى شاؤها عن عقيرة	لعاقرها فيها عقيرة عاقر
٤	فآنست خيلا بالرواق مغيرة	أوائلها مثل القطا المتواتر
٥	قتيل بني عوف فوا ترتا له	قتيل بني عوف قتيل يحابر
٦	توارده أسيافهم فكأنما	تصادرن عن حامي الحديدة باتر
٧	من الهندوانيات في كل قطعة	دم زل عن اثر من السيف ظاهر
٨	أتته المنايا بين زغف حصينة	وأسمر خطي وجرداء ضامر

9	على كل جرداء السراة وسابح	درأت بشباك الحديد زوافر
10	عوابس تعدوا الثعلبية ضمرا	فهن شواح بالشكيم الشواجر
11	فلا يبعدنك الله يا توب انما	لقاء المنايا دارعا مثل حاسر
12	فان تكن القتلى بواء فانكم	ستلقون يوما ورده غير صادر
13	وان السليل ان أبأت قتيلكم	كمرحوضة عن عركها غير طاهر
14	وان تكن القتلى بواء فانكم	فتى ما قتلتم ال عوف بن عامر
15	فتى لا تخطاه الرفاق ولا يرى	لقدر عيالا دون حار مجاور
16	ولا يأخذ الابل الزهارى وماحها	لتوبة عن صرف السرى في الصنابر
17	اذا ما رأته قائما بسلاحه	نقته الخفاف بالثقال البهازر
18	اذا لم تجر منها برسل فقصره	ذرى المرهفات والقلاص التواجر
19	قرى سيفه منها مشاشا وضيفه	سنام المهاريس السباط المشافر
20	وتوبة أحيا من فتاة حيية	وأجرأ من ليث بخفان خادر
21	ونعم الفتى ان كان توبة فاجرا	وفوق الفتى ان كان ليس بفاجر
22	فتى ينهل الحاجات ثم يعلها	فتطلعه عنها ثنايا المصادر
23	كأن فتى الفتيان توبة لم ينخ	قلائص يفحصن الحصا بالكراكر
24	ولم يثن أبرادا عتاقا لفتية	كرام ورحل قيل في الهواجر
25	ولم يتخل الضيف عنه وبطنه	خميص كطي السبت ليس بحادر
26	فتى كان للمولى سناء ورفعة	وللطارق الساري قرى غير قاتر
27	ولم يدع يوما للحفاظ وللندى	وللحرب يذكي نارها بالشراشر

وللخيل تعدوا بالكماة المساعر	28 وللبازل الكوماء يرغوا حوارها
قلاصا لدى واد من الأرض غائر	29 كأنك لم تقطع فلاة ولم تنخ
صريف خطاطيف الصرافي المحاور	30 جنوحا بمومأة كأن صريفها
بنا أجهليها بين غاو وساعر	31 طوت نفعها عنا كلاب واسدت
لعا لأخينا عاليا غير عاثر	32 وقد كان حقا أن تقول سراتهم
تخطيتها بالناعجات الضوامر	33 وداوية قفر تحار بها القطا
على مثله أخرى الليالي الغوابر	34 فتا لله تبني بيتها أم عامر
بغاز ولا غاد بركب مسافر	35 فليس شهاب الحرب يا توب بعدها
سان ومجدام السرى غير فاتر	36 وقد كان طلاع النجاد وبين الـ
دعاك ولم يهتف سواك بناصر	37 وكنت اذا مولاك خاف ظلامة
واب بأسلاف الكمي المغاور	38 فان يك عبد الله اسى ابن أمه
سباعا وقد ألقينه في الجراجر	39 وكان كذات البو يضرب عنده
وأنى وأنى عذر من في المقابر	40 فانك قد فارقته لك عاذرا
وأحفل من نالت صروف المقادر	41 فأقسمت أبكي بعد توبة هالكا
تبكي البواكي أو لبشر بن عامر	42 على مثل همام ولابن مطرف
من المجد ثم استوسقا في المصادر	43 غلامان كان استوردا كل سورة
على كل مغمور نداه وغامر	44 ربيعي حيا كانا يفيض نداهما
سنا البرق يبدو للعيون النواظر	45 كأن سنا ناريهما كل شتوة

1 I looked out, and below me was the elevated land of 'Amaya
and the interior of al-Rika'[41]—what a sight to behold

2 To perceive, from afar, if [my] sight does not fall short of them
—there is no shortage of news even if vision is my limitation—

3 Riders, diverted by a slain nobleman, rush
to his slayer, sounding the moan of a killer[42]

4 Then I discerned some horses in the premonitory galloping,
their forerunners in short succession like the sandgrouse

5 A murdered Bani 'Awf, alas what blood retaliation for him
A murdered Bani 'Awf is a murdered Yahabir[43]

6 Their swords flocked around him, then it was as if
they left him together sharp-edged, as hot as fired iron

7 With each blow of an Indian blade
blood slipped from the sword's prominent glitter

8 The Fates came to him amidst an impenetrable coat of mail
a spear, and a slender short-haired mount

9 against every bare-backed [mount] and every swift runner
strong-ribbed horses in their iron lattices rushed

10 Stern-faced, attacking the slender camels on the sly
mouths wide open with muzzling bits

11 May God not let you depart, O Tawba, for verily
meeting the Fates in armor [is the same as meeting them] without
helmet nor coat of mail nor turban

12 and if the slain ones are in retaliation then you all
will meet, entering a [battle] day from which there is no exit

13 and indeed, Salil, if I recognize him as [Tawba's] equal [in retaliation],
is like a laundered napkin, not pure of its menstrual blood

14 and if there are to be retaliatory killings then oh what a youth
of the clan of 'Awf b. 'Amir you have killed[44]

15 A young man whose friends did not overreach him, who did not
feed his family
without also feeding protected neighbors

16 Tawba's [white] camels bore no marks of sunstroke
[since they were] dispatched on night journeys in cold winds

17 When they saw him standing with his weapon
the nimble ones would extract the bone marrow for him from
the heavy

18 and when they yielded little milk, it would be apportioned to
    the best of the slender [horses] and the merchantable young
        she-camels

19 he would offer the cartilage to his sword and to his guest
    the hump of the big and heavy, lank-lipped camels

20 and Tawba is more modest than a chaste young woman
    and more daring than a lion hiding [in his lair] in Khaffan

21 If Tawba was a libertine, he was still an excellent young man
    and if he was not, then he surpassed them all

22 a young man who quenches desires, first once, then twice
    while praises for him spring up from the satisfied

23 as if the ultimate youth, Tawba, did not let young she-camels kneel
    to scratch the callosities on their breasts against the pebbles

24 as if he failed to offer cool, aged wine to the noble youths
    traveling, and resting during the hottest hours of the day

25 as if his guest was not made to feel at home and left [him] empty-
    bellied
    fatless like a fold in tanned leather

26 A young man who behaved nobly toward the *mawla* and honorably
    toward the night traveler, hospitable and un-stingy

27 [as if he was not invited] to celebrate feasts to attend assemblies
    to wage war— throwing kindling on its fire

28 and to a weaning big-humped teething she-camel, whose young
    one grumbles
    or to the horses running with the brave firebrands

29 as if you had not crossed a waterless plain and not made a
    young she-camel kneel in a sunken riverbed

30 trudging on through an abandoned waterless desert, the gnashing
    of her teeth
    like the creaking of the iron hooks of a mast against the pins of
    a pulley

31 Dogs [iron-hooks] had run out of use for us and they sicked their
    most ignorant
    on us among the [furious] and [rubber-necking] camels

32 It was indeed a duty for their generous lords to say *laʿan*[45]
    to our brother, lofty not staggering

33 many a waterless wild desert where the sandgrouse gets lost
     you traversed on swift and slender she-camels

34 By God Umm 'Amir will set up camp
     on his equal during the coming tail-ends of the nights[46]

35 For the comet of war, O Tawba, after that will not attack
     nor set off in the early morning with a traveling party

36 And he was of high stature, eloquent,
     [affectionate friend] of night travelers, un-stingy

37 and when your *mawla* feared an injustice
     he called you, and nobody else but you, to protect him

38 It was 'Abdullah who [tended to] his mother's son
     and returned with the skins of an iron-clad raider

39 and, like a camel with a tulchan, he was beating away from him
     the birds of prey which had cast him about with their beaks

40 But you abandoned him while he was defending you
     where and whence the excuse of those in the graves[47]

41 so I swore, after Tawba, not to weep for anyone perished
     nor shed copious tears for the one obtained by the vicissitudes
     of fate

42 It is over such an energetic effective man and for the son of
       Mutarraf and
     for Bishr Ibn 'Amir that the female mourners weep[48]

43 Two young men who arrived at every rank of glory
     then settled [flocked in camels] at the sources

44 They were two springtimes of rain,[49] their generosity overflowing
     on every fertile ground as well as every wasteland

45 As if the flash of their fire every rainy season
     was the flash of lightning showing to onlooking eyes

Modularity

All of these poems exhibit modular fluidity; that is their poets move in and out of familiar *topoi* and themes with structural versatility. Transitions from one section to another sometimes occur abruptly, and hence are easily identified and located. Other transitions take place gradually, as one image, allusion, or metaphor metamorphoses into another in a kind of structural movement that Sells's notion of the "dissembling simile" so aptly illustrates.[50] These less pronounced transitions yield multiple themes that collapse into each other, and it is not always easy to fit them into a functional and formal outline. Moreover, there are different recensions of the poems' texts in circulation, so the potential for structural variation between different versions of the same poem is extensive. Thus the following structural breakdowns of the three featured *marathi* are presented with the above provisos.

Su'da bt. al-Shamardal: *Amin al-hawadithi wa-l-manuni urawwa'u?*
Verses 1–3   *Nasib*
Verses 4–8   *Hikma*
Verses 9–13   Exhortation
Verses 13–27   *Ta'bin*
Verses 28–30   Death Announcement/Death Scene/*Tahrid*

al-Khansa': *Ya 'ayni judi bi-dam'in minki mighzari*
Verses 1–3   *Nasib*
Verses 4–5   Death Announcement
Verse 6   Exhortation
Verses 6.5–8   *Ta'bin*
Verses 9–10   Oath
Verses 11–14   Exhortation/*Hamasa*
Verses 15–18   Death Scene
Verses 19–24   Shaming/*Tahrid*
Verses 25–26   *Ta'bin*

Layla al-Akhyaliya: *Nazartu wa-duni min 'Amayata mankibun*
Verses 1–10   *Nasib*/Death Announcement/Death Scene
Verses 11–15   Exhortation/ *Hikma*
Verses 15–37   *Ta'bin/ Fakhr/ Rahil/Wasf*
Verses 38–40   Death Scene
Verse 41   Oath
Verses 42–5   Return to the *Nasib*

Rather than analyzing each poem individually, I will divide them into sections and then compare and contrast the poems through these sections. The terminology for the section headings comes from classical structural breakdowns of both the *qasida* and the *marthiya*. For example, I identify the opening of each poem as a *nasib*, even though they do not fit neatly into the category of 'amatory' or 'erotic' prelude associated with the *qasida*. I speak also of *hikma* and *wasf* (description) as subsections and transitional sections. I borrow the terms *tha'r* (blood vengeance) and *khabar* (or *na'y*: death announcement) from studies of the *marathi*, although I do not know of any scholar who discusses the *khabar* as a section in its own right. To these I have added *ta'bin* (encomium), which I relate to the *rahil* of the *qasida*, and what I call, for lack of a better term, 'death scene.'[51] By dividing the *marathi* into section and subsection, and by highlighting the transitions between them, I hope to explore the structural richness and modularity of women's elegies, thereby situating them in a broader aesthetic context.

Nasib

Each of the three poems opens with a *nasib*. I use the term, despite its conflation with a genre of erotic lyrical poetry, because terms such as *dhikr al-atlal* (remembering the ruins) are not inclusive enough to cover the *topoi* that occur here. I would not view them, after Pellat, as substitutions for the *nasib*,[52] because I see their function as more or less identical to the *nasib* of the *qasida*. That is, it situates the poet, in space and time, vis-à-vis her beloved/*gharad* (the deceased). Perhaps it is better to think of the *nasib* as a 'nostalgic'—after Jaroslav Stetkevych in *The Zephyrs of Najd*—rather than 'amatory' or 'erotic.' The *nasib*s of Su'da and al-Khansa' are relatively straightforward and conventional. They speak of, and in the case of al-Khansa' *to*, their eyes and of weeping. They speak of sleeplessness and pangs of grief. Al-Khansa' exploits the metaphor of 'pastor of the stars'—a common motif in both *marathi* and *qasidas*—[53] likening herself to a shepherd watching over the flocks, and by extension, perhaps, a *qasida* poet gazing over departing womenfolk.

Layla al-Akhyaliya's *nasib*, however, is an entirely different story, for she seems to be self-consciously modeling it after the *nasib* of the *qasida*, but with a few key and meaningful inversions. First of all, she does not speak of tears—in fact, she does not mention her own weeping until verse 41. Instead, she uses her eyes to gaze upon menfolk *(nazartu / li-unisa / fa-anastu)*—the horsemen who enter her frame of vision in verse 3 to retaliate for the death of Salil. Ingeniously, it is unclear whether the news *(akhbar)* of verse 2 refers to Salil's death (hence the background for Tawba's slaying) or to Tawba's death as she is about to envisage it. Continuing with the perspective of the gaze of verse 1, verse 2 ingeniously draws attention to the sex of the poet and to the transgression of her voyeurism. *Wa-l-tarafu qasiri*, which I have translated as "vision is my limitation," stands as a mirror image of the more common phrase *qasirat al-tarf*, which applies to a woman when she does not raise her eyes to return a glance—an image which forms a recurring trope of the *nasib*.[54] Quite subversively, Layla al-Akhyaliya here alludes to the stereotyped beloved of the *qasida* and distinguishes herself from that stereotype at the same time that she applies its terminology to her person. No sooner does Layla make herself the object of her audience's gaze than she resumes the voyeuristic posture of her *nasib*. For, when she describes the gruesome death of her beloved, she assumes a posture similar to that of the male poet watching his beloved and her kinfolk pack up their belongings and move on to the next camp-site; Layla, too, watches her beloved "depart."

With the transition away from the *nasib*, in what amounts to the equivalent of the *takhallus*, or 'disengagement,' the retrospective nature of the poem's temporal dimension begins to assert itself. The exhortation of verse 11, "may God not keep you far O Tawba," followed by the adage that death strikes down the armed man as well as the unarmed man, brilliantly evokes present and past simultaneously. In the present moment, it voices the grief of the poet at this irretrievable loss. In the past, more specifically at a point in the past that precedes Tawba's death, it voices the poet's anxiety at her lover's departure each and every time he went off to battle. This exhortation, *fa-la yub'idanka*, may be a cliché, but here it beautifully effects a transition between the *nasib* and the *ta'bin*. This section, verses 12–14, sets up the context of blood retaliation, explaining his death and exploiting the concept of *bawa'* (match or equal) to open the *ta'bin*, as if Tawba has no equal.

Curiously, the exhortation in the first hemistich of verse 6 of the poem by al-Khansa' also has a dual application that acts as a transition—this time between the *khabar* or news of the beloved's death and the first phrase of the *ta'bin*: "Go, then. May God not keep you far, a man such as you." First, she orders away the bearer of bad tidings, the messenger of Sakhr's death, then she addresses Sakhr and pleads for him to stay. Here the *fa-* in *fa-la yub'idanka* indicates a change of grammatical subjects rather than serving as a marker of tense. In the following hemistich the *ta'bin* begins.

The transition to the *ta'bin* happens more gradually in Su'da's poem. The shifts occur not so much in tense or person but rather in a semantic continuum from generalities to specifics. First, a section of *hikma* speaks of universal truths and her knowledge of them. She then asks herself, in verse 8, if she has never mourned the loss of a member of her people before. She then bemoans the losses of her tribe in the Battle of al-Risaf in verse 9 *(waylu m-min qatla bi-r-Risafi. . .)*. This segues into the fact of her brother's participation in that battle in verse 12 and finally into the *ta'bin* which begins in verse 13 *(waylummihi rajulan. . .)*. She opens the *nasib* with her *self*, abstracts upon that self through musings about the vagaries of Fortune and other universal laws, moves from universal laws to tribal memories, and finally to the individual commemoration of her brother.

Perhaps the most striking aspect of the *nasib*, and its particular incarnations in our three sample poems is the way in which poets construct gendered and, to some extent, sexualized stances for themselves in relation to both their beloved *marthi*s and their audiences. These stances are similar in the elegies of Su'da bt. al-Shamardal and al-Khansa', a fact which should not surprise us given the extra-textual context of their poems: they both elegize brothers; hence the longing for intimacy with the lost beloved must overcome the incest taboo. Su'da achieves this beautifully in the first hemistich of verse 2: *wa-abitu mukhliyatan ubakki As'adan*—"and I spend the night, withdrawn" or "alone" or "isolating myself, weeping for As'ad." She thereby invites the thought of As'ad into her bed while reiterating his absence from it as well as her loneliness. And although this kind of fraternal longing, that is the kind of longing displayed in the *nasib*s of Su'da and al-Khansa', is not sexual in a carnal sense, it is highly sensual, in accordance with a desire for physical intimacy appropriate to a sibling relationship. Beyond the moistness of tears, we feel the internal pain of Su'da (verse 3.5) and the mote in the eye of al-Khansa' (2.5). We hear the poets' sobs, voiced and unvoiced (Su'da, 2 and 3.5, al-Khansa', 1.5), and we feel the shifting covers against the skin of al-Khansa' (3). We, the audience, are invited to picture the poets alone, sleepless, at night—to be their emotional voyeurs, if you will. They then deflect our voyeurism, inviting us to see what they see. In the case of Su'da, it is the cloudiness of her bleary eye (3), whereas with al-Khansa', it is the stars of the nighttime sky (3).

In her *nasib*, Layla al-Akhyaliya, who here supposedly elegizes a lover rather than a brother or a platonic interest, constructs quite a different stance for her poetic persona. On the one hand, her *nasib* reads more like the amatory prelude of a tripartite *qasida* than the opening lines of the *marthiya*. On the other hand, it is less sensual and less erotic, except insofar as it is gruesomely violent. She, too, invites us to be voyeurs, but not, in this particular section of her poem, onto her own grief. Rather, she invites us to see through her gaze, and to visualize the context of her lover's death. It is curious that, while Suʻda and al-Khansaʼ announce their gender by applying the feminine adjectives *mukhliya* (2) and *sahira* (2) to themselves, Layla al-Akhyaliya provides us with no such overt grammatical cue. Her gaze may be sexualized, but it is almost pornographically morbid, for it invites us to picture the beloved's dead body. She does this not only in verses 6, 7, and 38, but also in the poem's opening line—the very framework of the *nasib*. She accomplishes this through plays on geographical terminology: *mankib* refers to 'elevated land' and to 'shoulder' while *batn* means both 'interior' and 'belly.'[55] The grief she thus expresses is less a romanticized angst, and more a gruesome shock.

Taʼbin

I have dubbed this section *taʼbin* because, on the surface, it seems to consist of a simple enumeration of the deceased's admirable qualities. Upon further consideration, however, the *taʼbin* involves much more. I compare it to the *rahil* because, like the journey section of the *qasida*, on a very basic level it usually depicts the elegized astride at least one mount facing the dangers of the road. Moreover, it is rife with animal imagery and 'dissembling similes.' It should be noted that it extends beyond the *rahil* into other *aghrad*, especially *fakhr* and *wasf*. Most importantly, however, the comparison stems from the *taʼbin*'s status as the spatial/temporal axis of the poem, just as the *rahil* is for the *qasida*. For while the *rahil* takes the (male) poet away from his beloved, his point of departure, if you will, forward in space and time, toward his *gharad*, or final purpose, the *taʼbin* takes the (female) poet back in time and lets her protagonist journey not through space but through her memory, back into the present, a present eternalized through recitation.

The *taʼbin* in the *raʼiya* by al-Khansaʼ is rather short, merely four and a half lines, hence it lends itself to a concise introductory analysis to the section. In Abu Suwaylam's recension of the poem, it begins in the second hemistich of verse 6, continues in verses 7 and 8, and then does not resume until verse 25 for the final two verses of the poem. It thus serves to frame the main body of the poem, that is of the text that follows the *nasib* and the *khabar*, and includes bits of *hamasa* and *tahrid* as well as a depiction of the death. The first phrase of the *ta'bin* in the poem by al-Khansa' is a good example of the kind of rhythmic pattern that tends to punctuate the encomium: *darraki daymin wa-tallabin bi-awtari* (one who prosecutes injustice and exacts retaliations). This half-verse partially exhibits the internal rhyme pattern often built on intensive adjectives of the *fa'al* pattern and active participles—appropriate vehicles for laudatory warrior epithets. This pattern punctuates the *ta'bins* of many elegies, including Su'da's. Observe the frequency of intensive adjectives and active participles in the following verses: (17) *sabbaqu 'adiyatin wa-hadi suryatin / wa muqatilun batalun wa da'in misqa'u* and (22) *jawwabu awdiyatin bi-ghayri sahabatin / kashshafu dawiyyi z-zallami mushayya'u*. Jones suggests that similar internal rhymes and rhythms in verses attributed to Janub al-Hudhaliyya serve to "add emotional pressure to phrases of simple praise."[56]

This dense convergence of epithets provides a formalistic, as opposed to merely metaphoric, parallel between the *ta'bin* of the *marthiya* and the *rahil* of the *qasida*; for, as J. Stetkevych has observed, the *qasida*, and the journey section in particular, is full of epithets for animals but rarely calls them by their precise names. In fact, the more important the animal in the greater scheme of the *qasida*, and the more centrally it figures in any particular section, the less likely it will appear by its scientific appellation.[57] The she-camel, for example, may appear as *damra'* (slender) or *jarba'* (scabby) or *zahra'* (white) but fairly infrequently as *naqa*, whereas the relatively minor figure of the sandgrouse almost always appears by its name, *qata*. Similarly, in the *ta'bin* section, the deceased is referred to primarily by epithets. In Su'da's poem, where the *ta'bin* is most clearly elaborated and delineated, the name of the elegized does not appear at all in the *ta'bin* section (verses 13–27), but, quite significantly, it does appear in the lines immediately preceding and following it (as "As'ad" in verses 11 and 28 and as "Ibn Majda'a" in verse 12). In contrast to the animals, and particularly the mounts of the *rahil*, who tend to be described with words denoting physical peculiarities, frequently conveyed through the *afal/fa'la'* pattern, the epithets of the *ta'bin* convey actions as well as more ephemeral, spiritual qualities. In Su'da we find the intensive adjectives and active participles *nassal* (swift runner, vs. 13); *sabbaq* (preceder), *hadin* (guide), *muqatil* (fighter), *da'in* (caller, vs. 17); *mut'im* (feeder, vs. 20); *jawwab* (responder), *kashshaf* (explorer vs. 22); and *mutahallib* (milky-palmed or generous, vs. 26). Toward the end of her *ta'bin* we find adjectives that are not active participles yet still convey physical energy: *anifun* (prominent) and *tuwalu al-sa'idayni* (high-forearmed, vs. 26), as well as softer epithets that connote gentleness: *amyath* (soft-hearted, vs. 26) and *samh* (selfless or compliant, vs. 27). These latter adjectives convey a sense of vulnerability that pave the way for the 'death scene' in the first hemistich of verse 30, "You left him on the Day of al-Risaf, knocked down *(mujaddalan)*," where a passive participle describes the deceased. Meanwhile, in between and among these clusters of epithets one finds metaphors and similes, *madh* and *wasf*, extolling the beloved's heroism, generosity, and strength.

The figurative fecundity of the *ta'bin* is most pronounced in Layla al-Akhyaliya's poem, and it is not surprising that her *ta'bin* should most closely resemble a *rahil*, given her authorship of a polythematic *qasida* featuring a *rahil*, and given her self-conscious rewriting of the *nasib* in this poem. It falls roughly between verses 15 and 37, that is between an exhortation against blood vengeance and a description of the beloved's death. In keeping with J. Stetkevych's description of the *rahil*, it teems with animals, including humans, and their epithets: *al-zahara* (white [she-camels], vs. 16); *al-khifaf* (the nimble ones), *al-thiqal al-bahazir* (the heavy [camels], vs. 17); *dhura al-murhafat* (best of the slender [horses]), *al-qilas al-tawajir* (the merchantable young [she-camels], vs. 18); *al-maharis* (big and heavy [camels]), *al-mashafir* (lank-lipped [camels] vs. 19); *qala'is* ([she-camels] vs. 23); *khamis* (empty-bellied [guest]), *hadir* (fatless [guest] vs. 25); *al-tariq al-sari* (night-traveling visitor, vs. 26); *al-bazil al-kawma'* (big-humped teething [she-camel], vs. 28); *qilas* (young [she-camel], vs. 29); *al-na'ijat al-dawamir* (slender [she-camels], vs. 33); and *Umm 'Amir* (hyena, vs. 34). In stark contrast to Su'da's elegy, very few epithets are applied to the deceased. He is, rather, referred to for the most part simply as *fata* (young man or noble[58] young man, vss. 15, 21, 23, 26), or as Tawba (vss. 16, 20, 21, 23, 35). Indeed, heroic epithets for Tawba do not appear in the *ta'bin* until its end: *shihab al-harb* (comet of war, vs. 35) and *talla' al-najad* (of high stature/tall). *bayyin al-lisan* (eloquent), and *mijdam al-sura* ([affectionate friend of] night travelers, vs. 36). This creates an exquisite tension between the hyperbolic assertions of Tawba's superiority on the one hand and his simply being a young man, like any other, on the other. What one finds, instead, is that the epithets are mostly reserved for the animals and humans who had the benefit of inhabiting his world.[59] In this way, Layla al-Akhyaliya's *ta'bin* formally resembles the *rahil* of the tripartite ode more than the encomium of the elegy, just as the opening of her poem resembles the *nasib* of the *qasida* more than that of the *marthiya*.

But there are differences between the two kinds of journeys: Layla al-Akhyaliya's *ta'bin* contains many scenes of *fakhr* that may be associated more with the outcome of the journey section rather than the journey itself. Verses 15–25 describe a young man who casually shares his sustenance with his neighbor, camel, guest, and even his sword. The images there are reminiscent of feasts and siestas. Verses 26–28 depict his ability and readiness to rise to the occasion for those who are in particular need: the breast-feeding camel, the night traveler, the warrior. Verses 29–32 then introduce a *de facto* journey, a habitual one, perhaps, in which the beloved, astride his camel, trudges along through a dry riverbed—the friction of the movement being captured in the sonorous simile comparing the camel's groans to the creaking of the pulleys on a sailing vessel. Then in verse 33, close to the very end of the section, the poet introduces a *waw rubba*—a particle which often signals a transition. But this *waw rubba* governs a desert to be crossed, an image that one would expect to find at the beginning, not at the end, of the journey; it is as if Layla al-Akhyaliya models her *ta'bin* on the *rahil* but in reverse. Metaphorically, this signifies that the beloved has embarked on a final journey through death; thus it is no coincidence that it is this image of a desert expanse governed by the *waw rubba* that leads into a depiction of Tawba's death in verses 38-40.

Death Scene

The principal death scenes come at the end of Su'da's and Layla's poems and in the middle of the poem by al-Khansa'. In Su'da's *'ayniya*, it is encapsulated in the first hemistich of the last verse in the poem, verse 30: "you left him, knocked down, on the day of al-Risaf" (*ghadartahu yawma r-Risafi mujaddalan*)—a line it shares with the poem's only reference to the *khabar*, or news of the death. This hemistich is enough to express the horror, isolation, and injustice of As'ad's death in battle and to shame his kinsmen who left him there. By contrast, the death scenes in the *ra'iyas* by al-Khansa' and Layla al-Akhyaliya are rather more developed, but they also convey the vulnerability of the deceased hero and the responsibility of his companions to stick with him in battle and tend to him after his death. The death scene in Al-Khansa' amounts to a slightly more elaborate and more graphic version of Su'da's: "You left him, knocked down." She compares her brother to a fierce lion who fights on, when others have retreated, despite his wounds: "As if they [that is, the Fates], on the day they all made a shooting match with him / shot at an intractable, carnivorous lion; such that the heroes dispersed, leaving a man alone / cut by swords but not disoriented; just above the breast, a foam boils over from him / followed by the belly's blood vessel bubbling up" (15–18).

Layla al-Akhyaliya's death scene (38–40), which resumes the description of Tawba's slaying of verses 6–8, is both extremely gruesome and immensely touching: she shows Tawba's brother, 'Abdullah, retrieving the deceased's remains (literally skins: *aslaf*) and shooing away the scavengers. She highlights the affection, both emotional and physical, that 'Abdullah feels for his brother by comparing him to a camel whose calf has died but whose body has been stuffed or somehow preserved for her so that she will continue to produce milk *(dhat al-baww)*.[60] This is actually the second feminizing comparison made in the poem; the first comes in verse 20 (and Tawba is more chaste than a chaste young woman). Such comparisons contrast nicely with others that draw attention to Tawba's masculine sexuality, as verse 20 considers his status as *fajir* (libertine, profligate, or adulterer). It is interesting to see how Layla al-Akhyaliya injects a bit of the female into the male in order to make him more heroic, especially in light of the tendency in elegies, and specifically those that include blood vengeance imagery, to portray menstrual blood as a source of pollution and to associate the feminine with weakness or shame.[61] This of course occurs in verse 20 of the poem by al-Khansa', where she exploits the reference as part of a *tahrid*, as well as in verse 13 of Layla al-Akhyaliya's poem, where she appears to exploit the trope to suggest that retaliation does not work—as if she is saying: You have killed Tawba in revenge for al-Salil, but al-Salil is [still] impure, like laundry soiled with menstrual blood.

Return to the *Nasib*

At the end of two of the poems, and in the middle section of the third, one finds allusions to and symmetries with the *nasib*. In Layla al-Akhyaliya's *ra'iya*, this return manifests itself formally and literally: the phrase *ayya nazrata naziri* of the poem's first line transforms itself into *li-l-'uyun in-nawaziri* in its last. This time it is not Layla as an individual who looks on, but rather the community, which has been bereft of two of its youths (*ghulaman*). The poet thus ends her personal elegy dedicated to Tawba with a collective elegy for the victims of the cycle of blood vengeance in general. The end of her poem brings formalistic closure but remains, emotionally, open-ended: it harps back to the first beginning at the same time that it marks a new beginning. To the extent that the elegy serves as a critique of the culture of blood vengeance, the new *nasib* compounds the grief of the old; for the elegized have doubled and the bereaved have multiplied.

The return to the *nasib* in the other two may be less overt, but they are no less poignant. Al-Khansa' exploits the imagery of fluid and orifice to effect her return. Whereas the poet's eyes overflow with tears in verse 2, her brother's breast boils over with blood in verse 17. The parallels between the orifices of the eye (*'ayn*) and the wounded belly (*jawf*) are strengthened by the visual imagery of intense colors of black, implied in *kuhilat* (lined with kohl), and red, suggested by the obvious reference to blood found in *niyat* (blood vessel). Similarly, these orifices all emit fluids: tears, foam, and blood. In a curious and paradoxical fashion, Sakhr's loss of bodily fluid, or at least the poet's visualization of it, provides some relief for the poet's audience, frustrated by her inability to summon tears. The extended rhyme in the *rawi*s of verses 2 and 17, *'uwwari* and *fawwari*—matched only by *khawwari* in verse 7—further strengthen the correspondence. Furthermore, each orifice suffers from a painful contusion, be it a mote or a stab wound. Unlike Layla al-Akhyaliya, al-Khansa' does seem to approve of the culture of blood vengeance; in fact she encourages it, first by shaming those who failed adequately to protect Sakhr (verses 19–21) and then by instigating them to avenge his death (verses 13, 22–24).

By contrast, Su'da's return to the *nasib* unrolls in a subtle and understated fashion. The return, which comes at the very end of the poem, and which manifests itself like that of al-Khansa', in the death scene, lies in the sense of loneliness and isolation, of disconnectedness from society, that pervades the mood of each section. As'ad has been abandoned (*mujaddalan*) on the battlefield, forsaken by his kinsmen. This invokes the image in Su'da's *nasib* of the poet grieving in solitude, away from her relations (*abitu mukhliyatan ubakki As'adan*). Her poem begins with the effect and ends with cause; in fact the news (*khabar*) of As'ad's death is not mentioned until the very last hemistich.

Conclusion

There is no question that these three elegies aptly illustrate the potentially complex modularity of the *marthiya* and its structural similarities to the so-called tripartite *qasida*. I think it is also fairly clear that the blanket-labeling of women's poetry as monothematic is an inaccurate assessment of the early poetic corpus. Here, I mean this intra-generically. That is, within the bounds of the *marthiya*, women embraced *hikma, fakhr, wasf*, and a host of other *aghrad* including, but by no means limited to, *tha'r/ tahrid*. In my opinion, it is this versatility of the genre and its paradigmatic resemblances with the celebrated *qasida* that ensured it a secure place in the literary canon. Yet an interesting distinction imposes itself between the two forms. In the *qasida*, the poet, or at least his persona, is, generally speaking, his own protagonist. Even in a praise poem, which is outwardly devoted to someone else, the poet starts from a certain position in space at a certain point in time, and travels through space and time to reach that someone else.[62] In the *marthiya*, the poet, or at least her persona, begins from a point in time and space from which she does not necessarily budge. The traversal of space and time, in her poem, belongs to another protagonist. Time is traversed in the past, but, in the present, time no longer progresses, at least not for the persona of the woman elegist. The woman poet of the *marthiya*, or what we might call the *poetess persona*, remains still and steadfast: she embodies the rootedness of her heroic subject, the receptacle of his immortality and worldly permanence. Curiously, the *marathi* here have all been composed by women who were not childbearers for the deceased; hence woman's role as an immortalizing agent is not simply a figurative function of the reality of her biological capabilities of reproduction.

It is tempting to see the poetess persona's stillness in space and time as a reflection of women's social and cultural circumstances: they did not wander about the desert unaccompanied; they did not mount camels except as passengers of a *hawdaj*; they did not fight in wars; they only had a public voice in ritually circumscribed states. The problem with this is that we know this not to be the case. As I have laid out elsewhere,[63] women were warriors, soothsayers, and priests too frequently to be dismissed as rare exceptions. Moreover, if women's experience of life was so confined, how could they have composed with such ease about what was outside their experience? Indeed, the case of the *marathi* provides an interesting contrast with contemporary or modern women's writing, which is often viewed—erroneously, in my estimation—as being more autobiographical than men's in part because women are more caught up in their own private worlds. Here you have a case of woman composing poetry that is almost entirely about a third person. True, she composes in the 'first-person' but mostly insofar as it narrates a kind of emotional framework for her grief and for her role as a vessel for the propagation of collective memory. In other words, she does not boast of her exploits, recount her achievements, or sing her own praises. She may be the *speaking subject* (the narrating agent), but the spoken subject (the narrated protagonist) as well as his importance in the community are the central topics of her composition. This differs, or *defers*, from the paradigm of the polythematic ode, in which a masculine poetic persona, even in the context of *madih*, does not usually completely disengage from his own self-centeredness. He has the past and the beloved on one side and the future and the *mamduh* on the other, but the course of poet's text and its traversal of *topoi* follows his own persona's path.

Women wept and they mourned the dead, either spontaneously and sincerely or professionally and by rote. This was part of their function in society. We do not dispute this. What we would dispute is that women's poetic contributions were somehow limited to this and somehow bound within its confines. Question: How did woman write about man's world? Answer: She knew it—either through personal experience or through study. She was charged with its preservation. In this primarily pre-literate society men *and women* were charged with writing memory. *Marathi* spring not only from emotional vulnerability and sentimentality but also from education and training. It is not only a question of sentimentality, ritual, and obligation, but of art and craftsmanship. They were, in effect, the obituary writers. Fortunately, the *marthiya* model provided the gifted among them with an outlet through which they could display their virtuosity across themes and genres.

Notes

1   This article is a revised version of the third chapter of my PhD dissertation, "The Poetics of S/Exclusion: Women, Gender and the Classical Arabic Canon" (Columbia University, 2003). It was the last piece of writing I produced under the direction of Magda Al-Nowaihi, who gave me her comments on the initial draft only a couple of months before she died. I am indebted to her for more than just her comments and suggestions, but for her friendship. Our bond, perhaps appropriately for an advisor and her advisee, was unusually bookish. Although we often chatted on the phone and gossiped over lunch, we enjoyed each other's company most in our co-engagement with texts, and so I see the present contribution as part of our ongoing dialogue. In addition to Magda, I wish to thank George Saliba, who graciously sponsored my dissertation defense, as well as Philip Kennedy, Elliott Colla, Muhsin al-Musawi, and Hamid Dabashi, the other members of my defense committee, who also had valuable comments and suggestions. My gratitude also extends to Geert Jan van Gelder and Dana Sajdi, especially for their careful reviewing of the poetry translations. If the translations remain rough around the edges, the fault is mine, not theirs!

2   Charles Pellat, "Marthiya," *Encyclopaedia of Islam. New Edition.* 12 vols. to date (Leiden: Brill, 1960–2004), 6:605.

3   See, for example, two articles by Renate Jacobi: "The Origins of the Qasida Form," in *Qasida Poetry in Islamic Asia and Africa*, ed. S. Sperl and C. Shackle (Leiden: Brill, 1966), 21–34, and "The Camel Section in the Panegyrical Ode," *Journal of Arabic Literature* 13 (1982): 1–22. See also M. M. Badawi, "From Primary to Secondary Qasidas: Thoughts on the Development of Classical Arabic Poetry," *Journal of Arabic Literature* 11 (1980): 1–31.

4   See J. A. Bellamy's "Some Observations on the Arabic Ritha' in the Jahiliyah and Islam," *Jerusalem Studies in Arabic and Islam* 13 (1990): 44–61, especially pages 44–45, where he discusses an article by Ignaz Goldziher entitled "Bemerkungen zur arabischen Trauerpoesie." See also Alan Jones, ed., *Early Arabic Poetry*, vol. 1: *Marathi and Su'luk Poems*, Oxford Oriental Institute Monographs, no. 14, vol. 1 (Reading: Ithaca Press, 1992), 25, where he states: "There is some evidence to show that the earliest *marathi* were rhymed chants uttered at funerals by women mourners and that the *saj'* used in them was of the same register as the utterances of the *kahins* [soothsayers]." For more information on the tradition of lamentation and the role of professional female mourners, see T. Fahd, "Niyaha," *Encyclopaedia of Islam* 8:64–65, and A. A. Muhanna, "Notes on Ancient Arabic Consolation (*ta'ziya*) and Lamentation (*niyaha*)," in a primarily Arabic-language volume edited by al-Muhanna, *Dirasat fi-l-adab al-'arabi wa-l-lugha muhda min a'da' hay'at al-tadris bi-qism al-lugha al-'arabiya wa-adabiha ila jami'at al-Kuwayt* (Kuwait: 1976–77), 64–37.

5   Ahmad Muhammad al-Hufi, *Al-Mar'a fi-l-shi'r al-jahili*, 2nd rev. ed. (Cairo: Dar al-Fikr al-'Arabi, 1963), 624.

6   Bellamy, "Some Observations," 54–55.

7   Ibid., 58. Bellamy seems to prefer the short *marthiya*, which he says "had reached a state of perfection" toward the end of the Jahiliya (55), over the long *marthiya*, in which he says "confusion seems to reign" with regard to the arrangement of *topoi* (56). Hence he does not equate the relative thematic simplicity of women's elegies with their authors' artistic inferiority, as al-Hufi does.

8   Rashida Binmas'ud, for example, believes that women's propensity for elegy stems from a taboo preventing them from addressing verses to a lover. She writes: "The explanation that comes closer to the truth, in our view, is that the silence imposed on lovers or spouses, at that stage, had opened a dialogue between the woman and members of her family, the brother or father who represented the knight *(faris)* in her mind." Rashida Binmas'ud, *Al-Mar'a wa-l-kitaba: su'al al-khususiya/ balaghat al-ikhtilaf* (n.p.: Ifriqiya al-Sharq, 1994), 10. Suzanne Pinckney Stetkevych puts forward a similar, albeit more elaborate theory. She argues that the noblewoman *(hurra)* normally lived in a state of protection and confinement and would not have voiced her concerns publicly. A threat to the mode of her protection, however, such as the unavenged slaying of a male relative, would empower her to break out of her confinement and express herself in a public forum. She explains: "Crucial to the argument at hand is that confinement and privacy thus constitute an expression of 'purity,' or in ritual terms, aggregation; hence, to be expelled, unveiled, to appear or speak in public, is an expression of 'defilement,' of liminality. It is therefore only in the liminal (defiled/sacral) states of a kinsman's death or of warfare that women of the warrior class have a public—and hence poetic—voice." Suzanne Pinckney Stetkevych, *The Mute Immortals Speak: Pre-Islamic Poetry and the Poetics of Ritual* (Ithaca, NY: Cornell University Press, 1993), 165. For more on the association of women with elegy, see chap. 2 of my dissertation, "The Poetics of S/Exclusion."

9   For a fairly exhaustive treatment of the metaphoric potential of the eye in Arabic Literature, see 'Abd al-Majid Juhfa, *Satwat al-nahar wa-sihr al-layl: al-Fuhula wa-ma yuwaziha fi-l-tasawwur al-'Arabi* (Casablanca: Dar Tubaqqal, 1996), 64–67. Incidentally, Juhfa cites the eye and the "arrow" of its glance as a key weapon at the disposal of what he terms the feminine element of the paradigm of passion.

10   See, for example, Kamal Abu-Deeb, "Toward a Structural Analysis of Pre-Islamic Poetry," *International Journal of Middle East Studies* 6 (1975): 148–84; Badawi; "From Primary to Secondary Qasidas,"; András Hámori, "The Poet as Hero," *On the Art of Medieval Arabic Literature* (Princeton: Princeton University Press, 1974), 3–30; Adnan Haydar, "The Mu'allaqa of Imru' al-Qays: Its Structure and Meaning," *Edebiyat* 2 (1977): 227–61 and 3 (1978): 51–82; Renate Jacobi, "The Camel Section in the Panegyrical Ode"; and Stefan Sperl, "Islamic Kingship and Arabic Panegyric Poetry," *Journal of Arabic Literature* 8 (1977): 21–35. See also books by Hassan El-Banna Ezz El-Din, *Al-Kalimat wa-l-Ashya': Bahth fi-l-taqalid al-fanniya li-l-qasida al-jahiliya* (Cairo: Dar al-Fikr, 1988); J. E. Montgomery, *The Vagaries of the Qasida: the Tradition and Practice of Early Arabic Poetry* (Cambridge: E. J. W. Gibb Memorial Trust, 1997); Jaroslav Stetkevych, *The Zephyrs of Najd: The Poetics of Nostalgia in the Classical Arabic Nasib* (Chicago and London: The University of Chicago Press,

1993); and Geert Jan van Gelder, *Beyond the Line* (Leiden: E. J. Brill, 1982). This list is far from exhaustive.

11   This point is not lost on Layla al-Akhyaliya, who, in the poem analyzed by Dana Sajdi, equates herself with the mount rather than the rider in the poem's journey section. See Sajdi's article "Trespassing the Male Domain: The Qasidah of Layla al-Akhyaliyyah," *Journal of Arabic Literature* 31, no. 2 (2000): 121–46, which has been revised and reprinted in this volume. For the parallels between the beloved and the riding mount, and the role of each in sublimating the poet's desires—sexual in the case of the former and primal and belligerent in the case of the latter, see Salah al-Din al-Munajjid, *Al-Hayat al-jinsiya 'inda al-'arab* (Beirut: Dar al-Kutub, 1958), 11–12.

12   Studies on the *marthiya* include: M. Abdesselem, *Le thème de la mort dans la poésie arabe des origines à la fin du IIIe/IVe siècle* (Tunis: University of Tunis, 1977); Bellamy, "Some Observations;" G. Borg, *Encyclopedia of Arabic Literature*, ed. Julie Scott Meisami and Paul Starkey, vol. 2/2 (London: Routledge, 1998), s.v. "Ritha'," 663–64; Jones, *Early Arabic Poetry*; Bushra Muhammad Ali al-Khatib, *Al-Ritha' fi-l-shi'r al-jahili wa sadr al-islam.* (Baghdad: Matba'at al-Idara al-Mahalliya, 1977); Henri Lammens, "Caractère religieux du tar ou vendetta chez les arabes préislamites," *Bulletin de l'Insitut Français d'Archéologie Orientale* 26 (1926): 83–127; Pellat, "*Marthiya,*" 6:605; and Mustafa 'Abd al-Shafi-l-Shura, *Shi'r al-ritha' fi-l-'asr al-jahili* (Beirut: al-Dar al-Jami'iya, 1983).

13   Mayy Yusuf Khulayyif, *Al-Shi'r al-nisa'i fi adabina al-qadim* (Cairo: Maktabat Gharib, 1991), 156.

14   One seminal exception to that rule is S. P. Stetkevych's work on pre-Islamic poetry of blood vengeance. See her *The Mute Immortals Speak*, esp. 161–238, as well as her article "Sarah and the Hyena: Laughter, Menstruation, and the Genesis of a Double Entendre," *History of Religions* 35, no. 5 (1996): 13–41, esp. 15–30. In these works, she lucidly explores the forms, structures, and imagery that characterize a particular strand of elegy, namely the one that includes a call for retaliation (*tahrid* or *tha'r*). I should note, however, that despite her analysis of the role of *tahrid* in the *marthiya*, Stetkevych herself does not contest the notion that women's poetry is "almost always monothematic." *The Mute Immortals Speak*, 164n.

15   Pellat, "Marthiya," vol 6, 605.

16   On this important point, see Jaroslav Stetkevych, "Name and Epithet: The Philology and Semiotics of Animal Nomenclature in Early Arabic Poetry," *Journal of Near Eastern Studies* 45, no. 2 (1986): 100.

17   Juhfa, *Satwat al-nahar*, 36.

18   Ibid., 47. While this assertion may be technically correct, in that the words *ana* and *nahnu* may be treated as masculine when employed as grammatical terms abstracted from their usual referential contexts, it is terribly misleading since the rules of gender agreement effectively acknowledge that 'I' and 'We' may be feminine.

19   Ibid., 138–39.

20   Jacques Derrida, "Différance," *Margins of Philosophy*, trans. and ed. Alan Bass (London: Prentice Hall, 1982), 11.

21 I personally cannot read Derrida without thinking about the *qasida*. His terminology alone is enough to evoke images from Imru' al-Qays. 'Trace,' 'erasure' and 'espacement' (that is spacing combined with temporization)—are these not the preoccupations of most of the *qasida* studies listed in note 10 above.

22 Joseph Adamson, "Différance/Différence," *Encyclopedia of Contemporary Literary Theory*, ed. Irena R. Makaryk (Toronto: Toronto University Press, 1993), 535.

23 In French, *différance* is phonetically indistinguishable from *différence*, the word for 'difference.' For this reason, *différance* actively illustrates the imprecise, equivocal nature of supposedly phonetic language systems: it 'differs' from difference in writing, but it 'differs' from difference in speech only through a deferral in meaning reception.

24 Derrida, "Différance," 16–17.

25 The term 'ungrammaticality' comes from Michael Riffaterre, *Semiotics of Poetry* (Bloomington: Indiana University Press, 1984), 2 and *passim*, and it alludes to the process whereby a text announces its hidden meanings by subverting the rules of grammar and other codes of meaning.

26 Many have examined the spatial and temporal aspects of the *qasida*, including J. Stetkevych in *The Zephyrs of Najd* and Hassan El-Banna Ezz El-Din in "The Aesthetics of Time in Poetry," *Alif* 9 (1989): 102–36.

27 The following excerpt from Dérrida deals with the origins of *différance*--the force behind the force, the player responsible for the play. I cite it here because it relates in some ways to what I like to call stance.

> What differs? Who differs? What is *différance*?
> In effect, if we accepted the form of the question, in its meaning and syntax [...], we would have to conclude that *différance* has been derived, has happened, is to be mastered and governed on the basis of the point of a present being, which itself could be something, a form, a state, a power in the world to which all kinds of names might be given, a *what*, or a present being as a *subject*, a *who*. And in this last case, notably, one would conclude implicitly that this present being, for example a being present to itself, as consciousness, eventually would come to defer or to differ: whether by delaying and turning away from the fulfillment of a 'need' or a 'desire,' or by differing from itself. But in neither of these cases would such a present being be 'constituted' by this *différance*. (Dérrida, "Différance," 14–15)

"The point of a present being" could be one definition of stance, connecting the speaking subject to different versions of itself (poet, poetic persona, the first person) as well as the various discrete positions it has assumed on both the spatial and the temporal axes.

28 For various versions of her name and appellations, see 'Abd al-Malik Ibn Qurayb al-Asma'i, *al-Asma'iyat*, ed. Ahmad Muhammad Shakir and 'Abd al-Salam Muhammad Harun, 2nd ed. (Cairo: Dar al-Ma'arif, 1964), 101n.

29 It is worth noting that the poem fairly closely resembles a renowned *'ayniya* attributed to the *mukhadram* Abu Dhu'ayb. Mohamed Al-Nowaihi, in his commentary on that poem, states that the opening line, *amin al-manuni wa-raybiha tatawajja'u / wa-d-dahru laysa bi-mut'ibi man yajza'u* (is it from the Fates and their

vicissitudes that you feel sorrow / when Fortune pays no heed to expressions of grief) reflects the sensibility of the new Islamic religion in its philosophical outlook (*al-Shi'r al-Jahili*, Part 2 (Cairo: al-Dar al-Qawmiya, 1966), 664–65). This would confirm the relative time-frame of Su'da's poem, since the *hikma* voiced in Abu Dhu'ayb's second hemistich on the uselessness of outward expressions of grief, is echoed in line 5 of her poem.

30 The text appears as it is cited in al-Asma'i, *al-Asma'iyat*, 101–04.

31 Shakir and Harun state that *waylummuh*, in this instance, is meant as an expression of wonder and praise rather than as a supplication (*du'a*) (al-Asma'i, *al-Asma'iyat*, 102n. 9).

32 "*Isma'alla al-tubba'u*" = "*irtafa'a al-zillu*" or the "shadow lifted," al-Zamakhshari, *Asas al-balagha* (Beirut: Maktabat Lubnan, 1996), 36. Note that this is when the sun is at its peak and when people are thirstiest.

33 According to Louis Cheikho, the Banu Bahz are a clan of the Banu Sulaym. Louis Cheikho, *Riyad al-adab fi marathi shawa'ir al-'arab* (Beirut: Catholic Press, 1897), 135n

34 'Umar Faruq al-Tabba', ed., *Diwan al-Khansa'* (Beirut: Dar al-Qalam, n.d.), 10.

35 Bint al-Shati', *al-Khansa'*, 2nd ed. (Cairo: Dar al-Ma'arif, 1963): 42–43.

36 This is the version of the poem that appears in Anwar Abu Suwaylam, ed., *Diwan al-Khansa' sharahahu Tha'lab Abu al-'Abbas Ahmad b. Yahya b. Sayyar al-Shibani al-Nahwi* (Amman: Dar 'Ammar, 1988), 290–302.

37 As Dana Sajdi has pointed out to me, the phrase 'go then' serves as a beautiful transition from the *khabar* to the *ta'bin*. Addressed to the reporter of the death, it reads as a rejection of bad news. Addressed to the deceased, it signals an acceptance of his departure from this world. It thus dispels the pain and grief at the same time that it initiates a string of pleasant memories and associations.

38 I believe, from the context, that this is a reference to the sub-clans of Sakhr's enemies.

39 See al-Sajdi's aforementioned analysis of the piece.

40 The text of this, most complete, version of the poem is found in Ibn Maymun, *Muntaha al-talab min ash'ar al-'arab*, ed. Fuat Sezgin, 3 vols. (Frankfurt: Ma'had Tarikh al-'Ulum al-'Arabiya wa-l-Islamiya, 1986–93), 1:45–46. See also the edition by Munir al-Madani, Sayyida Hamid, and Zaynab al-Qawsi, vol. 1 (Cairo: Dar al-Kutub, 1999), 116–20.

41 Al-Rika', with a *kasra* over the *ra'*, is the name of a place, possibly a *wadi*, and it is used similarly in the phrase *batn al-Rika'* in a poem by al-Ra'i. Rakka', with a *fatha* over the *ra'* and a *shadda* over the *kaf*, is also a place-name and one that occurs in juxtaposition to 'Amaya in a poem by Zuhayr. See Yaqut Ibn 'Abd Allah al-Hamawi, *Jacut's Geographisches wörterbuch*, 6 vols. (Leipzig: In Commission bei F.A. Brockhaus, 1866–1870). 2:808.

42 Clearly the poet is playing games with the root '-*q-r* and intends many meanings simultaneously. I have chosen to translate the line in this way because I believe the narrative thread of the poem demands it. The riders are approaching to avenge al-Salil. I read the first '*aqira* (عقيرة) as al-Salil's body and the second as a moaning

sound, and I read the first *'aqir* (عاقر) as al-Salil's slayer (Tawba) and the second as an avenging warrior. In the commentary of the *Aghani*, there are also rival interpretations of the line, but they each seem to assume that *'aqira* refers either to Tawba or al-Salil and that *'aqir* refers either to Tawba or his killer (Abu al-Faraj al-Isfahani, *Kitab al-Aghani*. 13 vols., 2nd printing. Beirut: Dar Ihya' al-Turath al-'Arabi, 1997. 6:149–50). Indeed, there are two slain and two slayers in this cycle of violence and the poet alludes to this beautifully in this brilliant instance of *jinas*. Incidentally, I read the *'-ha'* in *'fiha'* as refering back to *fawaris*, but it could also refer to *'aqira* or perhaps to something else.

43 Given the prevalence of bird imagery here, I think it is worth noting that *Yahabir*, the name of a tribal group, is also a broken plural for a bird called the *hubara* or the *yahbura* (bustard).

44 The sons of 'Awf b. 'Amir, al-Salil among them, were Tawba's rivals. See Abu al-Faraj al-Isbahani, *Kitab al-Aghani*, 2nd rev. ed., vol. 6 (Beirut: Dar Ihya' al-Turath al-'Arabi, 1997), 141. In these lines she argues that, by the logic of blood vengeance, they have effectively murdered one of their own, since Tawba's death, too, merits retaliation

45 *La'an* is said to someone who has fallen down.

46 *Umm 'Amir* and *Umm 'Amr* are epithets for the hyena. See E. W. Lane, *Arabic English Lexicon* (London: Williams and Norgate, 1863–67), s.v. *'-m-r*. I suspect that *tabni baytaha* here means to 'use as a mattress' (al-Zamakhshari, *Asas*, b-y-t). The image alludes to the hyena's supposed practice, attested to by al-Jahiz and others, of attempting to fornicate with dead bodies. See S. P. Stetkevych, *The Mute Immortals Speak*, 79–80 and "Sarah and the Hyena," 17.

47 If this were a typical *marthiya*, I would assume that here the poet was addressing the other men in Tawba's party (that is, not 'Abdullah) who left him on the battlefield, since it is common for the poet to accuse the slain's kinsmen of doing just that in order to shame them into exacting blood vengeance. But here it seems that she is addressing Tawba, accusing him of abandoning his brother while the latter was making such a valiant effort to defend him. It is a poignant ambiguity, especially given the poem's apparent stance against blood retaliation.

48 I believe that *hammam* here refers to Tawba, but it is also the first name of the Ibn Mutarraf of the second hemistich. The circumstances here are unclear to me, have these men already been killed, or is Layla implying that they will be killed in retaliation for Tawba's death? In either case, she ends her elegy with a new elegy, again capturing the grief of the cycle of violence in the system of *tha'r* and, through her dualization of the elegized, she even shows how it escalates.

49 Reading *rabi'ay haya kana* (they were two springs of a spring shower): here Layla seems to be inverting the phrase *haya al-rabi'* (the rain of spring). See al-Zamakshari, *Asas al-Balagha*, 99, for a definition of *al-haya* as the rain that brings life to the earth.

50 "The simile dissembles. What occurs is not so much description as its metamorphosis. Whenever we think we have the image pinned down, it changes. [. . .] In apparent digression the poetic voice outruns any descriptive point

through the indefinite extension of the simile or through chains of similes." Michael A. Sells, trans. and ed., *Desert Tracings* (Middletown, CT: Wesleyan University Press, 1989), 4–5.

51 Pellat acknowledges that many *marathi* contain descriptions of deaths, particularly violent ones, though, again, he does not speak of it as a 'section' or 'theme' proper. Pellat, "Marthiya," 605.

52 Ibid., 605.

53 See J. Stetkevych's discussion of this motif in "Meadows of the Sky," Chapter 4 in *The Zephyrs of Najd*, 135–67.

54 The motif of the languid eye and drooping eyelid that occurs so frequently in the *nasib* draws attention to the eye as an object of the poet's gaze, at the same time that it deflects or averts the return gaze of the beloved. Consider, for example, the second line of Ka'b b. Zuhayr's "Banat Su'ad":

وما سعاد غداة البين إذ ظعنوا   إلا أغن غضيض الطرف مكحول

And what was Su'ad, on the morning of separation, as the womenfolk prepared for departure

But a nasal-voiced (antelope) with lowered gaze, donning kohl

(Ibn Maymun, 27)

55 I find her use of these terms in *idafa* constructs with the place-names 'Amaya and al-Rikka' quite a poignant play on words. For the root '-*m-y* conveys blindness (hence eyes) wile *r-k-w* relates to water containers (hence tears). The encoded landscape she paints may thus be said to depict the poet crying over her beloved's body.

56 Jones, *Early Arabic Poetry*, 47. András Hámori, who makes the same citation from Jones (57n), describes this kind of internal rhyme as a "desolate thud." See his "The Silken Horsecloths Shed their Tears," *Arabic and Middle Eastern Literatures* 2, no. 1 (1999): 44. Similarly, in her commentary on this kind of *tarsi'* used sequentially over several verses, S. P. Stetkevych says it creates "an insistent and unrelieved hammering," *The Mute Immortals Speak*, 183.

57 He writes: "proceeding closely along the lines of the thematic and structural organization of the pre-Islamic Arabic poem, we notice that certain thematically relevant objects appearing in one section of the poem will more likely be more consistently, or even exclusively, referred to epithetically or descriptively, whereas other objects thematically tied to other sections of the poem will more likely be mentioned explicitly, by their substantival denotants. Such a structural-thematic perspective will also reveal that among the sections of the classical Arabic *qasida*, the indirectly referential and epithetic occurrence of key-words is the highest in the section of the journey, with its subthemes of the desert animals and the hunt, as well as in the kindred theme of the chivalrous chase on horseback." J. Stetkevych, "Name and Epithet," 100.

58 Ibn Manzur, in the *Lisan al-'Arab* (Beirut: Dar Sadir, 1955–56), cites verse 14 of this poem as an instance of the word *fata* meaning *karim*.

59 One animal who appears in the encomium but which does not figure in the beloved's animal entourage is the hyena of verse 34. This line amounts to a threat,

or perhaps a warning, to the killers of Tawba—harping back to the *fata* of line 14, the equal of Tawba in their clan who will be the next object of retaliation. In effect, it signals the beginning of the transition to the next section, the death scene. The hyena is a particularly ominous figure in Arabic poetry, for, in addition to its foreboding laugh, it was believed to have attempted sexual intercourse with dead bodies. S .P. Stetkevych, *The Mute Immortals Speak*, 79–80 and "Sarah and the Hyena," 17.

60　The death scene in Durayd b. al-Simma's *da'iya* elegizing his brother 'Abdullah has many parallels with the one here, including the use of the *dhat al-baww* motif. In this instance the poet compares himself to such a camel: *wa kuntu ka-dhat il-bawwi ri'at fa-aqbalat/ ila jaladin min maski saqbin muqaddadi* (And I was like a camel that has lost its foal and is terrified and has ventured forth to a hide stripped from the skin of a young one.) Jones, *Early Arabic Poetry*, 74. So it appears that the feminization of the hero who stays behind as a last defense for the fallen warrior is a trope of men's poetry as well. *Dhat al-baww* and its variant *umm al-baww* also appear in elegies by the Umayyad poets Arta b. Suhayya and Jarir for their children. See 'Abd al-Mu'in al-Malluhi, *Marathi al-aba' wa-l-ummahat li-l-banin wa-l-banat* (Beirut: Dar al-Kunuz al-'Arabiya, 1996), 67–68.

61　S. P. Stetkevych claims that a man whose slain kin lies unavenged, and therefore in a polluted state, is, in the poetics of blood vengeance, effectively feminized; see *The Mute Immortals Speak*, 196. While I would agree with her in many cases, this poem demonstrates the flexibility of the poetics of gender in the elegy. 'Abdullah is a heroic figure here; for he is the only one of Tawba's companions to have remained with him, and his feminization heightens that heroism. This could, of course, reflect Layla al-Akhyaliya's apparent rejection of the blood vengeance ethos, which would be in keeping with developments in early Islamic elegies and not necessarily refute Stetkevych's thesis with regard to pre-Islamic poetry.

62　This is sometimes the case even in men's *marathi*. In a renowned elegy by Muhalhil b. Rabi'a, for example, the poet makes a journey to the deceased's grave in a kind of condensed *rahil*:

فقالوا لي بسفح الحي دار 　　　　سألت الحي أين دفنتموه

وطار النوم وامتنع القرار 　　　　فسرت اليه من بلدي حثيثاً

ثوى فيه المكارم والفخار 　　　　وحادت ناقتي عن ظل قبر

I asked the tribe, "Where have you buried him?"
"At the foot of the tribal mount," they said, "is his abode."
I sped to him from my land, hastening:
sleep fled and I refused all rest.
My she-camel shied from the shade of a grave
in which nobility and pride lay buried.

(S. P. Stetkevych, *The Mute Immortals Speak,* 311, trans. on 217)

63　See the first chapter of my doctoral dissertation, "The Poetics of S/Exclusion."

8

Revisiting Layla al-Akhyaliya's Trespass

Dana Sajdi

This article revisits and revises my earlier study, "Trespassing the Male Domain: the qasidah *of Layla al-Akhyaliyyah."* [1] *I first thought about Layla's transgressive poetry while a graduate student in an Arabic literature class taught by Magda Al-Nowaihi at Columbia University. Magda encouraged me not only to publish the paper I wrote for her class, but also to write my PhD dissertation on Layla al-Akhyaliya. I followed the first part of Magda's advice (but not the second: I ended up writing my dissertation on eighteenth-century commoner histories from the Ottoman Levant), and the article on Layla came out in 2000 with a dedication to both Magda and my own sister, Luma, for these two young women's courageous battles against cancer. Magda, though, was not as fortunate as Luma. And now, five years on, I find myself revisiting Layla's exceptional literary corpus with a view to carrying out the second part of Magda's advice; to write a booklength study of Layla. The present article is the first fruit of my re-engagement with Layla, and it is only appropriate to re-dedicate it to Magda's memory.*

I have beheld you, with your verse strung like coupled pearls,
A line like a virgin, then a line like a woman deflowered;
One like the oration of Quss in the market of 'Ukaz,
Another like the lament of Layla al-Akhyaliya.

Abu Tammam [2]

185

Introduction

Some narrators said: Mu'awiya was walking when he saw a rider (faris). He said to one of his guards, "Bring him to me and take care not to scare him!" He [the guard] came to him [the rider] and said, "Report to the Commander of the Faithful!" He [the rider] said, "It is he whom I seek." When the rider approached, he lowered his face-covering and—lo, and behold!—it was Layla al-Akhyaliya.[3]

Layla al-Akhyaliya (d. ca. 704)[4] is one of the most prominent female poets of the first Islamic century. In the above report, Layla's gender identity is confused. She is mistaken for a man in one of his most 'manly' states, that of the rider. Her true identity as a woman only becomes apparent after she reveals her face. This report poignantly illustrates Layla al-Akhyaliya's literary career, which may readily be described as pushing the boundaries of gender-determined poetic norms. Although she is best known for her elegies *(marathi)*, the poetic form generally associated with female poets,[5] the image of Layla in the guise of a man is, in fact, aptly expressive of Layla's remarkable poetic corpus.[6] Possibly the most striking instance of gender transgression in Layla's poetry is her little known *ba'iya*[7] which, to the best of my knowledge, is the only *qasida* with a definitively masculine structure—that is, a *qasida* made up of the *nasib* (lamentation over the deserted encampments of the beloved's tribe), the camel section, and the *gharad* (the section that conveys the purpose or the subject matter of the poem, be it *hija'*, *fakhr*, or *madih*[8])—to have been composed by a female poet.[9]

The *qasida* as a poetic form serves to bring out the heroism of the male protagonist.[10] With his warrior qualities, courage, generosity, and ability to survive life-threatening situations, the protagonist, who is invariably male, emerges as the hero.[11] In addition to the values expressed in the content of the *qasida*, its myth-like tripartite structure has been understood to represent the male protagonist's performance of the initiation rites of passage into both manhood and full membership in the tribe. In other words, the *qasida*, as a poetic form seems to 'en-gender' the male persona.[12]

In light of the gendered division of poetic spaces, Layla al-Akhyaliya's *qasida* constitutes an instance of flagrant trespass in classical Arabic literature. This *ba'iya* is a thirty-six verse *qasida* (with a *nasib*, camel section, and *gharad*) composed, not as an elegy, but as a panegyric addressed to the Umayyad Caliph 'Abd al-Malik b. Marwan (d. 705). This article is primarily a study of the *qasida* of Layla al-Akhyaliya. Given that the *qasida* is a form reserved exclusively for male poetic expression, one immediately wonders what happens when a female poet such as Layla al-Akhyaliya attempts to enter this male domain. Does she compose the *qasida* in a mimetic manner, assuming the role of a male protagonist, or does she manipulate the *qasida* and inscribe it in such a way as to insert her own female voice? How does she tackle the male role that is defined by the structure of the *qasida*? And if Layla al-Akhyaliya does, indeed, manage to insert her female poetic voice, (how) is the resultant poem distinguishable from a male *qasida*? Does her composition manifest any distinctive features that could be attributed to a specifically female experience? In short, how does Layla, as a female poet, treat the exclusively male poetic form of the *qasida*? I will attempt to answer these questions in the first section of this article, "Transgressive Texts."

The reaction by contemporaries to Layla's transgressive *qasida*, if there was one at all, has not been preserved. However, what has been preserved is the response to one of Layla's other famous transgressions, her invective poetry attacking the well-known poet al-Nabigha al-Ja'di (d. 684).[13] Invective poetry, especially in this early period, was an unusual domain for women. Layla's lampoon of al-Ja'di elicited a riposte from the latter in the form of obscene and overly sexualized verses, which offer us a unique opportunity to assay the reaction of one of Layla's contemporaries and peers to her gender-related poetic trespasses. These will also be taken up in the first section of the paper.

The second section of this paper, "Post-Pre/texts," will explore some of the *akhbar* (reports) surrounding Layla's poetry and life. Layla's unconventional poetic output will be related to the ways in which some of the *akhbar* about her construct and emphasize particular images of her personality as a poet. As is typical of the genre of *akhbar* about poets, reports about Layla seem to be composed of information derived from her poetry (and from that of her admirer and kinsman, Tawba b. al-Humayyir) and woven into disparate narratives *ex post facto*.[14] As mentioned above, Layla is most famous for her elegies: indeed, most of her poetic corpus is made up of *marathi* for her kinsman, Tawba b. al-Humayyir (d. 674), which fact, when devoid of its historical and literary context, seems perfectly conventional. After all, as noted above, elegies for deceased kinsmen are the appropriate discursive space for women poets. However, what makes Layla's *marathi* unusual is the fact that Tawba's entire extant poetic output is made up of *'udhri* (platonic) love poetry for Layla. In this poetry, Tawba expressed his love for Layla, and in the *marathi* she composed after his death, she celebrated him and lamented his passing. One is immediately struck by the fact that, for once, the female object of *'udhri* love poetry finds a fully fledged poetic voice with which she reciprocates the lover, even though this voice is only acquired after the lover's death.[15] What, on the face of it, is an entirely legitimate and conventional poetical project—a woman's lamentation over a dead kinsman—is now transformed into something distinctly unconventional: a woman's lamentation for a departed lover.[16] The images of Layla contained in the *akhbar* were taken, along with her poetry, by medieval critics as evidence of an illicit relationship between her and Tawba. This section of the paper will explore the function of some of the *akhbar* as later narratives elaborated to absolve Layla of suspicions of sexual misconduct. Layla's connections to the Umayyads and their fearsome governor al-Hajjaj b. Yusuf (d. 714), as evidenced by her panegyrics to them, would be employed by later scholars as a vehicle for Layla's absolution. These figures are presented as the authorities who pronounce the dismissal of the charges against her.

It is evident from Layla's poetry and the reports about her that Layla was a maverick woman with a remarkable career.[17] Her transgression does not stop at the fact that she was a beloved who spoke, a woman who composed a masculine *qasida*, and who engaged in exchanges of invective (or flytings). Also remarkable is her heavy involvement in panegyric poetry: other than the *qasida* under study here, Layla's *diwan* contains many shorter panegyric poems. Layla's extensive composition of panegyrics is evidence that she was nothing other than a *professional* poet—that is, someone who actively sought patronage for, and profited from, her poetry. While women have always had a poetic voice, Layla's adoption of poetry as a profession, is, to the best of knowledge, unprecedented. She seems to have been the first professional female Arabic poet, after whom there were a precious few.[18] The questions that are immediately provoked by this remarkable fact are: What is it about early Islamic times that allowed such an extraordinary female figure to exist? And what is it about Layla's poetry that met the requirements for poetic success in her age? In the third section of this chapter, "Context: Flux as Opportunity," I will try to offer, to the extent possible, a historical siting to Layla's literary endeavors by attempting to relate her emergence to what we know about the political and social conditions in the early years of the Umayyad Caliphate that gave rise to the devastatingly competitive market of professional poetry in which the genres of invective and panegyric were the predominant currency, and in which arena the best male poets, or *fuhul*—literally 'stallions'—fought it out.[19]

Trangressive Texts
Layla's *ba'iya*: "I was overcome by emotion"[20]

1   I was overcome by emotion—though this is not time for
        emotions—
        for the tribe settled between 'Adh and Jubjub,[21]

2   of old; their encampment now a playground
        for tatters of wind [blowing] from every direction.

3   How often did their onlooker see there—and I saw him too—
        a generous uncle and father to me!

4   [They are] horsemen from the tribe of Nafada, they are lords,
        and from the line of Ka'b, they are masters, unsurpassed.[22]

5   How many a distant tribe did we raid in the morning,
        so not one of their tents passed the evening under the stars!

6   We launched on them every swift, lank-fleshed, relentless
        mare, rivaling their every swift steed;

7   [Their every] rough-throated [steed] which, when the reins
        draw across his foreshoulders, gallops over soft ground, raising and
            dropping his forelegs together.

8   On [every mare's] flank, from her speed [and the wind],
        a humming like that of a child's pierced top.

9   When [the mare's] sweat, hot water gushes
        from them like the leaking of a water-skin.[23]

10 But leave this! For how I wish for a rider who, when he
        speaks the truth, is not disbelieved!

11 For him I have a she-camel, wide-stepping in her jerky run
        And both her knees turn away from her chest.

12 When urged by his leg, she lowers her neck and goes swiftly
        forward
        like the hastening of the grouse when they arrive from every
            distant land,[24]

13 [Like] the hastening of the thirsty grouse when, in flocks,
    they approach the water spring from every direction.

14 They arrived in the early morning at Ajza', over Sawa'iq,
    at the flowing water of Dhat al-'Ayn, the sweetest of all waters.

15 They remained intoxicated around the springs like
    a group of drinkers who have just emerged from [the quarters] of a
        secluded Persian lord.

16 She drank a little, quenching her thirst, and hastened
    to a gathering place of hers between Shibak and Tandib.

17 She spent the night in a desert, and lingered there in the morning,
    among nest-holes of the hungry, the stomach-knotted.

18 She drew to [her] belly wing and breast,
    and carried a little [water] in a filled craw.[25]

19 When she slows the beating of her wings, she arranges
    [her offspring] on her side, shoulder to shoulder,[26]

20 And when the two [chicks] felt her pecking and writhed from
        hunger,
    and having realized that she had returned from whence she had
        gone,[27]

21 she bent down to the bald heads resembling a boy's
    toy balls made of cloth and rabbit hair.

22 And when night took its leave of her, [after] she had given the two
    the water of a water-skin hanging down still unpierced.

23 she emerged from night into morning like the pit from a date,
    and her offspring, who do not speak Arabic, gibbered and jabbered
        at her.

24 I wish that my rider not go astray
    depriving [the she-camel] of every richness![28]

25 [Then] the gatekeeper will let her through to her kneeling place,
    with his keys he will open the great bolted door.

26 If my she-camel is kneeled by Ibn Marwan [himself],
    then my riding her is not [intended] for [his] retainers.[29]

27 She trusted in my closeness to him, and he decreed in her favor
    a decree, uncontested and irrefutable.[30]

28 For you, after God, are her Commander,
    her protection from fear and from every frightful thing.

29 So, you judge, for, were it not for that I feared your every doubt
   and the least of your threats,

30 the unjust aggressor would not have wronged me,
   and I would not have been brought to this assembly.[31]

31 You confront the gossip of slanderers and you seek[32]
   to do her justice in each of her petitions.

32 When she journeyed through the night until she sighted dawn,
   she continued throughout the day until the setting of the sun.

33 When she saw the Commander [of the Faithful]'s palace she
      squinted at it,
   and I told her: You have [rightly] feared an awesome place,

34 [You have feared] the crowing of the roosters of the palaces,
   and [the yelling] of the guard, and the voice of the caller to prayer,
      calling repeatedly,[33]

35 and the voices of the enemies echoing
   from the rooftops and high portals.

36 The loudest resounds,
   as if a drone in a hive were humming incantations.

Layla begins her poem with the loaded verb *tariba*—meaning, to be overcome with emotion, either of joy or grief. Generally, to determine the meaning of such a verb, which means both a thing and/or its opposite, one remains in a state of suspense until the context is clarified or the semantic unit complete. In keeping with the convention of the *qasida* whose first sequence, the *nasib*, sets a mood of lamentation, grief, and loss, one would be justified in assuming that, in the present poem, the verb *tariba* must carry the meaning of 'grief,'[34] the more so since Layla provides a reason for grief that is conventionally used in *qasa'id*, namely, the departure of 'the tribe.' But, in spite of the conventionality of the theme of the departing tribe, to take *tariba* in the conventional sense of 'to grieve' appears, in the context of this particular verse, to be somewhat illogical. This is owing to Layla's insertion of the concessive clause, "though this is not time for *matrab*"—*matrab*, of course, is the state of being overcome by emotions of either joy or grief. Whatever the emotion Layla is experiencing—whether joy or grief—she clearly thinks that it is the inappropriate emotion for the moment. In other words, the concessive clause introduces an element of reproach. If we render *tariba / matrab* as connoting grief, Layla would be declaring her grief and reproaching herself for being overcome by it. This is somewhat unsettling for an audience accustomed to hearing (or reading) *qasa'id*, since the poetic function of the deserted campsite is precisely to create the occasion for grief, and the opening of the *nasib* is entirely the appropriate time and place at which to indulge in this emotion. Why would Layla reproach herself against an emotion that is normal, conventional, and suitable for the moment?

One possible solution for the apparent contradiction created by the concessive clause is to take it as expressing the conventional *nasib* sentiment of resolving not to dwell on grief after initially indulging in it. In this case, the line would mean something like: "I have grieved, though there is not time (available) for grief." The problem with this interpretation, however, is that the *qasida*'s structure demands that the place where grief ends is the place where the *nasib* ends. This is exactly the technical function of the *takhallus*—literally, the 'doing away with'—which is the structural transition that announces the end of the *nasib* and the beginning of the camel section: 'At last, the poet decides to stop brooding; he mounts his camel and rides away.'[35] In the present poem, the *nasib* (or Layla's version of it) will go on for another nine lines and she will provide the appropriate *takhallus* for it in verse 10: *fa-dhar dha*. In other words, from a structural perspective, understanding *taribtu* to mean 'I was overcome by grief' does not fit the structural requirements of the *qasida* genre.

The reading of *tarab* as grief fits, however, in the context of another poetic genre. The outpouring of grief and quick containment of it that is expressed in the first verse is characteristic of *ritha'* poetry, a form and theme which, as mentioned earlier, is the traditional ground of female poets. It might be suggested that Layla is utilizing this release and containment of grief so as to evoke the sentiments characteristic of *ritha'*, thereby rendering her poetic voice familiar and giving the impression that she is not in the male domain of the *nasib*, but in her own territory. This kind of conscious poetic inversion seems to be one of Layla's 'tricks of the trade.' In another poem of hers, a *marthiya*, she inverses this very same process by opening her elegy with what is almost a *nasib*.[36] Of course, such inversions between *nasib* and *ritha'* are not difficult to imagine; after all, both deal with the same subject of bereavement and grieving. But in the present *qasida*, Layla's invocation of the *ritha'* prefigures what we will find to be her general strategy in the poem, throughout which she evokes sentiments and conventions that belong to the female poetic sphere, thus taming the *qasida* to suit her female voice.[37]

The alternative reading of the verse is to render the meaning of *tariba* as 'to rejoice.' While this reading might appear even more disorienting for the listener/reader, it is, in fact, as plausible as the first. Having established that Layla is reproaching herself in the concessive clause, and is not resolving to put aside her grief, the logical rendition of *tariba* should then be that of joy. Layla, it would appear, is beginning her *qasida* with the unconventional sentiment of joy and, well aware of the unsuitability of such an emotion for that poetic moment, she immediately reproaches herself: "I rejoiced—though this is not time for joy—for the tribe settled between 'Adh and Jubjub." While this reading may be unconventional, or even counter-conventional, it does have the virtue of being perfectly logical in the context of the verse. Whichever reading we choose, Layla's opening verse remains ambiguous and maybe ambivalent. Her use of a verb that expresses both a conventional sentiment and its opposite creates a tension between 'conventionality' and 'unconventionality,' thereby situating her voice between the two states. She reiterates the norm vis-à-vis the poetic form by opening the *qasida* with a reference to the departure of the tribe, but confuses the emotional state that usually attends it. This dissonance of form and content functions as a striking announcement of difference at the very outset of what is to be an unconventional poetic venture.[38]

In verse 2, Layla follows the ordinary progression of the *qasida* to describe the state of the deserted encampments that she finds nothing but a playground for the blasting wind. One would expect Layla to continue describing the ruins for a couple of verses at least, in order that the lyrical mood of the *nasib* be fulfilled with images expressing isolation and desolation, but she does not. Layla's performance of this poetic duty is no more than a formality: one line suffices her.

The poet then proceeds to identify the departing tribe in verses 3 and 4. Of course, one immediately wonders who Layla's departed beloved/lover is going to be. Is Layla going to assume a male voice and describe a Mayya, a Su'ad, or a Fatima? Or is she going to remain true to her female voice and declare a male lover? Layla's solution, however, is not so simple: she neither assumes a male voice nor rests satisfied with a simple inversion of the gender of the beloved. Instead, in the place of the beloved, she mentions her own father and uncle: "How often did their onlooker see . . . a generous uncle and father to me." The object of Layla's loss and yearning is not a lover, but rather her own tribe. To Layla, then, the departure of the tribe represents the loss of the protection and security provided by male kinsmen.

Why, one asks, is it that Layla chose to speak of the loss of kinsmen rather than the loss of a lover? Why did she replace carnal love with filial love? An answer may be found on a purely poetic level. We have already noted the unconventionality of the idea of women composing love poetry: describing amorous encounters, even fictional ones, is, to say the least, untraditional in female poetic expression, despite the fact that it was virtually imperative in the realm of male poetry (viz., the *nasib* as a requirement in the *qasida*). The reader may ask, however, why it is that while Layla is willing to violate one important poetic norm—composing a *qasida*—she shies away from violating another, namely, composing love poetry. It will, in fact, be seen throughout this study that Layla repeatedly sets careful limits to her transgression, and that the specific junctures at which Layla decides to draw the line seem to be primarily expressive of her overriding concern not to impersonate the male experience.

There is, however, another plausible interpretation of this verse. If one can establish with certainty that the Ka'b mentioned in verse 4 is indeed related to Tawba b. al-Humayyir,[39] Layla's famous admirer, then one might be justified in suggesting that Layla is perhaps flirting with the *nasib*, as she had done in her elegiac *ra'iya*,[40] but this time, it is the *nasib* in its amorous form. As noted above, Layla happens to be the object of all of Tawba's extant *'udhri* poetry. If the departing tribe is that of Tawba, then Layla is definitely alluding to a loss of a romantic liaison. If this is the case, then Layla is using a seemingly innocent *nasib* (or rather a pseudo-*nasib*) to convey the original love sentiment found in the male *nasib*. Layla's *nasib*, however, is without the sexual content: it is, effectively, an *'udhri nasib* in exchange for Tawba's *'udhri* love poetry.

Whether or not Layla is alluding to the loss of a romantic connection, she refrains from opening her *qasida* by overtly describing a departing lover. Instead, she paints an image of herself as a vulnerable woman without the protection of kin. However, what is remarkable is that she accomplishes this by replacing the *nasib* 'icon of the lady' with the tribe as a new and different *dramatis persona*. Through this image of vulnerability, Layla actually manages to express a very similar sentiment to that of the male poet/protagonist in the *qasida*, namely that of reminiscence, loss, and yearning. Thus, in spite of the change of the cast of characters, the sentiment of the *nasib* is fulfilled.[41]

Having identified the departed tribe (the clans of Nafada and Ka'b),[42] Layla plunges into an unexpected *fakhr* sequence boasting of the warrior qualities of the tribe (beginning at verse 5).[43] She presents a battle sequence in which she juxtaposes her tribe's relentless mare and the enemy's swift steed (verses 6–9). As with the first line, the listener/reader is disoriented since, conventionally, a *fakhr* sequence should not appear in the *nasib*. Rather, *fakhr* may either constitute the *gharad* of the *qasida*, occupying the last part of the poem, or it may appear in flashes in the camel section, which falls in the middle part of the poem. Why does Layla introduce a *fakhr* sequence at this juncture, where it is not only structurally out of place, but also strikes a discordant note with the lamentory and contemplative mood of the *nasib*? The most plausible answer seems to be that by describing the superlative qualities of the departed tribe, Layla is able to emphasize the extent and nature of her loss. The tribe for which Layla yearns is not any 'run-of-the-mill' crowd, but an exemplary tribe whose warrior qualities provide the ultimate in protection and shelter. Since Layla cannot plausibly present herself as the warrior-hero of the *qasida*, she assumes the female role and laments the loss of a warrior-hero, thus echoing the theme which is rightfully hers, namely *ritha'*.[44] Again, Layla's *nasib* is effectively a *ritha'*: once again, we see her exploiting the parallelism between *nasib* and *ritha'* to domesticate the *qasida* and recast it in terms more poetically appropriate to her.

Quite conventionally, Layla begins the *takhallus* from the (pseudo-) *nasib* to the camel section with the phrase, "Leave this!" (verse 10). Like any poet-protagonist of a *qasida*, she resolves not to feel sorry for herself and decides to take the initiative. However, it is at this point that the poetic form would appear to be most resistant to her female voice. The camel section is, after all, expressive of a quintessentially male experience—that of the harsh desert journey of the heroic rider and his heroic mount (whose identities often converge in the course of their common trials), and thus of the male ideals of courage, endurance, and heroism which are displayed on the journey. Here, then, we have a head-on collision between two apparently incompatible elements. On the one hand, there is the poetic form, which demands that there be a camel section, and on the other, there is the above-noted heroic role of the protagonist which, on the poetic level at least, prescribes the desert journey and its ideals for males only. In responding to this dilemma, Layla would appear to have two options. One option is to take up the task of the camel section by setting out on the desert journey herself, in which case she will have to assume the male persona of the heroic rider. Her other option is to omit the desert journey altogether, thereby remaining within the norms of gender roles but irretrievably compromising the structural requirements of the poem. Layla's solution is an ingenious device through which she once again fulfils the structure and function of the male poetic form while recasting its *dramatis personae* to satisfy the restrictions of gender norms. She reconciles poetic form with gender role by literally creating an external mediator. Instead of going on the journey herself, Layla invents the character of a male rider (verse 10) to whom she delegates the task of the journeying through the desert. In other words, unable to plausibly undertake the journey herself, she simply sends someone else. The danger with this 'send someone else' scenario, however, is that in delegating ridership, Layla will automatically have to concede to the rider the role of the male hero, thereby delegating her own protagonist persona onto the rider and losing the agency of poetic voice that is critical to the *qasida*. Layla avoids this relegation of her role by redefining the conventional relationship between rider and camel in the camel section. As noted above, the shared experience of the desert journey conventionally results in a degree of convergence in the identities of rider and camel; the rider-protagonist identifies with his heroic mount.[45] In Layla's poem, however, no identification is made between the camel and the rider who, after all, must not be allowed to become the hero; instead, it is Layla's identity that is collapsed with that of the she-camel. By casting the camel as her alter-ego, Layla retains her protagonist role in the camel section, this despite the fact that she is not riding. The transference of identity from poet to she-camel is accomplished here, not through the conventional fact of companionship in journey, but by the explicit statement of the poet's ownership of the camel (*la-hu naqatun 'ind-i*, verse 11), which, in the conventional *qasida*, is presumed to be the property of the rider-protagonist. To be able to employ the camel as her alter ego, Layla specifies the fact of her ownership, rendering it the catalyst of identity transfer. Ingeniously, by a combination of an innovation (a delegate rider) and the re-alignment of an old theme (casting the she-camel as the poet's alter ego through ownership rather than companionship), Layla accomplishes the poetic performance of the camel section without impersonating the male role of the hero, but also without conceding this role to the rider, thereby retaining her agency as poet-protagonist. Thus, we find again that the form is fulfilled and her poetic voice preserved. We will see later that it is through her camel alter ego that Layla eventually appears at the destination of the journey.

As in other *qasidas*, once Layla mentions the she-camel, she proceeds to describe her (verse 11). She compares the swiftness of the camel's movement to that of a flock of sand grouse (*qata*, verse 12), and then launches into a series of sand grouse images that occupies the whole of the camel section. The first sequence is that of a flock of sand grouse as they approach a spring to drink and are intoxicated with the sweetest of all waters (verses 13–15). In the next series, the focus narrows to a mother sand grouse as she nurtures her chicks (verses 18–23). What is striking about the camel section in this poem is that the standard hunting scene is not present. Usually, through an extended simile, the she-camel is compared to a wild ass or wild bull, which courageously escapes being hunted down by dogs. Similarly, when sand grouse are used in the camel section as an extended simile for the she-camel, it is usually in a hunting motif where the grouse is presented as quarry being pursued by a bird of prey.[46] Both the hunted wild ass or bull and the pursued grouse are confronted by the proximity of death, but manage to escape it. These scenes represent a symbolic reenactment, or rather pre-enactment, of the male protagonist who, like the threatened bull, emerges from his ordeal as the survivor hero.

In her use of the grouse imagery, Layla does not present the birds as quarry. Instead, she employs images that, although not unusual per se, are not generally associated with the she-camel or the camel section. These are the stock images of the drinking grouse and of the hungry and helpless chicks awaiting the return of their mother.[47] Layla opts to employ neither the model of the male hero who survives the desert journey, nor its reenactment through hunting similes. Instead, she proffers a heroic model of her own: the mother grouse. In the first grouse series (verses 13–15), the poet portrays a satisfied and content community of grouse who are "intoxicated" with "the sweetest of all waters." The individual and collective survival and well-being of the grouse are dependent on the central role of the mother grouse (verses 16–23). The mother grouse is portrayed as being on full alert at all times, busy in the nurturing of her chicks. She travels long distances to bring water for her chicks (verses 16, 18, 21, and 22, respectively). When the mother grouse is not busy providing drink, she provides security and affection for her chicks by guarding them at night and keeping them physically close to her (verses 17 and 19, respectively). In the final verses of the grouse scene (verses 22 and 23) after she has done her maternal duties, night ends and the chicks are (happily) jabbering away. Thus, the second grouse scene moves from the sound of the chicks crying out of hunger (verse 20) to their convivial gibbering and jabbering (verse 23), and from night (verse 17) to day (verse 23)—in other words, the transition is from insecurity to safety. In Layla's version of the camel section, the similes serve as a reenactment of a female experience where it is the mother, not the male traveler, who emerges as the hero.

Although we do not know whether the embedding of these particular grouse images in the camel section was Layla's innovation, she was evidently regarded as an authority on the sand grouse in poetry, since she is recorded as having been sought out to serve as adjudicator in a grouse imagery competition among five poets.[48] But it does appear that Layla composed these images in inter-textual response to, or dialogue with, one of the greatest poets of the Arabic literary tradition: 'Alqama b. 'Abada (d. ca. 603).[49] In the camel section of his classic *mimiya*, 'Alqama proffers what is considered a rare scene for a camel section: a most exquisite depiction of a male ostrich hastening back to his offspring and 'spouse.'[50]

1   Until he remembers some eggs, disquieted by a day
    of a drizzle and wind and a covering of cloud
2   He quickens his pace, without strain,
    whisking along just short of all out, untiring
3   Split-foot flying past his bulging eye,
    as if he were wary of ill luck, fear-quickened
4   He doubles back to a down-cropped brood of nestlings
    that appear when they tumble over like a clod-covered root
5   Circling the nest hollow, circling again,
    searching for tracks . . .
6   Until he reaches as the sun's horn rises
    the next hollow and a heap of eggs

7　Beckoning to them with a crackling and a clucking
　　like a babble of Greeks in their fortresses,
8　Small-headed, thin-necked, wings and chest
　　like a caved-up heap of a tent set up wrong by a clumsy maid
9　A female draws near, long neck lowered,
　　responding with a warbling cry.[51]

The parent here is the male ostrich who, away from his offspring, "in two temporally separate flashes, race[s] back once to the eggs, another time to the chicks."[52] The fearful ostrich hastens, and arrives by dawn to find that the chicks are safe. He happily cackles and clucks at/with them. The camel sections ends with a convivial family scene, as the mother ostrich approaches to join in the babble.

Layla's grouse scene is a mirror image of 'Alqama's ostrich scene. Structurally, both conclude the respective camel sections. Thematically, both poets use birds as extended similes of the camel. Emotively, the sections are about parenting, where the main protagonists are parents who, fearful for the safety of their chicks, return to the nest. The conclusions are almost identical: a happy scene of a family in conversation. In both instances, bird speech is described as non-Arabic "gibberish": in 'Alqama's poem, the birds "*babble in Greek*," while in Layla's the chicks "*who do not speak Arabic, gibbered and jabbered* at her."[53] Layla does not only mirror, she sometimes humorously ripostes: for 'Alqama's ostrich, she provides a sand grouse; for his male protagonist, she provides a female; and if 'Alqama's use of ostrich scenes in the camel section is uncommon, then Layla's use of a grouse scene is even more so. It seems that Layla successfully rose up to the challenge of dialogue with a 'stallion' (*fahl*), as her engagement with 'Alqama was not without result: in the Arabic literary canon, he is considered an authority on ostrich description,[54] and she on the grouse.[55]

The ostrich tableau in 'Alqama's camel section thus provided Layla with a precedent and an important opportunity. If in the 'typical' camel section the protagonist is expected go through a 'liminal' stage where he is separated from the community,[56] and where he is fearful but fighting courageously, in the less common version of it, such as that of 'Alqama and now of Layla, the protagonist is at the center of community, nurturing needy offspring. This helps to shed light on the function of the camel section in general. If the 'typical' male heroism is about coming close to death, Layla's female heroism (facilitated by 'Alqama's precedent) is about sustaining life. Thus, whether the camel section is seen as a rite of passage (à la Stetkevych), or as a reflection of self and cosmos (à la Adonis), it is ultimately about the responsibility of the individual to the community. This point will be taken up later.

In the same way that Layla began the camel section by wishing for a rider who would faithfully accomplish the mission (verse 10), she closes it with a neat symmetry wishing that the rider not deviate from the appointed course (verse 24). While this type of symmetry between the *takhallus*es of the respective sections is quite conventional, it is particularly noteworthy in the present *qasida*. In moving from *nasib* to camel section, Layla used the *takhallus* to create the necessary device of the 'rider.' She now uses the *takhallus* at the end of the camel section to summarily dispose of him. His function and mission have now become clear, namely, to accomplish faithfully the desert journey and bring the camel safely to the caliph's gate where it can avail itself of caliphal riches (verse 24). Layla has no further use for the rider; he is not going to petition alongside her for caliphal favors, and will not appear in the *qasida* again. The mention of the caliph 'Abd al-Malik b. Marwan in the transition to the *gharad* brings us to the panegyric aspect of the *qasida*.

Panegyric poetry, especially in its post-Jahili phase, has generally been poorly regarded by contemporary scholars.[57] Its emergence has been posited as the historical marker for the rise of professional poetry where the poet uses his skills to earn a living, as opposed to an implicit notion of the poet as a creative, genuine, and free artist. In short, panegyric poetry is seen as a reflection of the sycophantism of the poet toward figures of authority, and thus of the debasing of poetry for material reward.[58] Putting such value judgments aside, there is no doubt that the authority of the caliph, ruler, or notable takes center stage in the panegyric. As has been shown by Sperl, it is in the first part of the poem that the bipartite Abbasid panegyric exhibits loss, hardship, decay, or whatever negative situation. This situation is transformed in the second part by the grace of the ruler through whom loss is compensated, hardship relieved, and decay replaced by rejuvenation.[59] In other words, the process that takes place in the final stage of both the tri- and bipartite panegyric *qasida*—namely, the successful reunion with society, or aggregation after 'liminality'—is only effected with the permission of the ruler.

Layla's panegyric, like its counterparts composed by male poets, is about loss and recovery, but the camel section in her *qasida* gives rise to a new view of the function of the camel section in panegyrics in general. While Ibn Qutayba sees the camel section as a display of the hardships undergone by the poet in order to provoke the sympathies of the ruler,[60] Layla al-Akhyaliya's *qasida* seems to understand the function of the camel section as the vehicle by which the poet presents proof of fealty to the ruler. Through the images of the mothering grouse, Layla has shown to the caliph that she, as a female, had done her duty toward her community, sustaining and nurturing its most vulnerable members, namely the infants. This view may also be applied to the male version of the camel section. Through the hunting scenes and the ultimate survival of the protagonist animal or bird, the poet shows his abilities as a warrior, thus demonstrating his performance of his duty as protector of his community. Both male and female protagonists emerge from the camel section as having shown their readiness to carry out their respective duties toward society. Hence, it is not only in the act of presenting the panegyric that the poet pledges his allegiance to the ruler, as demonstrated by Suzanne Pinckney Stetkevych,[61] but also in the content of the poem itself. More will be said about panegyric and the rise of professional poetry in the last section of this paper.

The *gharad* of Layla's *qasida* is the place where we will witness the reemergence of Layla as a participant character. Throughout the camel section and into the first couple of verses in the *gharad*, Layla was present, not as a character in her own right, but through her surrogate self—the she-camel. In verse 26, the she-camel arrives at the caliph's palace and, in verse 27, it is the she-camel—acting on Layla's behalf—who is in audience with the caliph. This is attested by the poet's use of the third person in referring to the she-camel (starting verse 25). However, in verse 28, Layla switches to begin addressing the caliph in the second person, as if she herself were now present at the caliph's court. Then in verses 28 and 29, Layla resumes the use of the third person in reference to the petitioner of the caliph, which leaves the listener/reader wondering whether she is referring to herself or to the she-camel. In verses 29 and 30, Layla finally refers to herself in the first person, reemerging as a character who is independent of and separate from the she-camel surrogate.

On her arrival at the palace, Layla approaches the caliph with hesitation and fear (verse 29), and pleads for his protection—which may or may not be granted. She is at the palace requesting a caliphal decree that would protect her from slanderers who have wronged her (verse 30). It should be noted that the motif of antagonism between the poet and the figure of the slanderer (*washi*, pl. *wushat*), is not particular to Layla. The *washi* is, of course, a standard character who figures in many famous panegyrics composed by men,[62] and who, in a given instance, may be a real person or a literary device. In Layla's case, we do know that she was involved in flytings with other poets, and hence may have indeed been 'slandered;'[63] however, Layla's invocation of the slanderer figure is particularly shrewd since, from a narrative standpoint, it renders the *gharad* consistent with the *nasib*. In the *nasib*, Layla loses kin protection, and this, in turn, results in the eventual emergence of slanderers threatening the unprotected woman in the *gharad*. In the male panegyric, there is less of a logical connection between the loss of the beloved in the *nasib* and the later emergence of oppressors in the *gharad*. So, while Layla's *qasida* is consistent with the male panegyric in terms of expressing a loss that is to be compensated by the caliph, it simultaneously exhibits a narrative element that renders the experiential and emotive aspect of the *qasida* more urgent and more real. She has lost the protection of the warrior (in the *nasib*), and though she has fulfilled all the requirements of fealty to the ruler (in the camel section), she is now defenseless against the slanderers (in the *gharad*): does she really deserve this fate? The denouement of Layla's predicament is finally at hand. The magnanimous caliph obliges: he confronts Layla's slanderers (verse 31), issues "in her favor a decree, uncontested and irrefutable" (verse 27), protects her from fear, and assures her satisfaction (verse 28). This, however, is not the end of the story, for there is a second part to Layla's *gharad* (verses 32–36).

After Layla describes the events of her meeting with the caliph in the first part of the *gharad*, she goes back in time to describe the moment of her physical arrival at the environs of the palace. In verse 32, the she-camel is on the last leg of her journey in the desert. In the next verse, she arrives at the environs of the palace, an urban setting with which she is probably unfamiliar and of which she is afraid. Layla describes the many discordant sounds that have frightened her she-camel: the call of the muezzin, the yelling of the palace guard, the crowing of roosters, and the voices of Layla's enemies echoing from the rooftops. While ' 'uphony may be frightening for the she-camel, these same sounds represent manifestations of security for Layla. In opposition to the *nasib*'s empty, windswept encampments, this space is full of human interaction. Layla is now close to her protector's abode (the caliph's palace), listening to noises that include the reassuring call of the muezzin. And while Layla does hear the voices of her enemies, these voices are cast back by the rooftops as if the urban structures themselves are keeping the enemies at bay. Layla concludes her *ba'iya* with an apparently ambivalent sound image: she compares the clamor *(dawiyy)* which has alarmed her she-camel to the sound of a drone humming incantations, which is an aural image of soothing quality. The ambivalent quality of this sound image reflects the tension between the she-camel's fear, on the one hand, and Layla's sense of security, on the other. This contradiction of feelings would seem to echo the ambivalence of the opening line of the *qasida*. The ambivalence in these last few verses is a subject that we will take up in the next section.

The *qasida* is considered to be representative of the male voice, and Layla's poem emerges as the exception that proves the rule. Her *ba'iya* is not a mimetic attempt at a *qasida*, it is rather a manipulation of a form that is experientially male. In this manipulation, Layla manages the poetic performance of all of the structural parts of the *qasida* without ever assuming a male role. Instead, she carefully domesticates the form in a manner that reaffirms the femaleness of her voice. Layla opens her poem with an ambiguous verse announcing her difference, and then proceeds to alter the *dramatis personae* of the *nasib* by exchanging the loss of the beloved for the loss of the protection of the tribe. In the camel section, Layla invents the character of the rider and collapses her identity with that of her she-camel. Also, instead of the model of the warrior hero, the poet adapts the image of the 'parenting bird' from one of the greatest poets in the tradition and alters it to offer the model of the mother heroine. In the *madih*, she uses the conventional figure of the slanderer (whether real or imagined) to provide a narrative element that would reinforce the notion of the loss of the protector, and thus render her predicament all the more urgent and convincing. Another trick Layla uses in her manipulation of the *qasida* is the evocation of poetical forms and themes that are legitimately female, such as the *fakhr* sequence in the *nasib*, which echoes *ritha'*. The *qasida* that emerges from these devices tells a story of a woman in search of a protector, whom she finds in the figure of the caliph. In her *ba'iya*, Layla 'de-genders' the *qasida* form and re-inscribes it with her own female poetic voice. In declaring her difference, Layla is effectively announcing the fact of her trespass, and thus acknowledging the exclusive male proprietorship of the domain of the *qasida*.

While Layla al-Akhyaliya's poetical transgression is carefully manipulated to avoid her assuming a male role, the fact of her composing a panegyric constitutes yet another violation, not only poetically, but also socially. With her composition of a panegyric, Layla is evidently behaving like a professional poet who earns a living from panegyric poetry; all indications are that this is squarely a male category. The scale of Layla's multiple transgressions can usefully be gauged with reference to Mayy Khulayf's representative assessment of the nature of women's poetry:

> Absent from her [the female poet's] poetry is the standard form
> of the panegyric with which the critics have occupied themselves,
> and through which they have defined the traditional form of Arabic
> qasida in terms of prelude *(muqaddima)*, desert journey *(rihla)*,
> subject *(mawdu')*, and conclusion *(khatima)*. For it seems that some
> of these elements are, in their very nature, incompatible with
> the female character of women's poetry. It is not befitting that a
> woman stand at the ruins and weep for the lover, nor that she woo
> a man, nor depict the departure of the tribe, nor even describe
> her journey across the terrifying desert to the individual whom
> the poet eulogizes, nor anything resembling such situations which
> are appropriate to the nature of men; especially to professional
> composers of panegyrics.[64]

Given this general impression of women's poetry, it is not difficult to see that Layla's appropriation of the *qasida*, as careful as it was, must have been construed as, at the very least, inappropriate. While we do not have any record of any reaction to Layla's ode by her contemporaries, we do, fortunately, have a response to another one of Layla's trangressions: her aforementioned invective against the poet, al-Nabigha al-Ja'di. Al-Ja'di, the object of Layla's invective, clearly views Layla's taking up satire as an intrusion on the male domain, and responds accordingly:

Greet Layla and tell her, "Whoa!"
she has committed a reckless, infamous deed;

She has eaten the herbage of a rotten plant
and drunk the urine of a mountain she-goat at the end of summer.
Leave the habit of satirizing men, and occupy yourself
with an uncircumcised man who will fill your anus with his penis!
How should I satirize a poet whose lance is his anus
whose fingers are hennaed, and who wears kohl?[65]

Although obscenity and sexually overt references form a part of the repertoire of male poetry,[66] al-Nabigha's riposte offers a topography that clearly demarcates the female discursive space. His attack on Layla is directed solely at her violation of poetic gender norms. He does not mock Layla's abilities as a poet, nor does he malign her tribe. Instead, he attacks her because she is a 'henna-fingered' woman who dares to commit the shameless act of satirizing men. He immediately sexualizes her act, presenting it as arising from sexual frustration. He portrays Layla as drinking the urine of a mountain goat, which is considered to be a sexual stimulant for women,[67] upon which, instead of engaging in sexual intercourse, she sets about satirizing men. For al-Nabigha, a woman satirizing a man represents the abnormal displacement of a sexual act. The first hemistich of the last verse is particularly revealing of the relationship between gender norms and poetry. Al-Nabigha is at a loss as to how to reply to a poet whose weapon is not penis but "anus." To al-Nabigha, a satirizing poet must be a man. Layla's satire is thus the poetic performance of sexual perversion.[68] If Layla's peer thought of her adventure in the male domain as a sexual aberration, what did medieval scholars of Arabic literature, who collected, transmitted, and codified the early literary tradition (in other words, who authored and authorized the canon), make of this extraordinary woman? This is the subject of the next section.

Post-Pre/texts

Who was Layla al-Akhyaliya in the eyes of the medieval students of Arabic literature? A ready answer is found in the poetry of the famous Abbasid poet Abu Tammam (d. 842) quoted at the outset of the paper. The line is found in a panegyric by the poet to one of his friends. In it Abu Tammam compares his friend's eloquence, on the one hand, to that of Quss Ibn Sa'ida, a contemporary of the Prophet, who is considered to be *the* orator *par excellence* in Arabic literary history, and on the other to that of Layla al-Akhyaliya in her poetry of lamentation *(wa ka'anna Layla al-Akhyaliyatu tandubu)*! Thus, two centuries after her death, Layla not only remained in the collective memory, but also was seen to possess exemplary poetic eloquence by no less a significant literary figure than Abu Tammam. By juxtaposing Layla's poetic prowess to Quss Ibn Sa'ida's rhetorical dexterity, Abu Tammam puts Layla's verbal achievements on a par with those of an established paragon of eloquence. However, Abu Tammam qualifies Layla's eloquence: it is of the lamenting variety. This qualification by Abu Tammam explains why medieval literati so readily compared Layla to the 'elegiac queen' of Arabic literature, al-Khansa' (d. 645).[69] Al-Asma'i (d. 831) thought that Layla was a better poet than *(ash'aru min)* al-Khansa',[70] while Ibn Qutayba (d. 889) favored the poetry of al-Khansa' over that of Layla.[71] Al-Mubarrad (d. 898) said that the two should not be compared since both were excellent and fully deserving of praise: "How many women excel at a craft? This is a rare occurrence!"[72] Thus, it is clear, from both Abu Tammam's poetry and the prompt comparisons with al-Khansa', that Layla was accorded her venerable place in the canon because of her elegies. In other words, it was the fact that Layla undertook poetic endeavors that are *legitimate* for a woman poet that she found a place in the canon. However, despite Layla's uncontested location in the Arabic literary tradition, the tradition also betrays considerable anxieties about her, which are directly related to her 'illegitimate' poetic exercises. This observation brings us to the problematic genre of *akhbar*.

Akhbar (sg. *khabar*) are narratives that frame the poetic text, purportedly providing the immediate context or occasion for the poetic composition.[73] The reliability of *akhbar* is suspect at best, since they often function as a myth-making apparatus. For example, the reports that include details about Layla's death are not only contradictory, but also marvellously dramatic. One report depicts Layla traveling with her husband, by chance passing by the grave of her lover Tawba, and promptly dropping dead at his graveside.[74] Another report portrays her, in old age, chasing al-Nabigha al-Ja'di all the way to Khurasan, until she dies during the chase.[75] Tragic or romantic endings aside, the unreliability of such reports does not rob them of utility. Rather, these reports reveal the attempts by their authors (whether authorship is individual or collective, and whether the reports are composed within a short period of time or

have accreted over generations) to make sense of the poetry being transmitted, and to resolve the contradictions therein. By framing poetic texts,
the narrative reports give coherence and rational order to both the poetry
and the lives lived behind it (whether these lives belong to the poets themselves, or the individuals and groups mentioned in the poetry). These
reports, then, allow us to view how later authors deduced the lives and
careers of the early poets from their poetry. Inasmuch as these reports
provide occasion or context, they provide a motive for the poet's composition. Thus, these narratives can also function as pretexts allowing the
poet to defend positions that seem morally or socially questionable; they
are texts that can function as *pretexts* composed *ex post facto* (hence, the
term 'post-pre/texts').[76]

In the case of Layla's *akhbar*, the situation is further compounded by
the fact that her lover Tawba was also a prolific poet. Thus, the reports are
not only numerous and concern the poets individually and severally, but
also attempt to reconcile the two poetic corpuses, and to understand each
corpus not only in terms of itself, but also in terms of the other. Naturally,
a comprehensive treatment cannot be undertaken here, but I will briefly
dwell on two reports of relevance to our study.

It will be remembered that in the report quoted at the outset, where
Layla is portrayed as an unidentified male rider in quest of Caliph
Mu'awiya, her gender identity is assumed to be male until she removes
her face cover to reveal that she is a woman. This report seems to reflect
not so much anxiety as full awareness both of Layla's appropriation and of
her manipulation of the *qasida*. In the report, like her *ba'iya*, which takes a
decidedly male poetic form, Layla appears in a male condition, but upon
careful viewing, both Layla and the *qasida* reveal their gender identity. Of
course, the image of the poet-rider's arrival at the caliph's palace is as a
standard motif dramatizing the beginning of the *gharad* in the generic
panegyric; in the present instance, this motif is relocated to a narrative
prologue to the presentation of Layla's panegyric *qit'a* to Caliph Mu'awiya.
It is ironic that while Layla went to great lengths in her poem to avoid
playing the male role of the rider, it would appear that by the simple fact
of her being a panegyrist, it is in this male capacity that one of her memories has been preserved.

However, the interest of this report lies not only in the gender confusion that reflects an awareness of Layla's transgressive career, but also

in the understanding of the relationship between panegyrist and *mamduh* (the object of the panegyric, or patron) being portrayed. Upon sighting the rider, the caliph is instantly curious, and subsequently fetches him (or rather, her) only to find that the rider herself is seeking the caliph himself. Given that the report does not state a rationale behind this coincidence of instant (and almost erotic) union, it insinuates a natural, subliminal attraction between patron and panegyrist. This mutual desire is in turn suggestive of the codependent or symbiotic relationship that Layla had with the Umayyad house. This point will be taken up later.

The gender confusion in the previous report is, nonetheless, quite innocuous in comparison to the allegations of sexual perversion made by Layla's contemporary, al-Ja'di, indicating that unlike her contemporaries, the later authors of reports about Layla seem to have been relatively unconcerned about the impropriety of Layla's professional career as a practitioner of panegyric and invective poetry. However, the later authors of reports do seem to have harbored great anxieties with regard to Layla's relationship with Tawba b. al-Humayyir. The fact that Layla chose not to play the role of the conventionally silent object of Tawba's love, but rather transgressed poetical norms by composing *marathi* to her lover, must have contributed to the circulation of reports conveying a public suspicion of her transgressing not merely poetic, but socio-sexual norms:

Haytham said: . . . he (Ishaq b. al-Jassas) told me on the authority of Hammad al-Rawiya: When Layla finished reciting her poetry, al-Hajjaj approached his companions and said to them, "Do you know who this is?" They said, "No! But, we have not seen a more eloquent [*afsah*] or articulate [*ablagh*] woman, nor a better reciter than she [*wa la ahsana inshadan*]!" He said, "This is Layla, the beloved of [*sahibat*] Tawba." Then he (al-Hajjaj) approached her and said, "By God, Layla, did Tawba ever do anything that you considered repugnant, or ask you (for) something shameful [*aw sa'ala-ki shay'an yu'ab*]?" She said, "By God, of whom I ask forgiveness, he never did anything of the sort [*ma kana dhalika min-hu qatt*]". He (al-Hajjaj) said, "If this was not (the case) [*idha lam yakun*] then may God have mercy upon us and upon him."[77]

This interrogation of Layla's most intimate personal affairs functions as a double-edged sword. On the one hand, the reports make its clear that there was a public suspicion of an illicit relationship between Layla and Tawba which was sufficiently widespread for the matter to be taken up by the highest social authority, the caliph [78] and his governor. On the other hand, it provides Layla with a platform from which to answer these suspicions, and thus functions as a pretext for the normalization of her sexuality. In defending herself, Layla was very likely helped by her high political connections, as evidenced by her extant panegyrics to the various members of the Umayyad ruling family, and their representatives.[79] It is this verifiable connection to the Umayyads that enabled later authors of reports about her life to furnish the court as the *mise-en-scène* for her trials. And once the highest authorities had absolved Layla of any suspicion of sexual misconduct, no one dared to cast further aspersions. It is interesting that the modern editors of Layla's *Diwan* seem to have shared the anxieties of their medieval counterparts regarding Layla's conduct. However, they too seem to have been convinced by Layla's purported defense, and devoted a whole section of their introduction to establishing "her chastity."[80]

One wonders if Layla ever thought that her panegyrics would continue to reap rewards not only for herself, but for her memory for centuries to come. Later authors seem to have found in her professional career, and the connections implied therein, the appropriate context to save her reputation as a woman who dared to publicize her love. Through the transmission of reports that confirmed Layla's relationship to Tawba as platonic, Layla's elegies were maintained in the 'pure' moral and literary status of a woman's lament over a fallen kinsman. These later authors' 'post scripts' not only functioned as pretexts by which Layla's sexuality was normalized, but also ensured that her place in the canon remained uncontested and unblemished.

Context: Flux as Opportunity

In many ways, Layla's poetic career is both unprecedented and unsurpassed. While the literary tradition has preserved the memory of some later professional female poets, none achieved Layla al-Akhyaliya's canonical status. And although her achievements must be attributed primarily to her literary prowess, one cannot help but ask the question: what is it about the early Umayyad period that allowed a woman to embark on, and succeed in, such an unusual poetic career? And what is it in Layla's poetic experiments that met the success standards of the age? Unfortunately, given that Layla's life is historically difficult to substantiate (the only relatively reliable documentation about her life is her extant poetry), and given our still limited knowledge about the Umayyad period, the answer to these questions must be speculative.

I suspect that a part of the answer to the question of what made Layla's poetic career possible may lie in the fact that Layla lived during a period of a great historical transition, when the nascent Muslim community, now informed by a new ethic and vision of the world, was attempting to establish an order that would actualize its vision. This was a period of profound political, social, and economic flux which witnessed a struggle for political power between various movements (Zubayrids, 'Alids, Kharijis, and Umayyads), accompanied by the maneuverings of individuals and communities attempting to insert themselves into the emerging order.[81] Layla would seem to be one such individual whose unique voice emerged in response to the opportunities provided by a situation of flux and transition in which community and order were in the process of formation. One such opportunity for self-insertion was provided by the rise of professional poetry under the early Umayyad state.

It has been widely noted that the panegyric *qasida* became the pre-eminent literary form in Arabic literature in the early Umayyad period (661–750).[82] On the literary level, eulogy was accompanied by its mirror-image invective, and the practice of flyting. On the social (and perhaps, economic) level, the paradigmatic status of the panegyric in the Umayyad period supported the phenomenon of 'professional poetry.' This search for patrons has been seen by modern Arab critics, following some medieval critics such as Ibn Rashiq, in pejorative crude terms as "the sale of poetry as a means to earn a living" *(al-takassub bi al-shi'r)*, whereby art is debased for material reward and the poet made servile to power. Also implied in this critique is an idea of the poet as an individualist who no longer acts as an altruistic spokesperson for the collective.[83] Such narrow vision of the Umayyad panegyric as merely a sale of a poem by a greedy sycophantic individual to a sovereign eager for flattery fails to see the full political and cultural implications of early Islamic poetry. What follows is a re-reading of early Umayyad poetry, which views the phenomenon of professional poetry not in terms of its debasement, but rather of its use as a *tool* in politics, whereby both individual and tribe are participating in the political process. Early Umayyad poetry is thus expressive of an important change in the nature and shape of the 'poetry market.'

It does not need restating that pre-Islamic poetry was not art for art's sake. In addition, by virtue of being the primary cultural product in pre-Islamic Arabia and the primary vehicle of public discourse, poetry also served a vital social and political function.[84] Poetry had the power to persuade, dissuade, oblige, and absolve; it served as the memory storehouse of the tribe, and the panegyric to the tribe functioned as a purposive means of forging and reinforcing tribal identity.[85] However, in the absence of a centralized state and its courts, the market for poetry was as diffuse as the political system that the poetry negotiated. With the rise of the buffer states of the Ghassanids and the Lakhmids, and then of the much larger Islamic state, these centers of powers acted as political and cultural poles, which as a result encouraged and attracted the various tribes to coalesce around them politically, and hence culturally. Thus, while all of the poetic capacities and functions—persuasion, dissuasion, obligation, identity formation, and so on—carried over to the Islamic period, the poetry market relocated to and became concentrated around the central and regional courts, as the different tribes offered political allegiance and negotiated their places with the new dispensation. The poetic functions were transposed into the new politics and society, with the new locus of performance being the court.[86]

The new Islamic political and social order did not emerge smoothly. It was riddled by civil wars and rebellions fought out between competing claimants to leadership.[87] In this era of contestation, not only did every political contestant need poetry to promote, legitimate, and defend his thesis, but every tribe and social group needed a poet-spokesperson to make a convincing case for a place within the new order.[88] Thus, the early Islamic poetry market became spatially concentrated at centers of power, politically polarized between competing groups, and individually competitive between poets vying not only, on the one hand, with other poets representing different political groupings, but also, on the other hand, with poets from the same political group all seeking preeminence at the court. This war of words reflected the different creeds of the various aspirants for the community's leadership, and was in turn reflected in the emergence of the genre of *naqa'id*, or poetic duels.[89] Although the poet might use his own personal voice in the poem, whether panegyric or invective, the tribe or group that the poet (or his opponent) represented is embedded in the poetic statement. Thus, the poetic exchanges in the early Islamic period represent a complex of mutual needs and transactions, where a patron needs the allegiance of a tribe conveyed through its representative poet, and the poet needs the support of the patron for an appropriate location for himself and the tribe. This codependence is picturesquely reflected in the natural attraction between Layla and the caliph depicted in the report quoted at the outset, and analyzed above.

Layla comes forward with her poetry not only as an individual, but as a representative of her family and tribe, the Akhaylis and the Banu Ka'b, respectively. In some of the surviving pieces of her panegyrics, such as in the *ba'iya* analyzed above, Layla includes a *fakhr* (boast) sequence extolling the virtues of her tribe, thus positing herself as their spokeswoman to the caliph. Layla and her tribe threw their lot in with the Umayyads; almost all of Layla's panegyrics are dedicated to Umayyad rulers, or their famous governor in Iraq, al-Hajjaj.[90] Interestingly, there is an elegiac piece attributed to her lamenting the passing of the third 'Orthodox' caliph, 'Uthman b. 'Affan (d. 652),[91] whose assassination ushered in the first civil war, and subsequently resulted in the rise to power of 'Uthman's relatives, the Umayyads. Whether Layla had composed this elegy immediately after the death of 'Uthman, or in a retrospective display of allegiance to the Umayyads in their rivalry with the 'Alids, is not clear. Either way, this elegy and her panegyrics serve to demonstrate a lifelong, unwavering dedication to the Umayyad cause. Naturally, Layla's invectives were hurled at the enemies of her patrons, chief among whom were the 'counter-caliph,' 'Abd Allah b. al-Zubayr, (d. 692), and the Kufan rebel, 'Abd al-Rahman b. al-Ash'ath (d. ca. 701).[92] Even her famous round of flytings with al-Nabighah al-Ja'di, which was framed in the *akhbar* as a personal dispute, in fact had larger political implications.[93] Two of al-Ja'di's panegyrics are dedicated to none other than 'Ali b. Abi Talib (d. 661) whose progeny and supporters constituted the strongest threat to Umayyad legitimacy, and the above-mentioned Ibn al-Zubayr, who proclaimed a counter-caliphate.[94] In sum, Layla and al-Nabigha's respective political allegiances were not only at odds, but diametrically opposed, and it is in this context of political struggles that their poetic duels should be read. The declaration that Layla was the winner of her duels with al-Nabigha may simply be a later and retroactive judgment transposing on the poetic arena the final Umayyad victory in the political arena.[95]

Al-Ja'di, then, was not merely Layla's personal enemy, but a political enemy who contested Umayyad suzerainty. This context illuminates yet another layer of meaning in Layla's panegyric *qasida* to 'Abd al-Malik b. Marwan, and may help us understand why Layla's poetry was considered worthy of patronage by the Umayyad house. It will be remembered from our analysis above that Layla's homage to the caliph constituted a pledge of fealty on her part, and a plea for protection from "slanderers" (verse 31). Although as mentioned above, the figure of the 'slanderer' is usually a literary device employed by panegyrists, it is entirely possible that the origin of the device lay in the real situation of political, and hence, poetic, competitions of the turbulent early Islamic times. In Layla's case, the slanderer in question may well be al-Ja'di, who composed a poem aptly entitled *al-fadiha* (the Scandalous) satirizing Layla's tribe.[96] Of course, al-Ja'di, as demonstrated above, was also an opponent of the Umayyads. Thus, by mentioning the 'slanderer,' Layla is further reinforcing the unity between her own tribe and the Umayyads by reminding the latter of their common enemy. After all, it was al-Ja'di who had issued threats against the Umayyad caliphs, Mu'awiya and Marwan b. al-Hakam, respectively, the great-uncle and father of Layla's patron, 'Abd al-Malik b. Marwan.[97] In short, al-Ja'di was the slanderer of both Layla *and* her patron. This might help to explain the ambivalence of the sound images in the last few verses of Layla's ode (verses 32–36), where Layla is in an urban setting near the caliph's palace. Although the caliph had just been depicted as having obliged Layla's request in the previous verse (verse 31), the general atmosphere described is one of clamor and cacophony that alarms Layla's alter ego, the she-camel. Even in the security of the urban enclosure, the sounds of the enemies do not disappear, but continue to echo (verse 36). Thus, although the poem had achieved its denouement with the magnanimous acts of the caliph toward Layla, the end of the poem does not announce a final end to the danger. Layla's suspenseful final lines serve not only to display her continued feeling of insecurity, but also as a warning that the caliph's rule has yet to silence his enemies. Thus, Layla's act of allegiance and fealty to the caliph is not mere submission, but a reminder to her patron that he too is in need of sustained and continued support. In this ode, then, Layla lays out the equation of the poetics of Umayyad politics, and the politics of Umayyad poetics: patron and poet are indispensable to one another.

This equation was also recognized by the ruler who, with each act of poetic homage, received a pledge of allegiance from the poet and his or her tribe. But, perhaps more importantly, the caliph's true reward is the vocabulary of legitimacy enunciated in poetry, which, as soon as it is recited, becomes a part of public discourse. In Layla's ode, the caliph is the supreme commander, *whose station is only superseded by God* (verse 28). In truth, the early Umayyads had to fight hard to retain their supremacy, but with each exaggerated discursive act such as Layla's, their hegemony was further reinforced such that they became the *effective* commanders after God. Thus, in the early Islamic period, poetry was far from being debased and poets sycophantic and servile: the poet enjoyed a power derived from an infinitely 'creative' weapon. Poetry constructed the ruler, and the ruler captured the potential of poetry. The result of the equation, then, was a co-institutionalization: the panegyric *qasida* and the caliphate of the Umayyads.[98]

Thus, for poets, the second half of the first Islamic century was a fortuitous time. Political uncertainty made poetry an urgent commodity, which assured the success of those who were able to oblige, including Layla. In this nascent 'Islamic order' that was still in the process of formation and definition, poets who would later be regarded to have 'suspect' or 'unorthodox' credentials were allowed ready entry into the poetry market. Thus, other than the example of Layla, there is al-Akhtal (d. ca. 710), who managed to become the poet laureate of the Umayyads despite being a Christian. And just as Layla's sexual unconventionality, exemplified in her poetic relationship with Tawba, would trouble the scholars of Arabic literature in the centuries after the formation of the 'cultural orthodoxy' of classical Islam, so would al-Akhtal's religion. In al-Akhtal's case, it was his fondness for wine that became emblematic of his religious nonconformity.[99] Both Layla and al-Akhtal attempted to negotiate for themselves a position in the new Islamic order, and both succeeded—not only in their own time, but gaining admission to the Arabic literary canon. But by the time the canon had formed, so had the parameters of Arab-Islamic cultural 'orthodoxy,' and we do not again encounter a professional woman poet or a Christian poet laureate.

Finally, it should be noted that neither Layla's circumstances nor her success are particular to Islamic history. Separated from Layla by religion and culture, by land and sea, and by a hiatus of a full eight centuries, Lavinia Fontana (1552–1614), a native of Bologna, possessed a talent similar in scope and power to that of Layla's in the context of her environment. Lavinia's art was not poetry, but one of the primary forms of cultural expression in early modern Italy: painting. Lavinia was "Europe's first female painter to attain professional success . . . in direct competition with male artists in her own city."[100] While there had been women painters at both convent and court, the public art market had been exclusively an arena for male competition. But Lavinia, as an artist whose gender identity relegated her to a marginal position, was, like Layla, fortunate enough to live at a time of crisis and critical transition: the beginnings of the Counter-Reformation. It was in the aftermath of the Council of Trent (1545–63), with its resolutions to reinforce Catholic dogma, that the Bishop of Bologna, Gabrielle Paleotti, wrote a treatise on sacred and profane images. Recognizing the potential of painting, the Bishop wrote his treatise as a manifesto, calling for doctrinally sound religious painting, and also for increased patronage of the arts. It was this urgent need for art as counter-propaganda that "gave incentive to a new generation of painters . . . including Lavinia Fontana."[101] Thus, Lavinia and Layla were both mavericks who capitalized on the urgent need of their respective crisis-ridden societies for tools for the manufacture of ideology. They both possessed powerful cultural—and hence political—weapons, which they skillfully employed to successfully trespass in a cultural marketplace that had hitherto been a male domain.

Appendix: Notes to the Arabic Text

Verse 1: The present rendition of the verse is from Abu 'Ubayd al-Bakri (d. 1093), *Mu'jam ma ista'jam* (ed. Mustafa al-Saqqa), 4 vols. Cairo: Matba'at Lajnat al-Ta'lif wa al-Tarjama wa al-Nashr, 1945, 2:364 (henceforth *Mu'jam*). In Ibn Maymun, *Muntaha al-talab* (henceforth, *Muntaha*): *taribtu wa ma hadha bi-sa'ati matrabi / ila al-hayyi hallu bayna 'Adhin wa Jabjabi.* In *Diwan Layla: Jubjubi.*

Verse 6: In *Muntaha: sharhabi.*

Verse 7: In *Muntaha: ajashshin hazimin*; in *Diwan Layla: ajashshun hazimun.* In *Muntaha, muqarrib* has both a *fatha* and a *kasra* on the *ra'* and the word *ma'an*—"together"—is written as a gloss above *muqarrib.* A margin note in *Muntaha* reads: *idha kalla sara 'inanu-hu 'ala awayila 'atfay-hi.* Another margin note in *Muntaha: fi sawti-hi bahhah.*

Verse 8: In *Muntaha: khafifun.*

Verse 12: In *Muntaha: rijlu-hu*, in *Diwan Layla: rihlatun.* Since *rijlu-hu* does fit in meaning, I opted not to change it. In *Muntaha*, the word *karkaratu-ha* [its sound], referring to the sand grouse, is written as a gloss above *tantahi.*

Verse 13: In *Muntaha: qaribna.*

Verse 14: In *Muntaha: sawayiqin.*

Verse 15: In *Diwan Layla: sharubin;* in *Muntaha: marzubanin.*

Verse 16: In *Muntaha: li-nadin* or *li-badin.* In *Diwan Layla: li-nadin la-ha* or *li-nadili-ha.* In *Mu'jam: li-nazilatin bayna al-Shibaki wa Tandibi,* 1:321.

Verse 17: A margin note in *Muntaha: wa yurwa al-ghabiyyi wa huwa al-khafiyyi* [a variant reading is *ghabiyy* which means hidden]!

Verse 19: A margin note in *Muntaha: janiba-ha* [its sides].

Verse 20: A margin note in *Muntaha: ya'ni firakhu al-qatati* [meaning, the offspring of the sand grouse].

Verse 21: A margin note in *Muntaha: min qabri al-aranibi* [from the grave of rabbits], which is almost certainly a scribal error for *min wabar al-aranibi* [from rabbit hair].

Verse 23: A variant reading in Ibn Qutayba, *Kitab al-ma'ani,* 1:327: *turatinu-ha dawiyyatun lam ta'arrabi.* In *Muntaha: lam ta'arrabi.*

Verse 25: In *Muntaha: yufriju.*

Verse 26: A margin note in *Muntaha: al-wusafa'* [servants].

Verse 27: In *Diwan Layla: lam.*

Verse 28: In *Muntaha: fi.* In *Muntaha* and *Diwan Layla: marghabi.*

Verse 30: This reading of the verse is from al-Marzubani, *Ash'ar al-nisa'*, 41. In *Muntaha* and *Diwan Layla*: *idha ma ibtagha al-'adi al-zalumu zulamatan / laday-ya wa ma istujlibtu li-al-mutajallabi.*

Verse 33: This reading of verses 33 and 34 is from al-Marzubani, *Ash'ar al-nisa'*, 41. In *Muntaha* and in *Diwan Layla*, the first hemistich of verse 33 was combined with the second hemistich of verse 34 to make one verse, while the rest was dropped. In *Muntaha*: *tahawasat.*

Verse 34: In *Ash'ar al-nisa'*: *hajiban.*

Verse 35: In *Muntaha*: *tarji'u.*

Verse 36: A margin note in *Muntaha*: *muzakhraf* [embellished].

Abu Tammam Text (Arabic)

تؤم فبكر في النظام وثيب	ولقد رأيتك والكلام لآلئ ١
وكأن ليلى الأخيلية تندب	فكأن قسا في عكاظ يخطب ٢

Notes

1   I thank the *Journal of Arabic Literature* for allowing me to republish a revised version of my article, "Trespassing the Male Domain: The Qasidah of Layla al-Akhyaliyyah," *Journal of Arabic Literature* 31, no. 2 (2000): 121–46. I also thank my co-editor, Marlé Hammond, not only for her valuable critiques, but also for insisting that I revisit and republish the article. And I am grateful to Shahab Ahmed for his careful reading and advice with translations. I should note that as this chapter went into press I discovered another short study of the poet by Renate Jacobi, "Layla al-Akhyaliyya—an Umayyad Feminist?" *Figurationen* 1, no. 5 (2005): 79–94. Despite overlap in some of the ideas, Jacobi seems to have been unaware of my 2000 article.

2   Abu Tammam Habib b. Aws al-Ta'i (d. 842), *Diwan Abi Tammam*, ed. Muhyi al-Din al-Khayyat and Muhammad Jamal (Cairo: al-Markaz al-'Arabi li-l-Bahth wa-l-Nashr, 1983), 39–40.

3   Abu Ishaq Ibrahim b. 'Ali al-Husri al-Qayrawani (d.1061), *Zahr al-adab wa thamar al-albab*, ed. 'Ali Muhammad al-Bajawi, vol. 2 (Cairo: 'Isa al-Babi al-Halabi, 1970), 932; *Diwan Layla al-Akhyaliya*, ed. Khalil Ibrahim 'Atiya and Jalil 'Atiya (Baghdad: Dar al-Jumhuriya, 1967), 51. This report is usually related to provide a context for a panegyric *qit'a* composed by Layla for the Caliph Mu'awiya which she describes herself riding toward him.

4   Two variant genealogies are given for Layla, the more common one being Layla bt. 'Abd Allah b. al-Rahhal b. 'Amir b. Shaddad b. Ka'b. The other is given by

Ibn Maymun as Layla bt. Hudhayfa b. Shaddad b. Ka'b; see in Abu Ghalib Ibn
Maymun (d.1200), *Muntaha al-talab min ash'ar al-'arab* manuscript, Istanbul, Laleli
1941, facsimile ed. (Frankfurt: Ma'had Tarikh al-'Ulum al-'Arabiya wa-l-Islamiya,
1986), 43, and *Diwan Layla*, 18.

5   For a discussion of *ritha'* as a female-specific poetic form, see Suzanne Pinckney
Stetkevych, *The Mute Immortals Speak: Pre-Islamic Poetry and the Poetics of Ritual*
(Ithaca, NY: Cornell University Press, 1993) 61–205; and Mayy Yusuf Khulayf,
al-Shi'r al-nisa'i fi adabi-na al-qadim (Cairo: Maktabat Gharib, 1991). Several
medieval scholars also identified *ritha'* as the principal domain for female poetic
expression. For example, Ibn Rashiq (d.1064) explained the connection between
female poets and elegy in the following manner: "Because of the great weakness
that God has placed in their nature, women's hearts sorrow more than (those
of) the rest of humankind when calamities occur; they grieve for the dead more
severely, and it is on the extremity of grief that elegy is built." Abu 'Ali al-Hasan
Ibn Rashiq al-Qayrawani, *al-'Umda fi mahasin al-shi'r wa adabi-hi*, ed. Muhammad
Qarqazan, vol. 2 (Beirut: Dar al-Ma'rifa, 1988), 817.

6   See Marlé Hammond's analysis of Layla's *ra'iya* in her contribution to the present
volume, "*Qasida, Marthiya,* and *Différance*."

7   *Diwan Layla*, 53–58. The most complete version of this *qasida* appears in Ibn
Maymun, *Muntaha al-talab*, 43–44. Al-Marzubani, Abu 'Ubayd Allah Muhammad
b. 'Imran (d.994) quotes 4 verses which are likely to be a part of Layla's *ba'iya* but
which are absent from both Ibn Maymun and *Diwan Layla*. See al-Marzubani, *Ash'ar
al-nisa'*, ed. Sami al-'Ani and Hilal Naji (Baghdad: Dar al-Risala li-l-Tiba'a, 1976),
41. The editors of *Diwan Layla* mistakenly take the panegyric to be dedicated to
Marwan b. al-Hakam. From the text of the poem, it is clear that the dedication is to
the Caliph 'Abd al-Malik b. Marwan. In verse 26 of the *qasida*, the poet mentions the
name of the eulogized as Ibn Marwan. Also, his rank is alluded to in verse 28: "For
you, after God, are her commander *[fa-inna-ka ba'da Allahi anta amiru-ha]*". The term
amir probably refers to the caliphal title *amir al-mu'minin* and not to that of governor.

8   Invective, boasting, and panegyric, respectively.

9   The fact of this *qasida* being the only one composed by a woman has been noted
by S.P. Stetkevych in *The Mute Immortals Speak*, 164 n. 11. I am grateful to Seemi
Ghazi for bringing this footnote to my attention. In my initial study of the
ba'iya, I followed received wisdom by further distinguishing between male and
female poetry as respectively 'polythematic' and 'monothematic;' see Ahmad
Muhammad al-Hufi, *al-Mar'a fi-l-shi'r al-jahili* (Cairo: Matba'at Nahdat Misr, 1954),
529; Khulayf, *al-Shi'r al-nisa'i*, 94–148, and 157; S.P. Stetkevych, *The Mute Immortals
Speak*, 164; and Ibrahim Wannus, *Sha'irat al-'arab* (Antelias: Myriam Publications,
1992), 139. However, Marlé Hammond has now successfully demonstrated that the
elegies of women poets were also complex polythematic ventures, which offered
tripartite parallels to their male counterparts. See her contribution to this volume,
"*Qasida, Marthiya,* and *Différance*."

10   In Arabic the term *qasida* is used to refer to any long poem; while in Western
scholarship, the qualification 'tripartite' or 'polythematic' is generally added to

distinguish the male ode with its *nasib*, camel-section, and *gharad* subdivisions. Since Hammond's study suggests that tripartite and polythematic qualities are not necessarily unique to masculine poetry, I am here abandoning these qualifications and using the unqualified term *qasida* to refer to the male ode comprised of *nasib*, camel-section, and *gharad*. The terminology currently in use clearly requires rethinking.

11 András Hámori, *On the Art of Medieval Arabic Literature* (Princeton: Princeton University Press, 1974), 3–30. The heroic aspect of classical Arabic poetry in general is discussed by Adonis ('Ali Ahmad Sa'id) in his *Muqaddima li-l-shi'r al-'arabi*, 4th ed. (Beirut: Dar al-'Awda, 1983), 15–19. One should qualify the heroic role of the *qasida*'s protagonist by noting that such heroic roles are as varied as the poems that they inhabit. For example, in the panegyric the protagonist seems to concede his heroism to the authority figure praised in the poem; see Stefan Sperl, "Islamic Kingship and Arabic Panegyric Poetry," *Journal of Arabic Literature* 8 (1977): 21–35. We will have occasion to discuss the relationship between the panegyrist and the *mamduh* later on in this chapter.

12 The seminal study of the classical *qasida* along gender lines is S.P. Stetkevych, *The Mute Immortals Speak*, 3–54. Marlé Hammond interprets the *qasida* as a form encoded with male sexuality, while the female *marthiya* with female sexuality; see her "The Poetics of S/Exclusion: Women, Gender and the Classical Arabic Canon" (PhD diss., Columbia University, 2003), especially chap. 2, "Gender Difference and Arabic Writing: Theorizing Endemic Conceptual Intersections of Sex and Language," 64–107.

13 *Diwan Layla*, 100–03. For a comprehensive study of al-Nabigha al-Ja'di's life and poetry, see Khalil Ibrahim Abu Dhiyab, *al-Nabigha al-Ja'di: hayatu-hu wa shi'ru-hu* (Damascus: Dar al-Qalam); also, Maria Nallino, *La Poésie di An-nabigha al-Ga'di* (Rome: Studi Orientali Publicati-Università di Roma, 1953).

14 Many of the *akhbar* about Layla have been cited by the editors of *Diwan Layla* in their annotations to her poems. Another valuable source, which was unavailable to the editors of the *Diwan*, is the chapter on Layla al-Akhyaliya in the *Nuzhat al-musamir fi akhbar Majnun bani 'Amir* of Ibn al-Mibrad (d.1503), edited and published separately with detailed appendices by Muhammad al-Tunji under the title *Nuzhat al-musamir fi akhbar Layla al-Akhyaliya* (Beirut: 'Alam al-Kutub, 1995). One of the more comprehensive sources on Layla is Abu al-Faraj al-Isbahani (d.966), *Kitab al-Aghani*, ed. Ibrahim al-Abyari, 31 vols. (Cairo: Dar al-Sha'b, 1969), 11:3990–4036. See also, al-Qayrawani, *Zahr al-adab*, 927–39; and Abu 'Ali Isma'il b. al-Qasim al-Qali (d.966), *Kitab al-amali*, ed. Isma'il Yusuf Diyab (Cairo: Dar al-Kutub al-Misriya, 1926), 86–90.

15 On the taboo on women announcing their love, see al-Hufi, *al-Mar'a*, 518–21. There are a few exceptions to this rule, most famously the Andalusian poet Wallada bt. al-Mustakfi (d. *circa* 1091), who composed love poetry for her poet-lover; see Hammond, "Poetics of S/Exclusion," 58–59. For Tawba's poetry, see *Diwan Tawba Ibn al-Humayyir al-Khafaji: Sahib Layla al-Akhyaliya*, ed. Khalil Ibrahim 'Atiya (Baghdad: Matba'at al-Irshad, 1968). Obviously, since Layla

composed elegies for Tawba, his love poetry to her is not contemporaneous to her laments over him. However, the *akhbar* do narrate one instance where Layla's poetry is in direct response to Tawba's; see al-Isbahani, *al-Aghani*, 11:3994.

16 Unfortunately, an analysis of this intriguing, complex, and rather prolific poetical exchange is beyond the scope of this paper, and I will be treating it fully in the future.

17 Even if one dismisses the reports as fictitious, they still indicate that she was *remembered* as a transgressive woman.

18 The Andalusian poet Sara al-Halabiya (*fl.* second half of thirteenth century), was also a professional poet. See Teresa Garulo, "Una Poetisa Oriental en al-Andalus: Sara al-Halabiyya," *al-Qantara: Revista des Estudios Arabes* 6 (1985): 155–77.

19 For an exciting discussion of the concept of *fuhula* in classical Arabic literature, see Hammond, "Poetics of S/Exclusion," 67–92.

20 In the *tawil* meter.

21 The more accurate translation of *taribtu* is 'I rejoiced/I grieved' since *tariba* means to be affected by the emotion either of joy or of grief. See E. W. Lane, *Arabic-English Lexicon*, 2 vols. (Cambridge: Islamic Texts Society Trust, 1984), 1:1835. The ambivalence of the opening line will be discussed below.

22 The Nafada, the Akhayil, and the Khafaja are the three branches of the 'Uqaylid clan of the Banu Ka'b tribe. It is unclear whether by "Ka'b" Layla means her own great-grandfather, or Tawba b. al-Humayyir's great-grandfather, or a common ancestor with the same name; see Hisham b. Muhammad Ibn al-Kalbi (d.819), *Gamharat an-nasab: das genealogische Werk des Hisam Ibn Muhamad al-Kalbi*, ed. Werner Caskel, vol. 2 (Leiden: E. J. Brill, 1966), 102, 103, and 106. I am grateful to Ihab el-Sakkout for sharing his extensive knowledge of genealogy with me.

23 The literal translation is 'when their vying overflows with hot water, they gush forth with it like a leaking water-skin' (*Jasha* [to overflow with much water]); see Lane, *Lexicon*, 2:2807.

24 *Janaha* (of the camel), lowering the forepart of the neck in running or, to go swiftly; see Lane, *Lexicon*, 1:468.

25 *Siqa'* (water-skin) is a common description of the craw of the sand grouse in poetry. See Abu Muhammad b. Ahmad Ibn Qutayba (d.889), *Kitab al-maani al-kabir* (Hyderabad: Majlis Da'irat al-Ma'arif al-'Uthmaniya, 1949), vol. 1, 319 and 322; see also descriptions of sand grouse filling their craws with water to give to their offspring, 311–12.

26 There is no direct mention of the offspring in this verse; however, they have been mentioned in passing in verse 17, and since "arranging shoulder to shoulder" requires more than one bird, I assume that this refers to her offspring. The image of the grouse arranging themselves side by side is not uncommon—in Humayd b. Thawr al-Hilali's (d.689) poem 2, verse 18: "[She is a] mother of seven who, when they follow each other [to] to seek food, [they] arrange [themselves] heads and sides (*fa-saffat ar'usun wa junubun*)", *Diwan Hamid b. Thawr al-Hilali*, ed. Muhammad Yusuf Najm (Beirut: Dar Sadir, 1995).

27   *Jars* (soft sound or pecking): Lane, *Lexicon*, 1:409.

28   The 'richness' is in anticipation of the reward of the patron to whom the panegyric is presented.

29   In the second hemistich of this line, مركب can only fit grammatically if it is taken to be as an abbreviation of مركبي (my riding her). *Habaniq* is plural of *habannaqa* (idiot), or *habnaq* (servant); see Jamal al-Din Makram Ibn Manzur (d. 1311), *Lisan al-'arab*, 20 vols. (Cairo: al-Dar al-Misriya li-l-Ta'lif wa-l-Tarjama, 1966), 'h-b-n-q,' 12:243–44. I take Layla to be saying, "I have undertaken this journey to meet the Caliph himself, and not his representatives." See Marlé Hammond's alternative reading of this line in "Poetics of S/Exclusion," 41.

30   *Naqada* from *naqd*: *al-mukhalafa, al-muradda,* hence "to contest"; see Ibn Manzur, *Lisan,* 4:436–37. *Ta'aqqaba*: *radda*, hence 'to refute'; see Ibn Manzur, *Lisan,* 2:102–15.

31   I opted to go with the reading in al-Marzubani, *Ash'ar al-nisa'* (see Appendix, verse 30), since it provides a conclusion for the conditional clause in the previous verse. Al-Marzubani gives an unsatisfactory explanation for this verse: "You are aggressive to whoever does injustice or lampoons so that I fear to lampoon and win, and have you turn against me" (I am reading '*la bal ta'di 'ala man zalama wa haja, fa-akhafu an ahjuwa wa antasir fa-ta'di 'alay-ya*' for the incorrect rendition by the editor of al-Marzubani's text: *la bal tu'di 'alay-ya min zulmin wa hija' fa-akhafu an ahjuwa wa antasira fa-yu'da 'alay-ya*). However, al-Marzubani's rendition serves to show to what extent Layla was perceived as a lampooner. The subject of her invectives will be taken up below. I have translated *mutajallab* (literally, 'the place to where things are brought') as 'assembly.'

32   I am reading *anba'* (news, gossip) for the less logical *abna'*.

33   *Fararij* (pl. of *farruj*) has no meaning other than 'offspring of the chicken'; Lane, *Lexicon*, 6:276. I am at loss as to whether to consider the verse corrupt or whether to understand Layla as being ironic by juxtaposing crowing *(siyah)*—a sound produced by roosters—with chicks (which certainly do not crow). Also, I was unsuccessful in ascertaining whether chicks formed a regular part of the entourage outside the palace! I translated *fararij* as roosters since the crowing of the rooster anticipates the description of the clamor in the last verses: *'uqur* (pl. of *'aqr*): palace; Ibn Manzur, *Lisan*, 9:317.

34   An example of the use of *tariba* to mean 'to grieve' is in a verse by Imru' al-Qays (d.545 AD): "Has grief come to your heart after calm, because of Mawiya, and the tears of the eye poured out? [*hal 'ada qalba-ka min Mawiyata al-tarabu/ ba'da al-huduwwi fa-dam'u l-'ayni yansakibu*]"; see *Diwan Imru' al-Qays*, ed. Muhammad Abu al-Fadl Ibrahim (Cairo: Dar al-Ma'arif, 1958), poem no. 74, verse 1.

35   Hámori, *On the Art*, 7. A similar description is given by Renate Jacobi in "The Camel-Section and the Panegyrical Ode", *Journal of Arabic Literature* 13 (1982), 1–22, here 5.

36   See Hammond's analysis of Layla's *ra'iya* in "*Qasida, Marthiya,* and *Différance*" in this volume.

37 By the terms 'domesticate' and 'tame' which I will use throughout, I do not mean that Layla renders the poem innocuous or harmless, but rather that Layla exercises her authority over the poem to turn it to her own ends.

38 Both conscious poetic ambiguity and announcement of difference or trespass seem to be another of Layla's professional 'trade marks.' On this, see again Hammond's analysis of Layla's *ra'iya* in *"Qasida, Marthiya,* and *Différance."*

39 For Layla's kinship to Tawba, see above.

40 Hammond, *"Qasida, Marthiya,* and *Différance".*

41 One is here reminded of the *nasib* of al-Shanfara's famous *Lamiyat al-'arab* which, like the present poem, is about the loss of tribe and in which the *dramatis personae* differ from those of the 'mainstream' *qasida.* While it would be interesting to compare Sa'alik *qasida*s with that of Layla on the basis that the respective composers are from marginalized groups, this is beyond the scope of the present chapter.

42 For Layla's relationship to these tribes, see note 22.

43 Layla does the same in her *ra'iya*: she inserts an unexpected *fakhr* sequence in the middle of journey section, rather than as an outcome of it. Hammond, *"Qasida, Marthiya,* and *Différance".*

44 A connection between *nasib* and *ritha'* in the male *qasida* has been established by Hasan al-Banna 'Izz al-Din, *al-Kalimat wa-l-ashya': bahth fi-l-taqalid al-fanniya li-l-qasida al-jahiliya* (Cairo: Dar al-Fikr al-'Arabi, 1988), 215–34; and Hammond, *"Qasida, Marthiya,* and *Différance".*

45 See also S. P. Stetkevych, *The Mute Immortals Speak,* 27.

46 Jaroslav Stetkevych, "Name and Epithet: The Philology and the Semiotics of Animal Nomenclature in Early Arabic Poetry," *Journal of Near Eastern Studies* 45, no. 2 (1986), 89–124, here 109 (including nn. 91 and 92).

47 I am aware of two instances where grouse imagery is utilized in a *qasida* in a manner similar to Layla's, that is to say where the bird is used as an extended simile for the she-camel without being presented as quarry. One of these is in an apparently incomplete *qasida* by a contemporary of Layla, Humayd b. Thawr al-Hilali, *Diwan Humayd b. Thawr,* poem no. 2, verses 15–28. The *gharad* section of this poem is missing. The second example, which is too late for our purposes, occurs in a similarly abbreviated *qasida* by al-Hakam al-Khudari, who was a contemporary of al-Asma'i, 'Abd al-Malik b. Qurayb (d.828) and whose poem is in al-Asma'i's collection, *al-Asma'iyat,* ed. 'Abd al-Salam Harun and Ahmad Muhammad Shakir (Cairo: Dar al-Ma'arif, 1964), poem no. 6, verses 4–8. While there are several other depictions of the grouse that are very similar to those of Layla, these are in *qita'* and do not seem to function as an extended similes; see al-Isbahani's account of a grouse imagery competition between five poets: al-'Ujayr al-Saluli, Aws b. Ghalfa' al-Hujaymi, Muzahim al-'Uqayli, al-'Abbas b. Yazid b. al-Aswad al-Kindi, and Humayd b. Thawr al-Hilali; al-Isbahani, *al-Aghani,* 8:3004–3009. Another two examples are presented by Abu 'Uthman b. Bahr al-Jahiz (d.869), as *qita'* (and not as part of *qasa'id*) with the result that one is unable to determine whether they function as similes or not. One *qit'a*, by al-Ba'ith, may have originated from a camel-section of a *qasida*, while the other,

which is either by one al-Marrar or by al-Ka'ibb al-Taghlibi (al-Jahiz is not sure) is presented without context; see *Kitab al-hayawan*, ed. 'Abd al-Salam Harun, vol. 5 (Cairo: Maktabat Mustafa al-Babi al-Halabi, 1966-69), 583–87. Unfortunately, the incompleteness of the above examples of sand grouse imagery makes it difficult to compare their use by the different poets.

48 This is the competition mentioned in the previous note.

49 For 'Alqama's life and poetry, see 'Abd al-Razzaq Husayn, *'Alqama b. 'Abada al-Fahl: hayatu-hu wa shi'ru-hu* (Beirut: al-Maktab al-Islami, 1986); and Yusuf b. Sulayman al-A'lam al-Shantamri (d. 1083), *Sharh diwan 'Alqama b. 'Abada al-Fahl*, ed. Hanna Nasr al-Hitti (Beirut: Dar al-Kitab al-'Arabi, 1993).

50 For the relative rarity of the use of ostrich similes, see Wahb Rumiya, *al-Rihla fi-l-qasida al-jahiliya* (Amman?: Ittihad al-Kuttab wa-l-Sahafiyyin al-Filastiniyyin, 1975), 347. This is corroborated by Jaroslav Stetkevych: "The ostrich, like the bird of the prey or the sand-grouse, turns up in only a limited number of pre-Islamic poems as the protagonist of a subtheme in the journey section." J. Stetkevych "Name and Epithet," 109. An ostrich scene parallel to that of 'Alqama appears in the *Mu'allqa* of 'Antara b. Shaddad (second half of sixth century); see 'Abd Allah al-Hasan b. Ahmad al-Zawzani (d.1093), *Sharh al-mu'allaqat al-sab'*, ed. Muhammad al-Fadili (Beirut: al-Maktaba al-'Asriya li-l-Tiba'a wa-l-Nashr, 1998), 205–206 (verses, 24–27), for an English translation, see Michael A. Sells, *Desert Tracings: Six Classic Arabian Odes* (Middletown, CT: Wesleyan University Press, 1989), 50. However, as noted by Sells, "'Alqama's [ostrich] comparison fits in perfectly with the erotic and humorous mood of the entire ostrich scene…In 'Antara, the ostrich performance is dominated by a more tragic mood . . . . " *Desert Tracings,* 11–12. Thus, while Layla (or both Layla and 'Alqama) may be also engaging in conversation with 'Antara, the conviviality of the bird scene in 'Alqama, in contrast to its dark mood in 'Antara renders the former more likely to be Layla's referent.

51 The English translation is by Sells, *Desert Tracings*, 16–17; for the Arabic, see al-A'lam al-Shantamari, *Sharh diwan 'Alqama*, 39–42, verses 20–28.

52 Sell, *Desert Tracings*, 11.

53 The second hemistich of verse 23 of Layla's poem is *turatinu-ha dhurriyatun lam tu'arrabi*. Similarly, in the ostrich scene in 'Antara's *mu'allaqa* the male ostrich is compared to a "foreigner who stammers and babbles." See Sells, *Desert Tracings*, 50.

54 See Rumiya, *al-Rihla*, 161.

55 See notes 47 and 48 above.

56 See S. P. Stetkevych, *The Mute Immortals Speak*, 26.

57 For an evaluation of the attitudes of the contemporary scholars toward the panegyric, see S. P. Stetkevych, "'Abbasid Panegyric and Political Allegiance," in *Qasidah Poetry in Islamic Asia and Africa*, vol. 1: *Classical Traditions and Modern Meanings*, ed. Stefan Sperl and Christopher Shackle (Leiden: E. J. Brill, 1998), 35–60.

58 Against this disparaging view, S. P. Stetkevych argues that the panegyric poem should be seen less as concession to authority and more as an equal exchange of gifts between poet and ruler where the value of the poem is commensurate with

the caliphal reward; S. P. Stetkevych, "Abbasid Panegyric." For S. P. Stetkevych's subsequent contributions to the study of the panegyric, see below.

59   S. Sperl, "Islamic Kingship."

60   Abu Muhammad b. Ahmad Ibn Qutayba, *Kitab al-shi'r wa-l-shu'ara'*, ed. M. J. De Goeje (Leiden: E. J. Brill, 1904), 14–15.

61   S.P. Stetkevych, "Abbasid Panegyric."

62   See al-Hutay'a's (d.661) poem no. 47, verse 22; *Diwan al-Hutay'a bi-sharh Ibn al-Sakit wa-l-Sukkari wa-l-Sijistani*, ed. Nu'man Amin Taha (Cairo: Mustafa al-Babi al-Halabi, 1958); also, Ka'b b. Zuhayr's (*fl.* 631) poem no. 1, verses 38–39; *Le diwan de Ka'b Ibn Zuhair*, ed. Tadeusz Kowalski (Krakow: Nakladem Polskiej Akademii Umiejtnosci, 1950); also, al-Nabigha al-Dhubyani, *Diwan de Nabiga Dhobyani*, ed. M. Hartwig Derenbourg (Paris: Imprimerie impériale, 1869), poem no. 1, verses 39–41.

63   I suspect that Layla and other early Islamic panegyrists did indeed have literary and/or political enemies who could be called 'slanderers.' However, there is not shortage of examples where the slanderer is merely a literary device of a sort that has numerous parallels in the tradition. For example, there is the standard character of the blamer/censor (*la'im*), who is constantly watching over the poet's moral conduct and who is invariably present when the poet is attending wine-gatherings. Another standard character is the *'adhil* who is jealous of lovers and is always trying to separate them. These three characters have similar functions, the *la'im* stands between the poet and his wine, the *'adhil* stands between the poet and his beloved, and the *washi* stands between poet and his *mamduh*.

64   Khulayf, *al-Shi'r al-nisa'i*, 115. The scholarship to which Khulayf refers is epitomized by Ibn Qutayba who defines the *qasida* as a panegyric: *Kitab al-shi'r wa-l-shu'ara'*, 14–15. In comparing between the (rather scant) panegyric output of women and that of men, Khulayf characterizes female panegyric as limited to the praise of departed family members, and thus as sincere and based on personal experience. Male panegyric, she says, is directed at living authority figures, and is self-serving and hypocritical. She relates this difference to the fact that male panegyrists were, more often than not, professional poets: Khulayf, *al-Shi'r al-nisa'i*, 113–22. It is interesting, however, that Khulayf remarks of one of Layla's panegyric *qita'* for al-Hajjaj that it is similar to male professional poetry precisely on account of its formulaic panegyric vocabulary: see Khulayf, *al-Shi'r al-nisa'i*, 115.

65   Al-Isbahani, *al-Aghani*, 5:1660–61. Lane translates the second hemistich of the first verse as "for she committed a notorious glaring deed;" Lane, *Lexicon*, 1:521. A variant reading of these verses, which is of a similar effect to that of al-Isbahani, is given in Ibn Qutayba's *al-Shi'r wa-l-shu'ara'*, 272.

66   According to Hammond, sexual innuendos are at the heart of the conception of *fuhula*; see her "Poetics of S/exclusion," 64–107.

67   *Ayyil*: 'thick urine of she-goats ; which, when drunk by a woman, excites her venereal faculty;' Lane, *Lexicon*, 1:128.

68   The reader may be interested to know that Layla is considered to have won this invective exchange; see al-Isbahani, *al-Aghani*, 5:166, and Al-Asma'i, *Kitab fuhulat*

al-shu'ara', ed. Charles C. Torrey, with an introduction by Salah al-Din al-Munajjid (Cairo: Dar al-Kitab al-Jadid, 1971), 17.

69 Hammond provides a table comparing the reception of the poetry of Layla as compared to al-Khansa' by medieval anthologists over the course of four centuries to find that the two poets started out on an equal footing, but for whatever reason, Layla's popularity slowly declined. See Hammond, "Poetics of S/Exclusion," 228, Appendix 7. It seems that Layla was readily compared to al-Khansa' because both were considered exceptions by virtue of the unusual length of their preserved *marathi*. The longer *marathi* preserved in the canon are usually composed by men. See S. P. Stetkevych, *The Mute Immortals Speak*, 146 n. 11. On the subject of the preservation of women's poetry and prose in the canon, see Marlé Hammond, "Literature: 9th to 15th Century," in *Encyclopedia of Women and Islamic Cultures*, ed. Suad Joseph, Afsaneh Najmabadi, Julie Peteet, Seteney Sahmi, Jacqueline Siapano, and Jane I. Smith, 5 vols (Leiden: Brill, 2003), vol. 1: *Methodologies, Paradigms and Sources*, 42–50.

70 Al-Asma'i, *Kitab fuhulat al-shu'ara'*, 19; cited in editors' Introduction to *Diwan Layla*, 35.

71 Ibn Qutayba, *Kitab al-shi'r wa-l-shu'ara'*, 271; cited in editors' introduction to *Diwan Layla*, 35.

72 Abu al-'Abbas Muhammad b. Yazid Al-Mubarrad, *al-Kamil*, ed. Muhammad Abu al-Fadl Ibrahim, vol. 4 (Cairo: Dar al-Fikr al-'Arabi, 1997), 46–47; cited in editors' Introduction to *Diwan Layla*, 35. Al-Mubarrad backs up this assessment of female capacities with appropriate references to Qur'an and Hadith.

73 As such, they seem to parallel the genre of *asbab al-nuzul* (occasions of revelation) for the text of the Qur'an.

74 See Ibn al-Mibrad, *Nuzhat al-musamir*, 22–23.

75 Ibid., 21.

76 Important contributions to the discussion of the function of *akhbar* are Suzanne Pinckney Stetkevych, "Pre-Islamic Panegyric and the Poetics of Redemption: *Mufaddaliya 119* of 'Alqama and *Banat Su'ad* of Ka'b b. Zuhayr,'" in *Reorientations/Arabic and Persian Poetry*, ed. Suzanne Pinckney Stetkevych (Bloomington and Indianapolis: Indiana University Press), 1–57; *idem, Mute Immortals*; *idem, the Poetics of Islamic Legitimacy: Myth Gender, and Ceremony in the Classical Arabic Ode* (Bloomington: Indiana University Press, 2002), 2; Marlé Hammond, "He said 'She said': Narrations of Women's Verse in Classical Arabic Literature. A Case Study: Nazhun's *Hija'* of Abu Bakr al-Makhzumi," *Arabic and Middle Eastern Literatures* 6, no. 1 (2003): 1–18; and *idem*, "Literature: 9th to 15th Century."

77 This report is from al-Isbahani, *al-Aghani*, 11:4035. Very similar reports are found in *al-Aghani*, 11:3993; al-Qayrawani, *Zahr al-adab*, 936; and Ibn al-Mibrad *Nuzhat al-musamir*, 21. One of these reports is usually related to a *qit'a* by Layla which reads: "And (you) who have a desire: do not divulge it/ as long as you live for there is no means to it. We have a companion whom we should not betray/ and you are to another a devoted husband" (al-Isbahani, *al-Aghani*, 11: 3993–94).

78 In the report in *Nuzhat al-musamir*, 21, the conversation is between Layla and the Caliph 'Abd al-Malik b. Marwan.

79 Aside from the present panegyric, she composed preserved encomiums to the Ummayad caliphs Mu'awiya b. Abi Sufyan and Marwan b. al-Hakam, and to al-Hajjaj; *Diwan Layla*, 28–29. Some reports depict an unusual degree of intimacy between Layla and important figures of authority. Layla's amicable relations with the Caliph 'Abd al-Malik b. Marwan can be detected in her rather presumptuous and sharp retort in the following report: "It has reached me that Layla al-Akhyaliya went into (the audience of) 'Abd al-Malik b. Marwan – that was when she had become old and weak. He ('Abd al-Malik) asked her, 'What did Tawbah see in you when he fell in love with you [*hawiya-ki*]?' She replied, 'What did people see in you when they placed you in authority [*hina wallu-ka*]?' 'Abd al-Malik laughed so (hard) that a black tooth of his, which he had been hiding, showed" (al-Isbahani, *al-Aghani*, 11:4026).

80 *Diwan Layla*, 22.

81 For a cogent historical background, see Hugh Kennedy, *The Prophet and the Age of the Caliphates*, 2nd ed. (Harlow: Pearson Education., 2004), 75–103.

82 For an overview of Umayyad poetry (although I disagree with most of her evaluations), see Salma al-Khadra al-Jayyusi, "Umayyad Poetry," in *Cambridge History of Arabic Literature*, vol. 1: *Arabic Literature to the End of the Umayyad Period*, ed. A. F. L. Beeston, T. M. Johnstone, R. B. Serjeant, and G. R. Smith (Cambridge: Cambridge University Press, 1983), 387–432. For the preeminence of the panegyric, see al-Jayyusi. "Umayyad Poetry," 389; Wahb Rumiya, *Qasidat al-madh hatta nihayat al-'asr al-umawi: bayna al-usul wa-l-ihya' wa-l-tajdid* (Damascus: Manshurat Wizarat al-Thaqafa wa-l-Irshad al-Qawmi, 1981), 16; and S. P. Stetkevych, *The Poetics of Islamic Legitimacy*, 80.

83 Wahb Rumiya claims that the Islamic panegyric (as opposed to its pre-Islamic counterpart) is individualistic, sycophantic, and "a commodity up for sale (*sul'a ma'ruda li-l-bay'*), *Qasidat al-madh*, 80. For an anti-panegyric manifesto, see Jalal al-Khayyat, *al-Takassub bi-al-shi'r* (Beirut: Dar al-Adab, 1970). For the famous "Chapter on Earning a Living by Poetry" by Ibn Rashiq, see his *al-'Umda*, 178–88.

84 See Khurshid Rizvi, "The Status of the Poet in *Jahiliya*," *Hamdard Islamicus* 6, no. 2 (1983): 97–110. Although the author's concern is to demystify the poet from the level of the supernatural to a "normal but important human being," (110), he brings together all the necessary evidence that attest to the power of the poet.

85 Almost all Suzanne Pinckney Stetkevych's numerous studies on the panegyric demonstrate the power of poetry in the creation of obligation. For the pre-Islamic period, see her, "Pre-Islamic Panegyric and the Poetics of Redemption," which also demonstrates the request for a concrete reward—in this case the ransom of an imprisoned relative—by the panegyrist. See also, Hammond, "Poetics of S/Exclusion", 19.

86 The poetics of politics in the panegyric is superbly demonstrated in many of S P. Stetkevych's works. For the period in question, see especially her "Pre-Islamic Panegyric."

87 For the historical context for the period in question, see Kennedy, *The Prophet and the Age of the Caliphates*, 75–103.

88　The negotiation of tribal position and rank is very well brought out by
　　S. P. Stetkevych in her study on the poetry of al-Akhtal, *The Poetics of Islamic
　　Legitimacy*, 80–109.

89　For the use of politics in Umayyad poetics, see Shawqi Dayf, *al-Tatawwur wa-
　　l-tajdid fi-l-shi'r al-umawi* (Cairo: Dar al-Ma'arif, 1965), 85–101, for the genre of
　　naqa'id , see 162–202; see also, K. A. Fariq, "Umayyad Poetry: Its Political and
　　Social Background," *Islamic Culture* 29, no. 4 (1955): 256–66.

90　None of these is a fully fledged *qasida*. One panegyric is dedicated to Mu'awiya,
　　another to 'Abd al-Malik b. Marwan (again the editors confuse the *mamduh* as
　　Marwan b. al-Hakam), and two to the Umayyad governor of Iraq, al-Hajjaj. See,
　　Diwan Layla, 51, 87, 63 and 120–22, respectively. Curiously, there is *qit'a* where Layla
　　addresses the wife of 'Abd al-Malik with an element of reproach, *Diwan Layla*,
　　122–23.

91　*Diwan Layla*, 92.

92　See *Diwan Layla*, 108–10, and 116, respectively. The former is sometimes
　　attributed not to Layla, but to her contemporary, Humayd b. Thawr al-Hilali.

93　al-Isbahani, *al-Aghani*, 5:1657–62. The invective exchange of Layla and al-Nabigha
　　is framed in the context of a rivalry between the latter, and a certain Sawwar
　　b. al-Awfa, a kinsman of Layla's (who is even suspected to be her husband).
　　Al-Nabigha had composed a poem, dubbed as *al-fadiha* (the scandalous) maligning
　　the tribe of Sawwar and Layla. For Layla's riposte to al-Ja'di, and speculation on
　　the relationship between Sawwar and Layla, see *Diwan Layla*, 100–101, and 24,
　　respectively.

94　See Abu Dhiyab, *al-Nabigha al-Ja'di*, 145, and 147, respectively.

95　See note 68 above.

96　See note 94 above.

97　See Abu Dhiyab, *al-Nabigha al-Ja'di*, 143–45.

98　As demonstrated by S.P. Stetkevych, *The Poetics of Islamic Legitimacy*, 80–109.

99　Ibid.

100　Caroline P. Murphy, *Lavinia Fontana: A Painter and her Patrons in Sixteenth Century
　　Bologna* (New Haven, CT: Yale University Press, 2003), 1.

101　Ibid.

9

Writing About Life Through Loss: 'A'isha Taymur's Elegies and the Subversion of the Arabic Canon

Mervat Hatem

I experienced Magda Al-Nowaihi's death in June 2002 as a double loss: the loss of a personal friend and of an intellectual interlocutor whose knowledge and critical perspectives on the Arabic language, its literature, and its poetry provided sources of inspiration and support. Before her death, Magda's work on the early history of Arabic elegy intersected with mine which focused on the life and work of the nineteenth-century poet 'A'isha Taymur, who also wrote elegies that were praised by modern literary critics. Taymur was one of the prominent women writers and poets whose works of fiction and poetry were published in the late 1880s and the 1890s and were well received. She also published a social commentary on the changing relations between men and women in the family that provoked an important public debate.

I never had the chance to discuss Taymur's elegies with Magda because her illness and my decision to leave poetry until the end of my study foreclosed that possibility. In one of the few conversations we had, however, about elegies written by Arab women poets, I recall being taken aback when Magda challenged the masculinist construction of the Arabic canon, reflected in its classification of al-Khansa' as the most prominent

Arab woman poet based on the elegies of her two brothers Sakhr and Mu'awiyya. My knowledge and interest in elegies written by Arab women was largely informed by the nineteenth-century discussions of the genre, which provided a context for understanding the works of the early poets and of Taymur. In these discussions, the strength of the precedent set by al-Khansa' was embraced by modern women poets to support their interest in poetry in general and elegy in particular.[1]

Magda's very perceptive critical observation directed my attention to how the praise of al-Khansa''s poetic prowess was indirectly based on its affirmation of Arab masculinity and the placement of men at the center of women's emotional lives. It invited students of gender to be critical of this aspect of her elegies in their evaluation of her status as a representative of the female canon in Arabic poetic tradition. Based on this innovative attempt to radically interrogate the canon, there is no doubt in my mind that Magda's work on this genre and the pre-Islamic women poets were going to transform our understanding of both.

In the above discussion of al-Khansa', I suggested to Magda that there was a modern take on the poet's elegies that was important to consider in this evaluation. Zaynab Fawwaz, a younger contemporary of Taymur, offered it in her nineteenth century biographical dictionary of women, *al-Durr al-manthur fi tabaqat rabbat al-khudur* [The abundant prose for the biographies of secluded women] (1894) that highlighted the role they played in Arabo-Islamic history, including their important contributions to its literary tradition. It underlined the status of al-Khansa' as a *mukhadrama* (a poet whose life span bridged the times of polytheism and Islam) and how her poetry asserted its independence in the face of the powerful defenders of the new faith who tried to discredit the pre-Islamic poetic traditions and their figures.[2] According to Fawwaz, Omar ibn al-Khattab, the second caliph, was critical of al-Khansa''s pre-Islamic mourning attire and her elegies that mourned brothers who were not Muslim. Al-Khansa' did not cower or demur in the face of criticisms from such a powerful source, insisting that he listen to her elegies before passing judgment. In this request, she clearly recognized that her elegies were being dismissed for considerations that were unrelated to poetry. Fawwaz informed the readers that Omar was moved by the poet's eloquence and suggested that she be left alone because her overwhelming grief remained undiminished.[3] One could see in his response an early articulation of women's depth of feeling, their emotional nature and ability to successfully articulate grief.

While the classical Arabic critics acknowledged that women were great elegists, they did not argue that they could not excel in other genres.[4] In contrast, the modernist critics, some of whom were women, claimed that women poets were only adept at this genre because of their emotional nature and character! Paradoxically, 'A'isha Taymur's family and friends, who were critical of her unorthodox literary interests, used her seven years of mourning her daughter, Tawhida, to underline her diminished rational capacity and unstable nature. They found a strong ally in modern medicine's construction of the hysterical woman, which condemned what they considered to be her transgressions and inappropriate forms of expression. Her grandson suggested that this led her children to isolate her (ya'zilunaha) an ambiguous reference that could be interpreted as having her institutionalized or simply locked up in the family home.[5]

Taymur wrote several elegies for family members, including her daughter, her father, her mother, and her sister. Surprisingly, she also wrote an elegy mourning Shaykh Ibrahim al-Saqqa, a distinguished member of the ulema class who most probably helped her research her important social commentary, *Mir'at al-ta'ammul fi al-umur* [A reflecting mirror on some affairs] (1892). What I propose to do in this paper is first examine why modernist literary critics associated women with elegiac poetry, singling out Taymur's elegies as examples of her best poetry. Second, I want to look more critically at how, in addition to the exploration of loss, Taymur's poems offered an appreciation of the lives of these important figures and how they impacted hers. Third, like the rest of her collected poetry, these elegies allowed her to share a great deal about her life, personal feelings, and relationships, challenging the uncritical assumptions that people make about the limited openness of nineteenth-century women. Finally, I will discuss how these poems subverted the modern Arabic canon that sought to restrict women's scope and forms of poetic expression.

I. Modernist Views of Women Poets and Elegiac Poetry

Taymur's collected poems (diwan) titled *Hilyat al-tiraz* [The finest of its class] was published in 1892. Zaynab Fawwaz informed us that it had a "great effect on the readers and enjoyed an additional favorable reception by the literary establishment."[6] While she did not attempt to comment on any of Taymur's poetry, Fawwaz underlined how the poet was greatly affected by the loss of Tawhida: "[she] was overtaken by extreme sadness and sorrow for [a daughter] who had taken over the management of her [mother's] household relieving her of the need to depend on others. She abandoned poetry and learning making elegiac poetry, wailing *(al-'adid)* and lamentation her habit/practice during seven years of mourning."[7]

Fawwaz characterized the special alliance between mother and daughter in functional terms, a theme that could be found in early modern elegies.[8] Because Tawhida was instrumental in allowing her mother to resume her literary studies, Taymur was understandably deeply affected by her loss. In addition, Fawwaz connected the way Taymur turned mourning into a habit and a practice with the existence of a class of hired female mourners who helped families process their grief in nineteenth-century Egypt, establishing grieving as a particularly feminine activity.

Paradoxically, Zaynab Fawwaz's dictionary, within which Taymur's biography appeared, offered a more complex representation of women poets and their contributions to the Arabic literary tradition. Fawwaz simultaneously praised the elegies of al-Khansa', especially those written for her brother Sakhr, as the best of their kind in the history of Arabic poetry,[9] but also shared many equally beautiful examples of all kinds of poetry written by other women poets in Ummayad Spain, Abbasid times, and beyond. In this way, the dictionary reacquainted the reader with a corpus that was generally not well preserved, circulated, or acknowledged.[10] Because of Fawwaz's awareness of the existence of women's diverse poetic interests, her discussion of Taymur's elegy for Tawhida suggested a certain ambiguity and ambivalence: she viewed the "habit of lamentation" as more appropriate to the working-class professional mourners and seemed critical of and puzzled by how a woman of Taymur's class standing was unable to sublimate her mourning poetically and/or engage in practical mourning with the "dignity" dictated by her class. Curiously, Fawwaz's earlier discussion of al-Khansa' showed how that great poet was also unable to maintain this class distinction in the face of significant personal losses.

Mayy Ziyada was the next major critic to thoroughly examine Taymur's poetry in the biography she published in 1923. Ziyada was a modern poet who published her works first in French, then in Arabic. As the daughter of a Christian Palestinian-Lebanese family that settled in Cairo in 1908, she used the support and presence of her family to create a space for herself in the sexually segregated literary establishment, presiding over a weekly salon that was attended by the leading male modernist poets and writers from 1913 onward.[11] Her French education and relations with members of the modernist literary establishment shaped her views of the previous generation of women poets, like 'A'isha Taymur and Warda al-Yaziji, whose biographies she published in the early 1920s.

Ziyada lacked the knowledge that Fawwaz possessed about the broad contributions that Arab women have made to Arabic poetry throughout history, and primarily used Taymur's work to offer a modernist critique of what she described as the pitfalls of 'traditional' Arabic poetry. In her assessment of Taymur's poetry, Ziyada declared "it lacked a system of organization . . . or a trace of history except in the historical poems which included a date in the last line. Even though it used the metaphors of those who preceded her . . . , her personality still came through transparent veils. She avoided the emphasis that some poets put on the pride of the family and/or tribe and she did not follow the pattern of beginning with praise and ending with verbosity. The sincerity of her emotions put her in the advanced ranks of the best poets. When she spoke about herself, she drew a picture of a sincere and sweet naiveté whose style was not as geometric as that of the advocates of classicism and more in line with what she categorized in French as "romantique," [a feature] which is typical of our age."[12]

In the above, Ziyada enumerated the problems she found in Taymur's poetry, like disorganization and continued reliance on familiar metaphors, which she attributed to traditionalism. Paradoxically, Ziyada also conceded that Taymur's poetry avoided traditional themes and styles of writing and was somewhat modernist in that her personality broke through the old limitations, making it consistent with the French romantic style. As far as Ziyada was concerned, the latter was not enough to challenge the traditional character of Taymur's poetry. Because Ziyada described Taymur as simultaneously following and departing from the traditional canon, there was no way she could in the 1920s appreciate the hybridity of its language and writing style, which M.M. Bakhtin defined much later as a state of having "double-accented" and "double-styled" language that allowed an author/poet to bring together, fuse, but also maintain the separation of two discursive voices.[13]

While Ziyada was generally critical of Taymur's poetry, she privileged her elegy for Tawhida as the most sincere of the poems she wrote about her family and an example of the best of her poetry.[14] In contrast to Fawwaz's discussion of the instrumental relationship between mother and daughter that had led Taymur to write eloquently about that loss, Ziyada offered a modernist abstract discussion of mothering as a woman's central role, and one that emphasized her relationship to nature and reproduction:

> Once a woman is born, all the conditions of her life are adjusted in preparation for this important reproductive role just as natural forces directed all rivers to the sea. A mother is always compared to nature, the greatest mother of all. All ancient religions treated femaleness as the symbol of Mother Nature and its wonderful reproductive function. The Egyptian deity, Isis, was first in a long series of goddesses that represented the impulse for divine reproduction and a divine mother who gave birth to all living things. All other mythologies followed suit in considering mothering to be the symbol of the power of a woman and a representation of her natural function and connection to life.
>
> Given this overwhelming social and natural emphasis on mothering, what happens to woman when she is confronted with the death of an offspring that she has created? That experience represented a crisis of cosmic proportion whose effects symbolized a dramatic reversal of all known things that lead parents to expect their demise before their youthful children.[15]

As a biographer of Taymur, Ziyada knew about the poet's ambivalence toward motherhood and domesticity, whose burdens she sought to escape, but she ignored this by representing Taymur's life as dominated by this important function. While Tawhida's death at the age of eighteen provided a sufficient explanation of the terrible blow that this loss represented, Ziyada's association between women and nature offered another modernist perspective that emphasized the view of women as emotional beings who found an outlet in grief.

Ziyada's admiration of Taymur's elegy for her daughter drew additional strength from the astonishing parallels she drew between it and Tennyson's *The May Queen*. Although Taymur did not know any English and Tennyson's poem was never translated into Arabic, Ziyada praised both poets for letting a deceased daughter address her mother regarding the rituals of death and mourning. Here, Ziyada's critical admiration of

Taymur's poem was enhanced by the fact that it mirrored Tennyson's poem. By making this comparison, she thus inserted English poetry in the discussion as a new standard for appreciating Arabic poetry.

Finally, Ziyada used her study of Warda al-Yaziji, published in 1924, to develop some of her views of Taymur's poetry and to use them as keys for understanding al-Yaziji, a Lebanese contemporary of Taymur. The literary establishments of both countries considered the two to be the pioneering poets of that generation, which inspired the two women to correspond with one another and to support each other's poetry by contributing introductions to each other's collected poems, as was the practice of the time.[16]

In Ziyada's study of al-Yaziji, she declared that it was difficult to discuss her poetry because it did not easily lend itself to the deciphering of "her temperament and its essential inclinations and/or interests."[17] Her study of al-Yaziji represented a continuation of the effort to explore the "temperament of the Oriental woman (al-mar'a al-sharqiya) so that her essence and genius could be appreciated." She considered al-Yaziji's elegies to be her best poetry[18] and categorized her as the elegiac poet par excellence; the elegies of family members, friends, and public figures that she produced constituted the bigger half of her *diwan*, entitled *Hadiqat al-ward* [The Rose Garden].[19] In this modernist/Orientalist construction, Arab women poets were treated as the carriers of the 'essences' of Oriental womanhood, which led them to become mistresses of grief and loss—a view that narrowly defined their legitimate scope of expression and undermined their ability to become great poets who explored a wide range of emotions and themes.

Finally, 'Abbas Mahmud al-'Aqqad, who maintained social and intellectual relations with Ziyada, was another political and literary critic who addressed himself to Taymur's poetry. As a liberal political writer, he was celebrated for his defense of the Wafd political party as a representative of the Egyptian political majority against royal privilege in the 1920s. Paradoxically, he was also known as a social conservative whose opposition to the rights of women earned him the title of 'aduwu al-mar'a (the enemy of the woman). With this in mind, al-'Aqqad used Ziyada's construction above to underline women's limited range of poetic expression and focused attention on femininity as an obstacle to their ability to excel in this field, with the exception of elegiac poetry. As far as he was concerned, the ability to excel in poetry was rare in general and was even scarcer among women:

A woman can be good at writing fiction, may be good at acting, and may be successful in artistic dancing, but she will never excel in poetry. [In fact], there is not a single great woman poet in the history of the world because femininity . . . does not lend itself to the expression of feelings and does not overpower other personalities it encounters. It is closer to the suppression of feelings and hiding them. A woman is inferior because she surrenders her existence to he who takes possession of her like a husband or a lover. And once a 'personality' loses true expression and the desire to be expansive, that is, to include and incorporate others, very little is left that allows for poetic greatness.

This does not deny [legitimacy to] our claim that a female can express sadness, because the latter reflects her willingness to surrender and her dependence on others. The only great woman poet whose genius is established in the Arabic language is al-Khansa', precisely because she cried and grieved. The other well-known slave and free women poets under the Abbasids and in the Andalus imitated others, and the sum total of their good poetry does not exceed a few pages.[20]

In the above, al-'Aqqad declared poetry, the most prestigious form of Arabic literary expression, to be closed to women because femininity discouraged them from the free expression of their feelings and expected them to surrender them to their husbands and lovers. Like Ziyada, al-'Aqqad considered this culturally defined role to be a reflection of an 'essential' feminine personality structure that was inferior to the masculine one. While men had overpowering personalities, women's were weak and inclined them to surrender. Men freely expressed their feelings while women hid theirs. As a result, women did not share the expansive frame of mind that made men at ease with the world, allowed them to incorporate others, and entitled them to greatness. Given this inferior nature, women could never produce great poetry.

According to al-'Aqqad, elegiac poetry was the exception that proved this general rule. The expression of sadness reflected women's lack of autonomy and their connectedness and dependence on others. Al-Khansa', the great Arab poet, provided an excellent example of women's poetic skills put in the service of expressing grief and shedding tears. In his view, the entire corpus of Arab women's poetry that dealt with other themes was very limited and only a few pages of it were actually good!

Despite this view of women's modest range of poetic expression, al-ʿAqqad placed Taymur third after Mahmud Sami al-Barudi, the nationalist poet of the ʿUrabi revolution, and Mahmud al-Saʿati, one of the poets of the royal court, in his evaluation of the leading poets of the 1870s and 1880s. In his explanation of this prominent ranking, he cited Taymur's elegy mourning Tawhida as an effective example of the sincere expression of a mother's pain at the loss of a daughter in the prime of her youth, with which readers from different national or cultural backgrounds and ages could identify. He dismissed her courtship poetry because she had dismissed it herself as a way of trying her hand in a different genre. Finally, he confessed to being unable to locate the poems that described her personal struggle with her fading eyesight in his interpretation of women's limited poetic range: they offered a counterintuitive expression of struggle that clashed with women's inborn disposition to surrender and accept the vagaries of life. In addressing this paradox, he decided that these poems were a reflection of the dissonance that Taymur experienced as a result of her prolonged mourning of her daughter. His familiarity with Taymur's early rebellion as a young child against the culturally specific ideal of femininity did not convince him that rebellion was a prominent theme in Taymur's life and work, rather than a product of dissonance. The death of a daughter before that of a mother ran against the laws of nature, which explains why natural forces like the sun and moon deviated from the norm.

In concluding, he suggested that Taymur's poetry represented the experience and views of secluded Egyptianized Turkish women. Even though he did not think that she described that experience in her poetry, he criticized her for not being able to break out of its constraints in her denunciation of the nationalist leaders of the ʿUrabi revolution. In contrast, he opined that men of her class (without being specific, but perhaps with Mahmud Sami al-Barudi in mind) were able to break out of their limiting class experience by mingling with men from the lower and upper classes. Had she not been the only woman poet of her generation, he thought she would still be peerless in her representation of the closed environment of her Egyptian-Turkish class.

These last commentaries of the contributions that Taymur's poetry made contradicted al-'Aqqad's view of women's limited capabilities for varied poetic expression. Even if one conceded that Taymur's critical views of 'Urabi's nationalist revolution reflected her Egyptian-Turkish milieu, her interest in political matters coupled with her struggle/rebellion against opthalmia offered a complex poetic personality. While al-'Aqqad gave weight to the fact that she was the only woman poet of her generation by placing her among the prominent poets of the time, he admitted that this was not the main reason for her prominent position. He suggested that she was entitled to our attention because of the broad social and thematic scope of her poetry.

II. 'A'isha Taymur's Elegies of Women and the Critique of the Modernist Feminine Sensibility

In this section, I want to examine the various elegies that Taymur included in her *diwan, Hilyat al-tiraz*, as part of the critique of the limiting modernist construction of that genre and its implicit belief in women's limited poetic scope of expression. I will show that beyond the grief and the tears, Taymur's elegies focused on the lives of these women and men and how they affected her own.

Taymur's elegy for Tawhida had been singled out by most literary critics as representing the most effective description of grief at the loss of a beloved young daughter. It began with a graphic description of her mother's raw emotional and physical reactions to this traumatic event, which distorted her perception of the surrounding world:

> The outpouring of a sea of tears from one's eyes protested the
>   injustice of fate and the betrayal of time.
> Each eye had a right to shed bloody pearls and the heart to experience
>   torment and ruin.
> A radiant light has been covered, the morning sun has chosen to veil,
>   and the beautiful moon quickly set after rising.
> The one I love has passed away leaving me drunk with pain and with a
>   inextinguishable flame in my heart . . . .
> If my pain were to travel back in time, no one would pay any attention
>   to the losses of Qays or Kuthayyir.[21]

If one were to judge lost love by the level of pain, then the pain felt by the best poets in the Arabic literary tradition would pale in the face of a mother's love and loss of a child. Not only did Taymur insert herself here into the Arabic literary tradition, but she sought to carve a unique place for herself in that tradition that has been largely focused on the pain that male poets felt from loss of a woman's love. Hers was a doubly unique contribution to the themes of love and loss in the Arabic poetic tradition.

Next, Taymur narrated the circumstances that surrounded the illness of her daughter. The symptoms appeared in the month of Ramadan, a festive time of year, which acquired a special sadness as Tawhida wilted like a flower and illness became her garb. Instead of enjoying the delicious juices and the deserts typically served in fancy cups during that month, her daughter sampled death quickly losing the bloom of youthfulness.

In a touching dialogue between daughter and mother, Taymur explained why Tawhida was special and why her loss was extremely difficult to bear. First, the ailing Tawhida asked the doctor for a quick cure for the pain, not for her own sake, but to spare her stricken mother. In this, Tawhida put the needs of her mother ahead of her own. Second, in this exchange first with the doctor and then with her mother, Tawhida's own poetic eloquence and skill were made clear. According to Taymur, the youthful Tawhida easily learned poetic meter and proved more skilled at it than her mother. Third, because she died at the young age of eighteen, her responses to her eminent demise reflected both maturity and childishness: she courageously faced death but also expressed fear at being torn away from her mother. Fourth, Tawhida's death during the preparations for her wedding and on her wedding night made the loss doubly painful for her mother:

O mother, I am sorry to leave you and tomorrow you will see my
    casket march like a bride.
It will stop at a tomb, which will be my home.
Tell the God of the tomb to be gentle with your daughter who came
    here as a young bride.
Be strong at my grave and linger there for a while to calm my
    frightened soul.
O mother, our early wish had come to a quick end and how lovely if it
    could have been easily realized.

It has become like a past dream in the face of this difficult day of
    truth.
Go back to your empty home and glorious exploits that will now
    unfold in my absence.
Preserve my bridal trousseau as a memento of a wedding and a wish
    for happiness.[22]

In the above, Tawhida made clear that mother and daughter shared
each other's hopes and dreams. Tawhida enthusiastically supported her
mother's wish to become a poet and a writer engaged in glorious deeds
and Taymur took joy in her daughter's desire for happy matrimony. While
Tawhida's death aborted her dream of a happy marriage, she encouraged
her mother to singly pursue the literary goals for which both had toiled.

In these verses, Tawhida emerged as much more than an instrument
of her mother's literary ambitions. Her relationship with her mother
was a symbiotic one in which their needs were intertwined, which contrasted with the instrumental view of outsiders, like Fawwaz and others,
who were unable to fathom the complex dynamics involved in such relationships combining mutual need, love, and admiration. This elegy and
the seven years that Taymur spent mourning her daughter's death cast
doubt on the instrumental view and supported a layered understanding
of that relationship.

The remaining part of the poem painfully described Taymur's reaction
to this loss and her daughter's final wishes. Her tears imprisoned her logic
expressing raw grief and regret. She pledged never to forget her and never
to tire from reciting the Qur'an and praying for her daughter as long as
the birds continued to sing on trees. She also promised never to forget the
sadness she felt when they laid Tawhida in the ground and to cry over her
loss until they met again.

In what was to become a significant theme of her elegies, Taymur
used her name, 'A'isha which literally meant living, to explore the effects
of the different losses on her life. When people reminded Taymur that
she had lived through (a'isha) the terrible loss of her beloved daughter,
she replied that her life and patience were effectively over, as only God
would know. Along with the ability to survive that her name signified
came the weighty obligation to mourn the loss of Tawhida, a mourning
that was to last seven years.

In this ruined life, Taymur reassured Tawhida that her mother's heart, eyes, and tongue were satisfied with her and that through them she would secure her a place of peace in heaven. Both mother and daughter made several references to the religious powers that mothers were said to possess. The daughter hoped that her mother's forgiveness and/or the religious rituals observed by families to memorialize their dead would entitle her to God's mercy. In response, her mother reassured Tawhida that her sacrifices will not be forgotten and that she would always have her prayers and religious approval. Because a *hadith* declared that heaven lay under the feet of mothers, both mother and daughter elaborated on different aspects of that belief in their hopes and promises to each other.

The description of the special relationship between Tawhida as a capable young woman and her poet mother provided real snapshots of the lives of two unusual women in 1877 (the date Taymur offered for this elegy). Taymur, who was deprived of a chance to complete her literary studies by marriage and children, turned to her daughter for support in realizing that dream. Through her literary mother, Tawhida grew up appreciating the new and old skills associated with femininity: poetry and embroidery. Lacking her mother's unfulfilled aspirations, Tawhida's attitude to marriage was also different: she looked forward to it instead of resenting the demands it would place on her. Mother and daughter also represented different generational and class responses to changes taking place in nineteenth century Egyptian society's definitions of women's roles. Unlike Taymur's mother, who discouraged her daughter's privileging of literacy over the feminine crafts for fear of social censure, this elegy offered an unusual theme in Arabic poetry, namely the solidarity of women as expressed by the unusual relationship between mother and daughter. Not only did they work with each other in the quest for their worldly hopes and aspirations, but Taymur used the prophetic privileging of motherhood to avail her young daughter, who was not herself a mother, of a place in heaven. This appreciation of a young daughter by her mother was unparalleled in Arabic poetry and reversed the very hierarchical relations between the young and the old and the treasured place that men (as brothers and lovers) occupied in the emotional lives of women, as expressed through elegies.

Taymur's elegy for her mother offered a marked contrast to the mother-daughter relationship described in her mourning of Tawhida. It described a different emotional dynamic of mother-daughter relationships within the same family. The defining event that shaped Taymur's relationship with her mother was the struggle between them over whether embroidery and needlework were more appropriate than reading and writing as the basis of the proper education for a young aristocratic girl. Mother and daughter represented two different ideals of femininity. While the former emphasized the importance of embroidery and needlework as part of a class-specific definition of feminine skills, the latter desired to learn how to read and write. Beauty was another feminine quality associated with this old definition of femininity and which Taymur clearly identified with her mother:

> O tomb, you must be delighted with the bright/shining pearl that you
> have acquired.
> She was betrayed by destiny and had to drink reluctantly from the
> cups of illness that left her thin and skinny.
> She had tasted bitter illness since childhood, living her days in pain.
> She finally bled to death, breaking one's heart with sorrow and pain.[23]

While most accounts of Taymur's life were silent on the history and life of her Circassian slave mother, the verses above volunteer some important information about this woman in contrasting bold strokes. The mother's external beauty, which was compared to a shining pearl, hid fate's betrayal, which was reflected in an underprivileged background and a life marked by a long history of illness without the means to treat it. Her thinness offered another piece of evidence of an impoverished childhood. Compounding this was the experience of being sold into slavery, which Taymur did not explicitly address, but which the informed reader knew.

As the concubine of 'Ismail Taymur, and mother of three daughters by him, she was eventually able to get the medical care she needed, but by then her many illnesses had worsened. Equally significant were the other unexplored wounds:

> How many nights did she stay up with the stars moaning about what
> she held inside?
> When God's order commanded her into the tomb, the order could
> not be reversed.

O God, provide her with paradise as a refuge and a home where she
can be happy and experience joy.[24]

On the surface, her mother's sleepless nights could be attributed to
her physical ailments, but Taymur also hinted that her moaning articulated other types of pain locked inside her: the experience of being taken
away from her family, sold into slavery, and having to hide the pain and illness that would have devalued her worth as the property of wealthy men.
When death came, her daughter's prayer summarized what she felt was
most important to her mother: a paradise that would serve as a refuge and
a home where she could be happy. The emphasis put on refuge and home
as sources of happiness seemed to suggest that her slave mother moved
from one home to another and that she was not always happy in them.

Taymur described the loss of her mother as a cause of sadness for the
family, provoking a stream of tears and allowing fortune to continue tor-
menting her grief and loss. It is fair to say, however, that this poem dealt
less with Taymur's feelings for her mother and more with the details of
her mother's physical and emotional pain. The picture it offered contradicted the assumptions popular in the literature about how white slaves
were exempt from emotional or physical suffering. Because of their
beauty and the fact that they sometimes became concubines of wealthy
men, there was a discursive tendency to dwell on their access to wealth
and comfort and to maintain silence on the painful effects that this form
of Ottoman slavery had on the lives of these white slave women.[25] Taymur
gently divested her readers of these romantic illusions, describing the
poor underprivileged background of her mother marked with ill health,
the experience of being sold many times over, a life of insecurity, and an
elusive quest for home and happiness.

Despite the sympathetic description of her mother's pain and exilic
experiences, Taymur's elegy for her mother lacked the depth of feeling
found in her elegy for her daughter. The most touching verses in this poem
were those in which Taymur prayed for her mother to find a final resting
place, a home in paradise where she could be permanently settled and
happy. The rest of the poem speaks of this loss in a very impersonal way,
counting it as one of many and failing to accord it any special significance.

Next, Taymur turned her elegiac skills to describing the emotional
impact of the loss of a younger sister. Like their mother, this sister was

described as a precious pearl, a beautiful girl. She died before she was old enough to put henna on her hands. Fortune assassinated her in its secluded headquarters as a lion would drag a young victim into his den.

Taymur used the same device she employed in Tawhida's elegy and allowed her sister to speak for herself. She felt frightened when the doctor declared that his efforts had failed. She also could not understand why she was to die before any of her peers, declaring herself cheated by time and defeated by her enemies and those who envied her.

Finally, Taymur shared with her readers that following her sister's death she suffered from severe anxiety attacks regarding her own mortality, which left her bedridden. She mourned her beloved sister without being able to understand the reasons for this early separation from a sibling. She longed to hug that sister whose body now belonged to the grave, which claimed this pearl of a sister who had so outshone her peers:

> O my beloved how can I be reconciled with this break which affected
> siblings and children. This life ('ayshati) half lived is something I
> would not wish on strangers or lonely people.[26]

Clearly, the effect of this early loss and trauma left its imprint on Taymur as a child. It was difficult not only to understand, but also to overcome. It denied her a sense of security and contributed to loneliness at an early age.

In her elegies for these female figures, Taymur provided the readers with vignettes about the women in her family and the way her dependence on and/or conflict with them shaped her emotional world. The result is a complex portrait of the lives of upper-class women in the nineteenth century.

III. 'A'isha Taymur's Elegies for Her Father and Shaykh al-Saqqa

Taymur wrote two other elegies that devoted attention to the loss of important men in her life: her father, Ismail Taymur Pasha, and al-'allama (an honorific adjective reserved for learned men) Shaykh Ibrahim al-Saqqa. While the women in her life contributed in different ways to a rich and complex emotional world, these men were associated with her literary interests. These were, of course, central preoccupations of Taymur's childhood and mature years and the focus of her ongoing struggles within and outside her family; she required the support of these important men in her quest to become a poet and a writer in the sexually segregated nineteenth century.

Her father was an early supporter of her unorthodox interest in reading and writing as alternatives to the feminine crafts emphasized by her mother. He wielded enough authority to persuade her mother to tolerate her novel preoccupations. While this made her relationship with him a special one, the poem eulogizing him revealed that theirs was a formal relationship. It began with a reference to his distinguished status:

> It was difficult for the inhabitants of the Earth to see him go like a
>   moon eclipsed in darkness.
> It was only right that the age should mourn the loss of its most
>   brilliant example of eloquence among the most well-spoken
>   class.[27]

The death of Taymur's father was not only a personal loss, but also a cosmic and temporal one underlining his distinguished status as a brilliant man of letters with a flawless literary Arabic style who stood out among the educated classes. Taymur clearly admired this part of her father's life and sought to emulate it in her literary writings.

While his health had been failing, affecting both his speech and then his constitution, he expressed a strong desire to live. Taymur confirmed her brother's account of how her father died outside his home at the palace of Crown Prince Tawfiq. This was how she described the news of his death:

> Calamitous news announced his loss and he was returned home
>   without hope.
> The female inhabitants of his palaces grieved as their prince lay in a
>   bed of condolences.
> The wailers spent the night surrounding him instead of his friends
>   and companions.[28]

The above provided explicit references to the wealth of her deceased father. Taymur was a rich man who had more than one concubine and/or wife settled in separate palaces. As another measure of his wealth, a very large number of professional wailing women surrounded his corpse, offering a contrast to the many male companions and guests who used to keep him company in his literary salon. While his daughter was not among the wailing women, female observers could note the grief in her eyes that betrayed her misery. Here, Taymur clearly adhered to the upper-class code of mourning that allowed women to cry, but not to engage in the lamentations that were reserved to the professional wailing women. Taymur added to this particular code through the use of poetry that described her feelings rather than act on them.

In her description of her feelings on the loss of her father, she mixed the use of the third person in outlining his relationship to his children and/or his role as a father with a more personal articulation of her feeling toward him. The former expressed the distance he maintained with his children and the latter indicated the special relationship between father and daughter:

> She said: by the oath of fatherhood, you provided the light of security to your children.
> Ever since I lost you, my gut has been on fire and my body has been enveloped in pain.
> You were the treasure of my hopes, the richness of my needs, my good fortune and the brilliance that filled my eyes.
> You soothed my pain, healed my sores, nourished my soil and were the river of my songs.[29]

According to Taymur, fatherhood was identified with being a good provider to one's children. In addition to commending him for the way he provided for his children, Taymur described her father as having been a good parent. In reference to the encouragement of her literary interests, she described him as representing the treasure of her hopes, the rich satisfaction of her needs, her good times, the soothing of her pain, the sustenance of her soul, and rivers of songs and poems. She also added that when she did not feel up to the task, she turned to him for help. In exchange, she placed immense importance on his approval:

> Your approval was the single most important accomplishment of my role as a daughter.

If I feel impatient to whom shall I complain, and after losing you
    whom shall I turn to for acceptance?
Would that I knew when you passed on, did I have your approval or
    disapproval?[30]

In exchange for his support of her wish to learn how to read and write,
Taymur spent her life seeking her father's approval and his good opinion. Following his death, she reported being haunted by whether or not
he was satisfied with her or if she had disappointed him. While Taymur
considered her father to have been a good parent, this was clearly a taxing
relationship in which she was not free to be herself, even if this meant his
disapproval.

She felt indebted to him and so she prayed that his soul be blessed.
She was confident of his immortality, however, because she counted him
among the martyrs—presumably because he died serving Crown Prince
Tawfiq. She ended this elegy by stating that her life without him would be
tormented for as long as she lived (ʿaʾisha).

Finally, Taymur's elegy for Shaykh al-Saqqa offers an interesting contrast to that for her father. According to Ali Mubarak, al-Saqqa was a
prominent member of the ulema of al-Azhar, where he taught Arabic,
fiqh, and exegesis.[31] How did Taymur know him, and what kind of a relationship did they have? The poem offered hints of an answer from the
personal note with which it opened:

Fate has substituted my comfort with hardship and replaced my
    blessings with misery.
Time took on such an appearance that obliged the eyes to mix its
    tears with blood . . . .
His mirror had been obliterated and its face made rusty after it had
    enjoyed a long period of clarity.[32]

In suggesting that the loss of Shaykh al-Saqqa substituted her comfort with hardship and blessing with misery, Taymur told the reader that
she knew the shaykh and that his loss was going to make a difference in
her own life, while also underlining how his loss was going to be historically felt. The reference to the obliterated and rusty mirror offered a
direct link to the title of her social commentary, Mirʾat al-taʾammul fi-l-umur,

which discussed the rights that men and women enjoyed in Islam, and how al-Saqqa might have provided her with some assistance in researching, selecting, and interpreting the Qur'anic verses that dealt with these issues.

She moved on to declare that the ulema would be saddened with the loss of his deep knowledge, which in his life he made available to others. Meanwhile, the ignorant would be happy to continue their nightly forms of gaiety, another theme that she tackled in *Mir'at al-ta'ammul fi-l-umur*. The shaykh was such a source of religious light that it was difficult to believe during his life that Imam al-Shafi'i, the founder of one of the four sects of Islam practiced in Egypt, was truly dead. He had deep religious and legal knowledge that richly guided humanity and made him one of its eloquent interpreters. He made sure that religious rituals were performed at the time of despair and offered his condolences to people, guarding the heart against error and from going astray. She played with his name, which meant 'to water,' likening his contributions to religious science to the watering of a colorful and splendid garden. Finally, she suggested that those who felt pain, like herself, would no longer find in him a source to soothe their tormented feelings.[33]

This last comment suggested that the shaykh might have served the religious needs of the family, providing religious counsel to its members and performing religious services in the event of death. Taymur suggested that he provided her with religious comfort in dealing with the many losses her family sustained:

> Who is going to perform the tireless rituals of the upright religion in
> the wake of anxious loss? . . . .
> His thoughts frequently healed the heavy hearts of those who were
> led astray . . . .
> Those who feel a deep sense of thirst will now have to suffer in the
> absence of the careful watering by al-Saqqa.[34]

In light of all the support and consolation Taymur attributed to the shaykh, the reader can well understand why she will suffer as a result of his loss.

In the above account, Taymur's description of the different roles played by the shaykh supported the claim made by Mayy Ziyada that elderly religious men were often asked to teach younger women language and religion in sexually segregated nineteenth-century Egypt. It was possible that the elderly al-Saqqa provided moral guidance to a mature Taymur, consoled her in the wake of family members' deaths, and discussed with her the Qur'anic verses that dealt with the rights of women in Islam. The personal tone Taymur used throughout the poem and the personal information she shared about the elderly man indicate that she knew him. He suffered from a variety of illnesses, but never complained or consulted any doctors. He performed his obligations as a member of the ulema by sharing his knowledge with others, and rightly received posthumous acknowledgment for it.

Taymur's admiration of the way the shaykh lived his life led her to conclude that not only did he deserve to occupy the highest ranks of his profession, but he was fit to be included in the ranks of religious martyrs. After having established that his was a life that was well lived and for which he would be religiously compensated, she discussed how she would miss him:

> He is in a blessed place, but we suffer greatly because of the distance
>   that separates us in times of hardship.
> My heart burned for him like smoldering embers and my grief
>   betrayed my misery and torment.
> I will shed tears of sorrow for him as long as I live ('a'isha) in my
>   annihilating seclusion![35]

This ending, with its personalized expression of loss, is very similar to the one Taymur used in her elegy for her father, which suggests that she perceived al-Saqqa as a father figure. Her expression of loss for the shaykh, however, was less burdened by the strong sense of duty and the need for approval that run through her elegy for her father. Thus, while Taymur considered her father to be her favorite parent, her relationship with Shaykh al-Saqqa, as a father figure, was less taxing, free as it was of the clear anxiety about whether or not she was meeting his expectations. Taymur played with her name in the last verse of this poem, as she had done in her elegies for other important people in her life, like Tawhida, her father, and her sister. Since Shaykh al-Saqqa was a man who was not related to her, she used his loss to criticize the stifling effects of her seclusion, which he had made more bearable. Through him she was able to maintain a link to the public world that she longed to join. Given the fact that all the other important men in her life had passed away including her father and husband, she promised to shed tears over him as long as she continued to live in her deadening seclusion *(ma dumt 'a'isha bi khadr fana'i)*. This is the only explicit denunciation of seclusion that can be found in Taymur's poetry, and it clearly indicates that her views on whether the seclusion of upper-class women is a mark of their virtue have changed.

Conclusion

An examination of Taymur's elegies for her daughter, mother, sister, and father and for Shaykh al-Saqqa offer very poignant vignettes of the lives of these women and men and how they intersected with hers. In giving attention to their lives, she made a persuasive case for why their loss should be mourned. Taymur transformed the classic Arabic canon represented by the legacy of al-Khansa' and the emotional centrality of her brothers, which Magda Al-Nowaihi criticized, by placing her daughter, mother, and sister at the center of poetic works. Not only did these women satisfy very important personal, work, and psychological needs, they were also central figures in the secluded feminine world of nineteenth-century Egypt. Her elegy of Tawhida had the unusual distinction of elevating a beloved daughter to a status that was unheard of in Arabic poetry. While Tawhida was special in her own right, her elegy provided a testimony to the special relationship between mother and daughter that was missing from that poetic tradition.

In contrast, the elegies for her father and Shaykh al-Saqqa underlined the important, but more secondary roles that they played in supporting her literary and social interests and concerns. These elegies also highlighted the changing attitudes that some nineteenth-century men had toward a new generation of young women who shared their literary interests. The result was a greater appreciation of the changes that were taking place in the lives of women and their relations with men. The complex emotional life and social world that emerged in these poems challenged the modernist claims made by male and female literary critics that the poetry of women was largely preoccupied with the traditional roles of shedding tears and articulating grief over the loss of loved ones in traditional forms. Taymur's elegies demonstrated that she was successfully able to manipulate this genre, insinuating her name, feelings, history, and interests into it and thereby contributing to its change and to the development of a Bakhtinian hybridity that made it anything but traditional.

Notes

1   I am grateful to Dana Sajdi for helping me develop this point.
2   Zaynab Fawwaz, *al-Durr al-manthur fi rabbat tabaqat al-khudur* (Kuwait: Maktabat Ibn Qutayba, n.d), 111.
3   See Magda Al-Nowaihi's reference to that discussion in "Resisting Silence in Arab Women's Autobiographies," *International Journal of Middle East Studies* 33, no. 4 (November 2001): 500 n. 32.
4   Marlé Hammond is the source of this assessment of the classical traditon.
5   Ahmed Kamal Zadah, "*Jaddati*," in *Hilyat al-Tiraz* (Cairo: Mataba'at Dar al-Kitab al-'Arabi, 1952), 18. Note that this volume, an anonymously edited collection of essays about 'A'isha Taymur's life and work, has the same title as her published collection of poetry (Cairo: n.p., 1892). The reader should note the author to distinguish between the two works.
6   Fawwaz, *al-Durr al-Manthur*, 304.
7   Ibid.
8   Dana Sajdi is the source of this observation.
9   Fawwaz, *al-Durr al-Manthur*, 110.
10 I am indebted to Marlé Hammond for this observation in an e-mail communication dated 9 February 2004. See her "The Poetics of S/Exclusion: Women, Gender and the Classical Arabic Canon" (PhD diss., Columbia University, 2003).
11 Salma al-Haffar al-Kuzbari, *Mayy Ziyada Aw Ma'sat al-Nubugh*, vol. 1 (Beirut: Mu'assasat Nawfal, 1987), 288.
12 Mayy Ziyada, *Sha'irat al-Tali'a, 'A'isha Taymur* (Cairo: Dar al- Hilal, 1956), 121.
13 M. M. Bakhtin, *The Dialogic Imagination*, cited by Robert J.C. Young, *Colonial Desire* (London: Routledge, 1995), 20, 22.
14 Ziyada, *Sha'irat al-Tali'a*, 131.
15 Ibid., 133–34.
16 Fawwaz, *al-Durr al-Manthur*, 305.
17 Mayy Ziyada, *Warda al-Yaziji* (Beirut: Mu'assasat Nawfal, 1980), 9.
18 Ibid., 10.
19 Ibid., 40, 43.
20 Abbas Mahmud al-'Aqqad, *Shu'ara' Misr wa bi'atuhum fi-l-jil al-madi* (Cairo: Maktabat al-Nahda al-Misriya, 1965), 151–52.
21 'A'isha Taymur, *Hilyat al-Tiraz* (Cairo: publisher unidentified, 1892), 17–18.
22 Ibid., 18.
23 Ibid., 31.

24 Ibid., 32.
25 Fadwa El Guindi, "Review Essay," *Journal of Political Ecology: Case Studies in History and Society* 6 (1999), 6–7.
26 Taymur, *Hilyat al-Tiraz*, 33.
27 Ibid., 28.
28 Ibid., 29.
29 Ibid., 29.
30 Ibid.
31 Ali Mubarak, *al-Khitat al-tawfiqiya al-jadida li Misr al-Qahira*, vol. 2 (Cairo: Al-Hay'a al-Misriya al-'Amma li-l-Kitab, 1982), 163.
32 Taymur, *Hilyat al-Tiraz*, 19.
33 Ibid., 19–20.
34 Ibid., 20.
35 Ibid., 21.

10

Sleep in Peace: Salah 'Abd Al-Sabur's Gentle Elegy on the Death of a Hero

Dina Amin

In the spirit of honoring the memory of my dear friend Magda Al-Nowaihi's scholarly and critical contribution as well as her humanistic legacy, I am contributing a study on modern Arabic poetry—a genre that was very close to Magda's heart—and am focusing on the work of a poet whom I know she admired greatly, Salah 'Abd al-Sabur. In this study, I will provide a close textual analysis as well as a translation of his poem *Sleep in Peace*.

I. Sleep in Peace[1]

(To the memory of my relative and friend, air force pilot Muhammad Nabil al-Baguri. He died a martyr on the sands of Gaza in September 1955)[2]

> He slept in peace
> His eyes shed a tear of joy
> It lit his noble face with a smile serene
> A smile that learned wise men cannot fathom
> He held out his palm, a lighthouse
> And cast a glance to bless life and the living
> With a smiling gaze, he engaged heaven in a chuckle

And without ceremony, that gentle soul departed life
He died a teacher and a paragon on the path of perfection
His disciples, who have spent their days in awe of his wisdom
They whisper in wonder
"Does the teacher smile?"
At that moment, the most gifted student responded
"Did our martyred professor not tell us the ultimate words of
  wisdom?"
Our teacher said, "Know thyself . . . O human being . . . ."
Having known himself, he died peacefully
He smiled
He has died for perfection, the ultimate endeavor
He had carried the end of his cross, his face frothing with anguish
In spite of the agony of that effort
In spite of the scorching heat tantalizing his bare body
He smiled
For he has given to life
He has given his fleeting days and strife
In order to heighten:
a lad's joyful smile,
a virgin's blissfulness,
and the glee parents experience in their child
So that, in the sky's cloud, a bird of peace can flutter

As for my brother, Muhammad Nabil
His funeral enveloped the streets of the city
On a sweltering summer afternoon, people with the heat were
  clobbered
Those who love him, those we love—dwellers of our old
  neighborhood
A lass wailing from a tired window
Soldiers marching in silenced gloom
Sad beatings of drums

Pointing her finger, an elderly lady questioned
"In this box, who is to be buried?"
"A young fighter; he died at twenty"

A syllable she did not utter—a strange woman
She is one of us; in her heart there are treasures
She has known compassions and numerous sorrows
She rushed howling into the funeral's crowds
Her aged flesh pushing against my arm and chest
Flesh of my shoulders sinking into the coffin
Everything was still at that moment, as if dying
In that death we all huddled

And in the graveyard resting in the midst of fields, there they put him
    away
Nothing was left of that handsome face but a handful of dust
Egypt's dust
You have returned to sleep in the arms of the dust
In the ground with our ancestors and our kin, and as such you shall
    sleep
Sleep in peace
In the eye of the sky, there was a haze of dusk
Red as blood
On the horizon, there were the blossoms of the fields
White as our hearts and his, white as the hearts of all those who are
    dead
Our own gentle *mujahidin*
Our own people, those who have blessed life[3]

II

This poem is an elegy written in memory of the early death of an exceptional air force pilot, Muhammad Nabil al-Baguri, who was killed in
battle along the Gaza strip, and is published in ʿAbd al-Sabur's famous
anthology, *al-Nas fi biladi* (People in my Country, 1965).[4] In it, he at
once elevates and simplifies the language of elegy composition. While
his effortless style communicates the heart-rending loss of a friend and
brings his humanity to the fore, ʿAbd al-Sabur's specific (and unforced)
choice of words tacitly transforms al-Baguri's life in two ways: from that
of a remarkable young man, role model, and teacher to the echelon of a
human being larger than life. ʿAbd al-Sabur does not only eulogize the

death of al-Baguri for his bravery and for making the ultimate sacrifice for his country, but, first, for having been a good person, an excellent teacher and role model, and, second, for having died a brave soldier. 'Abd al-Sabur's tone fluctuates from sadness over the loss of a beautiful soul to celebration, because a beautiful soul lives forever within our consciousness.

While the elegy is for a military hero, the emphasis is on the person: the loved friend, the highly respected teacher, the good neighbor. 'Abd al-Sabur does not dwell on the heroics that had shaped and defined the final moments of al-Baguri's life on the front; rather he focuses on his deceased friend's life, which had touched and improved the lives of so many. The poem does not begin with an expression of grief; on the contrary, it offers a picture of the fallen hero smiling, leaving us with a serene image of him as he departs:

> He slept in peace
> His eyes shed a tear of joy
> It lit his noble face with a smile serene
> A smile that learned wise men cannot fathom.

The image that the poet conveys of the departed reflects an astonishing and mysterious contentment. It is only through reading the rest of the poem that this satisfaction is unravelled and explained. The conduct and teaching of al-Baguri had a tremendous impact on people around him, which explains his elated departure, since he had helped so many. The poet places a special emphasis on the younger generation, al-Baguri's students, for they find consolation in what he had taught them. From this perspective, 'Abd al-Sabur's elegy comes through as a celebration of Nabil al-Baguri's life and its continuation through the memory of those who knew him and who will keep him in their consciousness; the poem itself is a testimony of that. In describing al-Baguri's passage from life to death, 'Abd al-Sabur uses larger-than-life poetic expressions to reflect the exalted place that hero holds in heaven:

> He held out his palm, a lighthouse
> And cast a glance to bless life and the living
> With a smiling gaze, he engaged heaven in a chuckle

Al-Baguri is alive in death; he holds out his hand in a gesture that suggests he embraces both life on earth and the afterlife. The glance that 'Abd al-Sabur describes seems to be the fallen hero's placid and serene farewell to life and the living; his chuckle with heaven symbolizes the beginning of a joyous journey to eternal life. The transition from the physical to the metaphysical world is represented in al-Baguri's easy harmony with and acceptance of his fate; his smile is almost a call to heaven to receive him and not vice versa. This indicates that death was a welcome (and an almost expected) path for the dead soldier; his choice to die in battle is implied clearly and repeatedly in the verses.

While al-Baguri seems to be journeying from one realm to another gracefully, the poem describes a sweeping emotional upset on earth, a sadness that has affected countless people upon hearing the news of that pilot's death. 'Abd al-Sabur weaves into the poem the sorrowful voices of al-Baguri's young protégés, their tones fluctuating between mourning and happy recollections. There is a sense that with him gone, his students have momentarily lost direction. However, when reminded of his valuable teachings, confusion is transformed into a reaffirmation of the path toward which he had led them.

At that moment, the most gifted student responds:

"Did our martyred professor not tell us the ultimate words of
     wisdom?"
Our teacher said, "Know thyself . . . O human being . . . ."
Having known himself, he died peacefully
He smiled
He has died for perfection, the ultimate endeavor.

The teacher who had lived and died by his own high standards of morality has, in the end, taught them his most valuable lessons: to know oneself is to live and die in peace, and to always aspire for perfection. In al-Baguri's case, this ideal is reflected in the manner of his death: without ceremony, he made the ultimate sacrifice for his country. This realization re-illuminates his students' path and allows them to celebrate his memory and his everlasting legacy instead of mourning his passing. This way, 'Abd al-Sabur manages to transfer sadness over the loss of a beautiful soul to a celebration in both heaven and earth: in heaven, because al-Baguri's death has graced it with his presence, and on earth, because his memory is so overwhelmingly sweet.

The hero's martyrdom is transformed in this poem from the loss of a brave soul to the birth of a hero whose death will preserve the security and happiness of the younger generation of his nation. His martyrdom also inscribes him forever within national memory as a *mujahid*, martyr, a place preserved in national history and religious perception to the finest of citizens. He will be forever remembered as a person whose sacrifice has improved the quality of present and future generations; parents can hope to raise their children in peace and the young can dream of a future full of possibilities:

He smiled
For he has given to life
He has given his fleeting days and strife
In order to heighten:
a lad's joyful smile,
a virgin's blissfulness,
and the glee parents experience in their child
So that, in the sky's cloud, a bird of peace can flutter

By dying in battle, al-Baguri's greatest legacy becomes peace. He is portrayed as a selfless man and soldier who had a short but meaningful life, one that ended with love of country, people, and tough valor. Yet, heroism is not praised per se; what is underscored is the self, the exceptional nature of the person who was lost and is considered a hero. Heroism is the least of his traits. A champion of truth and sincerity, a conscientious leader, a teacher instructing his students about life's most valuable lessons—he is much more than a brave air force pilot:

He died a teacher and a paragon on the path of perfection
His disciples, who have spent their days in awe of his wisdom
They whisper in wonder
"Does the teacher smile?"

'Abd al-Sabur stresses that the means by which al-Baguri has transformed life in his country is by way of ensuring that it has become a 'secure' one. He achieves that through his martyrdom, which according to the poem is 'the path of perfection,' thus changing the notion that the loss of a life (especially a young person's life) is a waste. It is not construed as such because al-Baguri's manner of death is in essence an act of giving. His death is perceived as heroic because it transcended fear, a human weakness; however, his heroism/martyrdom is not only measured by the reason for his death or extent of his sacrifice, rather it is identified by the positive impact it has left in the lives of fellow human beings, and his life is judged from the point of view of its significance.

With his modernist sensibilities, 'Abd al-Sabur has altered the traditional understanding of a battleground hero from one that highlights physical endurance, love of country, and sacrifice, to name just a few, to a humanistic heroism, evaluated by a person's compassion toward others and his or her integrity. 'Abd al-Sabur has transformed the memory of al-Baguri by humanising him and projecting his small victories outside the battlefield, not by way of portraying a timeless heroic image of him. In doing so, the poet by no means undermines the sacrifice or the magnitude of al-Baguri's suffering or his fortitude in battle. On the contrary, he compares the air force fighter's last moments on earth to those of Christ's agonizing crucifixion, thus raising the former to the level of a prophet/god. From the beginning of the poem, metaphors attributed to al-Baguri sustain transcendental qualities that elevate his status above those of humanity. The light that radiates from his palm, his serene smile, his exchanged chuckles with heaven, and his hauling of the cross are all iconographical images that support a divine-like distinction:

> He has died for perfection, the ultimate endeavor
> He had carried the end of his cross, his face frothing with anguish
> In spite of the agony of that effort
> In spite of the scorching heat tantalizing his bare body
> He smiled

And like Christ, al-Baguri is resurrected through the memory of those who love him and who are in this case a whole grateful nation, not only his friends and family. In a subtle merge between Christian and Muslim beliefs, 'Abd al-Sabur emphasizes al-Baguri's existence as simultaneously dead and alive. In comparing him to Christ, he reinforces the concept of his continued existence in death, which is a cross-religious belief; and in calling him a *mujahid*, he recapitulates the Qur'anic pledge that martyrs are not dead, but alive and prospering in the hereafter.

All the while, the image we carry about al-Baguri himself from the beginning to the end of the poem is his serene smile. Therefore, the significance in the poem is not the young man's pain, which he most certainly experienced before departing life, but rather that his sudden death has stunned an entire community, leaving them wondering whether to mourn his death or celebrate his life.

III

As a literary art form that helps deal with bereavement, the elegy helps find meaning in the life and death of the eulogized. Since death and the afterlife are by and large perplexing unknowns, the life of the departed becomes the only certain and tangible fact. While not bent on the traditional form of elegizing through aggrandizing, 'Abd al-Sabur obviously felt that no hyperbole was necessary to underscore the beauty of al-Baguri's life. Therefore, his words are not loaded with exaggerated descriptions and imagery. His elegy is simple and straightforward; its most striking features are its gentleness of tone and its subtlety of meaning. The dominant writing style and techniques employed in this elegy are best described as cinematic: the poetic narrative reveals the story of the death of Muhammad Nabil al-Baguri through a retelling of the reaction (scenes) of people in the street funeral. The poem comes through as a collage of responses to the death of the young fighter: students watching in wonder; a girl wails from a window, the unique reactions of an old lady to the news of the death of the young man in battle, the stillness in the air that the narrative voice describes. Moreover, the streets crowded with mourners on a stifling midsummer-day reveal with enormous economy the popularity that the deceased enjoyed. In spite of the heat and the crowd, both those who knew al-Baguri and those who did not joined the procession and found solace in connecting with a throng of strangers.

One of the most effective techniques in bolstering the animated description of the crowded funeral is the employment of dialogue, which 'Abd al-Sabur wove skillfully into his poetic narrative:

Pointing her finger, an elderly lady questioned
"In this box, who is to be buried?"

"A young fighter; he died at twenty"
A syllable she did not utter—a strange woman.

While the language is condensed to a bare minimum, shock value is expressed through nominal verbal exchanges and by way of writing silence. The old women's inquiry is juxtaposed with her abrupt silence when the age and occupation of the deceased are revealed to her. As she moves off, batting her way through the crowd in alarm, the narrative voice comments that her peculiar reaction made her seem strange. 'Abd al-Sabur, who subtly communicates that he too was in the midst of that crowded procession and was even a pallbearer, means to play on the double meaning of the phrase *imra'a ghariba* (a strange woman) possibly to point out both that her behaviour was peculiar and that although she was a stranger to the deceased, she was as disturbed by his death as those who knew him well. This emphasizes that the mourners flocking around the coffin were the kind folk of Egypt, who did not necessarily know al-Baguri at all, but who were nevertheless moved deeply by the loss of one of their own brave sons and soldiers.

IV

In describing the funeral, 'Abd al-Sabur deals with time and space in a very touching way, as though the temporal and spatial themselves are also in shock and mourning.

He divides the realms through which his subject traverses into soul and body, the metaphysical and the physical worlds. In the elegy, 'Abd al-Sabur deals with three forms of time: eternal/future, past, and present. The poem starts with the eternal, the soul, and ends with the perishable, the body, which is an effective means by which to depict loss. Between heaven, where al-Baguri's soul will continue to live (eternal/future), and earth, where his body is buried (past), there is the nation's reaction to the loss of a hero. The middle stanza of the poem represents the present moment.

The first part of the poem explores al-Baguri's strange exaltation in and welcome to death after a life that was well lived, albeit short. The metaphors reflect a joyful transformation as his spirit now emanates light; his image is one of smiles. The poem starts with what will endure and live on, the hero's soul; thus, in the first stanza, the tone is neither melancholic nor sorrowful as one might expect from the elegiac themes and tones; rather it exudes joyfulness. The hero's serene acceptance of death, his calm smile, and the light that is radiated from his image are all metaphors representing his metaphysical (almost mystical) transformation. Moreover, this transformation includes another eternal presence: his inscription in national memory, and history as a hero, which will continue forever.

In the second stanza, 'Abd al Sabur shifts his images from religious iconography to nationalism as he writes the dead into national narrative, which is a shift in perception too. In this section he writes about al-Baguri as a man/hero, not as a prophet/god or an ever-living soul of a martyr. He eulogizes the passing of the person and the loss of his physical absence in this world. He depicts the expression of bereavement over al-Baguri's death as one that has swept the streets of the nation and is experienced by all generations and across gender lines:

As for my brother, Muhammad Nabil
His funeral enveloped the streets of the city
On a sweltering summer afternoon, people with the heat were
    clobbered.

Rather, the streets become the center of mourning, and strangers are the grief-stricken mourners; space comes to represent communal feelings of immense loss. Bereavement is expressed through chaos and loss of direction, as the nation is beyond consolation. The mourners are not al-Baguri's kin; they are his neighbors, his students, and people who don't even know him personally. Like sorrow itself, the pain of losing that brave soul is seemingly everlasting and beyond containment.

In this section, grief and pain are expressed as an affliction of the living and the mourners, not of the deceased. Those watching the funeral procession from windows and those following the coffin are suffering the loss of their kind neighbor and brave fellow countryman. Grief is projected onto inanimate things: a damaged windowpane, wallowing music, a sad march, sweltering heat:

Those who love him, those we love—dwellers of our old
    neighborhood

A lass wailing from a tired window
Soldiers marching in silenced gloom
Sad beatings of drums.

The physical world seems shattered and in pain for the departed.
The wailing of the girl is contrasted with the silent march of soldiers.
Somberness prevails and there is a sense of suspended shock, not because
someone has died, but because a beautiful soul has departed. Earth is the
lesser and heaven the wealthier for the death of al-Baguri.

Conversely, however, as this stanza embodies the present moment,
the meaning conveyed is not a mournful one, for while al-Baguri's life has
ended, he has left his mark on earth forever, as other martyrs have. 'Abd
al-Sabur describes those martyrs later as, "Those who have blessed life."
This statement signifies that the ephemeral can actually affect the eternal, for sacrifices result in heroic narratives that are forever remembered
within the national memory and are passed down from one generation to
another. This continuum supports national (and nationalist) beliefs that
war is sometimes the only way to attain peace.

The last portion of the poem describes al-Baguri's final resting place,
the graveyard, another palpable symbol of loss and reminder of the perishable. However, this scene, while subdued, does not depict death as a
solitary journey shrouded in mystery, but rather as a union with other
good soldiers, other Egyptian *mujahidin* or martyrs:

On the horizon, there were the blossoms of the fields
White as our hearts and his, white as the hearts of all those who are
    dead
Our own gentle mujahidin
Our own people, those who have blessed life

Al-Baguri is buried alongside his ancestors in a field of white blossoms,
which is at the end a hopeful image of rebirth. The field symbolizes the
cycle of life, of which death is an integral part. The last message imparted
by 'Abd al-Sabur is that al-Baguri has united with similarly brave soldiers
in the vast Egyptian soil for a peaceful sleep, and that his Egyptian earth
will produce other blessed souls. The repetition of the noun "dust" is reminiscent of the biblical imagery that in death a person has returned "from

dust to dust." This image also resonates with Islamic reminders that God resurrects people from the dust at the end of time, which justifies the title *Sleep in Peace*, for, from this point of view, death is a but a temporary sleep within the cycle of life and afterlife. This cyclical nature of life and death represents an intersection that connects past and future: the continuous rebirth of *mujahidin* and the eternal life of martyrs in heaven seem to imply that neither heaven nor earth will ever be depleted of brave humans and souls. The eternal life in heaven, which is promised to martyrs, and the reproduction cycle on earth seem to reflect and complement each other. The discontinuity and pain of death are only felt by the living, who are not always conscious of the larger context of existence.

While Salah 'Abd al-Sabur employs metaphor to enforce the idea of the eternal nature of the spirit and the perishable (yet continuously reproduced) nature of the human body, he does not dwell on any consolations that might soothe the mourners. The poem is void of references to, for instance, prayers to calm the sadness that has swept the nation. While memories of the deceased sustain and console only those who knew him well, the broad majority of the population does not share that privilege. The inability of the living to find peace suspends the reader's sense of sorrow and prevents closure to the public mourning for the death of a hero. This inability to reconcile with death reflects two deep meanings: first, the tragedy of a young man's death; and second, the unquenchable sorrow that the death of Christ has affected in the hearts of the faithful. The final message is that while there is peace in heaven (future) and in death (past), there seems to be very little of it on earth (present); the dead lie peaceful, while living remain inconsolable and the sense of loss will stay in their hearts forever, even if the pain is bittersweet.

Notes

1   The Arabic title of the poem is "Nama fi-salam," which translates as 'He Slept in Peace.'

2   Salah 'Abd al-Sabur includes this dedication under the title of the poem.

3   This researcher was not able to find the exact historical documentation of Nabil al-Baguri's death. However, in 1955 there were a number of military skirmishes between Israelis and Egyptians along the borders of the Gaza strip. Those assaults were considered by Egyptians as a kind of provocation to engage Egypt in full-blown war. Anthony McDermott states in his *Egypt from Nasser to Mubarak: A Flawed Revolution* (London and New York: Croom Helm, 1988), 23–24, that one of the reasons that led to a coalition between England, France, and Israel in their tripartite aggression against Egypt in 1956 was that Britain construed Nasser's nationalization of the Suez Canal as an act of insubordination and France wanted to punish him for supporting The National Liberation Front in Algeria rebels in their fight for independence. Additionally: "As for Israel, hopes that peace might be possible with Egypt now that Nasser was in power had been dashed and replaced by resentment, antagonism and the feeling that he should be taught a military lesson. They were replaced also by concern at Egypt's acquisition of new arms and by increasing annoyance at cross-border guerrilla raids from the Gaza strip," McDermott, *Egypt from Nasser to Mubarak: A Flawed Revolution*, 24. Those raids resulted in the 'martyrdom' of some soldiers whose death was considered unsung heroism. Al-Baguri was one of them.

4   Salah 'Abd al-Sabur, *al-Nas fi biladi* (Beirut: Dar al-Adab, 1965), 115–19.

PART II

CROSSING BOUNDARIES

11

Historiography as Novel:
Bensalem Himmich's *al-'Allama*

Roger Allen

Introduction

In writing this contribution to a volume in memory of a much-respected
and much-loved scholar, Magda Al-Nowaihi, I have come to consider it
as something in the form of a debt repayment. During the early 1990s,
I had invited Magda to give a lecture at the University of Pennsylvania.
In accepting the invitation, she told me that she wanted to talk about a
Moroccan novelist, Muhammad Barradah, and his novel, *La'bat al-nisyan*.
While, like many other specialists on modern Arabic fiction, I was already
aware of the existence and even the importance of the ever-growing tradition of Arabic fiction in the countries of the Maghrib, my interest up
to that point was, I must confess, of a somewhat token nature. Indeed, I
can seek a certain refuge in the fact that even today there is extremely little written in English about the Maghribi novel by which to contextualize
the project as a whole. It was Magda's presentation that—typically—
presented that tradition as a significant factor in Arabic novelistic
creativity, one that could not be ignored. Listening to and later reading
that presentation, with its sophisticated analysis of Barradah's narrative
techniques, I became even more acutely aware of the need to study the
works of Maghribi novelists in greater detail.[1] This study of one of them,

Bensalem Himmich (that being the author's preferred spelling of his name in European languages, the final consonant being the Arabic *shin*), itself a direct consequence of my recent focus on Maghribi fiction, is thus a belated acknowledgment of Magda's role as both pioneer and astute critic of literary trends.

Al-'Allama

The novel in question is *al-'Allama*, the winner of the Naguib Mahfouz Prize for Fiction awarded by the American University in Cairo Press in 2002.[2] At the time the award was announced, I had in fact already been working for several years on the novels of Himmich and of other Moroccan and Maghribi novelists, and had completed a translation of one of Himmich's earlier novels, *Majnun al-hukm* (1989), a work that is devoted to a novelistic portrayal of the much-discussed reign of the Fatimid caliph al-Hakim bi-Amr Allah. I was invited by the American University in Cairo Press to translate *al-'Allama* into English (it has now appeared as *The Polymath*), and my earlier translation of *Majnun al-hukm* was published in 2005 (under the title *The Theocrat*). Since I have already discussed the latter novel elsewhere, I will concentrate my remarks here on *al-'Allama*.[3]

Bensalem Himmich, born in Meknes in 1949, teaches philosophy at the University of Muhammad V in Rabat, Morocco. He himself has written an academic study of Ibn Khaldun's philosophy of history, *al-Khalduniya fi daw' falsafat al-tarikh* (Khaldunism in the Light of the Philosophy of History, 1998). One can perhaps surmise that the process of preparing for and writing such a study may have provided at least part of the impetus for following it up with a novel devoted to the same basic subject. *The Polymath*'s focus assumes almost vertiginous proportions: a professor of the history of philosophy who is also a historical novelist here presents his readers with a novel that explores the later life, thought, and motivations of a world-renowned historian, Ibn Khaldun (d. 1406). Exiled from his native region of the Maghrib, Ibn Khaldun (or 'Abd al-Rahman, as he is described for much of the novel, using one of his forenames) spends his latter days in Egypt. He suffers a tremendous personal tragedy when his wife and children have drowned at sea on their way to join him in the Egyptian capital. The aged and lonely historian lives in Cairo and ekes out a modest living by teaching and serving as judge of the Maliki school of law—whenever, that is, he is not being dismissed because of the rigor that he brings to his judicial functions and his unwillingness to take external (that is, political) contingencies into consideration in passing judgment. To compensate for his loneliness and disillusion, he decides to revisit his earlier works on history and its science and to revise those sections of them that are in need of either reconsideration or complete rewriting in the light of the tumultuous events he himself experienced with rulers and tyrants in North Africa. In *al-'Allama* then, a historical novelist and philosopher of history is writing a novel about a historian rewriting his own historical record and his theoretical conclusions based on an analysis of its contents—a historiographical novel, one might suggest.

Himmich's novel begins with an 'opening' section, *"Fatiha,"* the name also given to the first sura in the Qur'an. This section sets up the narrative in a number of ways. The historical context is that of the Mamluk dynasty of Egypt, the remarkable institution made up of slaves imported from the Crimean region whose manumission was required for them to be eligible for the position of Sultan. In particular we are in the reign of al-Zahir Barquq, a notable builder in Cairo whose monuments continue to remind visitors to Egypt's capital of the splendor of his era. We are introduced to Ibn Khaldun, a renowned figure whose fame and controversial opinions have previously gained him prominent administrative and judicial positions with a variety of rulers in Spain and North Africa. From the machinations and intrigues involved in such a career, he has now retreated in the hope of spending his final years in relative tranquility in Cairo. In his house close to the River Nile we also encounter his faithful servant, Sha'ban, who takes care of the lonely widower—still grieving for his wife and children, whose loss has marred his plans for a happy retirement. Into this domestic scene comes another figure from the Maghrib: Hamu al-Hihi, initially requesting a legal opinion regarding the request of his young and beautiful wife, Umm al-Banin, to be allowed to take promenades along the banks of the River Nile and around Cairo's beautiful quarters, but thereafter offering his services as amanuensis to the great scholar as he revisits the theoretical issues confronting those who would write history.

The novel closes with a section entitled *"Tadhyil,"* which, like the *"Fatiha"* used for the opening segment, is a traditional term for the closing section of a text; the word *dhayl*, of which is it a derivative, means 'tail,' and thus it is linked to the use of the Italian word *coda* in musical notation. In this tail to the tale, as it were, things have come full circle.

Ibn Khaldun once again finds himself alone with his servant, as was the case when the narrative began. Intimations of his own mortality are becoming ever more insistent. Himmich assigns the narration of this closing chapter to Ibn Khaldun himself in the first person, thus replicating the second of the three central chapters in the narrative. As this second chapter's title, "Between falling in love and operating in the shadow of power," suggests, this other essay in first-person narrative combines the very personal story of Ibn Khaldun's increasing infatuation with Umm al-Banin, the widow of his amanuensis (whom he subsequently marries) and the subsequent birth of their daughter, al-Batul, with his accounts of the court of the Mamluk Sultan, al-Zahir Barquq. Extraordinarily detailed descriptions of buildings—palaces, mosques, stables, colleges, parks, and ceremonials—are linked with often highly critical opinions about the moral and political atmosphere surrounding the Sultan.

By contrast, the first of these lengthy central chapters finds a third-person narrator describing an entirely different scene inside Ibn Khaldun's house, as he meets at the end of each month with his amanuensis, Hamu al-Hihi. There is much concern here with texts and textuality, including the addition of several footnotes to the narrative itself. The two men discuss current political events; the dialogue format permits Ibn Khaldun to record his reflections on the various ways in which his previous writings on history, most notably the renowned *al-Muqaddima* (Introduction) to his work on history, *Kitab al-'Ibar*, and his autobiographical work, *al-Ta'rif*, are in need of revision or wholesale rewriting. In this process Himmich the novelist carefully crafts the role of al-Hihi as the deft poser of precisely the right kind of questions to provoke Ibn Khaldun into radical re-expressions of his earlier theories. This applies most particularly to the most significant and renowned of those ideas: that *'asabiya* (group solidarity) is a primary factor in the acquisition and maintenance of political hegemony and that such traits are to be found primarily among the inhabitants of desert regions, the Bedouin. The life of the city *(hadar)* leads inevitably to a weakening of such a sense of tribal identity and the virtues that go with it; as new and stronger tribal confederations emerge, the cycle of history repeats itself. During this chapter, with its seven nights of dictation and discussion, Ibn Khaldun thinks back on his own career in political and judicial service, a life of accommodation to intrigue, rebellion, and syco-phancy (including his own poems of hypocritical praise to various tyrant rulers), a life of imprisonment, high office, and survival that has eventually brought him to old age in the Mamluk capital of Cairo. Once more in and out of office as judge and teacher according to political whim, he is deter-mined to record in written form his reactions to everything he has been through by revisiting his previous ideas on history and historiography. At the very end of this lengthy chapter, the reader learns that Ibn Khaldun has been permitted to leave Cairo in order to make the pilgrimage to Mecca. He carries with him the prayers of Umm al-Banin, his amanuensis's wife, that she be blessed with the gift of children. In fact, our eminent histo-rian confesses to the reader that he spends entirely too much time during the holy pilgrimage thinking about his companion's beautiful young wife. Thus, when he returns to Cairo to discover that during his absence Hamu al-Hihi has died and he is now under some obligation to take care of her, it comes as little surprise that, once she herself has agreed to the idea, he takes little persuading to marry the much younger widow.

The chapter describing Barquq's palace and its protocol, mentioned above, had already made occasional reference to the looming menace of the Mongol invasions that had been threatening the West Asian region for some two centuries. This applies especially to its latest and dir-est manifestation in the much-feared figure of Timur Lang, known in the West—including in Christopher Marlowe's play—as Tamerlaine (or Tamburlain). The third of these central chapters is devoted to the encoun-ter between the proverbially ruthless and astute invader, Timur Lang, and Ibn Khaldun, the most renowned historian of his age. This particular seg-ment of the novel's narrative is recounted in the third person, although close to the beginning we have a further variant: Ibn Khaldun's late-night discussion of strategy with an ailing Sultan Barquq takes the form of a dramatized dialogue (albeit with occasional interpolations by the judge's somnolent colleague). It is not long afterward that the Sultan dies, leaving behind a young heir, al-Nasir Faraj, who is portrayed as not only subject to the rampant manipulation of his own courtiers but also—at the age of thirteen—a habitual drunkard. It is with considerable misgivings that Ibn Khaldun accompanies the young Sultan and his army to Damascus to await the arrival of the Mongol army. As time passes, the eminent historian's sense that a Mongol victory is inevitable only increases.

The novel now paints for the reader a detailed portrait of a city—Damascus—its people, its Citadel guards, its judges, its markets, as they all await their fate at the hands of a tyrannical invader whose savage treatment of other cities (including the already captured Aleppo) augurs nothing but the worst. Ibn Khaldun is, of course, consulted by the city's judicial authorities on matters political, juridical, and historical. He befriends one judge in particular, Ibn al-Muflih, a native of the city who takes his Maghribi colleague on an extensive tour of Damascus and its environs, thus affording Himmich's narrator the opportunity to display a considerable knowledge of the historical city, its rivers, gardens, monuments, hills, and restaurants. As tensions mount and political arguments flare, the Mamluk army gradually retires. Eventually the Sultan himself, al-Nasir Faraj, sneaks away with his retinue on the pretext of suppressing an incipient revolt against him in Egypt. The people of Damascus are now left to their own devices and at the mercy of Timur's infamous troops. Sober reflection among the judges and grandees of the city makes it clear that the city's only option is surrender in return for a guarantee of safety. The enormous repute of Ibn Khaldun is reflected in the Mongol Khan's specific request that he be present at the negotiations. The encounter between the great strategist and the scholarly historian is now set.

Once Ibn Khaldun has been admitted to the presence of the Great Khan and offered a sumptuous meal, it emerges that the Mongol leader is anxious to question the renowned sage about the linkage of Islamic belief and history. The historian thinks it wise to open with a sycophantic encomium of Timur's achievements—all duly translated for the Khan by his translator, Ibn al-Nu'man. Once discussion turns to more current and specific matters, the novel paints a wonderful portrait of Ibn Khaldun's internal calculations as he finds himself negotiating with both his own sense of what is judicious and the parallel sensitivities of the translator as to what opinions he is to put into words and how far he is permitted to go in his commentary on Timur's conduct toward Damascus and its people. Eventually agreement is reached to surrender the city to Timur's forces, and Ibn Khaldun has to watch as Mongol soldiers ravage much of the city. Even Timur himself expresses regret that the excesses of his fighting men have led to a disastrous fire in the Great Umayyad Mosque, one of Islam's most illustrious sites.

Throughout this lengthy process, Ibn Khaldun has been continuously aware of his lengthy absence from his young family in Cairo, a feeling made worse by a total lack of communication from them. In a touching scene, Timur compares Ibn Khaldun's longing for his wife in Cairo with his own feelings for his beloved consort in Samarqand. Ibn Khaldun is eventually allowed to return to Egypt, but his journey back meets disaster when the caravan is attacked by Bedouin marauders and the entire company is robbed and stripped.

The novel's "Conclusion" brings Ibn Khaldun eagerly back to his Cairo home, only to discover that his wife, believing rumors that he has died, has taken their daughter back with her to Fez in the far Maghrib. Messages are sent to the Maghrib to inform her that her husband is alive, but with no result. Every request that he makes to travel to the Maghrib himself is countered by the drunken Sultan al-Nasir Faraj who keeps appointing him judge, and, after dismissal a few months later, reappointing him (this happens on five separate occasions). Eventually, word gets through and Umm al-Banin returns, but without her daughter who is ailing. She receives a rather strange welcome: instead of rushing to greet his beloved wife, Ibn Khaldun spends a great deal of time in extra prayers and then proceeds to upbraid her for leaving in the first place. Once marital harmony is restored, she begs her husband to come back with her to Fez where their daughter is recuperating; she tells him that, at all events, she herself will have to return in a few months. Ibn Khaldun looks forward to the prospect of returning to the lands of his birth and packs up his books and belongings. However, a request to the Sultan for permission to leave is greeted by another appointment as Maliki judge in Cairo, and so Umm al-Banin returns westward without her husband—embracing him in Alexandria for what neither of them realizes will be the last time.

Ibn Khaldun is now left as a pawn in the frivolous hands of the Sultan. His judicial responsibilities—whenever he is not being dismissed for rigorous application of the law—prevent him from rejoining his family. He is struck down by a debilitating illness; a period of apparent recovery is followed by a relapse. The novel ends with that most permanent of closures, death, as the ever-cognizant religious scholar reflects on the evident decay of his own body and launches into a description of some of the phenomena of the Last Day, all recounted with a theologian's eye for detail and appropriate phrase.

History, Historiography, and the Novel

In *al-'Allama*, then, Ibn Khaldun is the central character, and his works are one of the principal topics. The novel is certainly one that fits into the category of historical novel, but, one might suggest, in a way that is somewhat different from many previous contributions to that subgenre. As noted above, there is a great deal of attention to detail: Ibn Khaldun's life experiences are set into the context of a bewildering succession of dynastic changes, of murders, imprisonments, and diplomatic missions, to all of which he was in one way or another a party (and I might note here that the preparation of the novel's translation required the production of an enormous glossary of names, places, and technical terms connected with his life's itinerary across the entire Maghrib and al-Andalus to Egypt and Syria). In terms of space, we learn a great deal about ceremonies and the buildings in which they take place (Sultan Barquq's weekly attendance of the Friday sermon, for example) and about the topography of Damascus and its environs. Readers of Ibn Khaldun's own writings, whether we are talking about *al-Muqaddima* or *al-Ta'rif*, will already be aware that his approach is characterized by an atmosphere of studious detachment, seen at its most obvious perhaps in the somewhat terse way in which he describes the loss of his family in the latter work (a passage duly included in the text of the novel itself):

> This situation coincided with a personal tragedy involving my
> wife and child. They were coming to Egypt from the Maghrib by
> ship. There was a storm, and they were drowned. With them went
> existence, home, and offspring. The pain of this loss was enormous.[4]

In the novel, however, this somewhat remote figure is personalized by the inclusion of the story of his love for Umm al-Banin and the birth of their daughter, al-Batul. This part of the novel seems to be a creation of the novelist himself, and it helps to tie this novel, qua historical novel, to earlier examples, not least those of the great pioneer in this subgenre, Jurji Zaydan (d.1914). Zaydan, who wrote some twenty historical novels beginning with *Jihad al-muhibbin* and *Istibdad al-mamalik* in 1893, would regularly insert into the particular historical era that was his primary topic a piece of 'local interest,' usually focused on a family and, more often than not, a love story. In *Sharl [Charles] wa-'Abd al-Rahman* (1904), for example, that particular love story involves the renowned affair between the poet, Ibn Zaydun, and the Umayyad princess, Walladah. In Zaydan's novels however, the love story is always ancillary to the main events of the historical narrative; the 'characters' involved may be directly affected by what is going on around them, but the love affair does not impinge upon the broader stage of history. At this early phase in the development of the Arabic novel, such a narrative strategy seems to have played a major role in popularizing the genre (not least through its publication in Zaydan's own magazine, *al-Hilal*) while at the same time providing his readers with a valuable series of accounts of their own history—an essential adjunct to the developing awareness of the need for an Arab national sentiment in order to counter the increasing role of British and French imperialism in the region. By contrast, what Himmich does in *al-'Allama* is to entwine the story of Umm al-Banin (and that of her highly problematic transvestite brother) into the framework of the account of Ibn Khaldun's residence in Cairo and his journey to Damascus to meet Timur Lang, thus enabling the author to insert elements of the fictional within the narrative framework of a highly authentic rewriting of Ibn Khaldun's account of his own later life. It needs to be added that even these fictional insertions are, as noted above, replete with carefully researched descriptions of the multifarious features of life in Cairo (and Damascus) in the late fourteenth and early fifteenth centuries.

So we are dealing here with a historical novel, one that depicts the later life of Ibn Khaldun, and, through his own recollections in the company of his amanuensis, a good deal of his earlier life as well. And yet it is also more than that, hence my use of 'historiographical' in the title above. As we have already noted, Ibn Khaldun is himself a historian (indeed Himmich, our novelist, is a student of his historiography). Such is Ibn Khaldun's repute that a very large number of scholarly studies have been published about his approach to history in both Arabic and European languages. One of the more interesting opinions on the topic is expressed by the great Egyptian critic, Taha Husayn (d. 1973), who in his doctoral thesis submitted to the Sorbonne in Paris ("La Philosophie sociale d'Ibn Khaldoun") suggested that, while the material in *al-Muqaddima* was clearly of enormous significance, the work of history itself displayed a surprising credulousness in the way that information was recorded (an opinion that, no doubt, also reflects the views of his French supervisors at the time, including Durkheim, Casanova, and Levi-Bruhl).[5] Whatever may have been Ibn Khaldun's approach to the compilation of the historical record itself, there is little doubt that his introduction to it *(al-Muqaddima)* has been the focus of the lion's share of attention among scholars who have seen it as a foundational stage in the establishment of the principles of social-scientific research. It is clearly this aspect of Ibn Khaldun's thought that also interests Himmich as both scholar and novelist. Following the *"Fatiha"* in which the historian's situation in Cairo is presented, it is to the principles involved that the substantial first chapter *(Fasl awwal)* is devoted—fully one quarter of the novel's text. Here too scholarship finds fictional expression, as Himmich uses his own knowledge of the philosophy of history in order to posit certain adjustments to statements made earlier in the text of *al-Muqaddima*. In such a context, Himmich's own statements on the role of history and its linkages to fiction give us some insight into his interests and motivations, as, for example, in this 'testimony' *(shahada)* at a novel conference, in which he draws attention to a number of examples of historical fiction (including Umberto Eco's *The Name of the Rose*) and then discusses his own approach to fiction:

> Authentic writing has no choice but to interact with precedents and with forms and styles that emerge from them, not so much in order to imitate them, but rather to place them within the fulcrum of change and thus enrich them with the added value of modernity.[6]

The American critic David Cowart has written a study on the tremendous contemporary relevance of such trends as these on a broader cultural scale.[7] His categorization of historical fiction includes a fourth type: "fictions whose authors project the present into the past." A clear illustration of this category within modern Arabic fiction is provided by the Egyptian writer Gamal al-Ghitani's famous novel, *al-Zayni Barakat*, 1971; English tr. *Zayni Barakat*, 1988). The novel is set in Cairo approximately one century after the events described in *al-'Allama*, but the real import of the novelist's accurate depiction of the activities of a secret-police force in sixteenth-century Cairo were not lost on Arab readers during the 1970s. *Mutatis mutandis*, the same comment may also be invoked to refer to Himmich's work under discussion here. The nature of good rulership, continuing turnovers of government, the place of religion and religious law within society, the theories behind the recording of what is termed 'history,' the possibility of speaking one's mind: these issues and others that confront Ibn Khaldun as he attempts to make a record of Islamic history, and to remake and revise it in the light of experience, are hardly irrelevant to the Arab world of the present day—in President Nasser's hackneyed phrase, the region that stretches "from the Ocean to the Gulf." And one might add that, when Western leaders can invoke the Crusades in the 21st century within the context of justifying military incursions into distant lands and cultures, is it surprising that inhabitants of the Arabic-speaking region as a whole should resort to texts depicting invaders of the past and that Arab novelists in particular should resort to history and its texts in order to challenge their present, both local and international?

To be sure, the scholar Himmich is as present in this novel as he was in the earlier *Majnun al-hukm*. Both works display an enviable knowledge of historical texts and an ability to work them into contributions to Arabic fiction that are interesting and complex examples of contemporary narrative. However, both novels also depict periods in the history of the Arabs during which struggles for power among ruling elites caused immense suffering to the peoples of the region and indeed, as *al-'Allama* makes very clear, rendered the task of recording accounts of historical events both complex and dangerous. In the context of the contemporary Arabic novel as it seeks for fresh modes and topics, and this particular novel about the theory of history, one is inclined to invoke: *plus ça change* . . . .

Notes

1   Magda Al-Nowaihi, "Committed Postmodernity: Muhammad Barrada's the *Game of Forgetting*," in *Tradition, Modernity, and Post-Modernity in Arabic Literature: Essays in Honor of Professor Issa J. Boullata* (Leiden: E. J. Brill, 2000), 367–88. Boullata is the translator of the English version of the novel, *The Game of Forgetting* (Austin, Texas: University of Texas Press, 1996).

2   Bensalem Himmich, *al-'Allama* (Rabat: Matba'at al-Ma'arif al-Jadida, 2000); English ed., *The Polymath*, trans. Roger Allen (Cairo: The American University in Cairo Press, 2004).

3   Roger Allen, "Lords of Misrule: History and Fiction in Two Moroccan Novels," *Middle Eastern Literatures* 9, no. 2 (August 2006): 199–29.

4   Himmich, *Al-'Allama*, 12; *idem*, *The Polymath*, trans. Roger Allen, 6.

5   An excellent study of this topic is: Abdelrashid Mahmoudi, *Taha Husayn's Education: From the Azhar to the Sorbonne* (London: Curzon, 1998).

6   See "Thaqafat al-riwayah: shahada," *Muqaddimat/Prologues* 13–14 (Summer–Autumn 1998): 136.

7   David Cowart, *History and the Contemporary Novel* (Carbondale: Southern Illinois University Press, 1989).

12

Sonallah Ibrahim's *Les années de Zeth,* or The Exportability of Contemporary Arabic Literature

Richard Jacquemond[1]

In 1992, just a few months after the appearance of my French translation of Sonallah Ibrahim's first novel, *Tilka al-ra'iha* (1966),[2] the Egyptian
author published *Dhat,* which many consider to be his masterpiece. A
convergence of factors—the bond that had developed between us during my translation of *Tilka al-ra'iha,* the fact that I was living in Cairo at
the time, and my enthusiasm for *Dhat*—then mobilized me to translate
this latter novel. Exactly one year later, in October 1993, *Les années de Zeth*
appeared in French courtesy of Actes Sud: an exceptionally brief delay, in
the context of contemporary Arabic literature, between the appearance
of the original and that of the translation. Now, I would like to revisit the
conditions of the experiment by exploring in greater detail the process of
translation itself, by entering, if you will, the kitchens of translation and
concocting recipes of a sort.

Continuing with the culinary metaphor, I will start by evoking the
golden rule of every chef: there is no good cuisine without good ingre-
dients. In other words, what is well written translates well. It is a matter
of some importance in modern Arabic literature. More than once I have
heard colleagues say they have had to rework at length the texts they were

281

translating in order to 'raise' them to a standard acceptable in French. Indeed, on first exposure, modern Arabic novelistic writing often gives an impression of looseness and imprecision—the text seems 'disjointed.' There are many reasons for this impression; some of them derive from the language itself. After all, modern Arabic evolved considerably in the twentieth century: old grammatical rules were abandoned, and new rules were coming into being; the lexicon changed at a tremendous pace; and the old method of discursive organization, in which texts are punctuated principally by connecting particles such as *wa*, *fa*, *thumma*, and so forth, was replaced by a modern method of punctuation which is based on symbols and which has yet to be completely codified. Other causes relate to the material conditions of the publication process: Arab publishers do not, as a general rule, carefully review and copyedit the manuscripts that they publish, but rather they content themselves with proofreading the manuscripts for grammatical mistakes and ensuring that they contain nothing which could provoke the censor to intervene.

Consider, for example, Gamal al-Ghitani's *Zayni Barakat*, which has been translated into a dozen languages, making it one of the most translated contemporary Arabic novels. Let us compare the French version of the novel, which was rendered into French by an excellent translator, the late Jean-François Fourcade, with the original version. In Arabic, the first twelve lines of the novel contain a single type of punctuation mark: the comma. In the equivalent French passage, one finds periods, commas, colons, semicolons, points of suspension, and even an em-dash. The text begins:

تضطرب أحوال الديار المصرية هذه الأيام ، وجه القاهرة غريب عني ، ليس ما

عرفته في رحلاتي السابقة ، أحاديث الناس تغيرت ، أعرف لغة البلاد ولهجاتها ،

أرى وجه المدينة مريضًا يوشك على البكاء ، . . . . .[3]

Ces derniers temps, le pays d'Égypte connaît de graves
bouleversements. L'aspect du Grand Caire m'est devenu
méconnaissable. Maîtrisant désormais la langue du pays, j'ai cru
comprendre depuis mon retour que les sujets de conversation avaient
bien changé. Cette ville me fait penser à un malade sans espoir, au
bord des larmes, . . .[4]

In the Arabic text, the narrator, a sixteenth-century Venetian traveler, could not be more affirmative: "people's conversations had changed,"
which he knows because he is "familiar with the country's language and
dialects." In French, the translator has deemed it necessary to clarify
that this familiarity is the fruit of a studied apprenticeship (maîtrisant
désormais, or "having already mastered"). He also conflates the pairing
language/dialect into a single word (no doubt because the contrast in this
dichotomy would not be immediately apparent to the French reader).
Finally, and most significantly, he introduces a strong element of uncertainty by adding the phrase "I believed I understood (j'ai cru comprendre)"
which has no equivalent in the original. The reasons for these interventions are fairly plain to see. The Arabic text is a kind of raw material that
needs to be "rationalized" and made more verisimilar (the first and third
interventions) at the same time that it is purged of anything that would
not be immediately explicit in French (the second intervention).

This type of rewriting is extremely frequent in the translation of contemporary Arabic literature. Experience tells me that it is in fact the rule
and not the exception. I do not wish to pass judgment on this state of
affairs. What interests me here, rather, is to draw attention to this gap
that it reveals between the conditions of production and reception of a
literary text translated from one language into another.

Now, in the case of *Dhat*, I was very quickly struck while I was undertaking the translation that the work of rewriting was going to be relatively
minimal compared to that of earlier translations I had done or to that I
had noticed in translations made by others. Here are the opening lines of
the text, in Arabic and French:

نستطيع أن نبدأ قصة ذات من البداية الطبيعية ، أي من اللحظة التي انزلقت فيها إلى

عالمنا ملوثة بالدماء، وما تلى ذلك من أول صدمة تعرضت لها ، عندما رُفعت في

الهواء، وقُلبت رأسًا على عقب ، ثم صُفعت على أليتها (التي لم تكن تنبئ أبدًا بما

بلغته بعد ذلك من حجم من جراء كثرة الجلوس فوق المرحاض). لكن بداية كهذه

لن يرحب بها النقاد، لأن الطريق المستقيم، في الأدب والأخلاق على السواء، لا

يؤدي إلى شيء ذي بال ، ولن يتمخض عنه في حالتنا هذه سوى إضاعة وقت كل

من القارىء والكاتب ، وهو الوقت الذي يستطيعان استغلاله مع التليفزيون ، على

سبيل المثال ، من موقعين مختلفين ، بما يعود عليهما بفائدة أكبر بكثير مما قد تجلبه

مئات الصفحات الورقية. [5]

> Nous pourrions commencer l'histoire de Zeth à son commencement
> naturel, c'est-à-dire à l'instant où elle glissa dans notre monde,
> souillée de sang, et au premier traumatisme qui s'ensuivit, lorsqu'elle
> fut soulevée en l'air, retournée de pied en cap et frappée aux fesses
> (qui ne laissaient en rien présager du volume qu'elles atteindraient
> plus tard, à force de séances sur le siège des toilettes). Mais un tel
> début ne serait pas apprécié des critiques, car le droit chemin,
> en littérature comme en morale, ne mène à rien qui vaille, et en
> l'occurrence n'aboutirait qu'à faire perdre au lecteur comme à
> l'auteur un temps qu'il pourraient aussi bien consacrer, par exemple, à
> la télévision, et avec infiniment plus de profit, pour l'un comme pour
> l'autre, que celui qu'ils peuvent retirer de quelques centaines
> de feuillets. [6]

One sees how the Arabic phrasing lends itself perfectly to a very faithful transposition. Both the punctuation and the propositional sequencing are reproduced identically, and there is no need to explain in French elements of the Arabic text, or conversely, to omit meanings that are not immediately accessible.

This proximity of the Arabic and French texts will sustain itself throughout the course of the novel, and from its opening lines one can divine the reason. Indeed, this opening sets the tone: we have a heroine who is an anti-heroine and whose story begins in the most ordinary possible way, and we have an omniscient narrator who adopts a maximal distance from her, amusing himself and the reader at the expense of her character not only by presenting her in a ridiculous light, but also and more significantly by intervening directly in the narrative first by way of a foretelling aside (duly signaled by parentheses) and then by a digression on the social function of literature and the status of the writer.

This opening throws into relief one of the novel's essential characteristics: its firm anchoring in the European literary tradition of the satirical novel, from *Don Quixote* to *Tom Jones* or *Tristam Shandy*, or even, for that matter, *Madame Bovary*. This, along with some other characteristics, tends to make the transposition of the novel from Arabic into French less a labor of translation than of a *return to the original*. It is as if the original Arabic itself is marked by the characteristics of a *translated text*.

These characteristics are, first and foremost, stylistic: the sentences are often long and laden with subordinate and relative clauses as well as some dangling ones. This is a kind of sentence that is prevalent in novelistic French prose, and much less common in Arabic prose—especially since the long sentences are articulated often without recourse to the habitual connectors and at times even deviating from syntactic norms. Such is the case with the following sentence describing an old friend of Zeth, a nominal sentence consisting of a series of nominal phrases or clauses in apposition with the subject *(mubtada')* without ever arriving at the predicate *(khabar)*:

صفية عباس، التي تكبرها بعدة سنوات، صاحبة الشفتين الناعمتين، اللتين كان

لهما مذاق سكري في أيام "أكتب اليك بالقلم الأحمر علامة الحب المشتعل"،

والمواثيق المؤكدة بالصداقة الأبدية، التي تحققت بدخول نفس الكلية، وأحلام

الزواج من شقيقين والسكنى في شقتين متجاورتين، التي لم تتحقق، لأن الاثنتين

وقعتا، بالطبع، في غرام نفس الشخص، عزيز عبد الله، الشيوعي، زميل

صفية في الصف الدراسي وضيف المعتقلات، الذي تزوجها بمجرد تخرجهما

وانتقل بها إلى الاسكندرية، مما دفع ذات إلى قبول الزواج من عبد المجيد أوف

كورس، . . . [7].

Safeya Abbas: son aînée de quelques années, aux lèvres douces et sucrées, à l'époque du "Je t'écris en rouge la flamme de mon amour," des serments d'amitié éternelle—tenus lorsqu'elles avaient intégré

la même faculté — et des rêves d'épouser deux frères et d'habiter
deux appartements voisins — jamais réalisés, toutes deux étant,
évidemment, tombées amoureuses du même garçon: Aziz Abdallah,
un militant communiste, hôte des camps d'internement et camarade
de classe de Safeya, qu'il avait épousée dès qu'ils avaient achevé
la faculté, puis emmenée à Alexandrie, convainquant par là Zeth
d'accepter le parti d'Abdel-Méguid Of Course . . .[8]

There is a gap here between the Arabic and the French: the Arabic
is constructed through a series of relative clauses (six relative pronouns
and particles, underlined above) which I preferred to render into French
by other means (of punctuation, principally) to avoid the heaviness of
the chain.

As Samia Mehrez notes, by maximizing in this way the distance
between the refinement of style and the extreme platitude of the subject
matter, Sonallah Ibrahim reproduces in a fashion the aesthetic program
of Flaubert in *Madame Bovary*: "to write the mediocre well."[9]

These stylistic characteristics of *Dhat* that make it read as a translated text are seconded in this regard by its lexical features, for the novel's
protagonists, Zeth and her companions, belong to an urban middle class
and move in a world of institutions, objects, and signs of foreign, that is
'Western,' origin. Indeed, one of the author's intentions is to criticize,
by way of satire, the effects of the material and symbolic domination of
the West on contemporary Egyptian society. Therefore the lexicon is not
a specialized one that denotes the cultural facts and artifacts of the culture or cultural milieu that he describes. Rather, it is a 'universal' *translated*
lexicon: a lexicon of current objects of consumption (televisions, refriger-
ators, washing machines, air conditioners, etc.) and of modern institutions
(the newspaper where Zeth works, the bank where her husband, Abdel-
Méguid, works). The author is completely conscious of this, and often
makes plays on these words:

أمام بركة البط في حديقة الميريلاند قالت له: غسيل الملابس لم يعد مشكلة بفضل

الأومو . قليل منه في طبق ماء من البلاستيك ، ويقلب حتى يصنع رغوة كبيرة ، ثم

تلقي الواحدة فيه بالقميص أو البلوزة وتنصرف لعمل الشاي أو الطبيخ . وبعد ذلك

دعكة أو دعكتين ، و لا حاجة إلى هري إلى هري الأصابع أو الغسالة (تقصد المرأة التي تغسل،

و ليس الآلة، التي لم يكن عصرها قد حل بعد).[10]

Devant la mare aux canards du Merryland, elle lui avait dit: "Avec
Omo, la lessive n'est plus un problème. Tu en verses un peu dans une
cuvette en plastique, tu remues jusqu'à ce que ça mousse, tu y jettes
la chemise ou le corsage et tu vas faire un thé ou préparer le repas.
Après, il suffit de frotter un peu. Pas besoin de s'user les mains, pas
besoin de laveuse." (Elle entendait par là, non la machine à laver, dont
l'heure n'avait pas encore sonné, mais la femme chargée de faire la
lessive).[11]

The lexicon is dominated by terms borrowed from foreign languages:
both proper nouns (Merryland, the name of a public park in Cairo, and
the brand "Omo") and common nouns (*bilastik* / plastic, *biluza* / blouse).
Ironically, it is in the one transposition of a foreign term into a 'purely'
Arabic word that becomes an amusing source of confusion: *ghassala*,
before it came to mean 'washing machine,' used to designate a laundress.

By citing these borrowings and loanwords with such frequency the
author very effectively scoffs at the consumerist aspirations and the submission to foreign fashions of the Cairene petite bourgeoisie that he
describes. Abdel-Méguid, in his desire to be trendy, peppers his speech
with English words: *of course, meaning*, etc. (This is why the narrator nick-
names him, as we have seen above, "Abdel-Méguid Of Course".) One of
the couple's friends, a doctor of science returning from Europe and a
great critic of the Cairene version of 'fast food,' recommends to them that
they eat only *fresh* products, and he is at once dubbed 'Dr. Fresh' (*duktur
frish*: a double borrowing) by Abdel-Méguid.[12] The example for this is set
at the very top by the president of the Republic himself. To those who
wish to know whether he leans more toward Nasser (that is to say toward
socialism and the USSR) or toward Sadat (in other words capitalism and
the USA), Sonallah Ibrahim has Mubarak volunteer: "*My name is* Hosni
Moubarak."[13]

It is certainly necessary to signal precisely the play on words for the
foreign reader through the use of italics, to signal that a certain word
or expression is, according to the consecrated formula 'in French' or 'in

English' in the text. But this is not so simple: as the above example illustrates, one cannot treat words that have been naturalized in Arabic, such as *bilastik* and *biluza*, in this manner, because their foreign origin is no longer apparent to their speakers, and because their usage, therefore, no longer has any distinctive social value.

It may seem simple, *a priori*, to distinguish between these two types of foreign words (between those, in other words, that signal to the reader that they are translated and those that do not). But in practice the distinction is not always clear; it is more a matter of a continuum the middle of which is occupied by terms that are too frequently used to have a distinctive social value at the same time that they are not completely generalized, notably because they exist concurrently with Arabic terms. Thus, in rereading myself I see that I translated *'asr al-mini* as "le temps des minijupes"[14] without italicizing the borrowing, and then, further on in the same chapter, I did italicize the borrowing in the case of its antonym, the *maxi*,[15] a word which is much more rare (even if as an item of clothing it is more common!), whereas a few lines above the *maxi*, I did not italicize *makiyaj* (*maquillage*/makeup). . . .

What is even more difficult—and sometimes simply impossible—is to render into French the author's neologisms, for which he likes to remold foreign words into Arabic morphological patterns: hence *sarmaka* (a verbal noun based on siramik) designates the painting of ceramics and *kandasha* (a verbal noun formed from the term [air-] conditioner, or, in the Cairene pronunciation, *kondishner*) the installation of air-conditioning. In such cases, I did not attempt to render the verbal invention into French.[16]

One will notice here the paradoxical position of the author who, in compounding these borrowings from foreign languages (French and English), intends to visibly stigmatize a certain 'cultural dependency' of Egyptian society (or at least its middle classes) with regard to the West, but who also, by forging an Arabic writing which is very largely informed by European literary references, exposes himself to the same criticism.

True, one can make the most of the fact that his project is legitimate in that he is not imitating a foreign model, but rather reappropriating it, even 'reinventing' it in his own way and rerooting it in Arabic literature. Could not the same be said, however, for most of the borrowings of the Arabic language and culture (in their Egyptian variety, which is what concerns us here)? Does not this aforementioned phenomenon of the naturalization of foreign terms signal precisely this reappropriation of exogenous material operated by the Arabic language? Here we are touching upon the dilemmas faced in any kind of social critique (and of literary or artistic undertaking) that is based on identity. . . .

Another characteristic trait of the novel's lexicon is the imitation, in the mode of parody, of the sort of wooden politico-administrative language that one finds in the Egyptian press and bureaucratic literature. Throughout the novel, one finds again and again terms that are borrowed from this administrative language being applied to characters and novelistic situations. Thus a conversation that Zeth has with a coworker or a friend is described as an 'emission' (*bathth*), and her office colleagues are called 'emitting machines' (*makinat al-bathth*). Zeth, who feels she is always incapable of rousing the interest of her colleagues because she does not have enough interesting 'subjects of emission' (*mawadi' al-bathth*) at her disposal, imagines that she is the victim of a "boycott" (*muqata'a*) on their part. There again, the repairs and renovations undertaken by the different occupants of the apartment building where she lives are described by a frequently repeated generic phrase: the "March of destruction and construction" (*masirat al-hadm wa-l-bina'*). These terms do not pose a particular problem in translation in that, once again, it is a matter of translating *translated Arabic*, for in modern Arabic the politico-administrative lexicon is copied by and large from its European equivalents. This then is another stylistic trait that gives the French translation of the novel its *return-to-the-original* feel.

This characteristic is not just a matter of the novel's lexicon, but also of its style, its rhetoric. Here is a particularly provocative example: the "war of attrition" waged in the conjugal bed by Chankeiti, the neighbor of Zeth and Abdel-Méguid, against his wife Samiha, who prefers her oneiric lovers to him. (In the political lexicon of Egypt, "war of attrition" refers to the low-intensity conflict in which Egypt and Israel were embroiled in the years following the all-out war of June 1967.)

استسلمت سميحة لعشاقها، بينما جثم زوجها إلى جوارها يتملى خطوته التالية .

كان يعرف أن فتح الثغرات يتطلب أن يكون المهاجم في وضع دفاعي ومسيطرًا

على مواجهات واسعة ثم يركز هجومه على مواجهة صغيرة إلى أن تنضم إليه

وحدات دعم. لكنه كان في وضع هجومي وليس دفاعيًا، ولم يكن مسيطرًا على أي

مواجهات ولا يتوقع دعمًا من أي وحدات، لهذا لم يبق أمامه سوى الانسحاب.

وكان الانسحاب تكتيكيًا، لا يعني التخلي عن الهدف الاستراتيجي.[17]

Tandis que Samiha se livrait à ses amants, son époux, allongé à côté d'elle, réfléchissait à sa prochaine initiative. Il savait, depuis la Guerre d'usure, que pour ouvrir une brèche, l'attaquant doit tenir une position défensive, s'assurer de la maîtrise d'un front étendu, puis concentrer son assaut sur un point précis jusqu'à ce que les unités de renfort le rejoignent. Or, il était en position offensive, ne dominait aucun front et ne pouvait compter sur aucun renfort. Il ne lui restait qu'une option: se retirer. Mais c'était un retrait tactique, qui n'impliquait pas qu'il renonçât à son objectif stratégique.[18]

Upon rereading, I see the imperfection of my work: the militaristic lexicon chosen by the author is present from the very beginning of the passage—in the verbs *istaslama* (to deliver oneself, but also to surrender to the enemy) and *jathama* (to be lying on one's chest, like a predator or a soldier preparing for an ambush). This does not come through in my translation.

One will notice, on the other hand, an added bonus in the translation: since French, in contradistinction to Arabic, makes use of upper case letters, I was able to put capitalization to good effect in many instances where I wished to highlight certain recurring terms that the author had borrowed from politico-administrative language: "la Marche de la destruction et de la construction," "la Guerre d'usure," etc.

The question of translating the politico-administrative lexicon leads me naturally to mention another aspect of the novel, and one which poses rather different problems for translation: its narrative structure. Formally, *Dhat* is composed of an alternation of chapters that are dedicated to narrating the life of the heroine and other chapters that consist of a collage of 'pseudo-documents' presented as press clippings. Out of a total of nineteen chapters, we have nine documentary chapters and ten narrative ones (because narrative chapters both open and close the novel).

The documentary chapters paint an extremely bleak picture of the state of Egyptian society in the 1980s in just about every sphere: political, economic, social, environmental, educational, etc. They consist, essentially, of press clippings that have been rewritten and/or summarized by the author to varying degrees that are difficult to appreciate. These documentary chapters are less accessible to the foreign reader for various reasons.

The problem lies, fundamentally, in the fact that the press, in Egypt as elsewhere, mentions on a daily basis all sorts of institutions, personalities, and events that are very well-known locally and that it does so in a de-contextualized, implicit manner. This does not bother local readers, as long as they read their papers frequently enough to be familiar with the idiolect, but it constitutes a major problem for foreign readers. This fact is not lost on foreign language instructors, who know that, even though journalistic language is supposed to be easier than literary or poetic language, it is as a general rule less accessible to students.

In order to resolve these problems without overloading the text with numerous footnotes, I found recourse in the classic solutions of the glossary and the timeline: at the end of the translation figure the "Petit dictionnaire de l'Égypte de Zeth" (Zeth's concise dictionary of Egypt, pp. 339–43), where the principal personalities and institutions mentioned in the documentary chapters are presented in a few lines, and the "Chronologie sommaire des années de Zeth" (Brief summary of the Zeth years), which gives the dates of the main events mentioned in these same chapters (which the author presents in chronological order without indicating any of the dates in question). The latter was what gave the editor the idea for the title of the novel: *Les années de Zeth*.

In the case of the Egyptian press, as a result of politically imposed restrictions on freedom of expression, the role of the unspoken, the understood, and the implicit looms large. Thus, for example, the press often deals with institutions or personalities in an indirect manner, without naming them, in the knowledge that they will be recognizable to an informed local reader. Sonallah Ibrahim does the same. Thus, in placing these two clippings one after the other:

C'est le ministre qui était consultant de la Femme d'Acier à 10 000
    livres par mois qui a facilité sa fuite [à l'étranger] . . . ,
and

> Le magazine féminin Hawwa rend visite au ministre de
> l'Administration locale, Dr Ahmed Salama, et l'interroge sur les
> valeurs dont il s'inspire dans l'éducation de ses enfants,[19]

he intends to signal to the reader that the anonymous minister of the
first clipping and the named minister of the second are one and the same
person.

These documentary chapters distinguish themselves from the narrative chapters in the quality of their language as well. Whereas the language of the novelistic narration is sophisticated and precise, that of the press—which the author has reproduced faithfully, for the most part—is often slack and inelegant, and, in any case, it has its own peculiar style of rhetoric, which is very different from that of the French press. In other words, in these chapters I found myself in a situation familiar to the translator of modern Arabic literature: forced to 'rewrite' my first attempt relatively radically in order to make the text 'readable' in French, but at the same time wary of taking the exercise too far, since the gap between these two levels of language, journalistic and literary, is manifestly intended by the author; hence it was necessary to render this gap perceptibly in French and to navigate judiciously between these two contradictory constraints. Here is an example:

التحقيق سرًّا مع ١١ من العاملين بإحدى المؤسسات الهامة لاشتراكهم في لجنة

التعاقدات التي اشترت ٢٩ طائرة معطوبة من مصانع بريطانية وصل منها ١٧

طائرة، وانفجرت اثنتان منها، ولقي قائداهما مصرعهما، خلال ٤ أيام وحسب.[20]

> Onze responsables militaires entendus à huis clos. Ils faisaient partie
> de la commission des contrats qui a décidé l'achat de 29 avions
> endommagés à des fabricants britanniques. Sur les 17 appareils
> d'ores et déjà livrés, deux ont explosé en moins de quatre jours, tuant
> leurs pilotes.[21]

The euphemism "institution of prime importance" (mu'assasa hamma) behind which the Egyptian reader would recognize the army, had to be explained ("onze responsables militaires"), and I preferred to speak of plane "manufacturers" *(fabricants)*, rather than factories *(usines/masani')*. Most of all, the sequencing of the sentence, barely passable in Arabic (especially the ending: *"wasala minha 17 ta'ira . . ."*) would have been inadmissible in French *("dont 17 sont arrivés, dont deux ont explosé, dont les pilotes ont trouvé la mort, en quatre jours seulement")*.

These problems, multiplied by nearly two hundred pages, led the French editor to intervene in the translation: judging these documentary chapters to be too rich in information of uneven interest and, in the end, too unreadable for a French audience, he asked us—the author and myself—to cut them by half! During the translation, we worked together to prune these chapters of what we considered to be the least essential, sometimes from his point of view, sometimes from mine. In the final tally, we cut 'only' less than a third of these pseudo-press clippings.

All of this had to be made explicit to the French reader in a brief foreword where we, again Sonallah Ibrahim and myself, assume the editor's choice and explained why we had to make some cuts in the clippings. We also offered the reader some indispensable tools for understanding them. Notably, we cited the aforementioned example of la Femme D'Acier and Dr Salama, and we explained the meaning of the word *dhat*, which is the proper name of the heroine (rendered 'Zeth' in French in order that its French pronunciation be as close as possible to its current Cairene pronunciation) as well as a common word with many significations in Arabic: of feminine gender, it is usually followed by another noun and serves to designate the owner of a thing or a quality (as in *Dhat al-himma*: 'one who has ardor'—the name of the heroine of a popular Arabic epic); on its own, it signifies the self or the subject, both in philosophical and in common parlance. One can see all the meanings that can be read into the heroine's 'first name.'

Was it necessary to amputate fifty pages from the novel? Purists will cry scandal. For my part, I am torn. On the one hand, the need to make contemporary Arabic literature familiar presupposes some compromises. They must be made in order that this literature be 'exportable.' This entails a certain submission to the norms of the European market. Literature, like tomatoes or potatoes, must be 'calibrated' to find its place in the market. In the case of *Dhat*, I had a product that adhered perfectly to the norms when it came to the narrative chapters, but that had to be 'recalibrated' in its documentary sections. Moreover, is it not possible to imagine that if the author had had a 'true' editor in Egypt, perhaps it is he or she who would have intervened and asked Sonallah Ibrahim to 'tighten up' the documentary parts? On the other hand, we must acknowledge that we yielded to a kind of censorship of the marketplace—less brutal, perhaps, than political or religious censorship, but even more pernicious and difficult to combat.

The lesser of two evils . . . .

Notes

1   Translated from the French by Marlé Hammond. Originally published in French as "Les Années de Zeth de Sonallah Ibrahim : Les conditions de l'exportabilité de la littérature arabe contemporaine," in Henri Awaiss et Jarjoura Hardane, eds, *Du pareil au même. La fidélité en traduction* (Beyrouth: Presses de l'Université Saint-Joseph 159–73). We thank the editors for permission to reproduce the article in English here.

2   '*Cette odeur-là.*'

3   Gamal al-Ghitani, *al-Zayni Barakat*, 3rd ed. (Cairo: Dar al-Mustaqbal al-'Arabi, 1985), 7.

4   Gamal Ghitany, *Zayni Barakat* (Paris: Editions du Seuil, 1985), 7.

5   Sonallah Ibrahim, *Dhat*. (Cairo: Dar al-Mustaqbal al-'Arabi, 1992), 9.

6   Sonallah Ibrahim, *Les années de Zeth*. (Arles: Actes Sud), 13.

7   Ibrahim, *Dhat*, 117-118.

8   Ibrahim, *Les années de Zeth*, 111-112.

9   Samia Mehrez, *Egyptian Writers between History and Fiction: Essays on Naguib Mahfouz, Sonallah Ibrahim and Gamal Ghitany* (Cairo: The American University in Cairo Press, 1994), 132.

10 Ibrahim, *Dhat*, 16.

11 Ibrahim, *Les années de Zeth*, 17.

12 Ibrahim, *Dhat*, 234 and Ibrahim, *Les années de Zeth*, 223.

13 Ibrahim, *Dhat*, p. 23 and Ibrahim, *Les années de Zeth*, 29. *My name is* appears in English transcription in the Arabic original.

14 *Les années de Zeth*, 15.

15 Ibrahim, *Dhat*, 24 and Ibrahim, *Les années de Zeth*, 30.

16 Ibrahim, *Dhat*, 153 and Ibrahim, *Les années de Zeth*, 141.

17 *Dhat*, 93.

18 *Les années de Zeth*, 88.

19 Page 48 in the Arabic and the French translation.

20 *Dhat*, 73–74.

21 *Les années de Zeth*, 73.

13

Tawfiq al-Hakim, Yusuf al-Qa'id, and the 'Mature' Arabic Novel

Christopher Stone

The Lebanese novelist and critic Elias Khoury has suggested that not a single detective novel exists in all of Arabic literature.[1] In making this statement, perhaps Mr. Khoury was not considering works like Tawfiq al-Hakim's *Yawmiyat na'ib fi-l-aryaf* (Maze of Justice, 1937) and Yusuf al-Qa'id's[2] *Yahduth fi Misr al-an* (It's Happening in Egypt Now, 1977), both of which have been compared to the detective novel in the West.[3] These two works share another similarity: they are both part of the century-long tradition of novelistic narratives about the Egyptian countryside. Despite these parallels, and also despite the fact that by all accounts al-Hakim is considered an important influence on al-Qa'id,[4] a comparative project of these two novels would seem to promise a study of contrasts. While it is undebatable that both novels contain elements of the police-novel genre and that the events of both narratives are firmly anchored in the Egyptian countryside, *Yawmiyat*, though almost universally praised, is from a time when the Arab novel was said to be in its early stages of development.[5] *Yahduth*, on the other hand, has been described as being more experimental than even the French *Nouveau Roman*.[6] In fact, there seems to be some debate as to whether or not Yusuf al-Qa'id's complex texts should even be called novels.[7]

Novel or not, in this chapter I examine the experimental nature of *Yahduth fi Misr al-an* in light of Fedwa Malti Douglas's article on similarities between *Yahduth* and the French *Nouveau Roman*. I then go on to suggest that *Yawmiyat na'ib fi-l-aryaf* can be read as being equally, if not more, 'experimental' than the al-Qa'id novel. This is not merely an exercise in identifying a paradox. An examination of these two novels, written some forty years apart, serves to remind us of the limitations of the developmental model of the history of the Arab novel, which traditionally has anthropomorphized the genre's history by describing it as passing through the various stages of life until maturity is reached somewhere in the 1960s. This discourse assumes that the models for modern narrative forms are already evolved Western genres with which these Arabic versions are constantly being compared as they strive to match the perfection and maturity of the former. Thus I use the term 'experimental' throughout this chapter relatively and in the sense that such terms are used by historians of the Arab novel in both Arabic and Western languages, that is, that experimentalism is but one rung on the ladder of literary evolution usually equivalent to characterizations such as 'mature.'[8] I argue that in such terms both novels are similarly experimental, and that at least in one aspect—the depiction of the Egyptian peasant—the 1937 novel outstrips the 1977 work. Both works, as mentioned above, are part of a tradition of writing the peasant that is as old as the Egyptian novel itself.[9] Despite all its narrative high jinks and despite al-Qa'id's well-known sympathy for the Egyptian *fallah*, I argue that his novel offers a rather one-dimensional depiction of the Egyptian peasant. Al-Hakim, on the other hand, presents the relationship between city and country—center and margin—in such a way that makes his *Yawmiyat* appear, according to the developmental model, more avant-garde than the avant-garde of today.[10]

It is perhaps equally important to state what this chapter is not. It is not, first of all, an in-depth study of either author or of either novel. Tawfiq al-Hakim is one of the most written about and translated twentieth-century Arab literary figures in both Arabic and European languages, and though he is known and written about more as a playwright than as a novelist, there are countless studies on *Yawmiyat*, as it is widely considered to be his best novel.[11] In comparison, while Yusuf al-Qa'id is generally regarded as one of Egypt's leftist literary dons and an important writer of the perhaps overused moniker 'sixties generation,'[12] he is, in my view, understudied and under-translated in English.[13] I have chosen these two works not only because a contrast of them illustrates the point I am trying to make about the historiography of the Arab novel but also because each novel in its own way is an example of the best of modern Arab narrative. If I spend more time on *Yahduth* than *Yawmiyat*, it is because the former has been much less studied than the latter.

I begin with the more recent *Yahduth* by al-Qa'id. On the simplest level the "*al-an*" (now) in the novel's title refers to the year 1974, and the main event implied by "*yahduth*" (it is happening) is the visit in that year of the U.S. president Richard Nixon to Egypt. The novel focuses on the impact of this visit on the Delta town of al-Dahriya, Yusuf al-Qa'id's own hometown. Presented in a polyphonic combination of reports and testimonies, the story unfolds as follows: Just prior to the American president's arrival in Egypt, aid in the form of foodstuffs is sent to the villages through which his train will pass. The arrival of this aid immediately presents a problem for the elite of al-Dahriya: how is it to be distributed? It is ultimately agreed that it should be given to the town's pregnant women, a task to be carried out by the author of this plan and the one best qualified to determine who is pregnant and who is not—the town doctor. It is eventually discovered that one of the women (Sudfa) who received the aid is not, in fact, pregnant. The Doctor, along with a police escort, goes to her house and takes what is left of the food. When the woman's husband (al-Dubaysh) discovers that the food has been confiscated he goes to the distribution center to protest. In the meantime, the reader is given insight into the process of rationalization that went into al-Dubaysh's decision to have his wife feign pregnancy: first, he reasoned that his wife was almost always pregnant anyway, and that it was sheer bad luck that she happened not to be at this particular moment; and second, he assumed that the town elite were using similarly dishonest means to procure their share of the aid. The confrontation at the clinic results in al-Dubaysh, a landless agricultural worker, assaulting the Doctor. Chaos ensues, and what food remains is stolen. Al-Dubaysh is arrested and is sent by the head of the village council (*Ra'is majlis al-qarya*, henceforth 'the Chairman') to the town police station to be placed in the custody of the chief officer (*Hadrat al-dabit*, henceforth 'the Officer'). That night al-Dubaysh dies. We later learn that he died from a severe beating. The Officer sees to it that no official reports are written (the reader later learns, however, that the doctor on duty at the hospital where al-Dubaysh was 'cared for,' did in fact write an unofficial report) and has the body of al-Dubaysh buried in an unspecified and unmarked grave. The Doctor, the Officer, and the Chairman then meet to discuss how best to cover up the incident. They arrive at two choices: to paint al-Dubaysh as a revolutionary who has escaped from custody and is working as part of a larger organization bent on disrupting the visit of the American President; or to claim that al-Dubaysh never existed at all. After some debate they decide upon, and then successfully implement, the seemingly absurd second option. They are able to pull off such a stunt because not a single written document establishing the existence of a man named al-Dubaysh 'Arayis exists. In other words, due to his extreme poverty and because of a series of bureaucratic paradoxes and Catch-22s (for example, he never obtained an identification card because he did not possess a birth certificate, and did not possess a birth certificate because his mother could not afford to make the necessary post-natal trip to procure one), it will be impossible for anyone to produce a written document confirming his existence. He does not even posses a picture from his wedding, not to mention any kind of written proof of the marriage. Meanwhile, a hospital worker who was the last to speak to al-Dubaysh before his death carries out his last request and comes to inform al-Dubaysh's wife Sudfa that he has died. The remainder of the novel is occupied by the fruitless attempts by some of al-Dubaysh's fellow workers to obtain justice, and by Sudfa's failed attempts to receive at least some compensation from a government that not only refuses to admit that her husband is dead, but also actually contends that he never existed. In the end, the train carrying Nixon does not even stop in the village, dashing the hopes of the ambitious Chairman who had expected his elaborately planned reception of the American president to catalyze a series of promotions that would have eventually catapulted him into the position of governor of the province of Alexandria.

While covering the basic plot, this summary in no way conveys a sense of the novel's complex structure. In her article, "*Yusuf al-Qaʿid wa-l-riwaya al-jadida*," Fedwa Malti-Douglas goes so far as to posit that not only do al-Qaʿid's novels resemble those of the French *Nouveau Roman* movement, but that in certain ways they even outdo their French counterpart in their experimental nature.[14] She bases her findings on the following: she says, first of all, that novels like *Yahduth* go further than other experimental Arab novels that tinker either with the narrative form, such as *Rim tasbagh sha'raha* (*Rim Dyes Her Hair,* 1983, by Majid Tubiya), or with the narrative events themselves, such as *al-Lajna* (*The Committee,* 1982, by Sonallah Ibrahim), or with a combination of the two, such as Muhammad Mustajab's *Min al-tarikh al-sirri li-Nu'man 'Abd al-Hafiz* (*From the Secret History of Noman Abd al-Hafiz* , 1982).[15] According to Malti-Douglas, however, Yusuf al-Qa'id does not stop there, for he

> finds a way to express a philosophy of the novel which approaches that of the Nouveau Roman movement. The similarity between the novels of Yusuf al-Qa'id and the Nouveau Roman can be boiled down to two essential points. The first point is represented by al-Qa'id's break from the traditional novel, a feat accomplished by a variety of literary means, including fragmented narration and ambiguity in the events of the novel. As for the second point, it is comprised of—in the Qa'idian novel—the continuous implied and explicit references to the plot of the police novel.[16]

What she means by the latter point is that both the novels of al-Qa'id and those of the *Nouveau Roman* movement simultaneously refer to and subvert the traditional Western police novel by twisting the smart-investigator-solves-the-crime paradigm (which is supposed to stand for the return of order to society), for example by ending their texts without the crime being solved or even, as in the case of *Les gommes* (The Erasers, 1953) by Alain Robbe-Grillet, with the investigator himself being the criminal. In these novels, in other words, the investigators, rather than imposing order on the world, render it in a state of "non-order."[17]

Yahduth fi Misr al-an certainly seems to fit these specifications, for the investigator, while not being the perpetrator of the crime being investigated (the stealing of the food aid) is the perpetrator of, or at least an accomplice to, a much more serious crime, that is, the killing of al-Dubaysh. He and his co-conspirators—the Chairman and the Doctor—do initially conduct an investigation of a nonexistent crime (that is, the escape of al-Dubaysh), but then they claim that he never existed so that there can be no investigation of their own crime. According to Malti-Douglas, the Qa'idian novel actually exceeds the *Nouveau roman* in its subversion of the traditional police novel, because whereas in the latter the inspector is generally a *non*-bureaucrat creating non-order by fighting against bureaucracy, in al-Qa'id's novels such as *Yahduth*, the inspector is often a *bureaucrat* creating non-order, which Malti-Douglas considers to be an effective way of criticizing bureaucracy as well as society in general.[18]

While I am not completely convinced that having an investigator who is also a bureaucrat is grounds for claiming the experimental edge over the French *Nouveau Roman*, I do find Malti-Douglas's argument about the similarities between the *Nouveau Roman*'s and al-Qa'id's use of the traditional police novel plot convincing. The examples she gives, however, to establish the *avant-garde* feature of ambiguity in *Yahduth* are less so. She cites the critic Jean Ricardou as differentiating between two types of ambiguity in the *Nouveau roman*: *réalités variables* (*al-haqa'iq al-mutaghayyira*; changing facts) and *variantes réelles* (*at-taghayyurat al-haqiqiya*; real variants). Simply put, the first kind of ambiguity calls into question the meaning of an occurrence in a given novel, whereas the second kind of ambiguity calls into question the existence of the occurrence itself.[19] As an example of both kinds of ambiguities in *Yahduth*, Malti-Douglas offers the apparent ambiguity that surrounds the question of the existence and nature of al-Dubaysh. By the novel's end, she claims, there are three choices for the reader: 1) that al-Dubaysh never existed; 2) that he is a dangerous anti-government rebel at large; or 3) that he is a normal peasant who merely wanted a share of the food assistance. She surmises: "Perhaps the reader will favor one reading over another for personal reasons, but the novel does not present a basis for certainty of this choice."[20]

I posit that the novel does offer grounds for certainty. Very early in the work, in fact, in a dramatic literary move to be discussed more fully below, al-Qa'id announces that the third reading, that is, that al-Dubaysh is just an ordinary man who was the victim of injustice and was killed at the hands of the authorities, is the correct interpretation. After informing us very clearly that al-Dubaysh is dead, he writes:

> The rules of the profession dictate that I should have hidden the news of his death. It would have been more interesting had I talked about the worker's [al-Dubaysh's] disappearance at night. Then we could have embarked with the Officer on the adventure of searching for him everywhere only to discover at the end of the novel that he had died. . . . But I revealed my secrets and uncovered my plan.

Despite this I do not request from you that you forget the death of the agricultural worker; rather I will remind you of it with each step forward in the novel.[21]

The existence of the two false reports, one claiming that he never existed and the other that he is an escaped rebel, not only fails to confuse the reader, it fails to fool any of the characters in the novel, for by the novel's conclusion everyone knows who al-Dubaysh was and more or less how he died. The only fact that remains a mystery to reader and characters alike is the inconsequential issue of the location of his grave. A question that remains unresolved for the reader, although not for at least some of the characters, is *how* al-Dubaysh was actually killed, for toward the end of the novel the author presents two possible scenarios which I will discuss at greater length below. I am suggesting, in other words, that the kind of ambiguity discussed by Ricardou in his work on the French *Nouveau Roman* is not a prominent feature of *Yahduth fi Misr al-an*.

The decision to inform the reader up front that al-Dubaysh is dead is part of a larger plan to, as al-Qa'id puts it, "surrender his weapons." It is evident that this is a technique he considers to be unconventional or experimental, particularly given the statement quoted above, in which he says that the "rules of the profession" demand such and such while implying that he will in fact do the opposite. This comes as no surprise. After all, the title of this section of the novel is: "The Author Surrenders to the Reader his Most Important Weapons."[22] A few sentences into the section it becomes clear that he considers this to be a radical technique: "But I—for many reasons—announce my surrender of all the weapons of the writers of both new and old novels."[23]

I would like to suggest that this claim to be surrendering all of his novel-writing weapons to the reader rings somewhat hollow. It is true that knowing right away that al-Dubaysh was killed and is not in fact a revolutionary fugitive does not add any ambiguity to the text. It does, however, seem like a direct subversion of the police novel, where suspense is the writer's main tool to keep the reader turning the pages. But just because al-Qa'id supplies us with this important piece of information does not mean that the novel, which as we have seen above contains very little ambiguity as defined by Ricardou, is completely devoid of suspense. Although the reader knows that al-Dubaysh has been killed, he or she does not know, as mentioned above, the details of the death, that is, how and when he died. And although the novel does subvert expectations and present us with two possible scenarios of his death (he was either killed by fellow prisoners, who were constantly being provoked to attack one another by the guards, or he was killed by the night guard when he protested an order to clean the station, including its bathroom),[24] the reader is left in the dark about his death until novel's end. The traditional element of suspense appears in other places as well. The author appends the reports written by both the Chairman and the Doctor with footnotes, a device whose function is to elucidate the falsehoods of each report. At the end of the Doctor's report we read: "What the doctor failed to mention [in his report] will become clear in what remains of the novel. . . ."[25] If the author were truly set on eliminating suspense from the novel, he would have told the reader immediately what these missing elements are.

Another experimental aspect of the novel that both Fedwa Malti-Douglas and the author himself point out is the latter's invitation to the reader to, as it were, co-write the novel with him, a device which Malti-Douglas sees as part of a larger overall plan to write his novel as self-consciously as possible. She writes:

> The role of the author appears more clearly in the novel Yahduth
> fi Misr al-an, in which at the beginning of the novel the narrator
> invites us to create the novel with him. There is, to be sure, no more
> effective way than this to alert the reader to the process of writing.
> The references to this invitation continue in the text, meaning that
> the reader does not forget the imposed-upon-him responsibility of
> creating the novel with the author.[26]

The very first lines of the novel, in fact, read as follows: "Just by your eyes falling on the beginning of this line, and until you reach that last word at the end of the last page, there will have been established between us a relationship revolving around a novel that we create together."[27] And, as Malti-Douglas explains above, this invitation is repeated several times throughout the novel.

While I do not take issue with Malti-Douglas's contention that the novel is very effectively self-consciously written, I am not convinced that this particular technique contributes to that effect. Even Malti-Douglas admits that the invitation cannot be a real one: "But this partnership does not have, naturally, a real presence, but rather represents textual sleight-of-hand *(khurafa nassiya)*." [28] Not only is the invitation a false one, but it should also be pointed out that the novel's very first sentence, quoted in the paragraph above, manages simultaneously to extend the invitation and to preclude it from becoming a reality. By mentioning in that sentence the last word at the end of the last page of the novel, al-Qa'id is admitting from the very beginning that the novel has already been written. Additionally, toward the end of the novel he writes: "We have approached the end of the novel, and thus we arrive at the final word, which was never a happy one." [29] This use of the perfect tense is further proof that the ending has already been determined, and that his invitation to the reader to create the novel with him is, in fact, an empty one. Malti-Douglas defends the device by claiming that when the reader finally understands the trick his or her attention has once again been drawn to the fact that this is a text with an author, that this is a text that has, in other words, been created. [30] Even if this were true, this stratagem appears to be a gimmick to this reader, especially when the novel is quite successful in other ways in drawing the reader's attention to the process of its authorship, about which I will say more below. [31]

Al-Qa'id also mentions several times at the beginning of the work that he is going to forgo the traditional novelistic introduction. In fact, the title of the first chapter's first section is "Instead of an Interesting Introduction." [32] Just after inviting the reader to co-create the novel, he writes: "I have said that we are creating a novel. And what kind of novel is it that does not have a beginning? But I, in the blank pages designated for the introduction or the opening *(muftatah)* in the language of the innovators among the narrativists *(qasasiyun)* of our time, I will begin my novel immediately." [33] To what kind of introduction is he referring? He certainly cannot mean either a pre-textual introduction by the author himself or by a noteworthy critic, since the edition used for this paper (the fourth) has both of these. Does he mean that after these two introductions the novel itself begins by an immediate immersion in the events to be narrated? This is not what we find either, for by merely writing that he is going to forgo an introduction, he is offering an introduction of sorts.

I should state clearly at this point that I do not see the above contradictions as distracting blemishes to an otherwise powerful work of narrative. What I did not attempt to highlight in my simple summary of the novel's plot is the book's biting sarcasm and irony, through which al-Qa'id repeatedly makes clear his disdain for Egypt's 'open door' *(infitah)* policy of the 1970s.[34] Yusuf al-Qa'id has always been clear about his criticism of the period of Anwar Sadat's rule. *Yahduth fi Misr al-an* is a stark example of this clearness, especially given the author's own analysis situating this as the first work in a period of more overtly political writing:

> This period began with the novel *Yahduth fi Misr al-an* in which my social concerns took on a political bent embodied by my rejection of dependency on America and my rejection of the detente with the Israeli enemy, along with a clear bias toward the poor of Egypt, and the total rejection of the wealthy, since I believe that underneath all wealth lies some great crime. It was a violent and clearly delineated period [of writing], which was against all of Sadat's attempts to invalidate the accomplishments of the July Revolution and of Nasser's revolution. It was a period marked by its rejection of the selling of all the accomplishments of the October War in return for an equalizing peace with Israel and America and in an alliance that leads the regressive wing of the Arab world, and by my rejection of the economic opening up that is happening in Egypt. . . . All of this I expressed completely in the novel *Yahduth fi Misr al-an*.[35]

Sarcasm is one manifestation of this rejection. It should come as no surprise that the target of his sarcasm is the village elite who plan to benefit from the American president's visit, an event which for al-Qa'id and most Egyptians, according to 'Ali al-Ra'i in his introduction to the novel, was the perfect example of the folly of the *infitah* policy and the sycophancy of the Egyptian government toward America: "In any case, Nixon's visit to Egypt was considered to be a big joke *(udhuka tuthir al-dahsha)*. It was considered so in the U.S. itself. And the Americans—both officials and non-officials alike—could not understand why the Egyptian government would open its arms to welcome a man who had been expelled from his own government. . . ."[36]

Perhaps no one is as much a target of sarcasm as the Chairman, who, as previously mentioned, hoped that his lavishly planned reception of the president, his embracing of this disgraced politician whom only Egypt would receive, would boost the trajectory of his career. The novel pokes fun at the man's unbridled ambition and imagination, for example, in a section that describes his having had a dream in which President Nixon presents him with a white rose. We ultimately learn that this dream is the basis for all of his elaborate expectations and astronomically high hopes. This section also sarcastically targets sycophancy, for once the Chairman has had this dream, many other people in the village claim to have the same or similar dreams about the Chairman, obviously hoping that reporting these dreams to the Chairman will win them political favor.[37] The other elite in the novel are shown to be equally opportunistic: sarcasm oozes from the pages during the meeting of the village council that is convened to determine how the U.S. food aid should be distributed. Al-Qaʻid skillfully demonstrates the lengths to which the wealthy are willing to go to justify having the aid distributed to themselves, arguing that if they look upon the food as a "gift" instead of "aid," then it would be extremely rude for them not to accept a portion of it, and that their non-acceptance of it, in fact, could spark an international diplomatic incident. They go so far as to cite a prophetic tradition urging the acceptance of all gifts.[38] Perhaps the most biting sarcasm comes when a law student, using the freewheeling financial language of the *infitah*, suggests to the poor farmers seeking some form of retribution that they turn the cause of al-Dubaysh into a "project" called the "The General Egyptian Organization to Keep Alive the Memory of the Martyr al-Dubaysh ʻArayis, and Co." He even suggests that they look for foreign investors and that they sell shares of the company.[39]

The novel abounds with irony as well. It is particularly sharp when al-Qaʻid wants to chastise Egypt for so quickly forgetting the role that the US, and hence Nixon, played in the 1973 war. The author mentions, for example, by way of depicting the frenzy of preparations that takes place prior to Nixon's visit, that a neighboring town was contemplating changing its name to 'Nixon.' The reader is meant to feel even more indignant when he or she learns that this same town had been contemplating changing its name to 'Village of Nixon's Martyrs,' just a few years before.[40] Very striking too is the image of the young girl—whose father died in that war—being dressed up to look like an American flag as part of the reception party for Nixon's visit.

Although I may disagree with Malti-Douglas about the efficacy of al-Qaʻid inviting the reader to co-author the text with him, I do agree that the novel's self-conscious style is effective, if not unique. The author does not, for example, merely appear in the text as a disembodied pronoun, but is actually a character named Yusuf al-Qa'id. He also, as Malti-Douglas points out, never lets you forget that what you are reading is a text that has been written,[41] or that it is a text written in the context of antecedents. When, for example, he explains the difficulty he has in describing Sudfa's reaction to learning of the death of her husband, he says that he should describe this moment, but that he is not quite sure how to proceed: "The situation is subtle and difficult, but how many novels have already described the same thing? I feel that it has become such a cliché that it will not move within you what the significance of the situation calls for."[42]

Not only does he constantly remind you that what you are reading has already been written, but also that it is going to be read, and by lay people and critics alike. At several points in the novel he tries to defend aspects of the work that he expects to be attacked by critics. At one point he even goes on the offensive in anticipation of criticism. Toward the end of the novel, for example, he writes: "A literary critic will come along who has spent his youth in endless frustration. He works in the morning as a government employee in one of the institutions that he himself describes as reactionary. And when the evening comes—and the night is good at hiding the truth of things—he becomes as much as he can a leftist who eats, drinks, and sleeps the revolution. In this way he can live off of the money of the right and the intellectual prestige of the left. . . ."[43]

Not only is al-Qa'id openly self-conscious about the process of writing, but he is also very much interested in the power of the written word, for ultimately it is al-Dubaysh's lack of any written documents that allows the Doctor, the Officer, and the Chairman (the three of whom are repeatedly and sarcastically referred to in the novel as "lifetime friends"), to successfully implement their plan to claim that al-Dubaysh never existed, just as the Doctor can, in a sense, make his rich friends' wives pregnant (or at least make them eligible to receive a share of the American food aid) by simply adding their names to the hospital pregnancy register. While alive, al-Dubaysh had always thought of his lack of documentation as a bit of a joke, except when it prevented him from joining the army, something he had wanted to do as a means to escape his abject poverty in the village.[44] In the end, however, this lack of written documentation is no joke at all. All it takes is a report claiming that al-Dubaysh never was, to throw serious doubt on his existence, because no one can positively prove otherwise. This means that the three friends cannot possibly be implicated in his death. So not only does al-Qaʿid constantly remind us of the writing of *Yahduth*, he also reminds us that in some cases Descartes' famous sentence can be rephrased: I am written, therefore I am. Yusuf al-Qaʿid thus criticizes the massive, self-contradicting, and even, in this case, human-erasing Egyptian bureaucracy of the late twentieth century. Such criticism may not make this novel more experimental than the French *Nouveau Roman*, but it certainly does present a tragic critique of modern government and modernity more broadly.

In discussing Tawfiq al-Hakim's 1937 *Yawmiyat naʾib fi-l-aryaf*, I would like, in a sense, to invert the argument I made for *Yahduth*. While *Yawmiyat* initially appears to be anything but experimental in form, I would like to suggest that if we apply some of Fedwa Malti-Douglas's criteria to it, such as the critique of society and bureaucracy via a rewriting of the traditional Western detective novel and the presence of textual ambiguity, we may be able to argue that it is in certain ways as experimental as *Yahduth*. I would then like to move on to examine the way the two novels treat the relationship between city and country, arguing that *Yawmiyat* may be the more 'experimental' of the two works in this regard.

Fedwa Malti-Douglas argues that al-Qaʿid's novels surpass the French *Nouveau Roman* in its appropriation and ultimate subversion of the traditional Western detective novel. The traditional detective novel, by having its crime neatly solved by book's end, represents the possibility of the existence of an orderly world. The French *Nouveau Roman* and the Qaʿidian text, in contrast, by twisting this convention in any number of ways, use the skeleton of the plot of the traditional police novel to champion what Malti-Douglas calls "non-order." She also, as mentioned above, considers the presence of narrative ambiguity another criterion for comparison to the experimental *Nouveau Roman*.

Tawfiq al-Hakim's *Yawmiyat* can be read as fulfilling both of these requirements. Samah Selim, in her work on the Egyptian village novel, captures well the ambiguity of the narrative at the same time that she offers a micro-summary of the plot:

> The narrator of *Maze of Justice* is a cynical and overworked district prosecutor assigned to a small Delta village. He spends his days

investigating the petty crimes committed by the locals, listlessly attending innumerable and interminable court sessions, and shuffling through endless legal dossiers while his solitary evenings are given over to his sole companion and refuge—his journal. . . . Eleven entries frame the time of the novel, narrating eleven consecutive days of his life, which focus on the mysterious circumstances surrounding the murder of a local peasant. The novel is thus a 'whodunit' of sorts, a hapless detective story in which murderer, victim, witness and motive form a cryptic constellation of characters and events that defy comprehension and resolution.[45]

If you did not know what novel was being described above, you could easily think it the summary of an Alain Robbe-Grillet or Claude Simon novel, not to mention the kind of text that Yusuf al-Qa'id might write. And like the investigator in the texts by al-Qa'id, the investigator in *Yawmiyat*, that is the prosecutor, is most definitely a bureaucrat, a bureaucrat who, armed only with laws totally unsuitable to the peasant population which does its best to resist their application, is unable, not only to create order, but also to make sense of any of the people or events that surround him.

The novel is a scathing critique of the inefficacy of the application of foreign laws implemented by city lawmakers on country folk who cannot be blamed for looking at the fines levied against them as a kind of extortion. Al-Hakim skillfully reveals the peasants' puzzlement over these imported laws: at, for example, having to pay fines for consuming some of the wheat that they have personally cultivated, for washing their clothes in the nearest water source, or for wearing clothes that have fallen off the back of a transport lorry.[46] And just as the peasants are frustrated by having these strange laws applied to their lives, so is the prosecutor in trying to enforce them: trying, in other words, to create order.

From the very beginning of the novel, the prosecutor's cynicism is clear. When summoned to go and investigate the murder that gives the text its police-novel character, he predicts sarcastically how the investigation will go:

No big deal. It's a simple thing that will take no more than two hours of my time, for the assailant is unknown, the victim cannot talk or rant on and of course the witnesses, the night watchman who heard the shot and went slowly and fearfully, found no one except a fresh corpse, the mayor will swear to divorce his wife if the perpetrator is a local, and then the family of the victim will say nothing so as to be able to exact revenge themselves.[47]

What actually happens is even more frustrating. Rim, the case's 'key' witness, sister-in-law of the victim, and, as it turns out, a stunningly beautiful girl, throws the investigation into chaos. She drives the police chief to the appearance of social impropriety when he insists that she stay with him and his family while the investigation is being carried out, and she drives the lonely narrator to insomnia. More baffling than her impact on the lives of these allegedly dignified officials is her disappearance, ostensibly with the assistance of the mystical Shaykh al-'Usfur, an enigmatic man who would often assist the police in their investigations using his psychic abilities. Eventually Rim and the Shaykh reappear, or so the beleaguered prosecutor thinks. When he has some men sent to arrest the pair within minutes of having spotted them himself, the men only find the Shaykh, who swears up and down that he has not seen the girl. The prosecutor starts wondering whether he had actually seen her. He starts to doubt, in other words, his own sanity. When Rim finally does turn up, it is as a corpse. The cause of death is discovered to have been strangulation. The novel thus ends with a mysterious and unsolved murder that precludes a solution to the original mysterious and unsolved murder. Detective novels do not get much less clear or more critical of bureaucratic inefficiency than this. By at least some of Malti-Douglas's standards, then, *Yawmiyat* can be read as experimental in the vein of the much later French *Nouveau Roman* school.

Having mentioned already the difficulties in applying city- and foreign-made laws to Egyptian country folk, as depicted in *Yawmiyat*, let us now turn to a comparison of the relationship between city and country in the two novels under discussion here. As mentioned above, both novels can be seen as contributions to the more than century-long Egyptian novelistic tradition of the writing of the village/peasant, a tradition that is often said to have started with *Zaynab* (1913)[48] and which continues in the present day, with one of the latest notable contributions being the Tawfiq al-Hakim-echoing *Yawmiyat dabit fi-l-aryaf* (Diary of a Village Officer, 1998) by Hamdi al-Batran, a controversial work about the recent treatment of

Islamists in upper Egypt by interior ministry security forces. Selim aptly describes the stylistic and chronological range of these works:

> From romanticism to realism to a variety of post-realist styles; from high colonialism to independence to the veiled neo-colonialism of the "open door" years, the village novel forms an elaborate intertextual subgenre with a variety of specific recurring structures, strategies, and motifs and has essentially and consistently engaged the seminal tensions and discourses that marks this century's central cultural and political project: the arduous task of negotiating modernity.[49]

Yusuf al-Qaʿid is thoroughly committed to this genre. The vast majority of his novels, in fact, revolve around the power and economic struggles of the village. And in what he calls the second stage of his writing, a more overtly political stage, his works deal in a very persistent way with the exploitation of the peasant at the hands of the wealthy:

> And the village [of all of his novels] is al-Dahriya . . . where the place is represented by the dominance of poverty and oppression and authoritarianism. The place in his works is not some frozen detached space which has no real hold over its occupants, rather the place (the inhabitants of which own nothing)—the village/interior— is described by its isolation from the city/exterior which practices domination and authoritarianism over the countryside. And in this place contact between the interior and the exterior can only happen via the mediation of the feudal lord who dominates the destitute peasants. . . .[50]

While this clearly stated agenda is certainly an admirable one, a look at the way al-Qaʿid depicts relations between the rich and the poor reveals, I would like to suggest, a somewhat naive oversimplification. Simply put, in the world of *Yahduth*, poor equals good and rich equals bad. Keep in mind, for example, his paraphrase of Balzac about the source of all wealth being some great crime, as well as his statement about his ever-present bias in favor of the poor. The poor, in this work as in his others, are almost without exception heroic, even if he adjusts the conventional definition of that word: "Every age has its heroes, and heroism today is defined by the person who is patient and can bear suffering, not by stubbornness, refusal, and boldness. . . . This does not mean that our age has become without men. In fact, the opposite is true."[51] Even the woman criticized for dressing her daughter up like the American flag to greet president Nixon is vindicated when we discover that the authorities had promised her that Nixon would solve all the woes of the Egyptian countryside.

In al-Hakim's *Yawmiyat*, relations between villagers and city folk, between rich and poor, between ruler and ruled are depicted as being much more complex. Everyone, in fact, seems to be both an oppressor and a victim—a feature which makes this novel stand out as much today as when it was written. The prosecutor, for example, feels like he is overworked, saying at one point, in a complaint about his heavy workload and the accompanying lack of sleep, that even soldiers in the trenches are treated with more respect. On the other hand, he also feels, as we saw above in the difficulties he faces in effectively applying these strange urban laws, that his efficacy is hampered not just by the ignorance of the peasants but also by their intransigence. *Yawmiyat*, then, effectively depicts the tension and power struggle in all human relations. Al-Hakim shows, for example, how the court scribes often have to intercede in cases to bail out young prosecutors, but at the same time resent never moving up the legal ladder.[52] He also demonstrates the complicated relations and at times subtle power struggles between the prosecutor and his assistant.[53] Ultimately, no one in the novel escapes criticism. As Selim points out:

No one is innocent in al-Hakim's village . . . the Cairene judge whose sole concern is the daily purchase of 'real country meat' in time to catch the 11 o'clock train back to the city, the chief surgeon who blithely holds court at the abattoir-like operating table, the miserly and obsequious shari'a court judge busy fattening his pockets through embezzlement, the police commissioner in charge of falsifying election results, all the way to the corrupt government of the moment in Cairo itself.[54]

What the novel shows, then, is that it is not always a problem of rich oppressing poor, but sometimes simply a general difficulty in dealing with 'the other.' It is not just that the prosecutor does not want to deal with criminals per se, but that he would prefer to deal with criminals who are more like himself: "I miss Cairo. I forget what the capital of my country even looks like! I want to change the type of crime [from what I am now working with] and work with criminals wearing jackets and pants."[55]

As I suggested above, al-Qa'id's *Yahduth* very simplistically depicts the wealthy as bad and the poor as good. The only well-to-do character who seems actually to be in the moral camp of the poor is, not surprisingly, the narrator/author himself, for as soon as he hears about the strange case of al-Dubaysh he rushes to the village to investigate and meets extensively with the dead man's wife and friends. Toward the end of the novel he describes, with a mixture of sympathy and condescension, how the whole ordeal has affected him:

> I returned to Cairo. I spent many days not knowing what to do. I discovered that I could not write. I lost my previous satisfaction with all that I had ever written. The murder of al-Dubaysh is the sentence of one class against another. Their simple minds did not understand what this meant. . . . My pen refuses to write calm and neutral words that will please everyone. . . . I decided to write. To exit the conspiracy of silence that has hidden from sight all that has happened and all that is happening.[56]

Is there not something self-aggrandizing about al-Qa'id writing for himself such a heroic role, the role of the one well-to-do character in the novel who is able not only to make contact with the peasants but who chooses to champion their cause so enthusiastically? Tawfiq al-Hakim, on the other hand, presents a narrator[57] who has a much more complicated relationship with the country poor, a brave thing to do when the norm at the time was to romanticize the peasant.[58] It has become common to read this novel as an expression of al-Hakim's disdain for the peasant, as a kind of glimpse into the subconscious of the normally pastoral-leaning urban intellectual of the time. An alternate reading is to see it as a conscious expression of the artificiality of the construction of the modern nation.

The result of presenting a more multi-dimensional and ambiguous view of the peasant and of human relations in general is—perhaps paradoxically—that one is left with the feeling that al-Hakim's peasant is scrappy and obstinate compared to al-Qa'id's mostly pliant peasant, who is reliant on the patronizing concern and the pen of the city-slicker writer. While there are a few occasions in *Yahduth* where the peasants talk back or act up, they are generally depicted either as being docile or—if like al-Dubaysh they do attempt to stand up for themselves—dead. This is contrary to what we find in *Yawmiyat*, about which Selim comments, in the context of comparing its peasants to those of *Zaynab*:

> the peasant voices [in Zaynab] are hollow and obedient, while those of the sundry peasant characters that people al-Hakim's village are loud, insistent and critical, this forming a sharp counterpoint to the hegemonic discourse of the narrative Subject, who, like the industrious little mouse that shares his lonely room, can only silently and solitarily nibble away, with pen and ink, at a lived reality whose totality and larger meaning must escape him.[59]

If we substitute the novel *Yahduth* for *Zaynab* in this analysis, it remains, I believe, a valid statement.

By proposing that *Yawmiyat na'ib fi-l-aryaf* can be read as equally subversive of the traditional Western detective genre as is Yusuf al-Qa'id's *Yahduth fi Misr al-an*, and that in certain ways Tawfiq al-Hakim's treatment of peasants or his treatment of peasant/urbanite relations is more sophisticated or nuanced, I do not mean to say that Tawfiq al-Hakim's is necessarily the better book.[60] My emphasis lies elsewhere. What I hope this chapter challenges is the sometimes overly simplistic use of evolutionary or anthropomorphic metaphors in the writing of the history of modern Arabic literature.[61] The most common metaphor is that of the Arabic novel having developed like a human being, that is, that it contains all stages of life from infancy to maturity, often with the implicit or explicit assumption that the parent of this child is the Western novel. In his informative *An Overview of Modern Arabic Literature*, for example, Pierre Cachia includes al-Hakim's novel in a section entitled "The Novel in its Infancy."[62] Other section headings complete the metaphor: "The Novel Coming of Age" (113) and finally "The Novel at a Mature Stage."[63] Hilary Kilpatrick also uses the infancy-to-maturity metaphor in her "The Egyptian Novel from *Zaynab* to 1980," writing, for example, that:

> It is because Egyptians are now collaborating in the worldwide enterprise of the novel on the same terms as, for instance, the Latin

Americans, that I believe the Egyptian novel has now entered into its period of maturity. Of course, as time passes and new generations of novelists appear this period of maturity will acquire subdivisions, but the starting-point will remain the same.[64]

And, similarly:

It is a far cry from Haykal's *Zaynab* to Edwar al-Kharrat's *al-Zaman al-akhar*, but thanks to the abundance of material it is possible to explain, at least in some measure, the relationship between the restrained and rather conventional grandmother and her adventurous and unbridled grandchild.[65]

This is not to say that the Arab novel has not changed and that one cannot trace trends over time, but rather to challenge the implicit suggestion that the Arab novel developed in a linear fashion along lines similar to the development of the novel genre in the West. The general problem with this type of historiography is that it is ahistorical, for it assumes that the Arabic novel has developed along the same lines as the English novel without considering that the two are born of very different socio-economic and historical circumstances.[66]

An alternate reading of the novels of al-Hakim or al-Qaʿid studied here is that they do not subvert the Western detective genre as much as they participate in creating the Egyptian detective novel. In a sense, then, Elias Khoury may have been correct after all in stating that Arabic literature does not know detective fiction, if by that he was referring to the predominantly urban or, if rural, country-estate setting of that genre in the West.[67] Moreover, while it is true that Arab authors were and continue to be influenced by other literary traditions, and an analysis which compares novels across multiple traditions can provide new and thoughtful insights, to study the Arabic novel on its own terms and in its own contexts is equally important. I hope, finally, that this chapter challenges the tendency of literary historians to assume that the Arabic novel developed along later but neatly parallel lines to the Western novel, that its stages can be divided into a childhood, an adolescence, and then finally a coming of age, for if that were the case Tawfiq al-Hakim's *Yawmiyat naʾib fi-l-aryaf* must be seen as a very precocious child indeed.

Notes

1   This statement was made at a lecture given at Princeton University in the spring of 1996.

2   His full name is Muhammad Yusuf al-Qa'id (sometimes given as al-Qu'ayd), but most of his works are signed Yusuf al-Qa'id.

3   Fedwa Malti-Douglas writes that one of the distinguishing features of Yusuf al-Qa'id's narratives is their constant inferred and explicit references to the police novel. See her article "Yusuf al-Qa'id wa-l-riwaya al-jadida," *Fusul* 4, nos. 3–4 (1984): 91. Samah Selim calls *Yawmiyat na'ib fi-l-aryaf*, a 'whodunit' of sorts;" see her *The Novel and the Rural Imaginary in Egypt, 1880–1985* (London: Routledge and Curzon, 2004), 120. P. H. Newby, on the other hand, who introduces the English translation to *Yawmiyat*, writes:

> It has been said that *Maze of Justice* is a detective story. True, there is a murder and an investigation but the reader's expectations would be aroused in the wrong way if he thought he was in for a whodunit. He would become impatient of the incompetent way the investigation is carried out and its failure to name the culprit. It is not that sort of novel at all. It is about man's inhumanity to man and the murder investigation is just a way of tying the different elements of the diary together. (P. H. Newby, Foreword, in Tawfik al-Hakim, *Maze of Justice: Diary of a Country Prosecutor*, trans. Abba Eban [Austin: University of Texas Press, 1989], 9)

4   In his introduction to the fourth edition of *Yahduth fi Misr al-an*, for example, 'Ali al-Ra'i writes that the novel bears a "close resemblance" to *Yawmiyat na'ib fi-l-aryaf*; see the Foreword in *Yahduth fi Misr al-an* (Cairo: Dar al-Mustaqbal al-'Arabi, 1986), 13. And, based on interviews with Yusuf al-Qa'id, Salih 'Abd al-'Azim lists Tawfiq al-Hakim among a group of writers who "represent for him [al-Qa'id] an influence on his writings and his view of the countryside;" see Salih 'Abd al-'Azim *Susiyulujiya al-riwaya al-siyasiya. Yusuf al-Qa'id namudhajan* (Cairo: al-Hay'a al-Misriya al-'Amma li-l-Kitab, 1998), 189. And though she does not mention al-Qa'id by name, it would be hard to imagine him not being intended in the following statement by Samah Selim: "Subsequent generations of writers would consistently look back to the discursive iconoclasm of *Yawmiyat na'ib fi-l-aryaf* for new ways of writing the village." Samah Selim, "The Divided Subject: Narrative Enactments of the Nation in the Egyptian Village Novel" (PhD Diss., Columbia University, 1997), 89.

5   In a note on Tawfiq al-Hakim in the English translation to *Yawmiyat*, for example, Roger Hardy writes that "*Maze of Justice*, while universal in its appeal as a social comedy, is a product of this formative period of Egypt's [intellectual] development." Roger Hardy, "A Note on Tawfik al-Hakim," in al-Hakim, *Maze of Justice*, 13.

6   Malti-Douglas, "Yusuf al-Qa'id," 200.

7   Luwis 'Awad, for example, calls al-Qa'id's works a kind of "literary-novelistic investigation" *(tahqiq adabi riwa'i)*, whereas Naguib Mahfouz characterizes them as "political pamphlets" *(mulassaqat siyasiya)* (in 'Abd al-'Azim, *Susiyulujiya al-riwaya al-siyasiya*, 193.)

8   In his recent book on the experimental novel in the Levant, for example, Stefan
     Meyer posits: "the Arabic novel has followed a pattern of development that has
     echoed or paralleled the development of the Western novel, moving roughly from
     romanticism to realism to modernist experimentalism." See his *The Experimental
     Arabic Novel: Postcolonial Literary Modernism in the* Levant, SUNY series on Middle
     Eastern Studies (Albany: State University of New York Press, 2001), 5.

9   For detailed studies of this phenomenon see, for example, Selim, *The Novel and
     the Rural Imaginary*; 'Abd al-Muhsin Taha Badr, *al-Riwaya wa-l-ard* (Cairo: al-Hay'a
     al-Misriya al-'Amma li-l-ta'lif wa-l-Nashr, 1971); Muhammad 'Abd al-Ghani Hasan,
     al-Fallah fi-l-adab al-'arabi (Cairo: Dar al-Aqlam, 1965); and Suhayr al-Qalamawi,
     "al-Rif fi-l-riwaya wa-l-masrahiya," *al-Hilal*, Vol 6 (June 1966).

10   For the use of this term and its Arabic synonyms in regards to Arabic literature,
     see Elisabeth Kendall, "The Theoretical Roots of the Literary Avant-garde in
     1960s Egypt," *Edebiyat* 14, nos. 1–2 (2003): 29–56.

11   In addition to his many plays, essays and short stories, al-Hakim wrote five
     novels other than *Yawmiyat*, including *'Asfur min al-sharq* (Bird from the East,
     1938) and *'Awdat al-ruh* (The Return of the Spirit, 1933). See Hamdi al-Sakkut, *The
     Arabic Novel: Bibliography and Critical Introduction, 1865–1995*, 6 vols. (Cairo: The
     American University in Cairo Press, 2000), 4:2056. For information on al-Hakim's
     life and works see, for example, Mahmud Amin al-'Alim, *Tawfiq al-Hakim
     mufakkiran fannanan* (Cairo: Dar Shuhdi li-l-Nashr, 1985); Charles William Richard
     Long, *Tawfiq al-Hakim, Playwright of Egypt* (London: Ithaca Press, 1979); William
     Maynard Hutchins, *Tawfiq al-Hakim: a Reader's Guide*. Boulder, CO: Lynne Reiner
     Publishers, a Three Continents Book, 2003; 'Ali al-Ra'i, *Tawfiq al-Hakim: fann
     al-furja wa-fann al-fikr* (Cairo: Dar al-Hilal, 1969); Ghali Shukri, *Tawfiq al-Hakim:
     al-jil wa-l-tabaqa wa-l-ru'ya* (Beirut: Dar al-Farabi, 1993); and Paul Starkey, *From
     the Ivory Tower: A Critical Analysis of Tawfiq al-Hakim* (Oxford: Ithaca Press, 1987).
     As far as *Yawmiyat* itself is concerned, for an example of how it is considered
     to be his best work, see Pierre Cachia, "Idealism and Ideology: The Case of
     Tawfiq al-Hakim," *Journal of the American Oriental Society* 100, no. 3 (1980): 225–35.
     Al-Sakkut lists eighty-two Arabic books and articles and thirty-three texts in
     Western languages that study this novel to various extents; al-Sakkut, *The Arabic
     Novel*, 3:1656–65.

12   Some prefer the label *al-hasasiya al-jadida* (the new sensitivity), coined by Edwar
     al-Kharrat, about this generation. Other labels included *al-jil al-jadid* (the new
     generation) and *jil al-yawm* (today's generation) (Kendall, "Theoretical Roots,"
     40, 46).

13   For a comprehensive study of his novels through the seventies, see Starkey, *From
     the Ivory Tower*, 1993. Al-Qa'id has written close to twenty novels and a large
     number of short stories. His only widely available novel in English translation
     is *al-Harb fi barr Misr* (1978) (War in the Land of Egypt, 1986). His first novel,
     Akhbar min 'izbat al-Manisi, 1971, was translated as *News from the Meneisi Farm*
     in Egypt in 1987. This lack of translation may be because, as had been noted
     by Janine Abboushi Dallal among others, Western publishing houses have not

shown much interest in the Arab novel that experiments with form but rather have been attracted to works that reinforce stereotypes about the region. See her article "The Perils of Occidentalism: How Arab Novelists are Driven to Write for Western Readers," *Times Literary Supplement*, April 24, 1998, 8–9. Al-Sakkut lists sixteen articles and books in Arabic that deal with *Yahduth*; the English list, at just three works, is much shorter (*The Arabic Novel*, 3: 1645–46). For an account of the difficulties al-Qaʿid had in publishing *Yahduth*, see Marina Stagh, *The Limits of Freedom of Speech: Prose Literature and Prose Writers in Egypt under Nasser and Sadat* (Stockholm: Almqvist and Wiksell International, 1993).

14   Malti-Douglas, "Yusuf al-Qaʿid," 191. For information on the *nouveau roman* movement in France, see Jean Ricardou, *Le nouveau roman: suivi de Les raisons de l'ensemble* (Paris: Seuil, 1990) or Arthur E. Babock, *The New Novel in France: Theory and Practice of the Nouveau Roman* (New York: Twayne, 1997).

15   Malti-Douglas, "Yusuf al-Qaʿid," 191.

16   Ibid., 191.

17   Ibid., 197.

18   Ibid., 198.

19   Ibid., 195.

20   Ibid., 195.

21   Yusuf al-Qaʿid, *Yahduth fi Misr al-an* (Cairo: Dar al-Mustaqbal al-ʿArabi, 1986), 26–27.

22   Ibid., 25.

23   Ibid., 25.

24   Ibid., 144.

25   Ibid., 47.

26   Malti-Douglas, "Yusuf al-Qaʿid," 194.

27   Al-Qaʿid, *Yahduth fi Misr al-an*, 19.

28   ʿMalti-Douglas, "Yusuf al-Qaʿid," 194. ʿAli al-Raʿi, on the other hand, seems to take the invitation at face value. He writes in his introduction to the novel that al-Qaʿid "invites them [the readers] to participate in the writing of the novel, benefiting from improvisation and audience participation, techniques used by the theater to connect the people with the events of the work of art." ʿAli al-Raʿi, "Foreword" to Yusuf al-Qaʿid, *Yahduth fi Misr al-an*. Cairo: Dar al-Mustaqbal al-ʿArabi, 1986, 9–13.

29   Ibid., 57.

30   Malti-Douglas, "Yusuf al-Qaʿid," 194.

31   This is not to say, of course, that the reading of this or any other text is a passive act, as Roland Barthes reminds us in *S/Z*. Barthes writes, for example: "I read the text. This statement...is not always true. The more plural the text, the less it is written before I read it." Roland Barthes, *S/Z*, trans. Richard Miller (New York: Hill and Wang, 1994), 10.

32   al-Qaʿid, *Yahduth fi Misr al-an*, 19.

33   Ibid., 19.

34   This policy was an effort by the Egyptian president Sadat to invigorate the Egyptian economy by liberalizing investment policy after the tightly state-controlled

economy of the Nasser years. Many feel that this policy resulted in the widening of the gap between the wealthy and the poor.

35 'Abd al-'Azim, *Susiyulujiya al-Riwaya al-Siyasiya*, 195.

36 al-Ra'i, "Foreword" to *Yahduth fi Misr al-an*, 9.

37 al-Qa'id, *Yahduth fi Misr al-an*, 88–89.

38 Ibid., 35.

39 Ibid., 163.

40 Ibid., 6.

41 Malti-Douglas, "Yusuf al-Qa'id," 194.

42 al-Qa'id, *Yahduth fi Misr al-an*, 165.

43 Ibid., 154.

44 This is an interesting reversal of the situation one usually finds in both fiction and non-fiction on Egypt. Both Timothy Mitchell, in his *Colonising Egypt*, and Yahya al-Tahir 'Abd Allah in his *al-Tawq wa-l-iswara* (1975) comment on how peasants would do almost anything to avoid military service, even self-mutilation. Mitchell, in fact, describes a whole nineteenth-century Egyptian Army brigade being made up of conscripts who had attempted to maim themselves enough to avoid service. See his *Colonising Egypt* (Berkeley: University of California Press, 1988), 42. Yusuf al-Qa'id also seems to have more than a fleeting interest in this subject as his *al-Harb fi barr Misr* revolves around a village headman who coerces his head guard into sending his son to the army in his own son's stead, with the tragic result that the guard's son dies. And, if that were not a bitter enough pill to swallow, the village headman, in a classic piece of Qa'idian irony, collects the payout that is given to the families of soldiers who die in battle.

45 Selim, *The Novel and the Rural Imaginary*, 119–20.

46 Ibid., 120.

47 Tawfiq al-Hakim, *Yawmiyat na'ib fi-l-aryaf*. Cairo: Multazim al-Tab'a wa-l-Nashr, n.d. 8.

48 Selim takes up the issue of the primacy usually granted to *Zaynab*: "Muhammad Husayn Haykal's pastoral romance, *Zaynab* is most often identified as the first fully constructed, authentic Egyptian novel. Recently however, scholars have begun to acknowledge significant narrative antecedents such as Muhammad Tahir Haqqi's incendiary *'Adhra' Dinshaway* (The Maiden of Dinshaway, 1906) and Mahmud Khayrat's pair of novellas, *Fata Misri/Fatat Misriya* (An Egyptian Youth ([m./f.], 1903-1905)—all of which explicitly deal with the life of the Egyptian village." Selim, "The Divided Subject," 22.

49 Ibid., 23.

50 Abd al-'Azim, *Susiyulujiya al-riwaya al-siyasiya*, 86–87.

51 Al-Qa'id, *Yahduth fi Misr al-an*, 145.

52 Al-Hakim, *Yawmiyat*, 64–67.

53 Ibid., 88–91, 142.

54 Selim, *The Novel and the Rural Imaginary*, 120.

55 Al-Hakim, *Yawmiyat*, 166.

56 Al-Qa'id, *Yahduth fi Misr al-an*, 171–72.

57 Though al-Hakim never names the narrator as himself, because of the parallels

between their two lives, the identity of the two has often been conflated, as Fatma Moussa-Mahmoud writes: "The author draws on his experience as a district attorney in the provinces and the readers find it difficult to discriminate between fact and fiction concerning the narrator himself." See her contribution to Roger Allen, ed., *Modern Arabic Literature* (New York: Ungar, 1987), 119.

58 Selim writes: "If *Zaynab* is the canonical Egyptian national romance, reprinted in the decades after the Second World War to inspire successive generations of young nationalists, Tawfiq al-Hakim's 1937 novel, *Maze of Justice*, can be read as a brilliant parody of Haykal's imperfect utopia." Selim, *The Novel and the Rural Imaginary*, 117. Elsewhere she writes: "There is precious little natural description in *Diary of a Country Prosecutor*—a notable omission considering the contemporary vogue for it (also evident in al-Hakim's earlier novel, *The Return of the Spirit*). *Diary of a Country Prosecutor* must consequently be marked as a pointed anti-pastoral." Selim, "The Divided Subject," 83n.

59 Ibid., 83.

60 I also do not mean to suggest that the peasant was always thus depicted in the writings of al-Hakim. For a discussion of the contrast between the peasant in *Yawmiyat* and *'Awdat al-ruh* (The Return of the Spirit, 1933), see Selim, "The Divided Subject," 80.

61 Selim discusses this phenomenon at length in a recent article on the formation of the Arabic literary canon. She points out that this orientalist discourse has been adopted by critics writing in Arabic as well. See her "The Narrative Craft: Realism and Fiction in the Arabic canon," *Edebiyat* 14, nos. 1–2 (2003): 109–28. An example of such discourse can be found, for example, in the title of Yahya Haqqi's *Fajr al-qissa al-Misriya* (The Dawn of the Egyptian Story, 1975).

62 Pierre Cachia, *An Overview of Modern Arabic Literature* (Edinburgh: Edinburgh University Press, 1990), 112.

63 Ibid., 113, 117.

64 Hilary Kilpatrick, "The Egyptian Novel from *Zaynab* to 1980," in M. M. Badawi, ed., *Modern Arabic Literature* (Cambridge: Cambridge University Press), 259.

65 Ibid., 223. This mode is not reserved for the novel. Here is Sabry Hafez on the Egyptian short story: "The arrival of Lashin on the Egyptian literary scene in the 1920s marked a turning point in the history of the short story: he was an outstandingly vigorous pioneer who developed the genre and brought its formative years to a close." Sabry Hafez, "The Maturation of a New Literary Genre," *International Journal of Middle East Studies* 16 (1984): 367.

66 On the English detective novel's temporary relocation to the countryside, see Raymond Williams, *The Country and the City* (New York: Oxford University Press, 1973), 249–50.

67 For two recent critiques of traditional historiography of the Arab novel and of the implications of the different historical circumstances in which it was born, see Selim, "Narrative Craft," and Hosam Aboul-Ela, "Writer, Text, and Context: the Geohistorical Location of the Post-48 Arabic Novel," *Edebiyat* 14, nos. 1–2 (2003): 5–19.

14

The Anti-Romance Antidote:
Revisiting Allegories of the Nation*

Mara Naaman

Introduction

By way of a point of departure, I would like to insert myself into a somewhat dated, but no less relevant literary debate of the mid-eighties. Aijaz Ahmad, in his response to Fredric Jameson's well-circulated 1986 article, "Third-World Literature in the Era of Multinational Capitalism,"[1] raises several points that deserve reconsideration for comparatists today. The debate centers around the sweeping arguments asserted by Jameson in his attempt to advocate for the integration of third world literatures into Western conceptions of canonized fiction.

Among his many comments, Jameson points out that one of the key differences between first world and third world literatures is the allegorical nature of the latter. Most non-Western fictions, he argues, are constructed as national allegories,[2] unlike "western realist and modernist novels" whose structures serve to reflect the capitalist culture from which they emerge. In Western fiction, this consistently results in "a radical split between private and public, between the poetic and the political, between what we have come to think of as the domain of sexuality and the unconscious and that of the public world of classes, of the economic, and of secular political power ... "[3] Jameson points to the limitations in Western fictions by arguing that allegorical mapping has been "discredited" by the West, resulting in a private sphere that is never viewed as doubling for a more political one (or at least not overtly) and that the domain of the public and economic never mirrors that of the sexual or unconscious. While he acknowledges the reductive and sweeping nature of such a line of argumentation, he also seems very much committed to taking his argument one step further. On the one hand, he posits that such discontinuities between domains in first world literature cut off the Western intellectual[4] from imagining him- or herself as a political subject in a larger political body. On the other hand, the third-world intellectual is always, in his formulation, a political intellectual because the act of writing for him or her is always a political act. The first-world intellectual is forever "crippled" by his "view from the top" and thus incapable of "grasping the social totality."[5]

In Hegelian terms, Jameson reminds us that the Western intellectual knows only the "truth of the Master" and, as a result, is forever removed from any true materialistic consciousness of his situation. What is problematic about this position for me is not so much his critique of the Western intellectual (whoever this unspecific category may refer to), or even his narrow reading of Third World texts as predominately allegorical (the heterogeneous nature of the many postcolonial works now in circulation is testament to the contrary); rather, it is Jameson's lack of tribute to any of the Western writers of the twentieth century, even aside from women and minorities, who have conceived of themselves for years as agents for change (or a moral conscience of sorts) and have infused their work with a keen sensitivity to the plight of the disenfranchised within first-world locations.[6]

In a fitting response, Aijaz Ahmad, in his essay "Jameson's Rhetoric of Otherness,"[7] points to the weaknesses in Jameson's hypothesis. While he spends much of the article debunking Jameson's absolutist typologies (that is, Third World Theory, First World Literature, Western Literature, Third World Literature, etc.) and clarifying the contradictions in his generalizations, he points out, at the close of the essay, the ways in which this method of allegorizing the nation has long been used by women and minorities within a first world, particularly U.S., context. From within the space of these literatures, there does not exist a radical division of the public and private or the poetic and the political. Rather, these more marginal literatures have employed many of the same techniques as their third world counterparts to *rewrite* or *reconstruct* what we might call a U.S. national narrative. Here it is crucial to add to Ahmad's examples those authors who have been committed to U.S. stories of labor or working-class fictions whose works also serve as revisionist allegories of the nation.[8] In this discussion, I hope to illustrate through an examination of two works, one Egyptian, one American, Ahmad's thesis that civilizational alterity does not exist as such along global lines. That is to say, the Egyptian is not the American's civilizational "Other." By way of conclusion Ahmad writes:

> I point out these obvious determinations of Jameson's text for three
> reasons. One is to strengthen my proposition that the ideological
> conditions of a text's production are never singular but always
> several. Second, even if I were to accept Jameson's division of the
> globe into three worlds, I would still have to insist, as my references
> not only to feminism and Black Literature but to Jameson's own
> location would indicate, that there is right here, within the belly of
> the First World's global postmodernism, a veritable Third World,
> perhaps two or three of them. Third, I want to insist that within the
> unity that has been bestowed upon our globe by the irreconcilable
> struggle between capital and labor, there are more and more texts
> which cannot easily be placed within this or that world. Jameson's
> is not a First World text; *mine* is not a Third World text. We are not
> each other's civilizational Others.[9]

What Ahmad so skillfully does here, and what I would like to explore further in this paper, is to show how first world or Western authors are, by necessity, also political actors whose works are not mere meditations on individuality and "private subjectivity" as concluded by Jameson, but reflect an awareness of the "social totality," resisting what Jameson describes as the "structural idealism which affords us the luxury of the Sartrean blink." In other words, as Jameson might have it, having reduced our literary output to a self-referential, aesthetic expression of our existential and Freudian angst, we, as Western writers, have obliterated the possibility of understanding our material reality relationally.[10] This described form of social myopia, I hope to argue, does not fairly characterize the whole of contemporary Western writing nor does this manner of situating diverse literary output into juxtaposing globes do justice to the parallels and overlaps that characterize the relationship between these traditions.

I would like to consider Latifa al-Zayyat's work *The Open Door (al-Bab al-maftuh)*[11] insofar as it is an example of a text whose structure is allegorical, linking the plight of the individual character to that of the nation. This work is at once a traditional, virtually formulaic romance that may be read allegorically as a kind of foundational fiction chronicling the birth of an independent Egypt. To further illustrate the validity of Ahmad's argument, I will analyze in comparison Mary Karr's two-part memoir *The Liar's Club*[12] and *Cherry*[13] in an attempt to present this work as an example of a revisionist, subaltern U.S. national narrative. Her work, which is very similar in some respects to that of al-Zayyat, seems to offer the anti-romance as a reflection of the bankruptcy of U.S. foundational mythologies. In other words, while al-Zayyat's work challenges traditional representations of female subjectivity, and is a feminist text in every respect, it undermines its own intentions by falling prey to a formulaic schema where "requited love is the foundational moment" for the birth of the nation.[14] This ultimate outcome, of course, only reifies the traditional valuing of women as mothers and wives, despite the protagonist's strong-willed determination to actualize herself as a liberated woman.

Here, on the level of plot, echoing the earlier work of Mahmud Tahir Haqqi,[15] Egypt as a nation is configured as a woman through the protagonist Layla (the conventional woman as object-figure).[16] The consummation of her love for Husayn comes to represent the coming together of both national and libidinal aspirations and marks the founding moment of an independent Egypt. More specifically, as Elliott Colla has pointed out, it is really only on the level of character and dialogue (that is, not through plot) that al-Zayyat "argues for a new—and recognizably feminist—figuration of woman as subject-figure."[17] Similarly, Karr's fictional memoir also tells the story of the nation through the personal by offering an edgy chronicle of her coming-of-age in a poverty-stricken family in Texas during the sixties and seventies. Thus this feminist work, written from the underbelly of the first world and replete with doomed love affairs, marriages, and predatory men, serves as a critique that threatens the stable, bourgeois nation-building impulses underwritten in other U.S. romantic fictions. This point will be taken up in greater detail later in the paper.

The Open Door as National Romance

Latifa al-Zayyat's *The Open Door*, published in 1960, may be considered a form of historical romance novel. Traditionally considered her *magnum opus*, this work narrates the coming of age of the young protagonist Layla alongside the burgeoning nationalist stirrings in Egypt during the 1940s and 1950s. Marilyn Booth, in her introduction to the English translation (from which I will be quoting), points to what she considers the revolutionary aspects of this work. She writes:

> Al-Zayyat's novel, which on the surface of it seems to participate fully and unequivocally in a realist approach to social critique, pointed to some of the ways in which the Arabic novel would develop away from that approach. The Open Door did so by privileging and interweaving two kinds of marginality, one social and one literary: the first, putting a female perspective at the center, within a context of family and community; the second, using everyday rather than literary diction.[18]

Thus to categorize this work as a romance is not to take away from its value as a crafty piece of social criticism; however, it does limit, on some level, the extent to which we can view this work as feminist (despite the fact that it would have been considered bold to construct a novel around a female protagonist in the late 1950s/early 1960s in Egypt). All the same, it must be noted that *The Open Door* was al-Zayyat's first novel and was written early in her career. In her later autobiographical works, *al-Shaykhukha wa qisas ukhra* (*Old Age and Other Stories*, 1986) and *Hamlat taftish: awraq shakhsiya* (*The Search: Personal Papers*, 1992) al-Zayyat experiments with form/formlessness and narrative voice.[19] In no way do these later works resemble the romantic formula of her first text, and in many respects they are more "ground-breaking," to use Marlé Hammond's word, as a result. However, while *al-Bab al-maftuh* will never resemble the formalistic complexity of al-Zayyat's later narratives and often indulges in moments of unbearable melodrama, the text, overall, is entertaining and engages us politically, most likely accounting for its appeal among Egyptians.

Such an obvious dissonance between the feminist nature of the text and the more conventional romantic overtones of the work are apparently quite common for readers of romance fiction. The critic Janice

Radway points to this contradiction in her work *Reading the Romance*, which examines a variety of commerical romance novels and the practice of romance reading from a combined literary and sociological perspective.[20] After interviewing an avid romance reader named Dot, Radway notes the following:

> At first glance, Dot's incipient feminism seems deeply at odds
> with her interest in a literary form whose ultimate message, one
> astute observer has noted, is that "pleasure for women is men." The
> traditionalism of romance fiction will not be denied here, but it is
> essential to point out that Dot and many of the writers and readers of
> romances interpret these stories as chronicles of female triumph. . . .
> Dot believes a good romance focuses on an intelligent and able
> heroine who finds a man who recognizes her special qualities and is
> capable of loving and caring for her as she wants to be loved. Thus
> Dot understands such an ending to say that female independence
> and marriage are compatible rather than mutually exclusive. The
> romances she most values and recommends for her readers are those
> with "strong," "fiery" heroines who are capable of "defying the hero,"
> softening him and showing him the value of loving and caring for
> another.[21]

Zayyat's *The Open Door* fits this formula almost exactly. The protagonist Layla is hardly a demure, obedient young woman. She internally questions the conventions of her middle-class Egyptian life and outwardly seeks to challenge them. For example, she speaks of womanhood as a kind of prison of which fathers and brothers are wardens and women are prisoners. Layla comes to understand this early in her adolescence: "she grew to the realization that to reach womanhood was to enter a prison where the confines of one's life were clearly and decisively fixed. At its door stood her father, her brother, and her mother. Prison life, she discovered, is painful for both the warden and the woman he imprisons."[22] Layla, aware of her own intellectual abilities and physical prowess, naturally seeks to question the prison to which she has been assigned merely based on her gender. She rebels against these limitations and resists her fated role as wife and mother. Still, all the while the novel pivots around her love interests, her admiring suitors, and the one man who eventually seems destined to convince her of her socially 'liberated' self and her fated union with him; that is, the engineer Husayn, part of the engineering team assigned to design the High Dam in Aswan. While the book might be considered a kind of meditation on the role of desire and love in a socially conservative middle-class Egyptian environment, it reaffirms many status quo ideas about the power of love as a liberatory and patriotic impulse, conquering traditional family mores and societal notions of marriage as the vehicle for social mobility. This reflects Sommer's notion that love or erotic passion, in some 'pure' form, often functions as a revolutionary impulse or, as she puts it, serves as "the cure to the pathology of social sterility," exploding the backwardness and constraints of the loveless marriage.[23] This latter point will be explored in greater detail later.

Allegorically speaking, this novel is at once the story of Layla coming into her own, the story of Egypt realizing her independence, and the story of true love realized on the soil of the newly emancipated nation. Thus this work functions both as romance and as a founding fiction for an independent Egypt. Doris Sommer explores the idea that while many of these romances may very well be interwoven into the rhetoric of nation building (that is, what Jameson has called "national allegories"), many of them "have no preexisting and eternal referentiality;" in other words, they are each other's effect or, as she puts it, "*Eros* and *Polis* are the effects of each other's performance" and produce themselves.[24] Love becomes a patriotic and erotic impulse at once and is heightened and made more urgent because of this doubling.

Both intrigues, then—that is, heteronormative love for another and love for country (and in this case also self-love)—facilitate the tension that escalates through the novel, making each of their purposes codependent on the outcome of the other. It does not matter, for example, that October 1956 did not mark a military victory for Egypt (as it is ambiguously portrayed at the close of al-Zayyat's work); rather, what matters is that it was, as Booth has noted, "a defining moment for the nation" and Nasser's political victory. Thus Layla's realization of her role and power as a patriotic freedom fighter occurs in horizontal time with her realization of her romantic destiny with Husayn and the glorious future awaiting an independent Egypt. For example, al-Zayyat depicts the famous Port Said battle in the final pages of her novel. She writes of this defining moment for Layla:

Before her eyes flashed the image of herself pushing forward onto the battlefield, the enemy retreating in front of her. She must, she must see the enemy retreat from Port Said. And she could. She could do anything. Nothing seemed impossible no. She jumped up from her bed excitedly, her eyes blazing. . . . She stopped right in the middle of the room, her eyes gazing forward, shining as if she had just seen the most beautiful of visions and had heard a voice calling. She turned, her arms out, and called, "Husayn." . . . But Husayn was with her, as he had never before been, as if he had suddenly become a reality, a tangible presence to which she could extend her grasp, a presence she could embrace.[25]

Here Layla comes to realize not only her undying commitment to the nation, but also the reality of her love for Husayn. Despite the obstacles that had prevented the lovers from coming together prior (namely, her engagement to Professor Ramzi, Husayn's engineering fellowship in Germany, and Layla's resignation to follow her family's wishes for her to marry up the social ladder), in the mayhem of the battle at Port Said, it all becomes clear to Layla. Sommer points to this as another example of the way "desire doubles itself at personal and political levels." She shows how the desire of the lovers to consummate their love and be together escalates alongside the construction of the nation. Of Latin American romances that follow the same prototype she writes:

What I find ingenious, indeed brilliant, about this novel productivity is that one libidinal investment ups the ante for the other. And every obstacle that the lovers encounter heightens more than their mutual desire to (be a) couple, more than our voyeuristic keenly felt passion; it also heightens their/our love for the possible nation in which the affair could be consummated.[26]

Here Egypt becomes the only site on which a conjugal union can be actualized, and conversely, this very union seems to reify the idea of a state beholden to her population engaged in Sommer's "patriotic passions," passions that inevitably must turn into state-sanctioned marriages. This is nowhere so evident as in Husayn's letters to Layla, which express the blurring of his desire for his country with that of his desire for her: "For you have become a symbol for all I love in my nation. When I think of Egypt,

I think of you; when I long for Egypt, I long for you. And to be honest, I never stop longing for Egypt."[27]

And yet, as neatly as this structural mapping works, al-Zayyat's novel can be read allegorically on multiple levels, not all of them in keeping with the formula of the national romance. For example, the notion of social mobility as reflective of the aspirations of the middle class is very much tied to Egypt's bourgeois vision of her own prosperous future. As further depicted in Sonallah Ibrahim's *Tilka al-ra'iha* and Mahfouz's *Cairo Trilogy*, the movements of Cairo's middle class (their bourgeois desires and passive acceptance of the class system) form the basis of Egypt's national character. The character of Dawlat Hanim (Layla's aunt) in al-Zayyat's work embodies this residual Victorian sensibility. After one of her daughters commits suicide because she is not allowed out of an unhappy marriage, Dawlat Hanim, unfazed, insists that her second daughter, Gamila, also marry for security over love. Layla observes, "she would fling an offhand comment in Gamila's direction, about so-and-so, that girl who'd married for love but then failed in her marriage, because after all material security was the foundation for every successful union."[28] In a more materialist variation of the national allegory, such a comment might reinscribe the notion that the establishment of a truly bourgeois citizenry marks the foundation of a successful nation. In such a reading, all libidinal energies (for the woman and man alike) are vested in the upward climb toward social mobility and the attainment of a husband (or wife, for that matter) with recognized status and capital. Such mobility would parallel, of course, the modernizing, Westernizing impulses of the fledgling Egyptian nation stepping into her own with class hierarchies mirroring those in the West.

Yet al-Zayyat does not allow her protagonist to accept Dawlat Hanim's imposed social norms. Rather, she contests them and actively challenges them in the novel. Layla, especially early in her adolescence, finds such notions of a materially secure domesticity as the very cause for the unraveling of female subjectivity and ambition. Such pacification is what she fears the most, as she finds it also a threat to the concept of true love; thus, she clings to her bold love for Egypt as a sign of her unique sense of self and her belief that some man may also recognize such unique selfhood. In the following passage, for example, she rejects the system of bondage inherited by the women of her mother's generation and in so doing critiques Gamila's decision to marry Ali Bey for his money:

It's no joke, Adila, . . . Are you just like your mother? Do you think exactly the way she does? Your mother married without love because she could not do anything else. She wasn't in a position to choose. And anyway, if she had chosen, she wouldn't have been able to marry the man she chose. Our mothers were the harem—things possessed by their fathers, who passed them on to husbands. But us?—we don't have any excuses. Education—we've gotten that, and we understand everything, and we are the ones who have to decide our own futures. Even animals choose their mates![29]

Zayyat brilliantly offers a critique of the way in which notions of class, gender roles, and social caste are entrenched in patriarchal conceptions of the family and the family's future. In so doing, she challenges parallel national allegories that would suggest the dream of Egypt is grounded in bourgeois notions of social mobility and the maintenance of middle-class, status quo values.[30] Egypt's future, in this schema, lies in the hands of the young middle-class couple, Layla and Husayn, who presumably will cast off the yoke of traditional gender roles as pioneering lovers in uncharted social terrain—just as Egypt, newly emancipated, must step up to her position as the vanguard nation in the Arab world.

The Liar's Club and Cherry as the Anti-Romance

The Liar's Club and the subsequent Cherry chronicle Mary Karr's childhood and adolescence growing up in a dysfunctional, 'white-trash' home in Leechfield, Texas. Like al-Zayyat, Karr tells the history of America through the eyes of a young girl struggling to come into her own and break out of the provincial Leechfield worldview. It is the story of the lives and obstacles facing America's working poor and the way such a position of lack reverberates in the quotidian lives of women. To use Ferial Ghazoul's term, this work is in every sense a subaltern autobiography[31] chronicling the history of rural poverty. Grounding her narrative in the music, TV shows, neighborhood personalities, and family battles emblematic of her childhood, Karr provides an alternative cultural and social history of America. Such a work might also fall under the rubric of what Michael Denning calls an American "proletarian literature," exploring the relationship between class and national identity, that is, rewriting the twentieth century labor-narrative from the point of view of a white female.[32]

To further contest Jameson, Karr's work is no less political than al-Zayyat's work in its ability to bring into relief the way the personal is very much part of the larger telling of the body *polis*—an American memoir as allegory of the nation. Not only does Karr achieve this through her prideful rendering of her home life, but she also shows the way a female's body is a political space, a space that wields power and also may be violated and exploited (Zayyat depicts the female body along similar lines). Her exploration of the multiple forms of violation that occur in this work reiterate the unsuspecting ways in which patriarchy and male hegemony continue to manifest themselves in the gendered tapestry of the U.S. national narrative.

On another level, this work is a kind of anti-romance. Not only does it undermine traditional idealizations of family, but it also illustrates the way in which the ideal state-sanctioned conjugal unit is a sham, essentially a way of institutionalizing disorder and dysfunction. Karr depicts her mother's marriage to her father as a desperate decision to cling to something that would give her a sense of place and identity outside of the mainstream (where she felt she couldn't belong). Thus marriage, in this formulation is less the climax of romantic tension and more a vision of a couple whose lives, for different reasons, did not fit into the mainstream narrative of the fifties. She writes:

> At my parents' wedding in the Leechfield Town Hall, Daddy concluded the ceremony by toasting Mother with the silver flask she'd bought him for a present. "Thank you for marrying poor old me," he said. He was used to carhops and cowgirls, and said Mother represented a new and higher order creature altogether.

The truth seems to be that Mother married Daddy at least in part because she'd gotten scared. As much as she liked to brag about being an art student in Greenwich Village during the war—and believe me, in Leechfield she stood out—she had racked up a frightening number of husbands, so frightening that she did her best to keep them secret. And her economic decline had been steady: over fifteen years she'd gone from a country house in Connecticut to a trailer park in Leechfield. Somehow all of her wildness didn't wash in the anesthetized fifties. She'd lost some things along the way and losing things scared her.[33]

In her gritty retelling of her life, Karr illustrates how her own perceptions of romance are shaped by the embittered experiences of her mother, a thrice-married artist who struggles throughout her childhood with alcoholism and manic depression. Her father, an oil worker with Gulf Oil in Texas, is a fairly mild-mannered blue-collar worker who has a knack for storytelling—making up tall tales (or telling lies) to a group of men at the local bar, a group Karr comes to call "The Liar's Club." Frequent labor strikes and union meetings, resulting in a generally inconsistent income, punctuate her father's on-again off-again work. Just as al-Zayyat writes of womanhood as a kind of prison sentence, Karr similarly writes of her mother and father's marriage commitment as another form of prison sentence to which they were both bound:

> Mother threatened divorce a lot of times, and Daddy's response to it
> was usually a kind of patient eye-rolling. He never spoke of divorce
> as an option. If I asked him worried questions about a particularly
> nasty fight, he'd just say I shouldn't talk bad about my mother, as
> if even suggesting they might split up insulted her somehow. In his
> world, only full-blown lunatics got divorced. Regular citizens in a bad
> marriage just hunkered down and stood it.[34]

While her parent's bond is certainly not depicted as bereft of love or passion, it is consistently threatened with rupture by alcohol consumption, violent fights, and economic hardship. Her father's willful commitment to bear out the difficulty lasts only a short while, as Karr's mother eventually decides to move the family to Colorado without him. A few years later they divorce.

For Karr, romance is understood through her own youthful libidinal impulses and those imposed on her by other young and older men.[35] Like Layla, she fabricates images of romantic interludes and connection, but for her these result in only affirming her aloneness. She is candid and explicit in her language, using coarse and vulgar descriptions to capture the banality of the male libido in the face of female desire. For example she writes of her experience with a college boy:

> Soon after you make love, you curl in the fetal posture in the narrow
> bed and fake sleep for hours, staring at the luminous dial of the

roommate's clock face. Once you think Phil's breathing deep and slow enough, you slink into the bathroom downstairs—on the girls' floor—with your ragged copy of *Anna Karenina*. You sit on the cold tiles in your sweatshirt and shorts and have just begun to ponder the lunkheadedness of the cuckolded husband when Phil appears in the doorway. He looks tousled and fond. He wants to make love again, and you swear to yourself that on future nights you'll lie still till dawn rather than risk these additional ministrations.

Once you're home, Phil sends flowers—a box of peach-colored gladioli. The florist's card with its calligraphy birthday wish contains a vow from him to love you forever. Your mother grinds up aspirin with a spoon back to mix in the water, to keep the blooms fresh. But the phone rings, so she forgets, and you just wipe the powder off the countertop with a sour sponge.[36]

In describing the national romance, Sommer remarks that the obstacles placed on the couple by society and the inchoate nation serve to "invest the love story with a sublime sense of transcendent purpose." In Karr, such transcendent romance is non-existent. She leaves out any trace of sentimentality in her scenes depicting male–female love. This undermines any romantic undercurrents and refashions a nation of broken families and soured love stories. To problematize Sommer, if allegorically speaking *Eros* is not the effect of *Polis* and vice versa—in other words, if the conventional founding mythologies of the nation cannot be reflected in the ideal conjugal union here—then Karr's gut-wrenching realism seems to suggest, like many who have come before her, that American national allegories reflect more about the undoing and demystification of foundational mythologies than they serve any underlying patriotic impulse. For example, the majority of American classic novels work to dislodge and unearth the contradictions underwriting patriotic ideals and notions of an American Dream.[37] Even the great American national romances like Margaret Mitchell's *Gone With the Wind* and F. Scott Fitzgerald's *The Great Gatsby* offer tragic endings. Thus, unlike the style of French and English national romances or Latin American types as suggested by Sommer,[38] the American literary coupling of *Eros* and *Polis* has, in a sense, been left undone, deliberately subverting the possibility for twentieth-century nationalist rhetoric to ground itself squarely in erotics.[39]

In *The Liar's Club*, TV shows like *I Love Lucy* and *Leave it to Beaver* constitute standards for normative bourgeois life that position Leechfield and Karr's family in stark contrast. Such notions of Americanness are further perpetuated by images of Jackie Kennedy and Jayne Mansfield. In contrast to al-Zayyat who uses the personal as a way to position her protagonist in the center of historical events, Karr shows how many of these events constituted the silent periphery of her adolescence. She writes the following:

> Anyway, while Lecia was trying to spit in my eye, Mother was driving
> across the Texas desert in Grandma's old Impala, heading from
> the hospital in Houston to Lubbock and the funeral. She says that
> she wore her black Chanel suit with Grandma's beige-and-ivory
> cameo, which her great-grandmother had brought from Ireland. She
> also wore pearl earrings, and a white pillbox hat of the type Jackie
> Kennedy had on when her husband was shot. (It is a sad commentary
> on the women of my family that we can recite whole wardrobe
> assemblages from the most minor event in detail, but often forget
> almost everything else . . .).[40]

Unlike Layla, who viewed her identity as very much bound to the burgeoning nation, Karr's world is inhabited, at least to some extent, by anti-establishment personalities. Such oppositional positions are heightened at the close of her memoir *Cherry* when the police arrest her best friend's brother for his affiliation with SDS, the Students for a Democratic Society (thought by the FBI to be linked to the Communist Weathermen of the mid-seventies). His subsequent imprisonment and Karr's own brief run-in with the police for drug use serves as one of the climaxes of the work: it is only here, when her narrative intersects with the fixity of the state, that Karr seems to realize the way her own subjectivity had developed oppositionally:

> Before the arrest, you believed neither brutality nor tedium in any
> measure could break you, for citizens of your region receive black
> belts in bearing up under both. There's some contrary regional pride
> in withstanding it all. Some kids leave elite prep schools like St. Paul's
> or Choate with entry into certain colleges, mastery of certain

protocols. In the same way, one leaves Leechfield with raw tales on which to dine out, a sense of having escaped, and the capacity for both pathos and pissed-off that would make for either an excellent nun or a fearless infantry soldier.[41]

While Karr's political consciousness is American in that it is grounded in a local, American reality, she hardly celebrates American ideals. Rather, she offers the reader an alternative vision of America, whereby her political consciousness makes her aware of her 'otherness,' her distance from a normative, status quo conception of a democratic, generous nation.

In this respect, however, Karr's work operates very much as a kind of national allegory where Leechfield (like Egypt for al-Zayyat) is the city with which Karr identifies; meanwhile, it is a city set geographically (and socially) apart from a mainstream center (if center is defined as the cultural and political establishment of the East Coast, or even the major metropolitan areas of Texas: Houston, Dallas, and Fort Worth). Thus if the national experience in Jameson's terminology can be said to operate centrally for the third-world intellectual, then we must also, in contrast to Jameson, consider its influence on first-world writers who view their lives as set apart or ineffectual in terms of the majority. Revising Jameson's reliance on the term 'nation,' we may embrace Ahmad's expanded definition of the nation as a "collectivity" or more generally a "community." With such a revision, Karr's national experience can be defined in relation to the small town of Leechfield. Her experiences of lack, poverty, and abuse may thus be viewed as 'national' experiences whereby her desire for personal actualization may also be interpreted as her desire to liberate and actualize Leechfield, to give voice and agency to a disenfranchised community. This motivation echoes, in many ways, Layla's identification with Egypt and her desire to rise alongside her idealized 'nation.' Here both the first-world and the third-world protaganist view their experiences as a critical part of the chronicling of the national experience. In this regard, the first-world writer shows us again that twentieth-century labor narratives do not necessarily offer a uniquely personal or overly psychologized first-world experience cut off from Jameson's "social totality." Karr's voice is the voice of an American majority, however silenced and shadowed it may be.

Conclusion

To be fair, Jameson recognizes that allegorical structures are not absent from first-world texts; however, he argues that they exist there on an unconscious level. Critiques of first-world hegemony and social myopia do occur in Western literature and film, but they must be teased out, as they are not overt to the same degree as found in third-world novels. It is this clumsy positioning of first-world writing against that of the third world that I have attempted to render as reductive and overly generalized. Through a close reading of two texts from disparate literary traditions, I have attempted to problematize and refute the "social and concrete gap" as proposed by Jameson. Both al-Zayyat's and Karr's works may be read as national allegories written from locations that are not unequivocally first or third worlds.[42] Both texts depict protagonists who struggle to realize themselves in locations that confine and limit them. For each of them, writing serves as the ultimate form of self-actualization. Where reading is their refuge from an unjust world of predatory men, writing becomes their self-selected escape—in essence, their means of living emancipated.[43] Layla muses:

> She had always wanted writing to be her profession; she wanted to
> give reign to her ideas, and to express the thoughts of those around
> her. She really had begun to write, and she had been told that she
> could write well. Even when she spoke, people noticed her meticulous
> powers of expression. One of her classmates had always been very
> enthusiastic whenever he heard her speak. "You must write," he would
> say. "You are a born writer." And she did write, and dreamed of the day
> when she would become a real writer.[44]

Of course, on some level, this transcendent notion of female self-actualization is eclipsed in al-Zayyat's work due to its melodramatic depiction of Layla's liberated destiny as bound to that of her submission to Husayn (who had all along seen her for who she *really* was). In this respect, Layla's ultimate pleasure, it would seem anyway, is finally reaching out to a man who loved Egypt as much as she. This once again affirms the aforementioned remark by a romance reader that so often, "pleasure for women is [still] men."

If we view al-Zayyat's work as squarely located in the genre of national romantic fictions, Karr's work then may be thought of as a response to the mythology of romance—a critique of the rhetoric of nationalism and the mythic bond of *Eros* and *Patria*. Still, one might argue that Karr's work offers a less orthodox romance in that *Cherry* celebrates the relationship of Mary to her closest friend Meredith, another Leechfield outcast with wild literary ideals. It is she who, like Husayn, at the close of the memoir helps Mary to see herself clearly, confidently:

> You're inside at the kitchen table wolfing cereal when she says, You
>   accomplished a great thing.
> And what would that be, Bwana? you ask, mouth full.
> You're your Same Self.
> The truth of this flickers past you gnatlike. For years you've felt only
>   half-done inside, cobbled together by paper clips, held intact
>   by gum wads and school paste. But something solid is starting
>   to assemble inside you. You say, I am my Same Self. That's not
>   nothing, is it?[45]

To read both of these works as romances, would, in my opinion, take away from the gritty realism of Karr's text that so lucidly critiques mainstream bourgeois notions of nationhood and Americanness. Furthermore, to read al-Zayyat's novel only as a romance would strip it of its value as an originary work of Egyptian, feminist writing grounded in the wit and cadence of Egyptian colloquial speech. What is clear, however, is that these works are hardly 'other' to each other; instead, they commonly seek to undermine traditional allegories of the nation, replacing them with sharp, critical representations of women's lives.

In short, these two works lend themselves to a comparative reading along the lines of what Edward Said might regard as their contrapuntal relationship. While different in terms of their cultural contexts, the marginality of their respective locations generates a similar sense of disenfranchisement for the protagonists (Egypt in the shadow of Europe and the U.S., Leechfield estranged from the social and cultural norms of the East Coast establishment). It is from this position of marginality that each author writes and desires to insert themselves into the historical teleology of the nation.

While numerous critics have offered comparative readings of Arabic works next to more traditionally recognized American classics (particularly those translated into Arabic, such as Hemmingway and Faulkner), few have examined the voices of fourth-world and minority authors whose issues and concerns often run parallel to those in third world locations.[46] In fact—and in this regard I am in agreement with Jameson—since Said's *Orientalism* and the rise of postcolonial studies, approaches to third-world literature (I am speaking for my part of Arabic literature specifically) have favored cultural differentiation as the dominant approach to literary analysis over a more humanistic universalism.[47] In other words, instead of seeking to examine the commonalities, overlaps, and differences between first- and third-world, or 'occidental' and 'oriental' texts, postcolonial scholarship treating contemporary Arabic works has drawn attention to the ways in which these texts "resist," "subvert," and "are liberated from" the hegemony of first-world/colonial narratives and authorship. Sadly, this has only further entrenched comparatists in critical habits of otherization (along an East/West axis) and celebrations of cultural singularity to the degree that literary comparisons between first- and third-world locations and their possibilities for generating a sense of universality have all but been outmoded. Indeed, I agree with Jameson that "one of our basic political tasks [as academics] lies . . . in the ceaseless effort to remind the American public of the radical difference of our national situations"[48] (and by this I think he means our *material* situations); still, culturally, there are many rich and insightful connections to be made through comparative projects that have been overlooked for this radical privileging of cultural difference. True, Latifa al-Zayyat and Mary Karr have presented us with narrators facing two seemingly polar cultural fronts, but the broader impulse to write a raw and dynamic *bildungsroman*, from the point of view of a precocious female adolescent, is the same. Similarly, their respective use of language—Zayyat's ear for the everyday rhythms of family dialogue and Karr's lively first-person narrative evoking the inner world of a child on the brink of adolescence—reflects the raw honesty and literary sophistication they each possess. These two works compel us to read them together, and in their midst require us to rethink our tendencies to singularize cultural circumstance and indulge, even revel, in the foreignness of one another.

Notes

* I would like to thank Elliott Colla for inspiring this work originally as a seminar paper for his course "Police and the Nation: The Modern Egyptian Novel" at Columbia in the Fall of 2002 and for his many comments, which were instrumental to my process of revision.

1 Fredric Jameson, "Third-World Literature in the Era of Multinational Capitalism," *Social Text* 15 (Fall 1986): 65–88.

2 In this context, Doris Sommer's definition of allegory seems applicable. She writes: "I take allegory to mean a narrative structure in which one line is a trace of the other, in which each helps to write the other." Doris Sommer, *Foundational Fictions: The National Romances of Latin America* (Berkeley: University of California Press, 1991), 42.

3 Jameson, "Third-World Literature," 69.

4 Jameson uses these ideas of first world and Western interchangeably as noted by Aijaz Ahmad. Aijaz Ahmad, *In Theory* (London: Verso, 1992), 106.

5 Jameson, "Third-World Literature," 74, 85.

6 A few good examples might be Theodore Dreiser, John Dos Passos, Sherwood Anderson, Upton Sinclair, Philip Roth, Thomas Pynchon, and Don Delillo. Of course there are many others.

7 Ahmad, *In Theory*, 122.

8 Here specifically I am thinking of authors more contemporary than Dreiser and Dos Passos, such as Dorothy Allison, Tobias Wolfe, and Mary Karr, not to mention more well-known authors of color such as Toni Morrison, Alice Walker, and Sandra Cisneros.

9 Ahmad, *In Theory*, 122.

10 Jameson, "Third-World Literature," 85.

11 Latifa al-Zayyat, *al-Bab al-maftuh* (Cairo: al-Hay'a al-Misriya al-'Amma li-l-Kitab, 1989). Henceforth all references will be to Marilyn Booth's English translation of the novel, Latifa al-Zayyat, *The Open Door*, trans. Marilyn Booth (Cairo: The American University in Cairo Press, 2000).

12 Mary Karr, *The Liar's Club* (New York: Penguin Books, 1995).

13 *Idem, Cherry* (New York: Viking Penguin, 2000).

14 Doris Sommer, *Foundational Fictions: The National Romances of Latin America* (Berkeley: University of California Press, 1991), 50.

15 See for example Mahmud Tahir Haqqi's *'Adhra' Dinshaway* (Cairo: al-Maktaba al-'Arabiya, 1906). In this short novella based on an actual incident in Egypt in 1906, four fellaheen are wrongly accused as bearing responsibility for the death of a British officer. Here the female protagonist, Sitt al-Dar, while witnessing her father's hanging comes to represent through her cries of injustice and despair the enduring and indefatigable spirit of Egypt. Her presumed marriage to the young fellah Muhammad al-'Abd suggests a romantic union that would necessarily further the nationalist cause.

16 See Beth Baron's "Nationalist Iconography: Egypt as a Woman," in *Rethinking Nationalism in the Arab World*, ed. James Jankowski and Israel Gershoni (New York: Columbia University Press, 1997), 105–24, for more on this early turn-of-the-century visual trope.

17 From a private discussion with Elliott Colla, "Police and the Nation," (Comparative Literature Middle East G4105, Columbia University, October 17, 2002).

18 Marilyn Booth, Introduction to *The Open Door*, xviii.

19 See Magda Al-Nowaihi's "Resisting Silence in Arab Women's Autobiographies," *Journal of Middle East Studies* 33 (2001): 477–502 and Marlé Hammond, "Formulating the First-Person (f.) in Two Stories of Egyptian authors Latifa al-Zayyat and May Telmissany," *The MIT Electronic Journal of Middle Eastern Studies* 4 (Fall 2004): 53–69, http://web.mit.edu/cis/www/mitejmes/intro.htm.

20 Janice Radway, *Reading the Romance* (Chapel Hill: The University of North Carolina Press, 1991).

21 Ibid., 54.

22 Al-Zayyat, *The Open Door*, 24.

23 Sommer, *Foundational Fictions*, 46.

24 Ibid., 47.

25 Al-Zayyat, *The Open Door*, 354.

26 Sommer, *Foundational Fictions*, 48.

27 Al-Zayyat, *The Open Door*, 217.

28 Ibid., 18.

29 Ibid., 77.

30 Along these lines, she depicts Layla's father and mother as resisting liberation, fearful that such rebellion would dismantle social norms. In this regard, they are also very committed to maintaining the status quo to safeguard against radical change and loss.

31 Ferial Ghazoul, "When the Subaltern Speaks," *Al-Ahram Weekly On-Line*, February 18, 1999, http://www.ahram.org.eg/weekly/1999/417/cu1.htm.

32 Michael Denning, *The Cultural Front: The Laboring of American Culture in the Twentieth Century* (New York: Verso, 1997).

33 Karr, *Liar's Club*, 13.

34 Ibid., 35.

35 Here I am referring to two instances of rape: one by a young boy from the neighborhood whom Karr used to play with—she was only seven at the time (66) and another by her mother's boyfriend Hector (245).

36 Karr, *Cherry*, 189.

37 I am thinking of novels such as *Moby Dick, Native Son, The Great Gatsby, The Adventures of Huckleberry Finn, Invisible Man, Their Eyes Were Watching God*, not to mention the epic war novels by Ernest Hemmingway, James Jones, and others that challenge the ethos of American capitalism and the patriotic values of freedom and democracy.

38 Sommer, *Foundational Fictions*, 46.

39 Of course, the opposite might be argued of American love stories on film where cinematic happy endings for the couple often coincide with the triumph of traditional American values and way of life.

40 Karr, *Liar's Club*, 101.

41 Karr, *Cherry*, 234.

42 al-Zayyat's own scholarly commitment to English literature attests to one of the ways in which identity constructions along first and third world axes are problematic or at the very least deficient.

43 Mary eventually gets a Master of Fine Arts and Layla yearns to become a journalist.

44 Al-Zayyat, *The Open Door*, 303.

45 Karr, *Cherry*, 276.

46 Professors Radwa Ashour, Michelle Hartman, and Lisa Suhair Majaj are notable exceptions.

47 Jameson, "Third-World Literature," 77.

48 Ibid., 77.

15

Self-Portraits of the Other: Toward a Palestinian Poetics of Hebrew Verse*

Lital Levy

An Unexpected Maelstrom

In 1986, a Hebrew-language novel called *'Arabeskot* (Arabesques) took the Israeli literary scene by storm.[1] For the Hebrew cultural establishment, the appearance of this complex narrative work by a Palestinian Arab author was a seismic event whose reverberations continue these two decades on to be experienced and measured. It is not the first time a Palestinian Arab had published in Hebrew;[2] in fact, the author, Anton Shammas, was already known in Israel as a journalist and poet before the novel established him as a writer of international renown. *'Arabeskot* became a watershed in the history of Hebrew literature due to the combination of factors it brought to fore: the sophistication of its narrative style, its virtuosic use of the Hebrew language, its sustained thematic engagement with Palestinian and Israeli identities and cultures—and not least of all because it is a critic's text, lending itself to a seemingly limitless array of interpretations. Even a cursory survey of the critical literature reveals that each of the studies performed by academicians of Hebrew (writing from Israel or the United States) employs a very different hermeneutic compass for the navigation of Shammas's labyrinthine narrative.[3] What underscores these diverse approaches, however, is their shared preoccupation with "*the* issue": namely, the question of Hebrew in an Arab hand, with all its attendant political and cultural ramifications. Faced with a novel of this power, Hebrew readers were unexpectedly confronted with the same dilemma of linguistic 'ownership' that has long plagued metropolitan languages in a 'post'-colonial age: is a language defined by (all) those who use it, or by the tradition with which it is associated—the dominant strand of its history? Suddenly, it seemed, Hebrew could no longer be considered simply a 'Jewish language,' nor Hebrew literature a 'Jewish literature'—a revelation at once discomfiting and exciting. Yet attempts to extricate Hebrew from Jewishness have been largely exercises in tautology; a convincing alternative has yet to be proposed. And so it seems that nearly two decades and hundreds of pages after the maelstrom of *'Arabeskot,* we are no closer to untying the Gordian knot that is the identity of the Hebrew language.

The combination of tenacious issue and loaded text makes for a formidable brew indeed. The Palestinian Arab writer of Hebrew is one of those seemingly inexhaustible topics, and Shammas's text is just as inexhaustible a font of intertexts and allegories, allusions and intimations, all waiting for excavation and dissection on the cold white page. Yet the prominence of Shammas's novel notwithstanding, I find it curious that all but one of these studies completely overlook the three volumes of poetry, two in Hebrew and one in Arabic, published by Shammas a decade earlier.[4] Nor do these studies give more than passing mention to other Palestinian poets in Israel, most of whom have also published bilingually.[5] Given these critics' persistent emphasis on the complementary issues of Palestinian identity in Israel and of Arab authorship of Hebrew, their elision of so many other sources for the investigation of this topic is quite puzzling.

By now a broader examination of Palestinian-Israeli writing—one that looks at a *group* of writers, that investigates poetry as well as prose, and that considers their Arabic alongside their Hebrew writings—is well overdue. The topic merits a full-length study; this chapter-length inquiry cannot offer an analysis of all or even most of the important Palestinian writers in Israel, and will be limited to a discussion of the poetry of Shammas and his contemporaries Salman Masalha and Na'im 'Araidi.[6] It also focuses almost exclusively on their Hebrew writing, with only a few brief glimpses of the Arabic as counterpoint. But in this interlude I will try to shift the approach to the 'Shammas question' in Hebrew literature from a clash of irreconcilable opposites toward a poetics of 'in-betweenness.' In so doing, I will reconsider the question of Hebrew's cultural agency and contested identity by reading the poetry of Shammas, 'Araidi, and Masalha from a bilingual perspective—that is, as a poetics formed *between* languages, cultures, and national traditions—and by means of a close examination of the internal, textual resources they draw upon in cultivating such an in-betweenness in their work.

My understanding of in-betweenness builds upon different articulations of this hermeneutic in critical work on bilingualism, translation theory, and cultural studies in postcolonial contexts.[7] As but one possible point of departure, we may turn to Homi Bhabha, who locates identity formation in the interstices, the 'in-between' places:

> What is theoretically innovative, and politically crucial, is the
> necessity of thinking beyond initial categories and initiatory subjects
> and focusing on those interstitial moments or processes that are
> produced in the articulation of 'differences' [. . .]. *It is at the level of*
> *the interstices that the intersubjective and collective experiences of nationness,*
> *community interest, or cultural value are negotiated. How are subjects formed*
> *'in-between,' or in excess of, the sum of the 'parts' of difference.*[8]

In Bhabha's exposition, within the articulation of differences (such as 'Palestinian' vs. 'Israeli') emerge cracks—"in between" places or moments that disrupt their boundaries, in which the collective experiences (such as what it means to be Palestinian or Israeli) are negotiated. Bhabha then asks how subjects are formed in those in-between spaces, those chinks in the allegories of difference, and what new forms of collective identification become possible through their displacement. If, as we learn from Lacan, subject formation takes place largely through a recognition of the self's own otherness and lack,[9] we can also extrapolate from Bhabha's postulations that this in-betweeness may be precisely the result of the dialectical negotiation of self and other through which both are continuously produced. In other words, the self cannot exist without its other, is defined by it and through it, and is, in deeper psychological terms, even constituted around a primal sense of difference or lack. In collective terms, if Palestinian-ness and Israeli-ness are constructed largely in (oppositional) relationship to one another, they must also be codependent. Bhabha asks what identities are formed "in between" and "in excess of" these "'parts' of difference." This too is what I seek to discover in my reading of poetry produced both in between and in excess of the Israeli and Palestinian, Jewish and Arab 'domains of difference.'

In another articulation of in-betweenness, Anuradha Dingwaney writes in her introduction to *Between Languages and Cultures*:

> The *between* of our title refers to that space of translation where the self or one culture encounters, and more importantly, *interacts* with an 'other' or another culture. It is a fertile space, and disquieting, because, if explored fully, it proves to be a sphere (or zone) *in which one both abandons and assumes associations.*
>
> Between also refers to *transculturación* .... *Transculturación*, insofar as it designates the space within which the dominant language and culture is rewritten, inflected, subverted by the 'subaltern,' functions as a form of resistance.[10]

Both the aspects of in-betweenness identified by Dingwaney—the productive and the resistive—are what I wish to explore. That the 'in-between' is a "fertile space" of cultural production will be obvious; what needs exploration and explanation is the *process* by which "one both abandons and assumes associations."[11] What, for the Palestinian writers of Hebrew, would those associations be?

I believe that the in-betweenness theorized by Bhabha, Dingwaney, and others might be particularly well illustrated through a focus on allusion in the Hebrew poetry of Palestinian Arab writers. Literary Hebrew is an intensely allusive idiom that draws widely and deeply from the Jewish canon, a vast body of scriptural and liturgical texts and commentary extending back to the Hebrew Bible.[12] In choosing to create literary works in Hebrew, the writers in question must thus contend not only with contemporary Hebrew as the language of political and cultural hegemony in Israel but with Hebrew's entrenched history as the language of Jewish thought, culture, and religious praxis.

To explore the interplay of these literary, cultural, and political factors, I will dwell closely on the language of a number of poems to examine both what they say and *how* they say it, to feel their allusive textures, to understand their stylistic choices, to notice their spaces—in short, to view the issue of Palestinian writing in Hebrew from the *inside* of the text. The criticism on Shammas's novel and the phenomenon of Palestinian-Israeli writing has treated this body of literature largely as a sociocultural or sociopolitical issue, foregrounding extraliterary, contextual discussions of production and reception. While such analyses are edifying, poetry demands a different, more textual critical approach. As poems, the texts under discussion in this paper are beholden to no single logic or unifying voice; different poems within the same collection may variously contradict or complement one another. To be sure, the precariousness of being a Palestinian Arab writer of Hebrew is manifest throughout this body of writing, to the extent that one critic has complained that "the obsessive preoccupation of Shammas and 'Araidi with their cultural identity" dominates their work to the exclusion of other important topics.[13] The predicament, perhaps, underscores everything; and yet, it too is multiple, shifting, unstable. It has also been read in terms of a classic Hegelian struggle/dialectic.[14] Perhaps, in the 'real world,' equations of power can be represented with mathematical certainty, and the players rendered as discrete Xs and Ys. But in the world of poetry, at least, there is no unified 'Arab' subject addressing a unified 'Jewish' reader (in a unified Hebrew language). Instead, we find different 'you's and just as many different 'I's, poetic subjects appropriating not only different idioms but also different identities. While, in broad strokes, the three writers in questions do maintain a sense of difference, do identify their poetic 'I's as Other from the audience they are addressing, this tendency is much more pronounced in some poems than others; and it could be argued with equal conviction that in all these poems, speaker and implicit audience are bound together in a shared community of readership, unified by a common symbolic language and sense of place. This tension between difference and sameness is salient in the works of all three poets; Masalha, for instance, writes numerous poems accentuating his difference, yet in other poems, appears eminently comfortable in an idiom of Israeliness that inscribes his speaker within the collective.[15] Shammas, as noted earlier, replicates a Bakhtinian multiplicity of voices in the novel, in which identity, as an ontological category, is depicted as unreliable and unstable (there are, for example, at least two different Anton Shammases in the narrative, and one may or may not be dead). This subject fragmentation, when maintained over the course of a single continuous narrative, becomes a literary conceit.

But when encountered across a collection of poems, such fragmentation seems to come with the territory of the genre. Each poem, constituting its own moment, its own self-contained world, makes us privy to another possible relation between speaker and language, speaker and place, and so forth. Modern Hebrew poetry, moreover, is distinguished by its intensively allusive relationship to the Hebrew Bible; it is, in fact, much more densely allusive than its prose counterpart.[16] For all these reasons it is all the more surprising that the poetry of Palestinian-Arab writers in Israel has not been tapped by scholars exploring the interrelationships of language and identity in this vexed context.

Here, before proceeding, I would like to step momentarily out of the role of the impersonal and invisible commentator. As this is an essay written to honor a person whose own life deftly interwove the personal and political with her academic commitments, it seems fitting to say something about the genealogy of my work on this topic, its relevance to my own scholarly development, and Magda's role in facilitating it.

I had the privilege of working with Magda on two projects as an undergraduate at Columbia. The first (which occasioned our meeting) was an independent study on the theme of language—as a bridge, as a barrier, as an object that is defended, derided, as a metonym for identity—in Palestinian and Israeli fiction (in English translation). The second was my BA thesis, which was a formative experience for me in every respect. The latter project focused on the question of language and identity in that most politicized of contexts, Israel/Palestine. As bilingual writers of Hebrew and Arabic, and as Palestinians living in the Israeli state, 'Araidi and Shammas exemplified the idea of the 'borderline' writer. How does one write in two languages that are so closely related and yet so distant: that are, in a sense, at war with one another? Fascinated by this question, I wanted to see how Shammas and 'Araidi mobilized Hebrew and Arabic as media of self-expression. That first question quickly proliferated into many: Who was the speaker in their poems in each of the two languages? Who were the implied readers? Did the poets use canonically Jewish allusions when writing Hebrew? What kind of identity was manifest in the Arabic? Did they attempt through their writing to 'Arabize' Hebrew or somehow bring the two languages closer? Can the two languages and cultural systems be entirely separated from one another in writing, or does the presence of one seep into the other? Can we consider Palestinian writing in Hebrew a facet of Palestinian literature? What determines the cultural identity of a text, anyway: the identity of the language or of the author?

Those were the questions I asked then, and which I sought to answer (although perhaps what I learned best was that many of these questions cannot be definitively 'answered'). Our work on it prompted Magda to suggest to me that I continue this kind of research in graduate school, and it was my deep respect for Magda that prompted me in turn to seriously consider her advice. I thus take this bittersweet occasion of writing an essay in Magda's memory as an opportunity to revisit the project I began under her supervision nearly a decade ago and that led me into graduate study of Hebrew and Arabic literatures. I think she would have agreed with the sentiment that our work, as our identities, is an always-evolving process; early phases are never really finished, but are reincarnated in the later ones.

Borders and Language

Borderlands are physically present wherever two or more cultures edge each other . . . . Living on borders and in margins, keeping one's shifting multiple identity and integrity, is like trying to swim in a new element, an 'alien' element—not comfortable but home.

— Gloria Anzaldúa, *Borderlands/La Frontera: The New Mestiza*[17]

By 'borderline,' I mean a place that is simultaneously inside and outside, a place that belongs to what it delineates while remaining altogether something else.

— Dzevad Karahasan, *Sarajevo: Exodus of a City*[18]

The borderline can be an apt metaphor for the situation of writers whose home is characterized by the intrusive, oppressive presence of borders and barriers and whose command of both languages and cultures also enables them to transcend, in some sense, these dividing lines. Following Anzaldúa's "borderlands," I suggest the term 'borderline literature' for texts produced by those working in the space between two languages/cultural systems, in which the condition of in-betweenness is produced. The border itself seems to migrate from an external presence to an existential condition; we find no lack of references in these poems to the sense of one's self being split in two, sometimes even of one half being pitted against the other. The condition of inhabiting the uninhabitable, of living and writing against an impossibility, becomes marked in space and on the body: it is spatialized as a junction, as a no man's land, as a treacherous road, as a map, as various portals of exile; it becomes internalized as possession by an alien essence, as a fold of the body, as a crucifixion; it is, at other times, a transcendent unification of worlds, cultures, selves, achieved sometimes through the sublimity of nature, sometimes through erotic love, and sometimes through the space of the city, most especially of Jerusalem.

But then, while the literature of Palestinian writers in Israel may seem to beg comparison with other borderline literatures, it is also an exceptionally extreme and troubled case. Rarely can it be said that two languages, with all their contemporary political baggage, are in such critical opposition as are Hebrew and Arabic—an opposition all the more poignant for their close linguistic ties. The activity of Palestinian writers in Hebrew may seem to beg comparison with the postcolonial "X-ophone" model, but the analogy is partial for a number of reasons. The postcolonial model is based on writing in metropolitan languages with a potentially global reach, while Hebrew is a non-metropolitan language read by a relatively miniscule and culturally specific group of people. Thus a Palestinian author who chooses to write in Hebrew has a very particular audience in mind: Israel's Jewish majority.[19] Historically, literary and cultural contact between Hebrew and Arabic did not originate with the colonial moment, but far predates it. Yet the revolutionary revival of Hebrew at the turn of the last century was linked to the Zionist movement, which sought to resettle Jews in Palestine and create a new, Hebrew-based culture. There is thus an extra nip of irony in Palestinian literature written in what Deleuze and Guattari called "the mythic language" of Zionism.[20]

Is Palestinian writing in Israel a minority discourse within Israeli literature or an offshoot of Palestinian literature (or both)? To what degree does this categorization of Palestinian-Israeli writing depend on language choice? These questions remain open for debate. The writers under discussion here were all born within five years of the establishment of Israel ('Araidi in 1948, Shammas in 1950, Masalha in 1953). Palestinians in the West Bank and Gaza remained connected to the larger Arab world and absorbed developments in Arabic writing between 1948 and 1967, while Palestinians living inside Israel during the same period were cut off from Arab life beyond the borders of the state. Immersion in the Israeli educational system and lack of access to current Arabic writings would inevitably have had to orient this group's developing literary sensibilities toward Hebrew, at least until access to current Arabic writing was restored. And indeed we know that one of Shammas's major influences was the Israeli poet Amir Gilbo'a,[21] while Na'im 'Araidi wrote his doctoral dissertation on the ultra-nationalist Hebrew poet Uri Tsvi Greenberg.[22] 'Araidi himself has grappled with this quandary:

> Na'im 'Araidi, a literary scholar, has tried to come to terms with Arabic literature written in Israel . . . . He hastens to point out that many Arab critics prefer to call it "Palestinian literature," thereby giving emphasis to the political struggle, obviating the 'Israel' connection, and placing that literature within the purview of literature written in the West Bank, Jordan, and other Arab countries and areas.
>
> 'Araidi argues that the Arabic literature produced in Israel cannot be considered 'Palestinian' because it was not created in a Palestinian state and was not influenced by the tradition of Palestinian literature in the pre-1948 era, when Palestine did exist. Only after 1967 was there a surge in the quantity of Arabic literature written in Israel. But 'Araidi takes note of the fact that many of the writers in question were educated by the State of Israel; their formative reading was in Hebrew literature and world literature translated into Hebrew—thereby giving to Arabic literature [produced in Israel] its 'Israeli' character.[23]

Yet this argument, while logical, seems unnecessarily reductive. Palestinians in Israel live under the hegemony of another language and culture. In this sense, the situation is comparable to that of writers in the Palestinian diaspora. Much as, for example, the English and Arabic poetry of Palestinians in North America could be seen as simultaneously belonging to two traditions, it is (at least in theory) possible to see the writings of this group as concurrently Palestinian and Israeli.

'Araidi's observation thus begs the question of what characterizes a literature. While language is the most obvious factor, it is but one (consider, for instance, what characterizes *beur* literature aside from its being written in French). The prominence of certain genres or thematic subjects and the recurrence of symbols and topoi in a body of writing eventually lead us, the readers/interpretive community, to expect them. For decades, Palestinian Arabic poetry displayed a keen identification with the Palestinian plight, and especially with the land, locating and reifying 'Palestine' both as geography (towns and villages) and as the collective Palestinian memory. The references to stock objects and symbols (orange, rose, rifle, olive trees/branch, etc.) served a unifying function, creating a shared metaphorical language of 'homeland' signifiers that could substitute for the signified in face of dispersion and exile. All the writers under examination here straddle a fence overlooking both this tradition and the Israeli poetic tradition, whose own roots are entwined with Jewish nationalism in its various manifestations, including Revisionist Zionism (for example, the poet Uri Tsvi Greenberg). Modern Hebrew in the early to mid twentieth century often positioned the lyrical self within collective (national) memory and identity, creating a language of reference that assumed a common experience binding poet and reader. For nationalist poets such as Greenberg, place was the embodiment of the redemption from exile, the link between the biblical Land of Israel and the modern-day state.[24] Hence two different poetic traditions lay claim, albeit in very different ways, to the same land. And both these histories—if not the land itself—are strikingly absent from the poetry of 'Araidi, Masalha, and Shammas.

We do not find in their poetry, in either language, the figurative re-mapping of lost and/or beleaguered Palestinian places (such as we find, for instance, in the poetry of Siham Daoud, another Palestinian-Israeli writer.[25] Rather, their spaces are personal, highly allusive; in terms of place, they take us to the childhood village, to Jerusalem, and in the case of 'Araidi, to the Carmel. While the love of the land is manifest in 'Araidi and Masalha's poems, it is a personal love that resists entrapment in the nationalist metaphors of either side. Masalha writes:

My father,
who was born on the slope of the mountain
and gazed down on the lake,
never had a passport.

Or even a laissez-passer.
He crossed the mountains
when the borders did not flow
in the river.
My father
never had a passport.
Not because he didn't have
a land and a seal.
Just because the land
always dwelt calmly
in the palms of his hands.
And just as the land
never slipped from his hands to travel
overseas,
Father—too.[26]

The father's love of the land does not recognize the accoutrements
of nationality. It is not so much that he lacks these trappings as that he
does not need them, because his is an organic connection to the land;
the land resides in him, and will not travel "overseas" by parting from
him. In this reversal of the land/body relationship, the father quite literally embodies the homeland. It is thus not a claim of possession but a
reflection on a relationship to place so profound as to blur the order of
subject/object relations.

All three poets also write poems to and/or about Jerusalem, but here
again, it is a personal and not a collectively symbolic Jerusalem.[27] In
Shammas's first Hebrew collection, a series of five love poems collectively
called "Five Gates of Jerusalem"[28] intertwines traits of the city, canonically Jewish allusions, and erotic imagery so freely that we cannot tell if
we are reading a metaphor of the city as woman or of the woman as city
(for example, "Snow in Jerusalem": "The ceremony of sprinkling coconut
on the cake / is complete. And now the contribution of the knife. Stains /
of my passion upon your body, as the stains / of cake on the tablecloth").[29]
The rejection of Israel's nationalizing allegories of land and language does
not lead these writers to embrace a Palestinian mode of territorialization
in their poetry. They remain islands unto themselves; in another one of
Shammas's poems, the speaker refers to himself as a "self-resident" *(toshav*

'atsmi).[30] These poets create their own geographies, their own retinue of symbols, and in a corollary sense, their own idioms.

Yet the fact remains that, even if they inhabit highly personal poetic geographies, in choosing to compose verse in Hebrew, these writers must nonetheless contend with the Jewishness of Hebrew letters—and, more specifically, Hebrew poetry. In particular, this means a relationship with the Bible. As Ruth Kartun-Blum puts it, for the modern Hebrew writer to engage in dialogue with the Bible "is not an option but a must; the choices are of an existential magnitude."[31] "How then," asks Miki Gluzman, "can an Israeli Arab writer participate in a Jewish literary tradition that perceives the writer as a biblical prophet, a 'watchman unto the house of Israel?'"[32]

Addressing more or less the same question, Hochberg suggests that language "does not belong to anybody and it cannot be possessed. As a cultural space that is always open to 'intrusions,' language can only possess."[33] Hochberg's point about possession is well taken, but even so, it is impossible to separate a language from its historic and cultural legacy; a language is not the equivalent of a lexicon, a value-neutral collection of words, but a more organic entity, a fluid and polyvalent cultural system. Similarly, the second part of Hochberg's argument, that "[t]he fact that [Hebrew] has always been used by Jews does not make it an exclusively 'Jewish language'" is incontrovertibly true of authorship and identity in the Israeli public sphere, but remains difficult to reconcile with the semantic system of cultural and religious associations that supports a Hebrew text, that imparts its meaning to its interpretive community. For most of its history, Hebrew was not simply "used by Jews" for quotidian purposes, but cultivated as a distinctly religious and cultural medium and as a *lingua franca* for world Jewry—somewhat closer, say, to how Latin was used by the Church than how French patois, and later standardized French, were used by the French.[34] Modern Hebrew literature, moreover, emerged in the late eighteenth century as "not just an aesthetic pursuit but a problematic renegotiation of the terms of Jewish collective identity."[35] One cannot deny the implications and reverberations of this centuries-old echo chamber even within texts written in the refurbished modern (that is, Israeli) Hebrew.[36] (How much of the multilayered Jewish textual past remains accessible and relevant to the contemporary Israeli reader—or, in another locution, whether modern literary Hebrew is not still too linguistically and allusively 'inflated,' is a separate issue.)[37]

At the other end of the interpretive spectrum, Reuven Snir, a distinguished Israeli scholar of Arabic literature, attributes Shammas's and 'Araidi's use of Hebrew primarily to a "conscious aesthetic preference."[38] It is this aesthetic preference for Hebrew that in turn

> demands absorption of the Jewish cultural and religious heritage. And indeed, despite their efforts for the 'un-Jewing' of Hebrew language and literature, Jewish heritage is evident in their works, although these works cannot be labeled as Jewish heritage.[39]

The end game is that, having exchanged their original cultural identity without integrating into the other, "they do not enter the gates of Hebrew literature as proud Arab-Palestinians" but "as lost and lonely people, slowly losing their connection with their roots and caught in an acute identity crisis . . . ."[40]

Snir reads Shammas and 'Araidi against the background of Shammas's oft-quoted statement: "What I'm trying to do—mulishly, it seems—is to un-Jew the Hebrew language . . . to make it more Israeli and less Jewish, thus bringing it back to its semitic origins, to its place;" for Hebrew, argues Shammas, is "the language of those who speak it."[41] For Shammas, deterritorialization of Hebrew as the Jewish language and its reterritorialization as the language of Israelis—the agenda he espoused throughout the 1980s and early 1990s—had explicitly political dimensions linked to his concept of an absolutely democratic Israel that would define itself not as "the Jewish state," but as the state of (all) its citizens.[42] Taking Shammas at his word (and assuming it applies to 'Araidi as well),[43] Snir concludes that Shammas and 'Araidi have failed in their endeavor to "separate Jewish heritage from Hebrew language;"[44] nor will their writing succeed (as Hannan Hever has averred) in penetrating the Israeli center and effecting a transformation of its cultural identity.[45] Snir's point that Shammas and 'Araidi fail to separate Hebrew from Jewishness speaks to the question of how identity affects language; his second point, that they do not appear in Hebrew as proud Palestinians, relates to how language reflects identity. That Shammas's and 'Araidi's use of Hebrew indicates a conscious aesthetic preference is conjectural (especially in light of 'Araidi's prolific Arabic activity, which more or less parallels his creative output in Hebrew).[46] The choice would seem to rest as much with the author's extra-literary objectives; certainly a work like *'Arabeskot*, written to engage the very dilemmas under discussion here, could not have been created in a language other than Hebrew. That loneliness and alienation permeate these poems, on the other hand, is indisputable; nor can one downplay the fact that their most persistent theme is the experience of being caught between two cultural spaces without fully belonging to either. But does this imply that they are any less 'Palestinian'—or does it reflect the reality of their situation? Ought we to expect Palestinians in Israel, severed as they have been from the Palestinian collective in the West Bank and Gaza, to wave the banner of Arab-Palestinian identity or of the Palestinian struggle in their work? If the identity of Palestinians in Israel is rife with fragmentation and internal contradictions, then it should come as no surprise to find those demons haunting the space of the text.

The trouble with the hermeneutic suggested by the "'un-Jewing' of Hebrew" is that Palestinian, Israeli, Jewish, and Arab identities are not univalent, nor are they fixed quantities locked together in a zero-sum game. In the context at hand, they are more like different interdependent and constantly shifting layers of a whole, some but not all of which will be thrown into relief at any given moment. Nor, for that matter, are 'Jewishness' and 'Israeliness' antinomies, so that making Hebrew more 'Israeli' would necessarily make it that much less 'Jewish.'[47] Shammas's statement thus creates a trap of expectations into which his critics fall by aiming either to affirm or to refute that he has realized through his literary project what is, in any case, a paradoxical objective.[48] This is not to deny that Shammas's literary and journalistic writings did in fact generate debate about the nature of Israeliness (most [in]famously through a heated exchange with the noted Jewish-Israeli writer A.B. Yehoshua)[49] and in other ways opened up new discursive possibilities for Israeli and Hebrew culture. Nor is it to downplay the importance of Palestinian authorship in Hebrew in destabilizing assumptions surrounding the terms 'Israeli,' 'Hebrew,' and 'Jewish,' both in relation to 'literature' and in relation to each other. But it is to question whether, rather than 'cleansing' (that is, emptying) Hebrew of its Jewishness, Shammas and his colleagues may be appropriating that Jewishness (and not just Hebrew) toward new ends.

What I am arguing here is that whether or not Palestinian 'possession' of Hebrew fundamentally destabilizes it as a Jewish language—or, to leave out the possession metaphor, whether or not the *presence* of Shammas et al. within Hebrew literature fundamentally disrupts its Jewish identity— is ultimately not a productive question. It may have been worthwhile to ask as an intellectual exercise, but over the past two decades it has led us in circles, and will only continue to do so. There is simply no way to conclusively determine whether or not 'Hebrew is Jewish.' But more to the point, why should this question, which seeks to close the hermeneutic circle, be the telos of inquiry? To my mind, the more interesting question—and one that opens up new spaces for interpretation—is how these (non-Jewish) writers appropriate and manipulate the semantic echo chamber of Jewishness (by which I mean Jewish textual culture and religious praxis) in their Hebrew work. How do canonically Jewish allusions and intertextuality contribute to the in-betweenness of their writing? How does Jewishness, when tapped and deployed by a Palestinian writer, create new meaning—and, perhaps, another textual 'afterlife' for the original, another level of associations that becomes part of its *own* ongoing story—a Palestinian midrash, as it were?[50] To overlook or deny that Shammas, 'Araidi, and Masalha do use the Jewish canon extensively—and, more to the point, *creatively*—is, I think, to miss the richness of their Hebrew poetry. It is also to overlook the subversive potential of allusion.[51] And here is also where the implied presence of the author, as well as the author's position relative to the target reading audience (the interpretive community)[52] and not just the choice of language itself, really matters. As Jeremy Dauber notes:

> Though allusions partake of, and indeed serve as the paradigmatic
> examples of, an intertextual system participated in by both readers
> and writers, the writers in question are also readers positioned
> similarly to their audience. Their authorial strength stems from their
> organization and contextualization of these texts, themselves linked
> with certain interpretations communally understood by virtue of
> both parties' common membership in a given interpretive community.
> In some cases, writers can and do employ this system not merely to
> establish group solidarity . . . but to subvert and to manipulate the
> system, simultaneously weakening and undermining communal bonds.
> Such employment may lead to one of two possible conclusions: either
> these liminal writers become "self-consuming," to use Fish's term, or

they create a 'minor literature,' differently understood, within the interpretive community.[53]

Indeed, the very point that has been elided from commentary on the presence of Jewish heritage in Palestinian Hebrew writing is the flexibility the writers gain by adopting an oppositional stance that moves referentially *between* a majority and a minority perspective. Minor literature, writes Caren Kaplan, "dismantles notions of value, genre, canon, etc. It travels, moves between centers and margins . . . . The value of this conception lies in the *paradoxical movement between minor and major*—a refusal to admit either position as final or static. *The issue is positionality.*"[54] That the movement is "paradoxical" is important for understanding how different poems by the same writer may reflect sharply different subject positions in relation to the Israeli center, as is the case for all of the writers under examination here. It is this movement between center and margins, the "refusal to admit either position as final" that endows their writing with the character of in-betweenness: irony softens the edges of what could otherwise seem dogmatic; subtle humor hints at the pain hidden between the lines; playful over-literality draws attention to the dichotomies and conflicts within the language itself.

Consider, for instance, Na'im 'Araidi's use of the famous 'Four Questions' from the Haggadah, the ceremonial text read by Jewish families at the annual Passover *seder* to recount the story of the exodus from Egypt. 'Araidi, who was interned for six months in 1972–73,[55] writes in a Hebrew collection published a few years later:

Answer me, guard
What makes this night different
from all other nights
What makes this night different
that all the nights
pass slowly
and this night passes slowly
Answer me, guard.[56]

During the *seder,* the four reasons why Passover is "different from all other nights" are enumerated aloud. 'Araidi's poem, while reproducing the question verbatim, inverts its meaning: it turns the Haggadah's *literal* question into a *rhetorical* one, for this night is in fact no different from the others, as all nights in prison pass equally slowly.[57] It also completely reverses the intertext's associations, as the Haggadah tells the story of the liberation from bondage in Egypt. Finally, in the context of imprisonment, the poem also inverts the interrogation process: here it is the Palestinian Arab prisoner who questions the Israeli Jewish guard. The deep irony of a Palestinian in an Israeli prison invoking the definitive Jewish story of liberation from bondage would not be lost on his audience. But this irony is a function of the movement between center and margins, majority and minority perspectives, so trenchant in this text. Indeed, the strategic intertextuality evinced by Shammas, 'Araidi, and Masalha depends on the reader's ability to recognize both the intertext and the author's relationship to the intertext's language, system of signification, and readership. For the full meaning to obtain from this double-edged use of cultural references, the reader must recognize the poetic subject as both part of and apart from the 'symbolic world' invoked by an intertext such as the Four Questions.

'Araidi's strategic use of Jewish heritage in this particular poem demonstrates anything but "a lost and lonely person . . . slowly losing his connection with his roots."[58] Rather, it is an instantiation of the cultural 'mimicry' that makes the colonial subject uncanny in the eyes of the colonizer.[59] This poem also recalls Samia Mehrez's analysis of "radical bilingualism" as a "subversive poetics," which "seeks to create a new literary space for the bilingual, postcolonial writer. It is a space that subverts hierarchies, whether linguistic or cultural; where separate systems of signification and different symbolic worlds are brought together in a relation of perpetual interference, interdependence, and intersignification."[60]

Borrowing from Benjamin, we could ask how such ironic appropriations of Jewish canonical texts affect their own textual afterlives: How, after 'Araidi's poem, do we read the Four Questions?[61] On the one hand, this ironic use of canonical Jewish material contributes to the ongoing desacrilization[62] of Hebrew enacted by Jewish-Israeli writers such as Yehuda Amichai, who penned a sardonic take on the Jewish requiem for the dead, *"El male rahamim"* (God Full of Mercy):

God is full of mercy,
Were God not so full of mercy

There would be some mercy in the world
And not just in Him.[63]

In a similar manner, 'Araidi's reworking of the Four Questions trans-
poses it from a traditional Jewish to a secular-national (that is, Israeli)
idiom. But there is a difference between the poetic iconoclasms of
Amichai and 'Araidi: Amichai's is a universal complaint with the way of
the world, not directly aimed at the state, whereas 'Araidi's is an argument
with the very terms of Israeliness. It is the luxury of the Jewish-Israeli
writer to be able to 'write off' Jewishness (literally and figuratively) in
favor of Israeliness, for as long as the ethos of Israel is based on the Right
of Return, which makes any person of Jewish descent an automatic candi-
date for Israeli citizenship (thereby conflating nationality and citizenship
with religion), any non-Jewish citizen of Israel will have to negotiate his
or her relationship to the Jewish state. 'Araidi's poem, in other words,
is simultaneously a Palestinian critique of Israeliness as much as it is an
Israeli naturalization of Jewishness.

Mirrors: Poetic Inversions

'Araidi seems to touch on something of this idea of refraction in an 'open
letter' to Shammas in the form of a Hebrew poem, "The Language of
Mirrors":

To Anton Shammas
What shall we say to whom
about people, about peoples,
about ourselves?
. . .
Look closely at the language of visions:
look far off—
behold
how the ancestor's knife
sharply fixes
its eyes on our eyes.
Look how they appear from afar—
old people, women, and children
in great anger

and in great delight
distancing the rams
from above us.
What shall say our Father who art in heaven
and our father who art on earth
if there is no miracle
and if fire does not burn?
Will we live to see
with our own eyes
the number of stars in whose multitudes
will be our descendants?
Oh, how hard waiting is by night
and how hard by day!
Which is the language of loneliness
of artists in the image of man?
Which is the poetry,
the art,
which is the best silence of all, that,
like Abel's cry from the blood,
will be able to truly explain
what I shall say to whom
in this most perfect of moments?[64]

"What," 'Araidi asks Shammas, "shall we say about ourselves?" The line plays on the classic Israeli Bible quiz question *"mi amar le-mi u-matay,"* (Who said unto whom and when?). Thus 'Araidi's opening question to Shammas—how do we write about ourselves, in Hebrew—is phrased as an inside joke about Israeli culture, and, moreover, one that alludes to the pedagogical apparatus of the Israeli educational system imposed upon the Palestinian-Arab sector. Finally, for readers of Hebrew, this cultural reference thematizes biblical intertextuality, immediately introducing the context of the Bible— and indeed, 'Araidi's poetic apostrophe to Shammas is replete with biblical allusions, to Genesis (the Abrahamian covenant, the sacrifice of Isaac, Cain, and Abel) and Exodus (the Burning Bush).

While set up as an answer to a question about identity and self-representation, this poem is very much about *vision*: about the limitations of ordinary human vision, the dangers of prophetic version, and the deception of grandiose visions. The phrase *sfat ha-mar'ot* (in the first line of the second stanza) could be translated either as 'the language of visions' or as 'the language of mirrors/reflections.' In Hebrew, 'the language of visions' *(lashon ha-mar'ot)*[65] is a fixed idiom that invokes the poetics of Hayyim Nahman Bialik, the most revered modern Hebrew poet, in one of his most famous poems, *Ha-Brekhah* (The Pond), of 1905, where poetic language is likened to the refraction of light upon water.[66] Throughout his career, Bialik also cultivated the trope of poet as prophet, a concept he adopted from Pushkin and infused with nationalist undertones.[67] In 'Araidi's hand, however, the object of the phrase *sfat ha-mar'ot* is not language in the universal sense, but specifically, the *Hebrew* language:

Re'eh
keytsad ma'akhelet ha-avot
no'etset be-ofen had
et 'eyneha be-'eyneynu

"Behold / how the ancestor's knife / sharply fixes its eyes / on our eyes," the speaker says, invoking *ma'akhelet*—the biblical word for the knife used in ritual slaughter—a term that, for the Hebrew reader, immediately invokes that knife which Abraham was to use in the sacrifice of his son Isaac. The action taken by this ritual knife is *no'etset,* a participle that literally means 'stabbing;' but when combined with "eyes" (as in *na'ats 'eynayim*), the verb forms an idiom meaning 'to stare at,' to set or fix one's eyes on (an object). The poem puns on the idiomatic and literal meanings of this collocation: the ancestor's knife in the poem has its own eyes, which it uses "sharply;" it can thus be read either as scrutinizing them, or, in a more literal reading, as actually stabbing their eyes. But in so doing, this mythical knife seems to transfer to 'Araidi and Shammas (as the projected speaker and addressee) its own vision, one that is almost prophetic in its perspicacity: like Moses, they have a panoramic view of the people in its totality, in its anger and pleasure. It is the people, as a collective, that is "distancing the rams / from above us."

That last line takes us directly into the story of the binding of Isaac, known in Hebrew as the *'akeydah*: "Looking up, Abraham saw a ram caught by its horns in a bush. Abraham took the ram and offered it . . .

in place of his son. And Abraham named that site Adonai-yireh, whence the present saying, 'On the mount of the Lord there is vision.'"[68] Does the fact that the people are distancing the rams from overhead mean that no sacrifice will be made in their stead—that it is 'Araidi and Shammas themselves who are to be sacrificed on the altar of the Hebrew language, in this place of deadly, divine vision? Because of Abraham's willingness to sacrifice his only son, God promises to make his descendants as "numerous as the stars" (c.f. Genesis 22:17). But, in his own rewriting of the story, 'Araidi doubts their poetic efforts in Hebrew will be rewarded, at least not in their lifetimes: "Will we suffice to see / with our own eyes / the number of stars in whose multitudes / will be our descendants?" 'Araidi's pessimism calls to mind Shammas's gloomy forecast that he may one day be held accountable for his Hebrew activities: "This whole thing is a kind of cultural trespassing," he has said, "and the day may come when I will be punished for it."[69]

Yet, at the same time, through his very rewriting of the 'akeydah story, 'Araidi inserts himself into a longstanding intertextual dialogue not only with the biblical text but with its numerous afterlives pulsing throughout the corpus of modern Hebrew poetry: as Kartun-Blum points out, there is hardly a modern Hebrew poet who has not made use of this most archetypal story, a foundational myth not only for modern Hebrew literature but for Israeli culture and collective consciousness.[70] Ultimately, then, 'Araidi's poem tells us that when a Palestinian-Israeli poet speaks to another Palestinian-Israeli poet[71] through one of Hebrew's textual lodestars, he uses the story as a foil, rewriting it in order to point out their *difference*; but the same intertextual act through which this difference is asserted implicitly situates them within the meta-narrative of modern Hebrew rewritings of the 'akeydah, acknowledging and affirming their place in the ongoing saga of Hebrew letters.[72]

Here we may also return to Gluzman's question about how a Palestinian-Israeli writer can participate in a tradition that views the poet as biblical prophet. 'Araidi's speaker initially assumes a prophetic viewpoint in the poem, only to reject it as futile. In so doing, 'Araidi implicitly rejects the romantic nationalism of the trope of poet as prophet (that is, as harbinger of national revival), as well as the use of the 'akeydah story as a Jewish, and later an Israeli, symbol of martyrdom.[73] The poem ends with the impossibility of its own articulation:

Which is the poetry
the art,
which is the best silence that,
like Abel's cry from the blood,
will be able to truly explain
what I shall say to whom
in this most perfect of moments[?]

The silence that is likened to the cry of Abel seems to answer 'Araidi's opening question to Shammas in the first stanza: "What shall we say to whom... about ourselves?" The truest form of self-explanation for the Palestinian-Arab writer of Hebrew, then, becomes silence. Yet the elaborately allusive route the poem takes to this conclusion suggests a meta-textual answer more akin to "We may not know what to say to whom, but we *do* know 'their' texts by heart." Hebrew as *sfat ha-mar'ot* is thus transformed in the poem from Bialik's language of prophetic, mystical vision into a language of mirrors and reflections a "language of loneliness."

This sense of loneliness and futility appears persistently throughout Shammas's poetry, where it is often coded through an inversion of Jewish textual and cultural references. Consider this poem from his first Hebrew collection:

Ani margish be-kefel (I Feel the Crease)

Sanctifies all that has transpired, in a flash,
from the roof drops tefillin, choking. Imagine
that all the glory is learned from books
and you boast of the empty pages.
A colonnade of lonely people. I thought
I'd go. There's no need to make a fuss. Truly.
And also by mistake. And what I'm doing here is making kiddush
over the white city. At times
I feel a crease going down my body. Once
you saw one like it going down the body
of Jesus, in an old print of the Last Supper.
Big deal.[74]

The poem contains two understated but distinctly Jewish references *(tefillin, kiddush)* discernible to any reader of Hebrew, followed by a more oblique reference to the crucifixion, first implied by the crease and then reiterated more explicitly through the invocation of Jesus at the Last Supper (that the Christian reference is spelled out in this manner indicates the identity of the interpretive community). As opposed to 'Araidi's poem, whose allusions invoked a biblical narrative that, while part of Jewish religious tradition, can also be read independently of Jewish religious praxis, here the two references are not to an intertext but rather to the ritual practices of Judaism; in other words, this poem deliberately employs Hebrew terms that cannot be divested of their Jewishness. The first of the two terms, *tefillin,* are prayer phylacteries whose ritual use is incumbent upon Jewish men. They consist of wooden cubes containing prayers, attached to black leather straps that are wound tightly around the arm and forehead. Choking, the speaker drops them from the roof onto the city below. "Sanctifying," in Hebrew, *mekadesh 'al,* evokes the blessing of the Sabbath candles or bread and wine (an activity referred to by English speakers as 'making the *kiddush.*'). Ironically, here the dropping of *tefillin* itself seems part of the speaker's inverted, private ceremony of 'sanctification' of his past. The poem's second mention of sanctification refers to the city: *"ve-mah she-ani kan 'oseh zeh le-kadesh 'al ha-'ir ha-levanah"* (And what I'm doing here is sanctifying [making the *kiddush* over] the white city). The "white city," a snow-blanketed Jerusalem, is a holy city purified by its white cover—recalling, in the context of the *kiddush,* the Sabbath tablecloth. It should also be noted that the Arabic name for Jerusalem, 'Al-Quds'—literally, 'the Holy'—is a cognate of the Hebrew *kadesh*; in a bilingual reading, then, the poem invokes the city's Arabic name as a subtext of the speaker's (Hebrew) sanctification of the city.

The speaker's position vis-à-vis all these (explicit or implied) ritual objects and actions is ambivalent: he drops the constricting *tefillin* from the roof while simultaneously performing (that is, appropriating) the sanctification benediction, and what he sanctifies is first his own history ("all that has transpired") and *then* the city, the place connected to his·present. He thus situates himself neither fully inside nor outside the cultural context that these references evoke, but in the 'in-between,' that interstitial space that later becomes re-territorialized (in a paradoxical, anti-territorial manner) as Shammas's "no man's land." In adopting the language of Jewishness, then, this speaker creates a kind of cognitive dissonance, destabilizing references such as *kiddush* and *tefillin* from their normative associations of ritual observance (while not quite explicitly reversing them *à la* 'Araidi's use of the Four Questions).

The poem instantiates Bhabha's description of "a strategy of ambivalence in the structure of identification that occurs precisely in the elliptical 'in-between,' where the shadow of the other falls upon the self."[75] There are really two lyrical voices in the poem: the dominant voice of the *tefillin*-dropper, the figure who stands over the white city desperate to express the depths of his loneliness and despair; and the sub-voice of the cynical 'intervenor' who undercuts and dismisses every attempt made by the speaker to tell us of his pain ("no need to make a fuss;" "Big deal"); the two voices are also marked by their different registers, wherein the diction of the first voice is literary while that of the second voice is colloquial slang. The crease along the speaker's body may be the tortured seam of these two 'I's, an internal borderline—a corporealized psychic split. The poem strategically uses resonant Jewish concepts to place the speaker within the fold (in both senses), which is what makes his 'schizophrenia' all the more compelling. This is a relationship borne of unbearable intimacy rather than tolerable distance (hence the speaker's need to free himself from the metaphorical chokehold of the *tefillin*).

Portraits: Self, Language, Body

If the experience of being caught in the power struggle between languages and cultures is the ubiquitous undercurrent of this poetry, it is at times a silent trickle, at others a roaring rush. The issue of language comes to fore most explicitly in the writers' poetic self-portraiture. "*Dyokan*" (Portrait), a poem by Shammas that appeared in a 1980 anthology of Hebrew poetry,[76] paints a visceral and rather frightening image of what it means to speak the language of the Other:

> I stand here in the azure light
> unwalled loneliness around me, as a candle's flame.
> And in my mouth, another tongue[77]
> not of my mother, and not in my blood.
> My blood paces in the emptiness of my arteries,
> a boat without oars.

And in my blood paces the spirit,
it comes and is borrowed from my body in the azure light.
And my body is full of rusty sores:
no turn will be made for me,
no pitiful mission.
And my body comes and is borrowed from another language,
with no love at all.
Another language is seeping into my body,
pressing my temples from within,
leaving fine fissures,
leaving sentries of darkness in my legs.
And I stand here in the azure light
growing in vain inside my portrait.
Sweat paces in my blood,
comes and is borrowed from my limbs.
And my portrait, it keeps retreating,
addresses me in a forgotten language.
Primal words drip from my fingers.
Foreign, unfamiliar, my legs quaver.
And my body, once the iron loses its edge, comes and is borrowed
    from my rusty sores.
And my body has a wish in its mouth—
May carob and a spring of water come forth.
A black rooster beating its wings. Jerusalem.[78]

As powerful as it is, this poem is also exceptionally difficult to unpack.
Its central themes of alienation and bifurcation come through with
unsettling force, but beneath the surface trickles an elusive stream of
intertextual references unfamiliar even to educated readers of Hebrew.
On the linguistic level, the text contains several opaque if not baffling
words and phrases: the repeated refrain of *ba ve-nishal,* 'comes and is asked/
borrowed;' the word *haluda'ot,* which does not exist in modern Hebrew
(and which I have rendered "rusty sores,") and the poem's closing lines,
with the enigmatic image of the black rooster and the mysterious, final
one-word sentence: "Jerusalem."

The untranslatable word *haluda'ot* and the reference to water and carob
work together to invoke the Talmudic story of Rabbi Shim'on bar Yohai,

who hid with his son Rabbi Ele'azar in a cave for thirteen years to escape a Roman death decree. While in hiding, the pair devoted themselves to study of Torah; when they ran out of nourishment, a spring of water and a carob tree miraculously appeared to sustain them. Studying with his son for thirteen years, with no other human company or diversions (and nothing but carob to eat), R. Shim'on bar Yohai attained mystical knowledge of the hidden (as opposed to the revealed) Torah, which, tradition has it, would form the basis for the *Zohar*—the foundational text of *Kabbalah*, the Jewish mystical tradition. Subtly, Shammas's poem evokes the atmosphere of a cave: the blue light, the language "seeping" *(mehalhelet)* and words "dripping" *(notfot)* like water, and even "stalagmites," the secondary meaning of the word *zekifim* (in the construct *zekifey hoshekh*, 'sentries of darkness').[79] Yet if there is the suggestion of a cave, it is contained in the speaker's body; all this imagery is internal to the speaker, as what we have before us in the poem is the speaker, the portrait, and the blue light.

Throughout the entire Jewish textual corpus (from the Bible on), we find the word *haluda'ot* only once, in a fairly obscure midrash[80] dealing with the story of Rabbi Shim'on bar Yohai: "R. Simeon b. Yohai and R. Eleazar, his son . . . spent time hiding in a cave during the thirteen years of the [Roman] repression, until their flesh was covered with *haluda'ot*"[81]—surmised, from the context, to be sores or lesions. The midrash is written in a difficult Aramaic idiom, and the word *haluda'ot* itself is not quite Hebrew.[82] To a modern reader of Hebrew, the word sounds like a corruption of *haludah* (rust); most likely, they share a common etymology linked to the idea of corruption or decay. (In biblical Hebrew, the same trilateral root connotes earthly existence and mortality.)[83] The word *haluda'ot* appears twice in Shammas's poem, both times in connection with the body: first, in the line "and my body is full of *haluda'ot*," followed by the line, "and my body, once the iron loses its edge [*im kahah ha-barzel*] comes and is borrowed from my *haluda'ot* [*ba ve-nishal mi-haluda'otay*]." While in the story of the rabbis, the *haluda'ot* appear *on* the skin, here the sores of loneliness, so to speak, are (again, like the cave itself) *inside* the body.

The speaker describes himself as trapped, isolated, defenseless—with no one coming to his rescue. The first two lines read: "I stand here in the azure light / unwalled loneliness around me, as a candle's flame." The phrase *bedidut-prazot sevivi* (unwalled loneliness around me) is a play on the biblical Hebrew term *'ir prazot*, denoting an unwalled (and hence vulnerable, unprotected) city; Shammas has split the idiom by replacing *'ir* (city) with *bedidut* (loneliness). Paradoxically, then, the speaker is surrounded by a barrier that affords him no protection. The simile *ke-shal-hevet ha-ner* (as a [lit., as the] candle's flame) completes the sentence with a complex and beautiful analogy: the speaker stands in the azure light and is surrounded by loneliness, like the blue inner part of a flame, which is surrounded (but unprotected) by the permeable outer border. The idea of penetration is central to the poem, which describes how the speaker's body is invaded by another language. Without the nourishing protection of his mother tongue, which has ceased to flow in his veins, he is vulnerable to the violent possession of his body by another language; in possessing him, it is slowly breaking his body down. Inverting the metaphor of linguistic possession (as discussed in the introduction to this chapter), the question explored by this poem is not what it means to *possess* a language—but rather, what it means to *be* possessed by one.

The central metaphor of the poem is, of course, the portrait. Also the title of the poem, the word *dyokan* (portrait) appears twice within the poem. The poem depicts the problem of identity through the relation of the speaker and the portrait, a relationship expressed both spatially and in terms of agency. At first mention of the portrait, the speaker is still inside it, saying he "grows in vain" *within* it; but two lines later, we find the portrait retreating ever further *away* from him, speaking to him in a "forgotten language." The speaker's traumatic confusion of Self and Other is expressed as physical paralysis: he stands rooted in place, and every action in the poem is enacted upon his helpless body. He does not speak, but rather, it is his image in the portrait that speaks to him, in his own (now forgotten) original language. Having become exiled from his own image, he is now losing even the "primal words" *(milim hiyuliot)* of that original language. Shammas's poetic vision of the fractured self reverses Lacan's mirror theory: here the portrait, in the function of the mirror image, *is* the real, primary, and original self, while the subject outside the mirror/portrait becomes its Other.[84] The portrait ultimately abandons its paralyzed and language-less subject. This poem, titled simply "Portrait", is thus a portrait of a portrait with a kind of infinite regress in which the subject simply disappears. In this eerie play on self and image, we may recall 'Araidi's "language of mirrors." Both poems suggest that in the experience of being a Palestinian writer of Hebrew, identity becomes not only unstable but un-*real*: a reflection without a fixed or tangible source, an uncanny simulacrum of a subject.

It is difficult to know what to make of the poem's cryptic final lines, which leave the subject and the portrait behind altogether and juxtapose allusions to the cave story (the carob and spring of water) with the seemingly unrelated image of the black rooster and the closing mention of Jerusalem. The image of the rooster would make most Hebrew readers think of *kapporot*, the ritual practiced by some Orthodox Jews on the Day of Atonement in which a live fowl is swung around the head as the devotee recites a prayer asking for the chicken to be considered atonement for his or her sins.[85] The *kapporot* image is easy to associate with "Jerusalem;" but in the *kapporot* ritual, the fowl is white. What, then, is the connection between the rest of the poem, the black rooster, and Jerusalem? Perhaps it is a personal association that worked its way into the poem: in Shammas's novel *'Arabeskot*, a legendary rooster known as Al-Rasad guards the hidden entrance to a deep cave hidden beneath the narrator's childhood village.[86] Shammas lived in Jerusalem during the time this poem was written; the mention of Jerusalem at the very end of the poem could be a connecting thread between the realm of metaphor and the realm of biographical experience. (This explanation, however, cannot be substantiated.)

Although its intertextual referent may be less elusive, the carob and water reference is also a puzzling choice, leading one to wonder: Why this intertext? Why would this poem, whose very subject is the pain of assimilating a foreign language and culture (which, in this case, happens to be Hebrew), invoke by way of metaphor a Rabbinic text, a Jewish text *par excellence*, let alone one as obscure as the Aramaic midrash containing the word *haluda'ot*? Israeli culture is suffused with the Hebrew Bible, which, embraced as an 'authentic' *erets-yisraeli* (Land of Israel) text imbued with a pre-diasporic national consciousness, was easily mobilized for—and quite central to—the national literary project. Rabbinic texts (Talmud and Midrash, written in a mishmash of Aramaic and Rabbinic Hebrew), emblematic of a diasporic and effete ethos, were consequently rejected and submerged. Shammas's contemporaries have not usually tapped these texts as an allusive resource. Yet why, then, would Shammas? If anything, it is the Bible that is the more 'Hebrew' (construed as 'Caananite,' semitic) and less 'Jewish' part of the canon. The deliberate manner in which Shammas interpolates Rabbinic language into this poem hardly implies that literary Hebrew needs to be deflated from its intensive textual allusiveness, to become 'thinner,' to be brought closer to a spoken, truly secular idiom—whence the "un-Jewing" of Hebrew. Alternatively, it is tempting to claim that his use of the Rabbinic language, in light of the stratification of the modern Hebrew canon into 'Israeli' and 'diasporic,' is an implicit rejection of the Zionist territorialization of Hebrew; but elsewhere in his poetry Shammas draws upon the Bible, too. In any case, what is clear is that Shammas's particular way of writing Hebrew neither shirks its Jewishness nor applies it according to the accepted modes. One might say it is an idiosyncratic relationship to the sources.

We find a strikingly different relationship between self and language in the portraits painted by Salman Masalha's Hebrew verse. A scholar of classical Arabic literature, Masalha published five volumes of poetry in Arabic before appearing in Hebrew (reversing the trend set by Shammas and 'Araidi). His first Hebrew collection, *Ehad mi-kan* (literally, 'one from here;' English title given as *In Place*)[87] appeared in 2004—three decades after the entrance of Shammas and 'Araidi into the Hebrew literary arena. Masalha's poetic idiom comes closest to realizing the stripped-down, layerless, and self-contained 'Israeli' Hebrew thought to have been advocated by Shammas. Yet Masalha's simplicity is highly deceptive; his poetic idiom brims with ambiguities, double meanings, and elisions. Neither does he forego the sources, but rather, he weaves them into his poems with subtlety and understatement.

At least four poems in the collection are portraits of different kinds. The first, *"Oto-portret"* (Self-Portrait) is a striking and imagistically lovely 'self-portrait' of—to the reader's surprise—an old, alcoholic man. The poem portrays its subject holding a glass of *'araq* in one hand and a cane in the other, and ends:

Only the man who sipped
his life slowly, it was himself
he hung up on the wall.
And no one is there to object.[88]

This ending is intentionally ambiguous; we think that "himself" is metonymic for "his portrait," but we can't be sure (the poem never actually mentions a portrait). Likewise, the verb *le-hasir* in the last line *(ve-eyn mi she-yasir)* can mean either 'to remove, take down,' or 'to object,' giving the sentence a poignant double meaning: there is either no one to object to his hanging (?), or no one to take down his portrait. The 'self-portrait,' then, while ostensibly the poem itself, riddles the reader on two levels: first, who exactly is the 'self' in this 'self-portrait' (is the old man a projection of the speaker's future self—or is this a paradoxical 'self-portrait' of someone else?), and second, does the "portrait" of the title in fact refer to what is being hung on the wall? This kind of playful linguistic indeterminacy is characteristic of Masalha's poetic self-portraiture throughout the collection.

The two poems that come closest to being genuine 'self-portraits' are, of course, not titled as such (although both do contain the word 'I' in the title). Both were published in the Israeli cultural journal *Hadarim* in 1996[89] and then reprinted in *Ehad mi-kan*. The first, *Ani meshorer 'aravi* (I Am an Arab Poet) recalls Mahmoud Darwish's famous "Identity Card" poem, in which the speaker, a Palestinian detained by an Israeli officer, defiantly states in the first line and again throughout the poem: *"Sajjil! Ana 'arabi!"* (Write it down! I am an Arab!).[90] Masalha's poem is also an identity card of sorts, whose first line declares: *"Ani hu meshorer 'aravi,"* (I am an Arab poet)—in Hebrew, without any qualification or explanation. While the poem never explicitly refers to Hebrew, this obvious elision cannot but draw our attention to the unspoken subtext (that is, 'I am an Arab poet who writes in *Hebrew*'), making the *absence* of the word not only conspicuous, but charged. 'Hebrew' is also a 'present absentee' in other ways: in the original, the poem's regular rhythm is based on anapestic trimester,[91] with a few deviations, and alternate lines rhyme (ABAB, CDCD).[92] Anapest is the natural spoken rhythm of modern (Israeli) Hebrew, which shifted Hebrew's stress pattern from the penultimate to the ultimate syllable. As such, the poem becomes a prosodic thematization of the language itself, a representation *in language* of the missing word 'Hebrew:'[93]

> I am an Arab poet
> Who paints everything in black.
> I will open the latch of my heart
> To a world that is spinning back.
> A poet composes his rhymes
> About brother dwelling with brother.

In his artifice he went just too far—
His father be cursed, and his mother.
And the sun will rise in the east
Upon an earth that is captive to dust
Blisters will blossom on hands, and al-
so the village girls must.[94]
To cherish his dreams the child
Wanted well before his betrayal.
When he was born, he found his hand
Clutching the spoon of Sheol.[95]
I am an Arab poet,
The word will suffer it all.
Letters sprouted in my heart
My leg, a peg to dance at the ball.[96]

The poem's strong cadences and regular rhythm and rhyme lull the
reader into a deceptive sense of simplicity or naiveté that is shattered by
its startling images and jarring language, so a sustained tension between
sound and imagery pervades the entire poem. From its very first stanza
("paints everything in black"; "world spinning back"), this poem is suffused with dark undertones.

The second stanza, beginning with *"meshorer yikhtov haruzim / 'al shevet ah ve-ahiv"* (a poet composes his rhymes / about brother dwelling with
brother), plays with the popular Hebrew folk song *"hiney mah tov u-mah
na'im / shevet ahim gam yahad,"* taken from Psalm 133:1: "How good and
how pleasant it is / that brothers dwell together." [97] In the continuation,
Masalha writes, *"ba-kazav hu me'at higzim / imo tekulal ve-aviv,"* (in his artifice he went just too far— / his father be cursed, and his mother [lit: may
his mother and father be cursed].) The Hebrew word *kazav* (כזב), 'fib' or
'lie,' is a cognate of the Arabic *kadhib* (كذب), 'lie,' which in classical Arabic
poetics was a term at the center of a polemic about the aesthetic versus
the truth value of poetry. The same concept in medieval Hebrew poetics refers to poetic *form* as an artifice, as in the expression *meytav ha-shir
kzavo* (the best part of the poem is its *kazav* [lie].) Here Masalha is pok-
ing fun at his own overuse of the poetic form (with the strong anapest
meter and regular rhyme scheme) in this text, while simultaneously alluding to the common poetic roots of Hebrew and Arabic versification. I

have translated *kazav* as 'artifice' in order to convey a sense of this idea of poetry as deceit. It is probable, however, that here the specific poetic artifice for which the poet's parents will be cursed is the 'lie' of brothers dwelling together—perhaps because, in the reality of Israel/Palestine, 'brothers' on opposite sides of the slash are more likely to shoot at one another than to congregate in mellifluous harmony. Is Masalha, in these lines, referring to his own poetic enterprise as an Arab writer of Hebrew?

The idea of the false or phony returns in the poem's last and most enigmatic line, *"ragli totevet le-mahol,"* literally: 'my leg is prosthetic to dance' or 'my leg is prosthetic for danc[ing]' (in my translation, "my leg, a peg to dance at the ball"). The syntax of the sentence, which sounds every bit as bizarre in the original Hebrew as it does in translation, leaves the poem's ending very much open to interpretation. The adjective *totevet* (prosthetic) is syntactically employed here as though it were a verb (for instance, *ragli rokedet* would be 'my leg is dancing,' hence *ragli totevet* sounds to the Hebrew reader like 'my leg is prostheticizing'). Read in context, where the speaker declares himself, in Hebrew, an Arab poet—and especially given the preceding lines of the last stanza—the "prostheticizing" leg seems to be the Hebrew language: an artificial limb, a borrowed or adopted body part, that enables the speaker to 'dance' the dance of Hebrew poetry, but is not organically his. The poem thus intimates a connection between the false leg, false expression (the *kazav* or fib), and false friends.

The connection between the dysfunctional or aberrant body and the speaker's experience of language resonates with the depiction of body and language we saw earlier in Shammas's poem. Similarly, in another poem-portrait, *"Mazal 'akrav"* (Sign of Scorpio), Masalha depicts his bilingualism as a snake's forked tongue (an idea that resonates curiously with Bhabha's personification of the discourse of English colonialism as one that "speaks in a tongue that is forked, not false"):[98]

> . . .
> And over the years I also learned
> to slough off my own skin.
> Like a snake that was caught
> between scissors and paper.
> Thus my fate was sealed
> in words cut from the roots

of pain. With a tongue forked
in two. One, Arabic—
to mother's memory entrust.[99] Second,
Hebrew—on a winter's night
to love.[100]

As in the previous poem, Masalha thematizes language. Here it is a subtle subtext, given away by the line "in words cut from the roots of pain" (*be-milim nigzarot mi-shorshey / ha-makh'ov*). Here the words *nigzar* (cut, as in cut from a pattern) and *shorashim* (roots) have a double meaning. In Hebrew, *shoresh* (root) is also a grammatical term for the trilateral root stem that forms the morphological basis for each lexeme. In this context, *nigzar* refers to the grammatical declension of words from the triliteral root. This line, then, plays with the technical language of Hebrew grammar, and in a sense, also the work of the poet: words are declined from the (linguistic) 'roots' of pain or heartache. Yet at the same time it may also be read as a statement about Hebrew–Arabic bilingualism; Arabic, like Hebrew, is a root-based language. Indeed, the lines that follow explicitly metaphorize the speaker's bilingualism, suggesting that Masalha is in fact referring to writing in Arabic and Hebrew, which are linked through their common origin in "the roots of pain." Finally, the word *nigzar* is also derived from the same root as *gzeyrah,* (sentence or decree, usually in a negative sense), thereby echoing the previous line ("thus my fate was sealed").

But another poem by Masalha (the second of the pair originally published in *Hadarim*) offers a far more optimistic view of being an Arab poet in Hebrew. Here, by contrast, Hebrew is not the poem's subtext, but its explicit subject. Moreover, while this poem also maps language onto the body, it does so in an entirely different manner:

Ani kotev 'ivrit (I Write Hebrew)

I write in the Hebrew language,
that is not my mother tongue,
to get lost in the world.
Whoever doesn't get lost won't
find the whole. Because everyone
has the same toes on their feet.

And the same big toe,
walking side by side with the heel.
And Hebrew, sometimes, I write
to cool the blood that streams without
pause from the heart. There are plenty
of chambers in the palace I built inside
my chest. And yet,[101] the colors
of the night that is spread on bare walls
are peeling off without knowing
what all this wonder is.
And I write Hebrew in order to lose
my way in my words. And also
to find a little interest
for my footsteps.
My strides are not over yet.
How many are the paths that I have furrowed.
Carved in my hands. I will yet carry
my legs in my hands
and will meet many
people. And make them all my friends.
Who is a stranger? Who is far and near?
There is nothing strange in the vanities of this world.
Because strangeness, for the most part,
is found in the heart.[102]

The idea of writing in Hebrew ("not my mother tongue") is connected to two parts of the body: the heart and the feet. Hebrew, in the first and third sections of the poem, is a path that leads the speaker into new vistas; and writing in Hebrew, in the second section, leads us, the readers, into the palace of the speaker's heart. This section is playing, of course, on the idiom of 'chambers' of the heart. In Hebrew, 'chest' (the body part) is *beyt he-hazeh*—literally, the 'house of the chest'—so the speaker has built his "palace" within his own body-house ("*hadarim yesh / be-shefa ba-armon she-baniti be-tokh / beyt ha-hazeh* [There are plenty / of chambers in the palace I built inside / my chest.]") Thus Hebrew leads the speaker both outward, to paths leading to eagerly anticipated unknowns, and inward, to the palace-in-the-heart, itself located within the house-of-the-chest.[103] Writing in

Hebrew, in other words, is a journey of both introspection and extroversion. In Hever's reading, "[t]he loss of orientation—linguistic and therefore of identity—is depicted in the poem as the only orientation possible in a world that is replete with violence."[104] "I Write Hebrew" is also a poem that insists on sameness rather than difference: everyone has the same feet; strangers are potential friends. The tone of this poem differs greatly from the skepticism we have seen earlier (such as in the wish that the poet's parents be cursed for the lies he composes about brotherly solidarity). It is also more positive than 'Araidi's apostrophe to Shammas, and, it is probably needless to say, quite the opposite extreme of Shammas's "Portrait" of the speaker who stands in total isolation, unable to move, slowly watching himself ebb away. Masalha's poems, then, express an ambivalent view of bilingualism as a condition in which one gains as much as one loses.

As a postscript to this discussion of portraiture, let us turn to Na'im 'Araidi's most cogent self-portrait, entitled *Na'im 'Araidi*. This self-portrait is contained in all of four lines:

> In all of these scores of poems
> There is if only one small spark—
> Your being
> Alone.[105]

The phrase *heyotkha levad* (your being alone) echoes God's words in Genesis 2:18, *"lo tov heyot ha-adam levado"* (It is not good that the man should be alone), whence the Lord decides to create woman. Once again, 'Araidi reverses the original meaning of his biblical intertext: his solitude is perhaps the only grace that this poetic journey has afforded him.

Space, Home, and Exile

[A]t once carrier of national and familial traditions and emblem of cultural and personal identity, language functions equally as an identity-grounding home under conditions of displacement and as a means of intervention into identity-fixing cultural agendas.[106]

Angelika Bammer assigns two functions to language: first, for language to act as "home," as a locus of self; and second, for language to act as a "means of intervention." This second function of language can be easily identified in the texts we have examined. But is it possible to locate in these poets' works moments in which language functions as an "identity-grounding home," not as a the site of illusions and reflections but as an icon of stability within the web of displacement, duality, and ambiguity that is the lot of the bilingual 'borderline' writer? How is the subject constituted through the language of place and space in these texts? After all, in the context at hand, *place* is at the very heart of these writers' dilemma. The concept of the 'borderline' writer, as one who inhabits a position of in-betweenness, is itself a manifestation of spatial tension.

We have already seen a number of spaces and places: there was 'Araidi's rereading of the biblical landscape of the *'akeydah* and the Abrahamian covenant; there was Shammas's cave, and his poems of Jerusalem (not to mention the conclusion of his 'portrait' poem with the one-word line, "Jerusalem"). Masalha's collection, as mentioned, is titled *Ehad mi-kan* (literally, 'one from here'); but its title poem presents a 'here' that, far from acting as a grounding center, is a node of instability and relentless violence:

One from Here
A poem for a late night's hour
It's changed so fast,
the world. And for me it's
now absurd. Things have reached
the point where I've stopped
thinking about the falling leaves.
Because, you see, from here,
there's nowhere to go.
And anyway, even in the park
the trees are uprooted and are
no more.
And these days, it's dangerous
here to go out on the streets.
The road is so wet.
Blood flows in the main artery.
I count them:
One from here, one from there.
I count them,
like sheep, until
I fall asleep. [107]

This is a poem about place, one that uses the most Israeli of collocations, *ba-arets* — literally, 'in the Land [of Israel]'; idiomatically, 'in Israel,' 'in this country' — to situate the speaker, as in the lines *"mesukan / la-tset ba-arets la-rehov"* (. . . it's dangerous / here to go out on the streets). This usage of *ba-arets* is most idiomatically rendered simply as 'here."[108] More importantly, this 'here' assumes a common frame of reference with the reader, in which both are part of the Israeli collective; in other words, the operating principle is one of inclusion, of *sameness* as opposed to *difference*. The language of the poem itself thus puts the speaker in a certain 'here' (or, perhaps more to the point, puts that 'here' in the speaker); and yet that 'here' of the poem, of the collection's title, and indeed, of the volume as a whole, is a place defined only in terms of change, absence, and loss. As Hever writes:

> [t]he identity with which the poet chooses to define himself is linked to place by virtue of the fact of his presence as a native there and not by virtue of any national connection: "And I was a Jew, before Jesus walked / on the Sea of Galilee . . . / And I was a Muslim in the land / of Jesus, and a Catholic in the desert." The homeland is [represented as] no more than an apartment house.[109]

But however conflicted they may be, home and a homeland have a palpable presence in Masalha's writing. His poetic geography also travels further than that of Shammas or 'Araidi; we find in the collection a love poem to a vanished and vanquished Baghdad (which, although clearly of the moment, draws upon the language of Psalm 137, *By the Waters of Babylon*);[110] and a poem from one of his Arabic collections describes *"al-Ti-fla min Ghazza"* (The Little Girl from Gaza).[111]

The poems of Shammas and 'Araidi deal with space and place, on the whole, more abstractly. They do not refer explicitly to Israel as a national space, nor do they invoke the violence associated with it. Instead, their poems overflow with spatial metaphors, symbolized most cogently by the no man's land for Shammas and the junction for 'Araidi. 'Araidi writes of the junction:

> The roads that meet in the junction
> are the roads that part ways in the junction.

. . .
Whence I am coming
to you
before I could cover my forsaken nakedness
for another
like those scattered
at all the junctions of my life—
now in Hebrew,
and then in Arabic.
And all the passersby will try
in vain to make corrections
according to the rules of the academy
of languages.[112]

In another poem, called "In the Middle of the Road," he writes:

Whoever stands in the middle of the road will be run over
by pedestrians before he can sit down
to verify on which side
he stands.
But whoever walks down the middle of the road
has a chance of being saved.
He just needs to pray
that all those walking on both sides
aren't following in his footsteps. . . . [113]

Whereas for Shammas:

I do not know.
A language beyond this,
And a language beyond this.
And I hallucinate in the no man's land.[114]

The no man's land is not only an existential metaphor. In the Israeli/
Palestinian context, the reader would immediately think of the no man's
land that divided East and West Jerusalem between 1948 and 1967. While
today, the erstwhile no man's land has become gentrified real estate, the city
remains divided into its Arab and Jewish halves. The idea of bifurcation is

echoed across his poetic *oeuvre* in other figurations; in poems in both Arabic and Hebrew, Shammas's speaker compares himself to the squeezed-out half shell of a juiced orange.[115] This is a particularly loaded metaphor, as oranges (synecdochical for the famous Jaffa orange) have been claimed by both sides as a national symbol, one that appears frequently in both Israeli and Palestinian literatures; it is not a stretch, then, to see something of the no man's land in the image of the self as an orange that has been sliced in two.[116]

Aside from the no man's land, which is both border and chasm, Shammas's poetry is full of gaps and spaces fraught with internal tension: doors, windows, apertures, passages. In his Arabic collection, *Asir yaqzati wa-nawmi* (Prisoner of my Wakefulness and Sleep), a blank page of paper becomes an empty white space; windows are openings for furtive stealings-in or escapings-out; gaps and voids are spaces through which the speaker flees. The persistent disassociation of self from surroundings is also expressed (as we have seen in the Hebrew poem) through experiences of the body.

As with Masalha, 'home' in the poetry of Shammas and 'Araidi is an unstable site of change and loss, albeit one somewhat more tangible and less abstract in the case of 'Araidi. 'Araidi's relationship to 'home' encompasses the spheres of his house, the village, and the people and scenery of the Galilee. For 'Araidi, rootedness is found in the wild beauty of the Carmel—in nature, not in language—and he claims, describes, and revels in this love for the Carmel in both languages. Home, on the other hand, has been lost through the changes wrought by time:

> I returned to the village
> where the dogs' barks died
> the aviary became a lighted tower.
> All the fellahin with whom I wanted to sing
> the song of the hay in a nightingale's tune
> have become laborers with smoke in their throat
> Where are all those who were and are no more?
> Oh, this heavy dream of mine.
> I have returned to the village
> as one who flees from culture
> and I came to the village as one
> who comes from exile to exile.[117]

If 'Araidi's landscape is outside, in nature, Shammas's landscape is decisively inside; what for 'Araidi is the topographical map of his soul is for Shammas the architect's plans. But 'home' is rendered impossible, not only because of the social and political conditions that have made him an exile, but because of the exile from childhood, which entailed the move from the village to the city (that is, from a traditional Palestinian community to a mixed, predominantly Jewish, urban environment) and the impossibility of a real return to the village. For Shammas, childhood is a murky and unpredictable presence, a mischief-making 'wild child' that runs through his work. The childhood home has Freudian undertones; its loss embodies the original, irreversible exile from self:

> My childhood village is swept away in the rain, not according to the
>   code of memory.
> And in my dreams, I barely manage to catch something of the field
>   of rye.
> I recite names that I knew, in the tranquil melody of oblivion.
> And only the house in which I was born follows me like a wild boy.[118]

In another poem in the same collection Shammas writes:

> My childhood home struggles inside me,
> I am struggling inside the empty house,
> and try to convince myself
> that here I am, a grown man.
> (A grown man, whose childhood home
> stuggles inside him, and he keeps quiet.
> and he struggles inside the empty house.)[119]

The impossibility of reconciling the lost past (entailing home, childhood, and wholeness) with the conflicted and fragmented present leads Shammas's speaker to make his declaration of private, internal 'citizenship.' Where Darwish's speaker commands his interlocutor, "Write it down! I am an Arab!" and Masalha's speaker affirms, "I am an Arab poet," Shammas's speaker pronounces:

I am a self-resident, a loyal citizen
to my loves. My loves that were,
and I touched them, with my hands.
The voice and not my hand is covered with a velvety down.
My Isaac has long since decided: it's not just the voice,
and not just the hands, but that it's not even the time.
But in the end I arrived, and here I am. And I would be happy
about this, if not for my childhood, stuck in the elevator
of memory, pressing
the alarm button.[120]

"*Ve-ḥiney ani kan*" (and here I am) says the speaker (in a modernized echo of the biblical *hineyni*); although (as in the case of Masalha's poems in *Eḥad mi-kan*), that *kan* (here) is far from a grounding, reassuring presence or force for the subject or *ani* (I). In this case, it is a 'here' whose constancy is threatened by that wild child, the suppressed childhood self trying to break out of the elevator of memory. As for that other face of home—exile—Shammas encapsulates it in a conversation with the Israeli writer David Grossman:

A line from a poem by Nizar Qabbani, the Syrian poet who
served his country as a diplomat in Spain, just came to me: "In
the narrow alleys of Cordoba I would extend my hand and look
for the keys to our house in Damascus." I don't feel that way
anywhere. You ask if I was "here." I understand the word 'here' in
its geographical-Hebrew sense. I was not here in the Arabic sense
of 'here,' because they have taken the ground out from under me.
When you say "Galil," what is that word for me? The Galil is yours;
for me it is the Jalil; the change in pronunciation makes all the
difference; without it my entire semantic security in my sense of
homeland is unsettled.[121]

Under these conditions, it is hardly surprising that he should declare himself a "self-resident." Doomed to residence in what will forever be the borderland of his semantic insecurity, Shammas, like 'Araidi, can only travel from exile to exile: "I feel an exile in Arabic, the language of my blood. I feel an exile in Hebrew, my stepmother tongue."[122]

Being in the borderline, within the seam of displacement, thus becomes a way of life. In a poem in his Arabic collection, Shammas writes:

And the woman waving a kerchief said:
"Open the map of the world as a razor
in the face of exile.
Search on its blade for an island
where they don't hang the people on
the traffic signs
and you will pass above the police barricades
because you are as the wind that comes from the sea."
And when they closed the window in his face
there was nothing on my eyelashes but algae.
Then how will the poem come?[123]

The image of an island on a blade: how isolated and precarious is this refuge from exile, this place in which one can float above the police barricades. If this poetic solution is the sought-after 'home,' it is but partial; the image gives new meaning to the expression 'living on the edge.'

Allusion and Illusion

In the 'self-portraits' we have observed, allusion is a double-edged sword, a means not only of describing the self and situating it in a world shared by the reader, but of establishing its difference by simultaneously inverting (and thereby defamiliarizing) many of those associations. It is a magician's tool kit, producing a vision that is at once real and unreal, familiar and unfamiliar, assonant and dissonant. Allusion, in this way, quickly becomes linked to illusion: a self-portrait retreating from its subject, a self-portrait of someone else, a self-portrait about solitude in the language of the biblical story about the invention of partnership; identity-grounding homes that have turned into sites of dream and memory, and the non-space of the no man's land becoming a surrogate 'home.' Allusion, in other words, enables these writers to reveal the underbelly of a reality that for them is paradoxical, unstable, an enigma wrapped up in a riddle.

Although these poems are written not just in the dictionary language of Hebrew but in the reader's cultural and symbolic idiom, they express a reality overlapping only in part—one that may be unfolding in the same time and place (as Masalha most cogently lets us understand, with his emphasis on the *kan* or 'here' of his title), but which, Janus-like, is also facing other experiences and memories, other associations of place. To be sure, the poems express these 'other' experiences too (for example, Masalha's exquisite image of the homeland nestled in the palms of his father), but by and large these are snippets, fragments of memory. Yet even so, these fragments of a Palestinian world, interpolated as they are within the Israeli-Hebrew text, foster the poetics of in-betweenness: "By focusing on 'events,' 'scenes,' 'memories that flash up in a moment of danger,' we hope to maintain a sense of the enactment of meanings . . . that become the insignia of the interstices. These are the spaces through which minorities *translate* the dominant designations of differences."[124] The 'in-between,' in short, is the space of translation of difference. In my reading, if the poetry of Shammas, 'Araidi, and Masalha does not empty the Hebrew language of its Jewishness, it does invert or transform its associations, thereby enacting a translation of meaning in relation to the source text—a process I have called Palestinian midrash.

My reading of Palestinian-Israeli poetry has attempted to transpose the hermeneutic framework from a question of 'which' ('which one,' 'either/or') to a question of 'how': from a politics of *claiming* to an aesthetic of *being*. This means asking not 'Israeli or Palestinian?' 'Hebrew or Arabic?' 'Israeli or Jewish?' but rather, asking what it means to *be* in-between 'Palestinian-ness' and 'Jewishness,' or in-between Hebrew and Arabic. This means also to ask not whether their writing succeeds in separating Hebrew from Jewishness, but rather, to ask how Palestinian identity in Israel has become irrevocably hybridized (and, for that matter, Jewish identity in Israel as well); and how Palestinian authors remake Hebrew culture through the symbolic domains of *both* Jewishness and Palestinian-ness: how do we find this fraught and yet productive crossing of experience expressed within the language of being? What I am advocating here, in short, is a productive rather than a reductive approach to cultural difference.

The lingering question for these borderline writers is that of reconciliation: can the two sides (of the self, to begin with) be unified; can the border be transcended; can in-betweenness be further translated into a holistic one-ness? Shammas's poetry does not entertain such a possibility. For 'Araidi, however, the possibility of reconciliation glimmers somewhere in sight, albeit just beyond reach. He writes in an Arabic poem entitled

Amal (Hope):

I am a friend of the friend of the sea
and an enemy of the enemy of the land
and there is nothing between them but air—
some of it is polluted by the speed of the wind
and some of it is as slow as the tortoise
and between the speed and the slowness
I breathe what is left of time.
The hour doesn't mean anything
but for one who wears a watch.
There's a time difference between the other side
of the sea,
and the other side
of the sea.
A place is only charted by its lovers
but I will chart my expectations
by the gallows of distant hope—
Once, here, and once, there,
and when the time comes
the hour will be without hands.[125]

As friend of both land and sea (between whom there is "nothing but air"), the speaker is poised to mediate between oppositional adversaries—a position echoed in "between the speed and the slowness / I breathe in what's left of time." This, in essence, is the same subject who embodies the junction, who goes down the middle of the road. Indeed, more often than not, 'Araidi's poetic 'I' is found being tossed back and forth, attached to a rope in a tug-of-war, or mediating between two opposing forces. But there is a time when this conciliatory movement will no longer be needed. The line "gallows of distant hopes" reflects 'Araidi's stubbornly optimistic pessimism—perhaps something like that which the late Emile Habiby coined "pessoptimism."[126] And sometimes 'Araidi's pessoptimistic shield cracks a bit, occasioning the expression of hopes without gallows (or, perhaps, without even gallows humor). This is the case in a 1975 poem called "*Shir shel Shalom*" (A Poem of Peace), which 'Araidi dedicated to the redoubtable Israeli poet laureate, Yehuda Amichai:

And what there is for me
and what there is for you
let us write in our beautiful books
in these two languages
of which neither
is the shadow of the other,
that the view that we have seen
together
not in dreams
is so very beautiful
so very shining
so very perfect.[127]

This poem also seems to tell us that while we ought not to forget
(and indeed the texts we have read do not let us forget) the assymetrical
power relations at play, we should also remember the ideal of bilingualism as a transcendent dissolving of borders between languages and
cultures—an ideal that does, nonetheless, inform their work, even if
only in shadow. For even the most profound expression of pain in their
Hebrew poetry is a means of bringing the Hebrew reader closer to a
Palestinian experience.

We will leave the final word on 'hope' with Masalha, who ends his
poetic tribute to the Hebrew language and his depiction of the reality
of life in the 'here' of his collection's title with a hair-raising poem called
Ha-Tikvah (The Hope)—a choice of title that could not possibly be more
fraught, given that it is also the title of Israel's national anthem. If this
essay has sought to illustrate how a Palestinian writer living in Israel may
use allusion, intertextuality, and a cultural standpoint of in-betweenness
to rewrite the language of Jewishness from within, the poem at hand
could serve as an exemplar—and, no less, as a powerful critique of life in
the self-defined Jewish state:

Ha-Tikvah (The Hope)

On the one-way street
leading to a wide-open field,
a corpse sprawled out to its soul.[128] On the edges of the street,

fragments of metal that fell from the heavens
of the spirit that fell silent. And the Spirit of God
hovers not over water;[129]
 over the blood.[130]
The trees, which suckled their mothers' milk,[131]
have already grown—false teeth
of the elderly city.[132]
How wonderful is the mulberry tree
Its roots—patriotic songs.
Soon fall
will awaken
Ha-tikvah, the hope—
falling
leaves.[133]

Notes

* I would like to thank Rutie Adler, Maya Barzilai, and Chana Kronfeld for their
   assistance with questions of translation; Shamma Boyarin for help with Rabbinic
   intertexts; Todd Hasak-Lowy and Chana Kronfeld for reading and commenting on
   the penultimate draft; and the volume's editors, Dana Sajdi and Marlé Hammond,
   for their careful readings, comments, and suggestions.

1 Anton Shammas, 'Arabeskot (Tel Aviv: 'Am 'Oved, 1986).

2 That distinction is credited to Atallah Mansour, author of Be-or hadash (Tel Aviv:
   Karni, 1966).

3 See, for instance, Hannan Hever, "Hebrew in an Israeli Arab Hand: Six
   Miniatures on Anton Shammas's Arabesques," in The Nature and Context of
   Minority Discourse, ed. Abdul JanMohamed and David Lloyd (New York: Oxford
   University Press, 1990), 264–93; Reuven Snir, "'Hebrew as the Language of
   Grace': Arab-Palestinian Writers in Hebrew," Prooftexts 15 (1995): 63–183; Rachel
   Feldhay Brenner, "'Hidden Transcripts' Made Public: Israeli Arab Fiction
   and its Reception," Critical Inquiry 26 (Autumn 1999): 85–108; Yael Feldman,
   "Postcolonial Memory, Postmodern Intertextuality: Anton Shammas's Arabesques
   Revisited," PMLA 114 (May 1999): 373–85; Gil Hochberg, "'The Dispossession
   of Hebrew': Anton Shammas's Arabesques and the Cultural Space of Language,"
   in Crisis and Memory: The Representation of Space in Modern Levantine Narrative,
   ed. Ken Seigneurie (Wiesbaden: Reichert Verlag, 2003), 52–66; and Michael
   Gluzman, "The Politics of Intertextuality in Anton Shammas's Arabesques,"
   Journal of Modern Jewish Studies 3, no. 3 (November 2004): 319–36. As for critics
   of Arabic literature, see Yumna al-'Id, Tiqniyat al-sard al-riwa'i fi daw' al-manhaj

al-bunyawi (Beirut: al-Farabi, 1990); also al-'Id, "Arabesques," *Al-Karmel* 35 (1990): 83–84, and a review by Muhammad Siddiq, "al-Kitaba bi-l-'ibriya al-fusha: taqaddum riwayat *'Arabisk* wa-hiwar ma' Antun Shammas" , *Alif* 20 (2000): 155–67.

4   To date, the only criticism of Palestinian writing in Hebrew that addresses poetry (in this case, that of Shammas and 'Araidi) and refers to their Arabic creative production is Snir's "'Hebrew as the Language of Grace,'" (see note 3, above).

5   When Shammas is discussed alongside other writers, these are nearly always the novelists Emile Habiby and Atallah Mansour (with the aforementioned exception of Snir's article "Hebrew as the Language of Grace").

6   Because of considerations of length, this article will not, for instance, discuss Siham Daoud, another Palestinian poet in Israel. According to 'Ami 'Elad-Bouskila, Daoud also has the distinction of being the only Palestinian-Israeli writer aside from 'Araidi to have begun writing in Hebrew and switched to bilingual writing in Hebrew and Arabic: *Modern Palestinian Literature and Culture* (London: Frank Cass, 1999), 44. For more on Daoud and an analysis of her poetry, see Lital Levy, Lena Salaymeh, and Adriana Valencia, "Poetic Structures on Contested Space: The *bayt/bayit* of Siham Daoud and Shelley Elkayam," *Critical Sense* 9, no. 1 (Winter 2001): 9–54, http://criticalsense.berkeley.edu/archive/winter2001/levy.pdf. For a comprehensive overview of the phenomenon of Palestinian writers in Israel (and more on Daoud, 'Araidi, and Shammas), see 'Ami 'Elad-Bouskila, *Modern Palestinian Literature and Culture*, chaps. 1–3 esp. chap. 2, "The Other Face: The Language Choice of Arab Writers in Israel," 32–62. It should also be noted that this essay will not consider the works of Sayed Qashu' (alternatively spelled Kashua; b. 1975), an important writer whose work takes up the second generation of Palestinians in Israel, for the simple reason that Qashu' has not published poetry. He has published two Hebrew novels to date: *'Aravim rokdim* (2002) and *Va-yehi boker* (2004), as well as numerous essays in the Hebrew press.
    Concerning the transliteration of 'Araidi's name: standard transliteration rules would render it 'Araydi; Snir spells it as 'Arayidi in his article. 'Araidi himself and most of the criticism spells it alternately 'Araide' or "Araidi,' so I have compromised by employing the latter version.

7   See Tejaswini Niranjana, *Siting Translation: History, Post-structuralism, and the Colonial Context* (Berkeley: University of California Press, 1992); Alfred Arteaga, ed., *An Other Tongue: Nation and Ethnicity in the Linguistic Borderlands* (Durham, NC: Duke University Press, 1994); Jacques Derrida, *The Monolingualism of the Other; or, The Prosthesis of Origin* (Stanford: Stanford University Press, 1998); Anuradha Dingwaney and Carol Meir, eds., *Between Languages and Cultures: Translation and Cross-Cultural Texts* (Pittsburgh: University of Pittsburgh Press, 1995); and Sherry Simon and Paul St. Pierre, eds., *Changing the Terms: Translating in the Postcolonial Era* (Ottowa: University of Ottowa Press, 2000).

8   Homi Bhabha, "Frontlines/ Borderposts," in *Displacements: Cultural Identities in Question,* ed. Angelika Bammer (Bloomington: Indiana University Press, 1994), 269; my emphasis.

9   See Jacques Lacan, *The Seminar of Jacques Lacan*, ed. Jacques-Alain Miller (New York and London: Norton, 1988); *The Four Fundamental Concepts of Psychoanalysis*, ed. Jacques-Alain Miller, trans. Alan Sheridan (New York and London: Norton, 1998 [1981]); and *Ecrits: A Selection*, trans. Bruce Fink, Heloise Fink, and Russell Grigg (New York and London: Norton, 2002).

10 Anuradha Dingwaney, "Introduction: Translating 'Third World' Cultures," in Dingwaney and Meir, *Between Languages and Cultures*, 8; emphasis in original except for the phrase "*in which . . . associations.*"

11 In a similar locution, Mary Louise Pratt identifies "contact zones" as "social spaces where disparate cultures meet, clash, and grapple with each other, often in highly assymetrical relations of domination and subordination." See her *Imperial Eyes: Travel Writing and Transculturation* (London and New York: Routledge, 1992), 4.

12 We may understand this to include the Hebrew Bible, the Rabbinic corpus (Talmud and midrashic literatures), liturgical and ceremonial texts, prayers, *piyyutim* (devotional poetry), and even certain well-known secular compositions by medieval Hebrew writers.

13 Snir, "Hebrew as the Language of Grace," 169.

14 Hever writes of Shammas's *Arabesques:* "In principle, what we are dealing with here is a variation on the Hegelian paradigm of the master-slave relationship, whereby the master's consciousness of himself as master is conditioned by the slave's acknowledgment of the master's superior status." This section of the study then extends its Hegelian analysis of the narrative. Hever, "Hebrew in an Israeli Arab Hand," 285; repr. in Hever, *Producing the Modern Hebrew Canon: Nation Building and Minority Discourse* (New York: New York University Press, 2002), 194–95.

15 This point will become more evident in my readings of Masalha's poems "*Ehad mi-kan*" and "*Ha-tikvah*" later in this chapter.

16 For more on this relationship, see Ruth Kartun-Blum, *Profane Scriptures: Reflections on the Dialogue with the Bible in Modern Hebrew Poetry* (Cincinnati: Hebrew Union College Press, 1999); I will be referring to this relationship (and to Kartun-Blum) more extensively in the body of this chapter.

17 Gloria Anzaldúa, *Borderlands/La Frontera: The New Mestiza* (San Francisco: Aunt Lute Books, 1987), 19–20, quoted in Marianne Hirsch, "Pictures of a Displaced Girlhood," *Displacements: Cultural Identities in Question*, ed. Angelika Bammer (Bloomington: Indiana University Press, 1994), 71.

18 Dzevad Karahasan, *Sarajevo, Exodus of a City*, trans. Slobodan Drakulic (New York: Kodansha America, 1994), 89.

19 Of course, the readership of Hebrew includes Israeli's Arab minority as well, but given that this group (many of whom prefer to read in Arabic) comprises a small minority of readers within an already limited target audience, it is safe to assume that Shammas, 'Araidi, Masalha, and other Palestinian-Israeli authors write in Hebrew with a primarily Jewish readership in mind. This is corroborated both internally, through the use of canonically Jewish allusions (and the relative paucity of Palestinian, Arabic, Muslim, and Christian cultural sources and references) in their Hebrew writing, and externally, through, for instance, footnotes explaining

Arab(ic) references to the reader (for example, 'Araidi's poem "Farid al-Atrash," whose footnote identifies the subject as "One of the great Arab composers and singers. Of the Druze faith, he was born on the Mount of Druzes and went into exile in Egypt with his brother and sister. He died in 1974;" but Farid al-Atrash is almost universally known among the Arab public.) 'Araidi, *Hazarti el ha-kfar* (Tel Aviv: 'Am 'Oved, 1986), 15.

20 Gilles Deleuze and Félix Guattari, *Kafka: Toward a Minor Literature*, trans. Dana Polan (Minneapolis: University of Minnesota Press, 1987), 25.

21 Shammas dedicates a poem to Gilbo'a in his first Hebrew collection. See his "*Koridah*," in Shammas, *Krikhah kashah* (Tel Aviv: Sifriat Po'alim, 1974), 13.

22 'Araidi writes a poem about Greenberg, "*Uri Tsvi Greenberg*," in *Ulay zo ahavah* (Tel Aviv: Ma'ariv Book Club, 1989), 24. 'Araidi is also a scholar of Arabic literature, and has published scholarly studies in Arabic.

23 Gila Ramras-Rauch, *The Arab in Israeli Literature* (Bloomington: Indiana University Press, 1989), 194.

24 Consider, for instance, these verses published by Greenberg in 1954:
> Outside – Jerusalem...and the moaning of God's trees
> Cut down there by enemies in all generations...
> Heavy-rivered clouds: within them lightnings
> And thunderings, that to me on a night of rain are tidings
> From the mouth of the Almighty till the end of generations.
> (Uri Tsvi Greenberg, "*Be-leyl geshem bi-rushalayim*" , trans. Arieh Sachs, *The Modern Hebrew Poem Itself*, ed. Stanley Burnshaw, T. Carmi, and Ezra Spicehandler [Cambridge, MA: Harvard University Press, 1989], 62–63)

But it should be noted that other Hebrew poets, even of Greenberg's generation and earlier, wrote poems of place in far less inflated, symbolic, and/or nationalist terms. A case in point is Lea Goldberg's "*Tel Aviv 1935*" (also anthologized in Greenberg, *The Modern Hebrew Poem Itself*, 130). Greenberg is thus representative of only one strain of modern Hebrew poetry, one with nationalist leanings.

25 We can make this claim as far as the Hebrew poems of all three poets are concerned; as for the Arabic poems of Shammas and 'Araidi, I believe it holds as well. But I have not located any of Masalha's Arabic collections and am therefore am unable to comment upon them.

26 "*Abba gam*" in Masalha, *Ehad mi-kan* (Tel Aviv: 'Am 'Oved, 2004), 25. Translation of poem by Vivian Eden, http://israel.poetryinternational.org/cwolk/view/23548.

27 Siham Daoud, for example, writes a poem about Jerusalem that, while incorporating personal elements, as well as an 'I' and 'you,' lies heavily on Christian symbolism and contains explicit references to the city's contested political status: see Levy, Salaymeh, and Valencia, "Poetic Structures," 37–39.

28 The word for 'gate' in Hebrew, '*sha'ar*' (שער is a homograph of the Arabic word for poem, *shi'r*, شعر); creating an interlingual pun. Bilingually, then, the poem can be read as either "Five Gates of Jerusalem" or "Five Poems to Jerusalem."

29 Shammas, "*Sheleg bi-rushalayim*," *Krikhah kashah*, 9. In Shammas's Arabic collection, *Asir yaqzati wa-nawmi* (Jerusalem: Al-Sharq, 1974), published in the

same year as *Krikhah kashah*, some poems express a similar intertwining of the lover and the city, but utilize a more Islamo-Arabic cultural idiom, for example:

> You were two poems away from me, or
> even closer
> within my lips and my reach.
> But when the climbing paths wound behind me,
> toward childhood,
> the wilderness poured down on me suddenly, and my sadness
> dashed forward.
> So I became the minaret of emptiness.
> And you ebbed away like dawn's call for prayer.
>
> (Shammas, *Asir yaqzati wa-nawmi*, 34. Translation adapted from Salma Jayyusi, ed., *Anthology of Modern Palestinian Literature* [New York: Columbia University Press, 1992], 303).

30 Shammas, *Shetah hefker* (Tel Aviv: Ha-kibbutz ha-me'uhad, 1979), 6.

31 Kartun-Blum, *Profane Scriptures,* 3. In her introduction, invoking the idea of linguistic possession, she writes: "In poetic and political terms, a filial struggle for identity means a struggle over the possession of language and the crucial right to interpret the present moment in new terms," Kartun-Blum, *Profane Scriptures*, ix.

32 Gluzman, "The Politics of Intertextuality," 323 and n. 67.

33 Hochberg, "The Dispossession," 64.

34 In his essay "Israeli or Jewish Literature?" Yonatan Ratosh (a right-wing figure influenced by the Canaanite movement in Israeli culture led by Aharon 'Amir) considers the issue from a different perspective—not the current but rather the historic production of Hebrew literature by non-Jews:

> Hebrew was undoubtedly the holy tongue, the language of the culture, thought, and science of the Jews for generation upon generation, just as Latin was that of the people of Europe throughout the Middle Ages. But Jewish literature does not exhaust itself in Hebrew, is not bounded by Hebrew, is not identical to Hebrew literature.
>
> It may help to expand our perspective a little if we recall that...in the Middle Ages Hebrew was at times one of the general languages of science – rather than a Jewish language alone. This was true in medicine, for example, and every doctor . . . might have been presumed to know Hebrew, as with Latin in our day. We might also remember that in the sixteenth century in Hungary, not only Jews but learned nobility and other Gentiles were supposed to know Hebrew no less than Latin and Greek. They even wrote poems in Hebrew as part of the learning process. Therefore, not only is Jewish literature not limited by Hebrew, but to be accurate, literature in Hebrew is not exclusively Jewish [...]
>
> And if we view Judaism as a unique form of existence, singular among the world's nations, whose laws are inapplicable to it – in short, in the same light as Judaism sees itself – it will be difficult for us not to conclude that the very uniqueness of Israeli literature lies in the fact that it is not *Jewish* (Yonatan Ratosh, "Israeli or Jewish Literature?" in *What is Jewish Literature?* ed. Hana Wirth-Nesher

[Philadelphia and Jerusalem: The Jewish Publication Society, 1994], 89–90; emphasis in original)

In short, Ratosh demonstrates that while there is an obvious overlap between 'Israeli' and 'Jewish' literatures, neither can exclusively 'contain' the other. Ratosh, however, is debating the identity of Hebrew literature rather than that of the Hebrew language. He does not comment on whether or not he considers Hebrew a 'Jewish' language, or what it would mean for a language to be 'Jewish' when it is utilized by Gentiles. He also admits in his conclusion that "[i]t may be difficult even to determine where Jewish literature ends and this new, national literature begins" (Ibid., 90).

35 Robert Alter, *The Invention of Hebrew Prose* (Seattle: University of Washington Press, 1988), 3; quoted in Gluzman, "The Politics of Intertextuality," 322.

36 It should be mentioned, however, that Israeli Hebrew literature has privileged the biblical over the rabbinic layers of Hebrew. More on this will follow below.

37 For Kartun-Blum, it is this very diachronicity embedded within the synchronic that enables the sort of intertextual discussion under consideration in this chapter:

> The intimate and quarrelsome dialogue with the Hebrew Bible in modern Israeli literature is possible not only because of the historical parallels between the ancient narrative and contemporary reality that converge in the same geographical space, but also because of the unique position of the Hebrew language – the fact that in Modern Hebrew there is no difference between the synchronic and the diachronic dictionary; that modern Hebrew words can be used in both the contemporary and the ancient registers and so burden even the so-called colloquial register with various associations and connotations of three thousand years of semantic history. Moreover, since the Bible is a part of the Israeli code, the poet can also rely on the fact that the addressee will be able to recapture the multilayered information. (Khartun-Blum, *Profane Scriptures*, 7)

38 Snir writes early in his article "Hebrew as the Language of Grace," that "[Shammas] justifies writing in Hebrew as a mission, since 'as an Arab it is important to say what I want to say to the Jews,' although it seems more likely that it is best attributed to a conscious aesthetic preference" (167). The rest of the article presents the "conscious aesthetic preference" as point of fact. The phrase appears in the article repeatedly (167, 172, 173, 175) and as "conscious aesthetic cultural choice" (176). Snir, "Hebrew as the Language of Grace."

39 Ibid., 175.

40 Ibid., 174–75.

41 Ibid., 165; reprinted from the periodical *Kol ha-'ir* (Jerusalem) 27, no. 2 (1987): 58.

42 This was a position Shammas advocated throughout the 1980s in his weekly column in a local Jerusalem newspaper, *Kol ha-'ir*, a project Yael Feldman refers to as a "one-man campaign" ("Postcolonial Memory," 385 n. 6). In recent years Shammas has not actively supported this position, appearing to have moved away from the Israeli political and cultural field altogether.

43 Snir, "Hebrew as the Language of Grace," 174. It should also be noted here that I have not seen evidence that 'Araidi himself ever referred to the separation of

Judaism from Hebrew as part of his own literary agenda. Snir's article seems to assume or infer that 'Araidi shares this goal, and I do not know whether or not this is the case.

44 Ibid., 174. Snir follows his point about "the failure of 'Arayidi and Shammas to separate Jewish heritage from Hebrew language" with a comparison to the Lebanese poet Sa'id 'Aql, advocate of the "Phoenician" ideology: "Like 'Aql, who tries to sever the link between Arabic culture and Islam, Shammas strives to purify Hebrew literature of its Jewish features and relics" (174). As will be discussed at length in this chapter, I do not find evidence of this program in Shammas's writing, which, to the contrary, makes extensive, strategic use of Jewish features.

45 Adding to this point, Snir writes, "The nature of contemporary Hebrew literature and the directions of its development, like those of Arabic-Palestinian literature, do not leave any room for doubt that the hope to expand the boundaries of Hebrew literature and to create a new Israeli cultural identity is nothing but a daydream" (Ibid., 174). Hever, in a 1989 article, espouses the opposite viewpoint:

> During the last two decades, literature written by Israel's Arab minority has slowly begun to infiltrate the Hebrew literary canon. From the far-off margins of the culture of the Arab ethnic minority it is gradually percolating into the authoritative culture of the majority [...].
>
> As the minority literature becomes increasingly cognizant of its potential, it may find its place much closer to the canon. In so doing it will also gradually leave behind its marginal role . . . and will be incorporated – so we may hope – as a legitimate and potent partner in Israeli literature. (Hannan Hever, "Israeli Literature's Achilles' Heel," *Tikkun* 4, no. 5 [September–October 1989], 30–33)

46 In one of his poems, 'Araidi's speaker refers to himself as "the intermittent Arabic-Hebrew Hebrew-Arabic poet" ("*Abba Ema*" ["Mother Father"], in *Ulay zo ahavah*, 49.) And in fact, 'Araidi has published poetry about equally in both languages; his only novel, *Tvilah katlanit* (Fatal Baptism, 1992) appeared in Hebrew. (The novel, however, did not receive much critical attention, and 'Araidi remains known primarily as a Hebrew poet). As to the question of language choice, 'Araidi writes:

> Just as I wanted to prove to my [Jewish] teachers and parents that I could meet their expectations [of mastering Hebrew], so I wanted to prove to my people that I could also write in Arabic. And so I can, but the way I write in Hebrew is very different from the way I write in Arabic. [...] I am not sure if the Jewish people in Israel are aware of what I think of the Hebrew language, and this does not concern me. It is not for them that I write in Hebrew, but because of them. As to the question of whether or not I am a Hebrew poet, the answer is very simple; a Hebrew poet, yes, but not a Jewish poet, just as I am too a Druze and an Arab poet. (Na'im 'Araidi, "Dreams, Ideas and Realities [Cultural Dialogue in the Middle East]," *The Jerusalem Review* 1, no. 1 [April 1997]: 208–13, 210)

47 Ratosh, for example, concludes: "And perhaps this is the real question: not *Israeli* or universally Jewish literature, an illusory opposition that a little reflection reveals to be without foundation, but *Jewish* or *non-Jewish* literature, *Jewish*

literature or *national* literature." Ratosh, "Israeli or Jewish Literature?," 90, emphasis in original.

48 For example, Hochberg writes: "Fortifying the static image of Hebrew literature as a Jewish literature and of Israeli culture as Jewish culture, Snir ascribes the 'identity crisis' to non-Jewish writers of Hebrew (Shammas and 'Araidi), denying the 'identity crises' of Israeli-Hebrew culture. He thus overlooks the productive effects of non-Jewish writings in Hebrew, which as Shammas describes it, 'Un-Jews the Hebrew language, making it more Israeli," and thus 'bringing it back to its semantic origins – back to its place;'" Hochberg, "The Dispossession," 56. Although Hochberg begins by taking her argument in a new and interesting direction, that of the internal identity crisis in Israeli Hebrew culture, she short-circuits this thread by falling into the same 'trap' as Snir, whom she criticizes from the opposing perspective.

49 See Brenner, "Hidden Transcripts," 97; also, *idem*, "The Search for Identity in Israeli Arab Fiction: Atallah Mansour, Emile Habiby, and Anton Shammas," *Israeli Studies* 6, no. 3 (2001): 91–112; 101–102; and Hochberg, "The Dispossession," 51. Yehoshua's notorious statement 'advising' Shammas to pick up his belongings and move a hundred meters to the East has appeared in a number of sources, including, in Hebrew, A. B. Yehoshua, *Ha-kir ve-ha-har* (The Wall and the Mountain) (Tel Aviv: Zemorah Bitan, 1989), 188, and in English in Bernard Horn, *Facing the Fires: Conversations with A. B. Yehoshua* (Syracuse: Syracuse University Press, 1997), 48. See also Gluzman, "The Politics of Intertextuality," 324. Shammas's response originally appeared in his weekly column in *Kol ha-'Ir* 13, no. 9 (1985).

50 In "textual afterlife," I am drawing on Walter Benjamin, "The Task of the Translator," *Illuminations,* ed. Hannah Arendt, trans. Harry Zohn (New York: Schoken Books, 1986); more on this will follow below. The term 'midrash' refers both to a body of literature (the Midrash, books of biblical exegesis written by rabbis in antiquity) and to a practice (midrash, a non-literal, creative reading, often in narrative form, often employing techniques such as parable or allegory, that seeks to explain or to elucidate a biblical passage or narrative or explain a Jewish law). According to Daniel Boyarin, 'midrash' is the practice of reading that we find in the Midrash; it is an inherenterly intertextual hermeneutic act, "a portrayal of the reality which the rabbis perceived in the Bible through their ideologically colored eyeglasses," *Intertextuality and the Reading of Midrash* (Bloomington and Indianapolis: Indiana University Press, 1990), 15. The term is used in a more contemporary sense to denote a creative interpretative reading of traditional Jewish texts. My suggestion of 'Palestinian midrash' is based on the idea of modern midrash: see David Jacobson, *Modern Midrash: The Retelling of Traditional Jewish Narratives by Twentieth Century Jewish Writers* (SUNY Press, 1987). What I mean here is how Shammas or 'Araidi's use of, for example, the narrative of the *'akeydah* (sacrifice of Isaac) becomes one more layer of a story whose textual life begins with the Bible, is reabsorbed through rabbinic literature and midrash, and enters into Israeli literature as an archetypal paradigm, where it acquires new (allegorical)

meaning as a literary metaphor (cf. Amir Gilbo'a's "Isaac," on the Sho'ah; for more on rewritings of the *'akeydah,* see Jacobson, *Modern Midrash,* 1–5, and Kartun-Blum, *Profane Scriptures,* 15–62 and 70n). A Palestinian reading of the Isaac story thus becomes one more of the biblical story's textual afterlives, part of the story's own ongoing 'history'—potentially influencing how we (re)read the original as well.

51 For an excellent discussion of allusion, see Jeremy Dauber, "Allusion in a Jewish Key: Literary Theory and the Study of Haskala Literature," chap. 2 in his *Antonio's Devils: Writers of the Jewish Enlightenment and the Birth of Modern Hebrew and Yiddish Literature* (Stanford: Stanford University Press, 2004), 32–66, esp. 36–57.

52 See Stanley Fish, *Is there a Text in This Class? The Authority of Interpretive Communities* (Cambridge, MA: Harvard University Press, 1980), esp. 161–73 (on reading reception theory).

53 Dauber, *Antonio's Devils,* 56–57; my emphasis. How intriguing that a study on the *maskilic* use of canonical Jewish texts—intensely subversive in its own context, aimed at a Jewish readership in Europe—resonates so loudly with the Palestinian use of the same canon in the 'Jewish state' over a century later.

54 Caren Kaplan, "Deterritorializations: The Rewriting of Home and Exile in Western Feminist Discourse," in JanMohamed and Lloyd, eds., *The Nature and Context of Minority Discourse,* 357–68, quotation from 358; my emphasis.

55 According to David Grossman, 'Araidi "spent six months in jail in the 1970s because he knew about but did not report the Syrian spy ring led by Israeli [Jewish] radical Udi Adiv." Grossman, *Sleeping on a Wire: Conversations with Palestinians in Israel,* trans. Haim Watzman (New York: Farrar, Straus, and Giroux, 1993), 286.

56 The original Hebrew reads: "*'Aneh li shoter/ mah nishtanah ha-layla ha-zeh/mi-kol ha-leylot/ mah nishtanah ha-layla ha-zeh/ she-kol ha-leylot le'at 'ovrim/ ve-ha-layla ha-zeh le'at 'over/ 'aneh li shoter [...]*" The repetition of "*mah nishtanah ha-layla ha-zeh,*" the refrain of the Four Questions, immediately triggers the intertext for readers of Hebrew. This poem, labeled "C. 'Ir'on. January 1973," is from a group of four poems collectively titled "*Mi-shirey batey ha-ma'atsar*" , each identified by date and place, that appear in 'Araidi's volume *Hemlah va-fahad* (Tel Aviv: 'Akad, 1975), 28–29.

57 In many (primarily Ashkenazic) traditions, the Four Questions (and their answers) are chanted by the youngest (able) child present. Reading this custom into 'Araidi's poem further enhances the ironic disjuncture between the poem's very political context and the rhetorical posture of innocence associated with the intertext.

58 Snir, "Hebrew as the Language of Grace," 174–75.

59 Cf. Homi Bhabha, *The Location of Culture* (London: Routledge, 1994), 86.

60 Samia Mehrez, "The Subversive Poetics of Radical Bilingualism: Postcolonial Francophone North African Literature," *The Bounds of Race: Perspectives on Hegemony and Resistance,* ed. with intro. by Dominick La Capra (Ithaca, NY: Cornell University Press, 1991), 255–77; 260; quoted in Dingwaney and Meir, *Between Languages and Cultures,* 13.

61 Here I borrow from Walter Benjamin's idea that the translation imparts a new life to the source text: "For in its afterlife – which could not be called that if it were

not a transformation and a renewal of something living – the original undergoes a change"; the original language is "powerfully affected" by the foreign tongue; Benjamin, "The Task of the Translator," 76, 81.

62 "desacrilization": Snir, "Hebrew as the Language of Grace," 165–66; cf. Aharon 'Amir. Also, Kartun-Blum enumerates the characteristics of the relationship of the modern secular writer to the biblical text, including: "quotation and distorted quotation, an aspiration to the sublime and a descent to the ironic, and the mocking sanctification of the profane, which merges with the profanation of the holy," *Profane Scriptures*, 17.

63 The original appears in Amichai's *Shirim: 1948-1962* (Shoken: Tel Aviv, 1977). The authorized English translation by Barbara and Benjamin Harshav reads: "*God-Full-of-Mercy*, the prayer for the dead. / If God was not full of mercy, / Mercy would have been in the world, / Not just in Him." *Yehuda Amichai: A Life of Poetry, 1948-1994*, trans. Barbara and Benjamin Harshav (New York: HarperCollins, 1994), 31.

64 'Araidi, *"Hazarti el ha-kfar,"* 13–14, my translation, partially adapted from Karen Alcalay-Gut, http://karenalkalay-gut.com/Araidi.html.

65 Hebrew has two words for 'language,' *lashon* and *safah*, *lashon* literally meaning 'tongue' and *safah* 'lip.' See also note 77 below.

66 Hayyim Nahman Bialik, *Kol shirey Hayyim Nahman Bialik* (Tel Aviv: Dvir, 1966), 361–69.

67 In his recent article "The Politics of Intertextuality," Michael Gluzman uncovers and analyzes Shammas's extensive use of Bialik's *"Ha-Brekhah"* in a section of *Arabesques*. Gluzman argues that "the passage in which Shammas rewrites Bialik is the text's most crucial moment," and that "his act of rewriting 'The Pool' should in fact be seen as intervening in the national discourse of contemporary Hebrew literature" (322). Gluzman's identification of this one passage as *the* singularly most important statement of the text is questionable, not least because this reading of the novel unequivocally privileges the issue of Israeli/Hebrew literary culture over the novel's extensive engagement with the Palestinian tragedy (the *nakba*, the Palestinian diaspora and the refugee situation, the occupation, and so on), resulting in a limited, 'Hebraicentric' reading of this very polyvalent text. There is no doubt, however, that it is *an* important moment, and that Gluzman has given us a valuable reading of it. I raise this point here because toward the beginning of his essay, Gluzman writes: "Shammas's acute awareness of the Jewishness of Hebrew literature compels him to expose its exclusionary ideology. Calling for the emergence of an Israeli literature that would treat him as an equal, Shammas advances a critique of the Jewishness of Hebrew literature" (323). Gluzman then proceeds to quote Shammas from a 1985 Hebrew-language essay:

> Today one can speak of an American literature, but it is doubtful if one can speak of an Israeli literature. A Hebrew, Jewish literature exists...but an Israeli literature, in a different mold [. . .] does not exist except perhaps in the writings of Sami Michael and Shimon Balas [*sic*], and a few others who reached these regions from another, that is, Sephardic orientation. (323)

The question, however, remains: if Shammas intended to critique the Jewishness of Hebrew literature, why would he rely so heavily upon allusions from the Jewish canon? See Shammas, *"Ha-mifgash she-hayah, ha-mifgash she-lo yihyeh,"* *Moznayim* 59, no. 3 (1985): 30–32; repr. in Gluzman, "The Politics of Intertextuality," 323 (trans. Gluzman). It is also worth noting that Shammas published a poem by the title *"Ha-Brekhah"* in his first collection, *Krikhah kashah*; yet this poem shows no obvious thematic or intertextual relationship to Bialik's poem, except that the speaker discusses trying to "stick" *(le-hadbik)* names to objects in his room (making it a poem about language). See Shammas, *Krikhah kashah*, 36.

68 Translation from Jewish Publication Society, Hebrew-English *Tanakh* (Bible) (Philadephia: Jewish Publication Society, 1999), 40.

69 Snir, "Hebrew as the Language of Grace," 167.

70 According to Kartun-Blum, the *'akeydah* "remains indisputably the most prominent and most powerful of all these biblical topoi" in modern Hebrew literature, and its persistence in modern Hebrew culture "borders on obsession;" *Profane Scriptures*, 18; "[t]here is scarcely a poet who does not use or abuse this narrative in his work" (19). For an extended reading of the *'akeydah* in modern Hebrew poetry, see chap. 2, "A Double Bind: The Sacrifice of Isaac as a Paradigm in Modern Hebrew Poetry," in *Profane Scriptures*, 15–62.

71 'Araidi is part of the Druze community, while Shammas (though non-practicing) was born to a Christian family; while not directly relevant to the text, this background information should be noted in the broader context of their identities vis-à-vis each other as mediated through Hebrew. The question of religious background plays a more significant role in each of their respective novels.

72 It should also be noted that the use of a biblical intertext in order to reject its traditional interpretation or to distance oneself from the collective is a common feature of contemporary Hebrew poetry. Kartun-Blum notes: "Indeed, much of the political poetry written in Israel since the 1970s – and especially in the 1980s, after the war in Lebanon – is concerned with stating what is not; prosing itself as 'not x' where x is a biblical intertextual referent"; she adds, "The question is always: In relation to what does one define one's own identity? In Israeli culture the Bible becomes the *intimate other*." *Profane Scriptures*, 5–7; emphasis in original. What distinguishes 'Araidi's "negative presupposition," however, is that the insider/outsider relationship that the poem carves out is not simply about political orientation but much more viscerally, about the place of a non-Jewish poet within a Jewish tradition.

73 Kartun-Blum elaborates on allegorical uses of the *'akeydah* in poems about war and national sacrifice as well as poems on the Sho'ah (Holocaust); again, see chap. 2 of *Profane Scriptures*. To be sure, there is also the Islamic version of the story, in which Ishmael figures as the Abrahamian son in question. Given the specifically biblical intertextual usage of the story, I do not think 'Araidi is invoking the Qur'anic version, but it should be noted that the story has a shared tradition in Hebrew and Arabic textual cultures.

74 Shammas, *Krikhah kashah*, 30; my translation.

75 Bhabha, *Location,* 60; emphasis in original. The point refers to theoretical concepts of the subaltern.

76 I thank Chana Kronfeld for bringing this poem to my attention.

77 Both of modern Hebrew's two words for 'language,' *safah* and *lashon,* are also the names for parts of the mouth: *safah* means 'lip' and *lashon* 'tongue.' (These terms also both have closely related Arabic cognates: *shafa* and *lisan.*) In the original Hebrew, the poem's use of *safah* connotes both language and tongue. Elsewhere throughout the poem I have translated *safah* as 'language;' but I have rendered this particular line "And in my mouth is another tongue," to best convey the emphasis on corporeality.

78 Shammas, *Shirah tse'irah: antologiah* (Young Poetry: an Anthology), Hannah Ya'oz, Ya'akov Beser, Itamar Ya'oz-Keset, eds. (Tel Aviv: 'Akad, 1980), 258–59; my translation.

79 "The Cave" is also the title of *Surat al-Kahf,* Chapter 18 of the Qur'an, in which we find a parable about *ashab al-kahf,* the Companions of the Cave: a group of youths who, seeking refuge from religious oppression, flee to a cave where Allah puts them into a centuries-long slumber. The parable is thought to be based upon an apocryphal story of Christian youths in the time of the Emperor Decius. In short, the cave has been a mystical symbol in all three monotheistic faiths. (Of course, we also find the parable of the cave in Plato's *Symposium.*)

80 'Midrash': see note 50 above.

81 Midrash Esther Rabbah, Parashah Gimmel. Trans, Jacob Neusner, *Esther Rabbah I: An Analytical Translation,* Brown Judaic Studies 182 (Atlanta, GA: Scholars Press, 1989), 88.

82 It is a kind of Aramaic-Hebrew hybrid, as is common in the language of Talmud and Midrash.

83 From the same root, *heled* is a biblical Hebrew world meaning 'the world,' 'human existence' ("*kol-yoshvey heled,*" "all the people of the world," Psalms 49:2) and by derivation, the duration of life, such that the expression *yamey heldi* (literally, 'the days of my *heled*') idiomatically means 'my mortal days.'

84 Jacques Lacan, "The Mirror Stage as Formative of the *I* Function as Revealed in Psychoanalytic Experience," in *idem, Ecrits: A Selection,* trans. Bruce Fink (London: W. W. Norton, 2004), 3–9.

85 The prayer's words are: "This is my substitute, this is my exchange, this is my atonement. This fowl goes to death and I shall enter a long, happy and peaceful life." (Roosters are used for men and hens for women.) The chicken is then slaughtered and it (or its cash value) is given to the poor. In Christianity, of course, the rooster represents Peter's denial of Christ and subsequent repentance, but this idea does not seem related to the poem. It has also been suggested to me that the black rooster is an apocalyptic image, but I have not found textual corroboration to support this interesting idea.

86 Shammas, *'Arabeskot,* 17, 174, 238.

87 The title idiomatically suggests 'Someone local,' 'one of us.'

88 Masalha, *Ehad mi-kan,* 9; my translation.

89 *Hadarim* 12 (1996): 147–48; the second poem is "*Ani kotev 'ivrit*" (I Write Hebrew), to be discussed shortly.

90 *Diwan Mahmud Darwish*, vol. 1. (Beirut: Dar al-'Awdah, 1977), 121–27.

91 Two unstressed followed by one stressed syllable; three stressed syllables per foot.

92 So for instance, the first stanza reads: "*a-ni* **hu** *me-sho-rer* '*a-ra-vi*/ *she-tso-ve-*'*a ha-***kol** *be-sha-***hor**/ *ef-***tah** *et segor li-***bi**/ *la-*'*o-***lam** *she-so-vev le-a-***hor**."

93 I thank Chana Kronfeld for this wonderful observation about the poem as a prosodic thematization of modern (Israeli) Hebrew.

94 The sentence is incomplete in the original.

95 *Sheol*: 'the underworld.'

96 Masalha, *Ehad mi-kan*, 14; my translation.

97 Translation from JPS *Tanakh*, 1580. King James renders it: "Behold, how good and how pleasant [it is] for brethren to dwell together in unity!"

98 Homi K. Bhabha, "Of Mimicry and Man: The Ambivalence of Colonial Discourse," chap. 4 of his *The Location of Culture* (London: Routledge, 1994), 85–92, 85.

99 *zekher ima la-*'*arov* (literally, 'to guarantee the memory of mother'): the verb *la-*'*arov* (to guarantee, be a guarantor for) is declined from the root '*a-r-v*, the basis for Arab, Arabic, and so forth, punning on the shared root to convey the idea of Arabic as mother tongue.

100 Masalha, *Ehad mi-kan*, 12; my translation, adapted from Vivian Eden, http://israel. poetryinternational.org/cwolk/view/23548. Of this poem, Hannan Hever writes: "In 'Sign of Scorpio,' a self-portrait, poetic diction grows like a bifurcated tongue in the presence of this profound awareness of disaster...The writing of poetry is like the snake's reaction to the danger it encounters... The snake sheds its skin – and the response is a tongue which is bifurcated like a snake's." Hever, "Not My Mother Tongue," *Haaretz* 5, no. 3 (2004); reproduced in English, http://israel. poetryinternational.org/cwolk/view/23548.

101 The word *ulam*, which I have translated as 'yet,' also means 'hall,' so that the sentence could be rendered; "And a hall, the colors of the night [. . .]"; it is a play on words contributing to the stanza's architectural metaphor of the house and heart.

102 Masalha, *Ehad mi-kan*, 15; my translation.

103 The word *nigar*, from the verb *le-nager* (to pour or flow from), in the phrase "*ha-dam she-nigar le-lo*/ *heref min ha-lev*," shares the root of *nagar*, "carpenter," further extending the stanza's architectural metaphor (also in the double meaning of *ulam*; see note 101).

104 Hever, "Not My Mother Tongue." Unsigned translation of text.

105 'Araidi, *Ulay zo ahavah*, 29; my translation.

106 Angelika Bammer, Introduction, in *Displacements*, xvi.

107 Masalha, *Ehad mi-kan*, 40; my translation except for "it's now absurd," which I borrow from Vivian Eden's translation. The poem does not specify whether these are victims of car accidents on Israel's notoriously dangerous roads or victims of terror. The answer is probably something of both—a comment on the general state of violence and bloodshed that characterizes the "here" of the poem's title.

108 Vivian Eden elides the collocation *ba-arets* from her translation altogether, rendering it: "[...] it's dangerous/ to go out in the streets."

109 Hever, "Not my Mother Tongue."

110 Masalha, *Ehad mi-kan*, 61.

111 Http://israel.poetryinternational.org/cwolk/view/23340; the poem was originally published in 1999.

112 'Araidi, *"Tsomet"* (Junction), *Ba-hamishah memadim* (Tel Aviv: Sifriat Po'alim, 1991), 15; my translation.

113 'Araidi, *"Ba-emtsa' ha-derekh"* in *Ba-hamishah memadim*, 14; my translation.

114 Shammas, *"Yud-gimel drakhim le-histakel be-zeh,"* in *Shetah hefker*, 46; my translation. These are the final lines of the last poem in the collection.

115 For example: "Sleep is an orange/ like an unexpected phone ring that stops when you get up / that's how the fragrance of oranges comes to you/ from the grove. And sleep is a bird / that catches your attention when it flies from the sill. No / sleep is an orange. I'm / its squeezed half." *Asir*, 56; from the Arabic. "On your walls, with a wandering brush. / I paint passwords: your charm / will fall in a voice of curses. / I lean on the wall / as the half of an orange/ the juicers of domes above me." *Krikhah kashah*, 10; from the Hebrew.

116 To name but two examples: Palestinian author Ghassan Kanafani's Arabic short story, 'The Land of Sad Oranges', and Israeli author Dalia Ravikovitch's Hebrew poetry collection, *The Love of an Orange* (which itself, of course, is itself an allusion to the Prokofiev.)

117 ' Araidi, *"Hazarti el ha-kfar,"* in *Hazarti el ha-kfar*, 8; my translation. The volume's cover features a black-and-white photo of an olive tree (well-known as a symbol of Palestine) torn down the middle: another image of bifurcation.

118 Shammas, *"Halakhti 'ad sof ha-geshem,"* in *Shetah hefker*, 15; my translation.

119 Shammas, *"Yud-gimel drakhim le-histakel be-zeh,"* in *Shetah hefker*, 44–45; my translation.

120 Shammas, *"Ani mitnatsel"* in *Shetah hefker*, 6; my translation.

121 David Grossman, *Sleeping on a Wire*, 252. (I have made two minor changes in Watzman's translation: from 'Galilee' to 'Galil' and 'Kabani' to 'Qabbani'.)

122 Ramras-Rauch, *The Arab in Israeli Literature*, 198; also in Hever, "Hebrew in an Israeli Arab Hand," 289.

123 Shammas, *Asir*, 14; my translation.

124 Bhabha, "Frontlines/ Borderposts," 270; my emphasis.

125 The word "aqarib" (عقارب) for hands of a watch or clock also puns with 'stings' or 'pricks' (of a scorpion, in particular.) 'Araidi, *Hunalika da'iman umniya* (Haifa: Maktabat Kull Shay, 1994), 6–7; my translation.

126 Cf. Emile Habiby, *al-Waqa'i' al-ghariba fi ikhtifa' Sa'id abi al-Nahs al-Mutasha'il* (Cairo: Dar Shuhdi, n.d.); in English, *The Secret Life of Saeed the Pessoptimist*, trans. Trevor Le Gassick and Salma Khadra Jayyusi, 2nd ed. (New York: Interlink Books, 2002).

127 'Araidi, *Hemlah va-fahad*, 10; my translation.

128 *Gvi'ah mutelet le-ruha*; idiomatically, 'a corpse sprawling/ cast/ left to itself;' also a play on *le-kol ha-ruhot!* ('Damnation!', 'The hell with it'!')

129 Cf. Genesis 1:2: "*ve-ru'ah elohim merahefet 'al-pney ha-mayim*" (And the spirit of God was hovering over the water.) This is a common translation, although JPS renders

it "And a wind from God [was] sweeping over the water" (JPS Hebrew-English *Tanakh* 1).

130 This line, "*'al ha-dam*" (on/ over the blood) invokes a complex network of intertextual associations. The original intertext is the biblical law "*lo tokhlu 'al ha dam*" (You shall not eat anything with blood): Leviticus 19:26 (JPS 252). The same phrase *('al ha-dam)* is taken by the famous Hebrew poet Saul Tchernihowsky as the title of one of his sonnet cycles. The epigraph at the head of Tchernihowsky's sonnet reads "*Ve-nikayti damam lo-nikayti* (Joel 4:21)", which is the concluding line of the following verses from the Book of Joel:

> (4:18) "And in that day, the mountains shall drip with wine, the hills shall flow with milk, and all the watercourses of Judah shall flow with water; a spring shall issue from the House of the Lord and shall water the Wadi of the Acacias. (4:19) Egypt shall be a desolation, and Edom shall be a desolate waste because of the outrage to the people of Judah, in whose land they shed the blood of the innocent. (4:20) But Judah shall be inhabited forever, and Jerusalem throughout the ages [from generation to generation]. (4:21) *Thus I will treat as innocent their blood which I have not treated as innocent*; and the Lord shall dwell in Zion." (JPS 1307–08; my emphasis)

The line in question is emended in the text as "their unavenged blood shall be avenged." In the context of this poem about the shedding of innocent blood, this phrase becomes highly significant. *'Al ha-dam," Kol kitvey Tshernihovski, kerekh alef: shirim ve-baladot: The Collected Works of Saul Tchernihowsky*, vol, 1: *Poems and Ballads* (Tel Aviv: 'Am 'Oved, 1990), 242–53.

131 The phrase *haleyv imam* (their mothers' milk) continues the poem's play on the biblical laws concerning blood (bloodshed, ritual purity, and so on) and its antithesis, milk, by alluding to another biblical dietary injunction "*lo-tevashel gedi ba-haleyv imo*" (You shall not boil a kid in its mother's milk), which appears first in Exodus 34:26 and repeated in Deuteronomy 14:21 (JPS, 190, 407). These two rules forbidding the consumption of blood and the mixing of milk and meat are cornerstones of the laws of *kashruth* (ritual dietary law).

132 *Ha-'ir ha-zkenah*: the adjective *zkenah* (old, aged), which is used only for people, personifies the city as an old lady.

133 Masalha, *Ehad mi-kan,* 68; my translation.

A List of Magda Al-Nowaihi's Publications

Books
The Poetry of Ibn Khafaja: A Literary Analysis. Leiden: E.J. Brill, 1993.

Articles
"Committed Postmodernity: Mohamed Berrada's *The Game of Forgetting.*" *Critique* 15 (Fall 1999): 1–24. Reprinted in *Tradition, Modernity, and Postmodernity in Arabic Literature*, eds. Kamal Abdel-Malek and Wael Hallaq. Leiden: E.J. Brill, 2000. 367–88.

"Constructions of Masculinity in Two Egyptian Novels," in *Intimate Selving in Arab Families: Gender, Self, and Identity*, ed. Suad Joseph. Syracuse, NY: Syracuse University Press, 1999. 235–63.

"For a Foreign Audience: The Challenge of Teaching Arabic Literature in the American Academy." *Middle East Studies Association Bulletin* 35, no. 1 (Summer 2001): 24–28.

"Memory and Imagination in Edwar al-Kharrat's *Turabuha Za'faran.*" *Journal of Arabic Literature* 25 (1994): 34–57.

"The 'Middle East'? or ... /Arabic Literature and the Postcolonial Predicament," in *A Companion to Postcolonial Studies*, eds. Henry Schwarz and Sangeeta Ray. Malden, MA: Blackwell, 2000. 282–303.

"Re-envisioning National Community in Salwa Bakr's *The Golden Chariot.*" *Arab Studies Journal* 7/8 (Fall 1999/Spring 2000): 8–24. Reprinted in *Gender, Nation, and Community in Arab Women's Novels*, eds. Lisa Suhair Majaj, Paula W. Sunderman, and Therese Saliba. Syracuse, NY: Syracuse University Press, 2002, 68–93.

"Resisting Silence in Arab Women's Autobiograhies." *International Journal of Middle East Studies* 33, no. 4 (November 2001): 477–502.

"Tadris al-adab al-'arabi fi Amrika: taqrib bayn al-hadarat am tawsi' li-l-huwwa baynaha?" *Al-Adab* 49, no. 5 (June 2001): 93–95.

"Unheard in English," in *Magda Al-Nowaihi (1958–2002): In Memory*, eds. Joseph Massad, Samia Mehrez, and Maha Yahya. *The MIT Electronic Journal of Middle East Studies* 4 (Fall 2004): 23–29. http://web.mit.edu/cis/www.mitejmes.